C++ Without Fear

Second Edition

C++ Without Fear

Second Edition

A Beginner's Guide That Makes You Feel Smart

Brian Overland

PRENTICE
HALL

Upper Saddle River, NJ • Boston • Indianapolis • San Francisco
New York • Toronto • Montreal • London • Munich • Paris • Madrid
Capetown • Sydney • Tokyo • Singapore • Mexico City

Many of the designations used by manufacturers and sellers to distinguish their products are claimed as trademarks. Where those designations appear in this book, and the publisher was aware of a trademark claim, the designations have been printed with initial capital letters or in all capitals.

The author and publisher have taken care in the preparation of this book, but make no expressed or implied warranty of any kind and assume no responsibility for errors or omissions. No liability is assumed for incidental or consequential damages in connection with or arising out of the use of the information or programs contained herein.

The publisher offers excellent discounts on this book when ordered in quantity for bulk purchases or special sales, which may include electronic versions and/or custom covers and content particular to your business, training goals, marketing focus, and branding interests. For more information, please contact:

U.S. Corporate and Government Sales
(800) 382-3419
corpsales@pearsontechgroup.com

For sales outside the United States please contact:

International Sales
international@pearson.com

Visit us on the Web: informit.com/ph

Library of Congress Cataloging-in-Publication Data
Overland, Brian R.
  C++ without fear : a beginner's guide that makes you feel smart /
Brian Overland.—2nd ed.
        p.   cm.
  Includes index.
  ISBN 978-0-13-267326-6 (pbk. : alk. paper)
  1. C++ (Computer program language) I. Title.
  QA76.73.C153O838 2011
  005.13'3—dc22

                                                    2011004218

ISBN-13: 978-0-13-267326-6
ISBN-10:   0-13-267326-6
Text printed in the United States on recycled paper at Edwards Brothers Malloy in Ann Arbor, Michigan.
Third printing, August 2012

For Colin

Contents

Chapter 3   *The Handy, All-Purpose "for" Statement*   67

Chapter 10 *New Features of C++0x*   243

Chapter 11 *Introducing Classes: The Fraction Class*   277

Chapter 12 *Constructors: If You Build It...* 307

Chapter 15   *Two Complete OOP Examples*   389

Chapter 16   *Easy Programming with STL*   413

Chapter 17   *Inheritance: What a Legacy*   435

Chapter 18   *Polymorphism: Object Independence*   453

Preface

Many years ago, when I had to learn C overnight to make a living as a programmer (this was before C++), I would have given half my salary to find a mentor, a person would say, "Here are the potholes in the road...errors that you are sure to make in learning C. And here's how to steer around them." Instead, I had to sweat and groan through every error a person could make.

I'm not just talking about programmers who can write or writers who can program. Each of those is rare enough. Much rarer still is the person who is programmer, writer, and *teacher*—someone who will steer you around the elementary gotchas and enthusiastically communicate the "whys" of the language, including why this stuff is not just useful but, in its own way, kind of cool.

It's hard to find such a person. But way back then, I swore this is the person I'd become.

Later, at Microsoft, I started in tech support and testing and worked my way into management. But my most important job (I felt) was explaining new technology. I was sometimes the second or third person in the world to see a new feature of a programming language, and my job was to turn a cryptic spec into readable prose for the rest of the universe to understand. I took the goal of "make this simple" as not just a job but a mission.

About This Book: How It's Different

What's different about this book is that I'm an advocate for you, the reader. I'm on your side, not that of some committee. I'm aware of all the ways you are "supposed" to program and why they are supposed to be better (and I do discuss those issues), but I'm mostly concerned about telling you what *works*.

This book assumes you know nothing at all about programming—that you basically know how to turn on a computer and use a mouse. For those of you more knowledgeable, you'll want to breeze through the first few chapters.

The creators of C and C++—Dennis Ritchie and Bjarne Stroustrup, respectively—are geniuses, and I'm in awe of what they accomplished. But although C and C++ are great languages, there are some features that beginners (and even relatively advanced programmers) never find uses for, at least not for the first few years. I'm not afraid to tell you that information up front: what language features you can and should ignore. At the same time, I'm also eager to tell you about the elegant features of C++ that can save you time and energy.

This is a book about practical examples. It's also a book about having fun! The great majority of examples in this book either are useful and practical or—by using puzzles and games—are intrinsically entertaining.

So, have no fear! I won't bludgeon you to death with overly used (and highly *abused*) terms like *data abstraction*, which professors love but which forever remain fuzzy to the rest of us. At the same time, there are some terms—*object orientation* and *polymorphism*—that you will want to know, and I provide concrete, practical contexts for understanding and using them.

Onward to the Second Edition

The first edition has sold increasingly well over the years. I believe that's a testament to the variety of learning paths it supplied: complete examples, exercises, and generous use of conceptual art. The second edition builds on these strengths in many ways:

▶ **Coverage of new features in C++0x:** This is the new specification for C++ that will be standard by the time you have this book in your hands. Compiler vendors either have brought their versions of C++ up to this standard or are in the process of doing so. This book covers well over a dozen new features from this specification in depth.

▶ **Examples galore, featuring puzzles and games:** By the end of Chapter 2, you'll learn how to enter a program, barely a page long, that not only is a complete game but even has an optimal strategy for the computer. Just see whether you can beat it! But this is only the beginning. This edition features puzzles and games, much more so than the first edition.

▶ **Generous use of conceptual art:** The use of clarifying illustrations to address abstract points was one of the biggest strengths of the first edition. This edition has substantially more of these.

▶ **Even more exercises:** These encourage the reader to learn in the best way...by taking apart an example that works, analyzing it, and figuring out how to modify it to make it do your own thing.

▶ **No-nonsense syntax diagrams:** Programming and playing games is fun, but sometimes you need straightforward information. The syntax diagrams in this book, accompanied by loads of examples, clarify exactly how the language works, statement by statement and keyword by keyword.

▶ **Introduction to Standard Template Library (STL):** Although I lacked the space to do a complete STL manual, this edition (unlike the first) introduces you to the wonders of this exciting feature of C++, showing how it can save you time and energy and enable you to write powerful applications in a remarkably small space.

▶ **Expanded reference:** The appendixes in the back are intended as a mini desk reference to use in writing C++ programs. This edition has significantly expanded these appendixes.

▶ **Essays, or "interludes" for the philosophically inclined:** Throughout the book, I detour into areas related to C++ but that impact the larger world, such as computer science, history of programming, mathematics, philosophy, and artificial intelligence. But these essays are set aside as sidebars so as not to interfere with the flow of the subject. You can read them at your leisure.

"Where Do I Begin?"

As I mentioned, this book assumes you know nothing about programming. If you can turn on a computer and use a menu system, keyboard, and mouse, you can begin on page 1. If you already have some familiarity with programming, you'll want to go through the first two or three chapters quickly.

If you already know a lot about C or C++ and are mainly interested in the new features of C++0x, you may want to go straight to Chapter 10, "New Features of C++0x."

And if you know C and are now starting to learn about object orientation with the C++ language, you may want to start with Chapter 11, "Introducing Classes: The Fraction Class."

Icons, Icons, Who's Got the Icons?

Building on the helpful icons used in the first edition, this edition provides even more—as signposts on the pages to help you find what you need. Be sure to look for these symbols.

These sections take apart program examples and explain, line by line, how and why the examples work. You don't have to wade through long programming examples. I do that for you! (Or rather, we go through the examples together.)

After each full programming example, I provide at least one exercise, and usually several, that builds on the example in some way. These encourage you to alter and extend the programming code you've just seen. This is the best way to learn. The answers can be found on the book's Web site (*www.informit.com/title/9780132673266*).

These sections develop an example by showing how it can be improved, made shorter, or made more efficient.

As with "Optimizing," these sections take the example in new directions, helping you learn by showing how the example can be varied or modified to do other things.

This icon indicates a place where a keyword of the language is introduced and its usage clearly defined.

C++0x ▶ This icon is used to indicate sections that apply only to versions of C++ compliant with the new C++0x specification. Depending on the version of C++ you have, either these sections will apply to you or they won't. If your version is not C++0x-compliant, you'll generally want to skip these sections.

What Is Not Covered?

Relatively little, as it turns out. The two features not covered at all are bit fields and unions. Although these features are useful for some people, their application tends to be highly specialized—limited to a few special situations—and not particularly useful to people first learning the language. Of course, I encourage you to learn about them on your own later.

Another area in which I defer to other books is the topic of writing your own template classes, which I touch on just briefly in Chapter 16. Without a doubt, the ability to write new template classes is one of the most amazing features of state-of-the-art C++, but it is a very advanced and complex topic. For me to cover it adequately and exhaustively could easily have taken another 400 or 500 pages!

Fortunately, although templates and the Standard Template Library (STL) are advanced subjects, there are some good books on the subject—for example, *C++ Templates: The Complete Guide*, by David Vandevoorde and Nicolai M. Josuttis; *STL Tutorial and Reference Guide: C++ Programming with the Standard Template Library, Second Edition*, by David R. Musser, Gillmer J. Derge, and Atul Saini; and *Effective STL: 50 Specific Ways to Improve Your Use of the Standard Template Library*, by Scott Meyers.

And remember that Chapter 16 does introduce you to using STL, which provides extremely useful, existing templates for you to take advantage of.

Getting Started with C++: A Free Compiler

Although this edition doesn't come with a CD with a free compiler on it, that is no longer necessary. You can download some excellent shareware (that is, free) versions of C++ from the Internet that not only have a free compiler (that's the application that translates your programs into machine-readable form) but also a very good development environment. And they install easily.

To download this free software, start by going to the book's Web site: *www.informit.com/title/9780132673266*.

As mentioned earlier, you will also find downloadable copies of all the full program examples in the book, as well as answers to exercises.

A Final Note: Have Fun!

Once again, there is nothing to fear about C++. Yes, there are those nasty potholes I started out discussing, but remember, I'm going to steer you around them. Admittedly, C++ is not a language for the weak of heart; it assumes you know exactly what you're doing. But it doesn't have to be intimidating. I hope you use the practical examples and find the puzzles and games entertaining. This is a book about learning and about taking a road to new knowledge, but more than that, it's a book about enjoying the ride.

Acknowledgments

I am likely to leave many deserving people out this time, but a few names cry out for special mention. The book's editor, Peter Gordon, not only took the initiative in arranging for the new edition but did a lovely job of nursing the book through all its stages along with the author's ego. His long-suffering right hand, Kim Boedigheimer, was a better person than we all deserved, coming to the rescue again and again and kindly aiding the author. I'd also like to extend a special thanks to Kim Wimpsett and Anna Popick, who unexpectedly have been an absolute delight to work with in getting the book through its final tense stages.

Closer to home in the Seattle area: I also want to make special mention to veteran Microsoft programmers John R. Bennett and Matt Greig, who provided superb insights about the latest directions of C++. Some of the more interesting new sections in the book came about directly as a result of extended conversations with these experts.

About the Author

Brian Overland published his first article in a professional math journal at age 14.

After graduating from Yale, he began working on large commercial projects in C and Basic, including an irrigation-control system used all over the world. He also tutored students in math, computer programming, and writing, as well as lecturing to classes at Microsoft and at the community-college level. On the side, he found an outlet for his lifelong love of writing by publishing film and drama reviews in local newspapers. His qualifications as an author of technical books are nearly unique because they involve so much real programming and teaching experience, as well as writing.

In his 10 years at Microsoft, he was a tester, author, programmer, and manager. As a technical writer, he became an expert on advanced utilities, such as the linker and assembler, and was the "go-to" guy for writing about new technology. His biggest achievement was probably organizing the entire documentation set for Visual Basic 1.0 and having a leading role in teaching the "object-based" way of programming that was so new at the time. He was also a member of the Visual C++ 1.0 team.

Since then, he has been involved with the formation of new start-up companies (sometimes as CEO). He is currently working on a novel.

Your First C++ Programs

There's nothing to fear about C++ programming—really! Like all programming languages, it's just a way to give logically precise directions to a computer.

C++ can get as complicated as you want, but the easy way to start learning is to use it to solve the fundamental programming tasks. That's the approach here.

In the first couple of sections, I review the basic concepts of programming. If you've programmed in any language, you might want to skip these. But if you stick around, I promise to not be too long-winded.

Thinking Like a Programmer

Programming may not be exactly like any activity you've ever done. Basically, you're just giving instructions—but doing so in a logical, systematic manner.

Computers Do Only What You Tell Them

Computers do only what you tell them: This is the most important rule in this book, especially if you are new to programming. By using a computer language, such as C++, Visual Basic, Pascal, or FORTRAN, you give the computer a list of things to do; this is the *program*.

A computer needs information, of course—that's program *data*. But it also needs to know what to do with that data. The instructions that tell it what to do are called program *code*.

Determine What the Program Will Do

So, to get a computer to do anything, it has to be told exactly what to do.

1

So far, you've probably used a computer by running programs that other people have written for you. To this extent, you've been an *end user*—or *user*, for short.

By writing programs yourself, you'll promote yourself into the next higher echelon of computer people. Now, you'll decide what a program does. You'll make things happen.

But a computer—more so than Dustin Hoffman in *Rain Man*—is the ultimate idiot savant. It can never guess what you want. It can never make independent judgments. It is extremely literal and will carry out precisely what you say, no matter how stupid. Therefore, you have to be careful to say what you mean.

You can't even give the computer a command that might seem relatively clear to a human, such as "Convert a number from Celsius to Fahrenheit for me." Even that's too general. Instead, you have to be more specific, writing down steps such as these:

1 Print the "Enter Celsius temperature:" message.

2 Get a number from the keyboard and store it in the variable ctemp.

3 Convert to Fahrenheit by using the formula ftemp = (ctemp * 1.8) + 32.

4 Print the "The Fahrenheit temperature is:" message.

5 Print the value of the variable ftemp.

If you have to go through this much trouble just to do something simple, why even bother? The answer is that once a program is written, you can run it over and over. And though programs take time to write, they usually execute at lightning speed.

Write the Equivalent C++ Statements

After you've determined precisely what you want your program to do, step-by-step, you need to write down the equivalent C++ statements. A statement is roughly the C++ equivalent of a sentence in English.

For example, say you want your program to do the following:

1 Print the "The Fahrenheit temperature is:" message.

2 Print the value of the variable ftemp.

You'd translate these steps into the following C++ statements:

```
cout << "The Fahrenheit temperature is: ";
cout << ftemp;
```

Remember, the goal of programming is to get the computer to do a series of specific tasks. But the computer understands only its own native language—*machine code*—which consists of 1s and 0s. Back in the 1950s, programmers did write out instructions in machine code, but this was difficult and time-consuming.

To make things easier, computer engineers developed programming languages such as FORTRAN, Basic, and C, which enable humans to write programs bearing at least some resemblance to English.

To write a program, you may want to start by writing *pseudocode*—an approach I often use in this book. Pseudocode is similar to English, but it describes the action of the program in a systematic way reflecting the logical flow of the program. For example, here's a simple program written in pseudocode:

If a is greater than b

Print "a is greater than b."

Else

Print "a is not greater than b."

Once you've written pseudocode, you're not far from having a C++ program. All you need to do is look up the corresponding C++ statement for each action:

```
if (a > b)
    cout << "a is greater than b.";
else
    cout << "a is not greater than b.";
```

The advantage of a programming language is that it follows rules that allow no ambiguity. C++ statements are so precise that they can be translated into the 1s and 0s of machine code without guesswork.

It should come as no surprise that programming languages have strict rules of syntax. These rules are more consistent, and usually simpler, than rules in a human language. From time to time, I summarize these rules. For example, here's **if-else** syntax:

```
if (condition)
    statement
else
    statement
```

The words in bold are *keywords*; they must be entered into the program exactly as shown. Words in italics are *placeholders*; they represent items that you supply.

The application that translates C++ statements into machine code is called a *compiler*. I'll have a lot more to say about compilers in the upcoming section "Building a C++ Program." First, however, let's review some key definitions.

Interlude

How "Smart" Are Computers, Really?

When I ran a computer lab in Tacoma, Washington, some years ago, I came across some interesting characters, some of them right off the street. One of them was a rotund little man in a straw hat, ill-matching clothes, old shoes, and a big smile, who carried around a copy of *The Daily Racing Form* like it was the Bible.

He came up to me every other day with his horse-racing newspaper. "I got this idea," he kept saying. "We'll make a million. All we have to do is put this information into the computer and have it pick horses. I'll supply *The Daily Racing Form*. You write the program. We'll be rich!" I smiled but mumbled something about feasibility problems.

What he forgot—or probably never understood—is that no real knowledge exists inside the computer itself. There's no magical being inside that answers your questions like the ship's computer in *Star Trek*. Just entering raw data into a computer does nothing. What a computer needs first is the right *program*...a series of instructions that tells it how to move, copy, add, subtract, multiply, or otherwise evaluate data.

The real trick in getting a computer to properly pick winning horses at the racetrack, of course, would be to come up with the right *algorithm*...an algorithm being a systematic, step-by-step technique for evaluating data and getting a result, that is to say, the right formula. If you could come up with the right algorithm for picking horses, I don't deny it could make you rich. But in that case, finding a computer would be the least of your problems. You could use any computer as long as it could hold the data required.

As for finding a programmer, well, if you could get such a person to believe you really had the right algorithm, it would simply be a matter of offering to split the first 10 million dollars in winnings. I know any number of people who would go for that.

Or better yet, you could use the techniques in this book to write the program yourself.

Some Nerdy Definitions—A Review

I like to avoid jargon. I really do. But when you start learning programming, you enter into a world that requires new terminology. The following are some definitions you need to survive in this world.

application

Essentially the same thing as a program but seen from a user's point of view. An application is a program that a user runs to accomplish some task. A word processor is an application; so is an Internet browser or a database manager. Even a *compiler* (defined in a moment) is an application, but of a very special kind, because it's used by programmers. To put the matter simply, when your program is written, built, and tested, it's an application.

code

Another synonym for "the program," but from the programmer's point of view. The use of the term *code* stems from the days in which programmers wrote in machine code. Each machine instruction is encoded into a unique combination of 1s and 0s and is therefore the computer's code for doing some action.

Programmers have continued to talk about "code" even when using languages such as C++, Java, FORTRAN, or Visual Basic. (See the definition of *source code*.) Also, the term *code* is used to differentiate between the passive information in a program (its data) and the part of the program that performs actions (its code).

compiler

The language translator that takes C++ statements (that is, C++ source code) as input and outputs the program in machine-code form. This is necessary, because the computer itself—its central processing unit (CPU)—only understands machine code.

data

Information operated on by a program. At its most basic level, this information consists of words and/or numbers.

machine code

The CPU's native language, in which each computer instruction consists of a unique combination (or *code*) of 1s and 0s. It is still possible to program in machine code, but this requires looking up each instruction, as well as having elaborate knowledge of the CPU's architecture.

Languages such as C++ provide a way to write programs that is closer to English but still logically precise enough to be translated into machine code.

program

A series of instructions to be carried out by a computer along with initial data. As I mentioned earlier, a program can take time to write, but once it's completed, it usually executes at lightning-fast speed and can be run over and over.

source code

A program written out in a high-level language such as C++. Source code needs to be translated into machine code before it can actually be run on a computer. Machine code is typically represented in hexadecimal (base 16), so it looks something like this:

```
08 A7 C3 9E 58 6C 77 90
```

It's not obvious what this does, is it? Unless you look up all the instruction codes, such a program is incomprehensible—which is why almost no one writes in machine code anymore. In contrast, source code bears at least some resemblance to English. The following C++ statement says, "If salary is less than 0, print error message":

```
if (salary < 0)
    print_error_message();
```

statement

A simple statement usually corresponds to one line of a C++ program, and it is terminated by a semicolon (just as an English statement is terminated by a period). But C++ supports compound statements, just as English does, and these can take up multiple lines. Most C++ statements perform an action, although some perform many actions.

user

The person who runs a program—that is, the person who utilizes the computer to do something useful, such as edit a text file, read email, explore the Internet, or balance a checkbook. The more official name for user is *end user*.

When I was at Microsoft, the user was the person who caused most of the trouble in the world, but he or she was also the person who paid the bills. Even if this hypothetical person was a nontechnical "bozo," there would be no Microsoft without users buying its products. So when you start designing serious programs, it's important that you carefully consider the needs of the user.

What's Different About C++?

Most of the things I've just said about C++ apply to other programming languages such as Pascal, Java, FORTRAN, and Basic. These are all *high-level languages*, meaning they do not correspond closely to machine code but use keywords (such as "if" and "while") that bear some resemblance to English.

Each language was developed for a different purpose. Basic was designed to be easy to learn and to use. As a result, it permitted loose syntax that unfortunately can lead to bad programming habits. Still, Microsoft developed Visual Basic into a powerful, convenient, quick application-building tool for Microsoft Windows and cleaned up some of its sloppiness.

Pascal was developed for use in academic environments, to teach sophisticated programming concepts. Pascal is more elaborate than Basic, but it cannot do everything that C or C++ can.

The legendary computer scientist Dennis Ritchie originally designed C for help in writing operating systems. It's a clean language that supports shortcuts and makes it possible to write more concise programs. The straightforward but comprehensive syntax of C has proven popular with programmers throughout the world. Another advantage of C is that it imposes fewer restrictions than other languages do.

So what about C++?

The major difference between C and C++ is that C++ adds the ability to do *object-oriented programming*. This is an approach especially well-suited to working with complex systems, such as graphical user interfaces and network environments. As an object-oriented programmer, you would ask the following:

1 What are the major kinds of data (that is, information) in the problem to be solved?

2 What operations should be defined for each kind of data?

3 How do the data objects interact with each other?

In learning object-oriented programming, I've found it's easier if you've mastered basic statement syntax first. Therefore, I don't focus on object orientation until Chapter 11.

But I do introduce some objects—pieces of data that can respond to operations—early in the book. For example, in this chapter, I use **cout**, a data object not part of the C language. In C, you'd print information by calling a function, which is a predefined series of statements. But when you use **cout**, you're sending data to an object that—in a real sense—*knows how* to display information.

This turns out to a superior way of doing things: **cout** knows how to print many kinds of data. Best of all, you can extend your own, custom-made data types (classes) to work smoothly with output objects like **cout**. You couldn't do that (not easily) with C.

Building a C++ Program

Writing a program is only the first step of creating an application. First, you enter the program statements.

Enter the Program Statements

To write a C++ program, you need a way to enter the program statements:

▶ You can use a text editor, such as Microsoft Word or Notepad. If you use this approach, you must save the document in plain-text format.

▶ You can enter text in an integrated development environment (IDE). A development environment is a text editor combined with other helpful programming tools. Microsoft Visual Studio is a development environment.

Build the Program (Compile and Link)

Building the program is the process of converting your source code (C++ statements) into an application. This is usually as easy as pressing a function key. The process actually has two steps: compiling and linking (which brings in standard functions that have been written for you). If these steps are successful, you are ready to run the program.

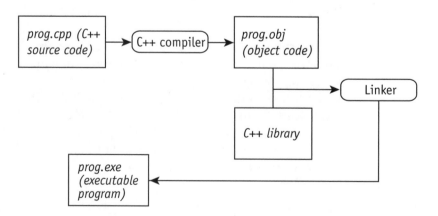

If the build was successful, you can pat yourself on the back; neither the compiler nor linker found errors. Does that mean you're done? No. The compiler catches syntax errors, as well as errors in program structure. But there are many errors it cannot find. Consider this analogy...suppose you have the following sentence:

The moon is made green cheese. [sic]

This is not a grammatically correct sentence in English. To fix the grammar, you'd insert the word *of*:

The moon is made *of* green cheese.

Now the sentence has no syntax errors. But does that necessarily mean it's a true statement? Of course not. You'd need to insert the word *not* in this case:

The moon is *not* made of green cheese.

Programming languages are similar. The C++ compiler determines whether you have a syntactically correct program, and if you don't, it reports the exact line at which the error occurred. But the larger question...the question of *whether the program behaves correctly in all cases*...is not as obvious, which brings us to the next step...

Test the Program

After you've succeeded in building a program, you need to run it to verify that it does what you want it to do. In the case of a serious program—a program to be given or sold to other people—you may need to test it many, many times.

The errors you look for at this stage are *program-logic errors*. These can be far more elusive than syntax errors. Suppose the program prints the wrong number or stops executing for no apparent reason. Which statement caused the problem? The process of testing and determining the source of a problem is called *debugging*.

Revise as Needed

If the program runs correctly, you're done. But if it has program-logic errors, you need to determine the source of error, make changes to the program, and rebuild it.

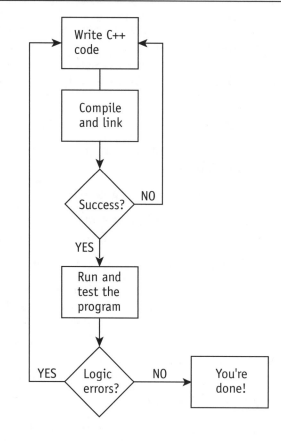

With complex pieces of software, you may need to go through this cycle many times. Such a program may take a good deal of testing to verify that the program behaves correctly in all cases. Until you've done with such testing and revision, the program isn't really done. But with simple programs, you can usually get away with a moderate amount of testing.

Installing Your Own C++ Compiler

The Pearson Web site (*www.informit.com/title/9780132673266*) contains a link to free shareware compilers that you can download, such as the Dev-C++ environment (which I strongly recommend); it includes a complete development environment in which you can write, compile, and test your programs.

Example 1.1. *Print a Message*

To start programming, open a new source file, and enter the following code:

```
print1.cpp

  #include <iostream>
  using namespace std;

  int main() {
      cout << "Never fear, C++ is here!";
      system("PAUSE");
      return 0;
  }
```

Note ▶ You have to do a couple of things differently with Visual Studio or Dev-C++, so don't expect the code to compile correctly until you consult that section.

Remember that exact spacing does not matter, but case-sensitivity does.

If you are using Visual Studio or the Dev-C++ environment, some extra lines of code will appear; leave them in. Also, you will need to open a new project.

If you are using the Dev-C++ environment, go to the File menu, choose New, open a new project, and select Console Application as the project type and pick a project name. Then click the source file main.cpp in the Project window (on the left of the screen). Dev-C++ creates the following code for you:

```
  #include <iostream>
  #include <cstdlib>

  using namespace std;

  int main() {
      system("PAUSE");
      return 0;
  }
```

In this case, you just need to insert the statement that begins with **cout**; insert it right below the line that reads `int main() {` and right above `system("PAUSE");`. Leave the other lines alone.

After entering the program, save it as print1, compile, and run it. Here's what the program prints when correctly entered and run:

```
Never fear, C++ is here!
```

If You're Using the Dev-C++ Environment

If you installed the shareware version of C++ described in the previous section, here's how to run the program:

1 Press F9 to build and run the program.

2 If you don't receive any error messages, the program compiled and linked success-fully. Congratulations! If you received error messages, then either you didn't install the compiler successfully or you mistyped part of the example. Go back and check to make sure you typed every character—including the punctuation—exactly as shown.

If You're Using Microsoft Visual Studio

If you're using Microsoft Visual Studio to write C++ programs, you need to do a couple of extra things. Visual Studio is an excellent tool for writing programs, but it's designed primarily for creating serious Windows applications, not sim-ple programs (which are the first things you should really be doing if new to C++).

To write a program in Visual Studio, you first have to set up the right kind of project. (*Project* is Visual Studio lingo for all the files that go together to form a program.)

1 From the File Menu, choose the File submenu, and from there, choose the New com-mand. Or you can click the New Project button if it is currently displayed near the middle of the screen.

2 Fill out the dialog box by clicking Console Application as the project type. Also, enter the program name—in this case, print1—and click OK.

3 If the file print1.cpp is not displayed, look for it in the list of filenames on the left side of the screen, and double-click it.

Before you enter any C++ code, first delete all the code you see in the print1.cpp file except the following:

```
#include "stdafx.h"
```

This statement needs to be included in console applications (that is, non-Windows applications) created with Visual Studio. If you're using Visual Studio to follow this book, remember to always insert this line at the beginning of every program.

The print1.cpp code should therefore look like this (with the added line shown in bold):

```
#include "stdafx.h"
#include <iostream>
using namespace std;

int main() {
    cout << "Never fear, C++ is here!";
    return 0;
}
```

To build the program, press F7. This launches both the compiler and the linker.

If you succeeded, congratulations! You're on your way. If the program did not build successfully, go back and make sure you entered every line verbatim.

To then run the program, press CTRL+F5. Although there are other ways to run the program from within Visual Studio, this is the only way that avoids the problem of the MS-DOS window flashing input on the screen and then disappearing immediately. Pressing CTRL+F5 (Start without debugging) runs the program and then prints a helpful "Press any key to continue" message so that you have a chance to look at the output.

Note ▶ The line of code reading `system("PAUSE");` is needed to keep a console app from disappearing too quickly. However, if your operating system is not MS-DOS or Windows, this statement might not work, and you'll need to delete it.

How It Works

Believe it or not, this simple program has only one real statement. You can think of the rest as a template for now—stuff you have to include but can safely ignore. (If you're interested in the details, the upcoming "Interlude" discusses the **#include** directive.)

The following syntax shows standard, required items in bold. For now, don't worry about why it's necessary; just use it. In between the braces ({}), you insert the actual lines of the program—which in this case consist of just one important statement.

```
#include <iostream>
using namespace std;

int main() {
    Enter_your_statements_here!
    return 0;
}
```

This program has one only real statement (which you insert into the fifth line shown previously). Don't forget the semicolon (;)!

```
cout << "Never fear, C++ is here!";
```

What is **cout**? This is an *object*—that's a concept I'll discuss a lot more in the second half of the book. In the meantime, all you have to know is that **cout** stands for "console output." In other words—it represents the computer screen. When you send something to the screen, it gets printed, just as you'd expect.

In C++, you print output by using **cout** and a leftward "stream" operator (<<) that shows the flow of data from a value (in this case, the text string "Never fear, C++ is here!") to the console. You can visualize it this way:

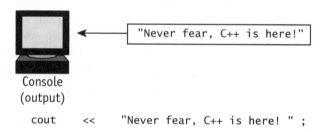

```
    cout      <<      "Never fear, C++ is here! " ;
```

Don't forget the semicolon (;). Every C++ statement must end with a semicolon, with few exceptions.

For technical reasons, **cout** must always appear on the left side whenever it's used. Data in this case flows to the left. Use the leftward "arrows," which are actually two less-than signs (<<) combined together.

The following table shows other simple uses of **cout**:

STATEMENT	ACTION
cout << "Do you C++?";	Prints the words "Do you C++?"
cout << "I think,";	Prints the words "I think,"
cout << "Therefore I program.";	Prints the words "Therefore I program."

EXERCISES

Exercise 1.1.1. Write a program that prints the message "Get with the program!" If you want, you can work on the same source file used for the featured example and alter it as needed. (Hint: Alter only the text inside the quotation marks; otherwise, reuse all the same programming code.)

Exercise 1.1.2. Write a program that prints your own name.

Exercise 1.1.3. Write a program that prints "Do you C++?"

What about the #include and using?

I said that the fifth line of the program is the first "real" statement of the program. I glossed over the first line:

```
#include <iostream>
```

This is an example of a C++ *preprocessor directive*, a general instruction to the C++ compiler. A directive of the form

```
#include <filename>
```

loads declarations and definitions that support part of the C++ standard library. Without this directive, you couldn't use **cout**.

If you've used older versions of C++ and C, you may wonder why no specific file (such as an .h file) is named. The filename iostream is a *virtual include file*, which has information in a precompiled form.

If you're new to C++, just remember you have to use **#include** to turn on support for specific parts of the C++ standard library. Later, when we start using math functions such as **sqrt** (square root), you'll need to switch on support for the math library:

```
#include <cmath>
```

Is this extra work? A little, yes. Include files originated because of a distinction between the C language and the standard runtime library. (Professional C/C++ programmers sometimes avoid the standard library and use their own.) Library functions and objects—although they are indispensable to beginners—are treated just like user-defined functions, which means (as you'll learn in Chapter 4) that they have to be declared. That's what include files do.

▼ *continued on next page*

Interlude

▼ *continued*

You also need to put in a **using** statement. This enables you to refer directly to objects such as **std::cout.** Without this statement, you'd have to print messages this way:

```
std::cout << "Never fear, C++ is here!";
```

We're going to be using **cout** (and its cousin, **cin**) quite a lot, so for now it's easier just to put a **using** statement at the beginning of every program.

Advancing to the Next Print Line

With C++, text sent to the screen does not automatically advance to the next physical line. You have to print a *newline* character to do that. (Exception: If you never print a newline, the text may automatically "wrap" when the current physical line fills up, but this usually produces an ugly result.)

The easiest way to print a newline is to use the predefined constant **endl.** For example:

```
cout << "Never fear, C++ is here!" << endl;
```

Note ▶   The endl name is short for "end line"; it is therefore spelled "end ELL," not "end ONE." Also note that **endl** is actually **std::endl,** but the **using** statement saves you from having to type **std::.**

Another way to print a newline is to insert the characters \n. This is an escape sequence, which C++ interprets as having a special meaning rather than interpreting literally. The following statement has the same effect as the previous example:

```
cout << "Never fear, C++ is here!\n";
```

Example 1.2.   *Print Multiple Lines*

The program in this section prints messages across several lines. If you're following along and entering the programs, remember once again to use uppercase and lowercase letters exactly as shown—although you can change the capitalization of the text inside quotation marks, and the program will still run.

```
print2.cpp
    #include <iostream>
    using namespace std;

    int main() {
        cout << "I am Blaxxon," << endl;
        cout << "the godlike computer." << endl;
        cout << "Fear me!" << endl;

        system("PAUSE");
        return 0;
    }
```

Save the program as print2.cpp, and then compile and run it as explained earlier, for Example 1.1.

How It Works

This example is similar to the first one I introduced. The main difference is this example uses newline characters. If these characters were omitted, the program would print

I am Blaxxon,the godlike computer.Fear me!

which is not what was wanted.

Conceptually, here's how the statements in the program work:

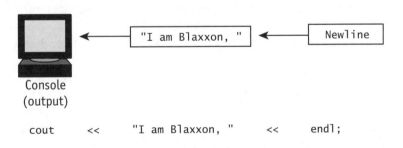

You can print any number of separate items this way—though again, they won't advance to the next physical line without a newline character (**endl**). You could send several items to the console with one statement:

```
cout << "This is a " << "nice " << "C++ program.";
```

which prints the following when run:

```
This is a nice C++ program.
```

Or you can embed a newline, like this:

```
cout << "This is a" << endl << "C++ program.";
```

which prints the following:

```
This is a
C++ program.
```

The example, like the previous one, returns a value. "Returning a value" is the process of sending back a signal—in this case to the operating system or development environment.

You return a value by using the **return** statement:

```
return 0;
```

The return value of **main** is a code sent to the operating system, in which 0 indicates success. The examples in this book return 0 most of the time.

EXERCISES

Exercise 1.2.1.   Remove the newlines from the example in this section, but put in extra spaces so that none of the words are crammed together. (Hint: Remember that C++ doesn't automatically insert a space between output strings.) The resulting output should look like this:

```
I am Blaxxon, the godlike computer. Fear me!
```

Exercise 1.2.2.   Alter the example so that it prints a blank line between each two lines of output—in other words, make the results double-spaced rather than single-spaced. (Hint: Print *two* newline characters after each text string.)

Exercise 1.2.3.   Alter the example so that it prints two blanks lines between each of the lines of output.

Interlude   ## What Is a String?

From the beginning, I've made use of text inside of quotes, as in this statement:

```
cout << "Never fear, C++ is here!";
```

Interlude

▼ *continued*

Everything outside of the quotes is part of C++ syntax. What's inside the quotes is data.

In actuality, all the data stored on a computer is numeric. But depending on how data is used, it can be interpreted as a string of printable characters. That's the case here.

You may have heard of "ASCII code." That's what kind of data "Never fear, C++ is here!" is in this example. The characters *N*, *e*, *v*, *e*, *r*, and so on, are stored in individual bytes, in which each is a numeric code corresponding to a printable character.

I'll talk a lot more about this kind of data in Chapter 7. The important thing to keep in mind is that text enclosed in quotes is considered raw data, as opposed to a command. This kind of data is considered a string of text or, more commonly, just a *string*.

Storing Data: C++ Variables

If all you could do was print messages, C++ wouldn't be useful. The point is usually to get new data from somewhere—such as end-user input—and then do something interesting with it.

Such operations require *variables*; these are locations into which you can place data. You can think of variables as magic boxes that hold values. As the program proceeds, it can read, write, or alter these values as needed. The upcoming example uses variables named ctemp and ftemp to hold Celsius and Fahrenheit values, respectively.

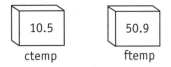

How do values get put into variables? One way is through console input. In C++, you can input values by using the **cin** object, representing (appropriately enough) console input. With **cin**, you use a stream operator showing data flowing to the right (>>):

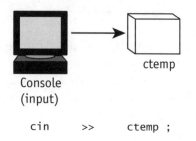

Console
(input)

ctemp

cin   >>   ctemp ;

Here's what happens in response to this statement. (The actual process is a little more complicated, but don't worry about that for now.)

1 The program suspends running and waits for the user to enter a number.

2 The user types a number and presses ENTER.

3 The number is accepted and placed in the variable ctemp (in this case).

4 The program resumes running.

So, if you think about it, a lot happens in response to this statement:

```
cin >> ctemp;
```

But before you can use a variable in C++, you must declare it. This is an absolute rule, and it makes C++ different from Basic, which is sloppy in this regard and doesn't require declaration. (But generations of Basic programmers have banged their heads against their terminals as they discovered errors cropping up as a result of Basic's laxness about variables.)

This is important enough to justify restating, so I'll make it a cardinal rule:

  In C++, you must declare a variable before using it.

To declare a variable, you have to first know what *data type* to use. This is a critical concept in C++ as in most other languages.

Introduction to Data Types

So, a variable is something you can think of as a magic box into which you can place information—or, rather, *data*. But what kind of data?

All data on a computer is ultimately numeric, but it is organized into one of three basic formats: integer, floating-point, and text string.

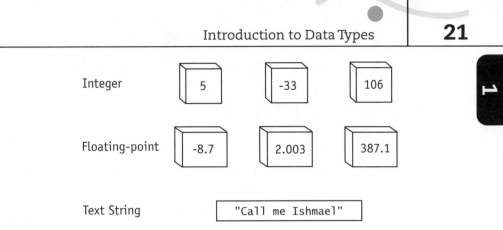

Integer

Floating-point

Text String

"Call me Ishmael"

There are several differences between floating-point and integer format. But the main rule is simple:

If you need to store numbers with fractional portions, use a floating-point variable; otherwise, use integer.

The principal floating-point data type in C++ is **double**. This may seem like a strange name; it stands for "double-precision floating point." There is also a single-precision type (**float**), but its use is rare. When you need the ability to retain fractional portions, you'll get better results—and fewer error messages—if you stick to **double**.

A **double** declaration has the following syntax. Note that this statement is terminated with a semicolon (;), just as most kinds of statements are.

```
double  variable_name;
```

You can also use a **double** declaration to create a series of variables:

```
double  variable_name1, variable_name2, ...;
```

For example, this statement creates a **double** variable named aFloat:

```
double  aFloat;
```

This statement creates a variable of type **double**.

aFloat

The next statement declares four **double** variables named b, c, d, and amount:

```
double  b, c, d, amount;
```

The effect of this statement is equivalent to the following:

```
double  b;
double  c;
double  d;
double  amount;
```

The result of these declarations is to create four variables of type **double**.

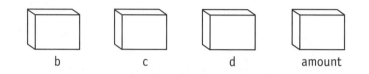

| b | c | d | amount |

Interlude

Why Double Precision, Not Single?

Double precision is like single precision, except better. Double precision supports a greater range of values, with better accuracy: It uses eight bytes rather than four.

C++ converts all data to double precision when doing calculations, which makes sense given that today's PCs include 8-byte co-processors. C++ also stores floating-point constants in double precision unless you specify otherwise (for example, by using the notation 12.5F instead of 12.5).

Double precision has one drawback; it requires more space. This is a factor only when you have large amounts of floating-point values to be stored in a disk file. Then, and only then, should you consider using the single-precision type, **float**.

Example 1.3.   *Convert Temperatures*

Every time I go to Canada, I have to convert Celsius temperatures to Fahrenheit in my head. If I had a handheld computer, it would be nice to tell it to do this conversion for me; computers are good at that sort of thing.

Here's the conversion formula. The asterisk (*), when used to combine two values, means "multiply by."

```
Fahrenheit = (Celsius * 1.8) + 32
```

Now, a useful program will take *any* value input for Celsius and then convert it. This requires the use of some new features:

▶ Getting user input

▶ Storing the value input in a variable

Here is the complete program. Open a new source file, enter the code, and save it as convert.cpp. Then compile and run.

convert.cpp

```cpp
#include <iostream>
using namespace std;

int main() {
    double  ctemp, ftemp;

    cout << "Input a Celsius temp and press ENTER: ";
    cin >> ctemp;
    ftemp = (ctemp * 1.8) + 32;
    cout << "Fahrenheit temp is: " << ftemp;

    system("PAUSE");
    return 0;
}
```

Programs are easier to follow when you add comments—which in C++ are notated by double slashes (//). Comments are ignored by the compiler (they have no effect on program behavior), but they are useful for humans. Here is the commented version:

convert2.cpp

```cpp
#include <iostream>
using namespace std;

int main() {

    double ctemp;    // Celsius temperature
```

▼ *continued on next page*

convert2.cpp, cont.

```
    double ftemp;    // Fahrenheit temperature


    // Get value of ctemp (Celsius temp).

    cout << "Input a Celsius temp and press ENTER: ";
    cin >> ctemp;


    // Calculate ftemp (Fahrenheit temp) and output.

    ftemp = (ctemp * 1.8) + 32;
    cout << "Fahrenheit temp is: " << ftemp << endl;

    return 0;
}
```

This commented version, though it's easier for humans to read, takes more work to enter. While following the examples in this book, you can always omit the comments or choose to add them later. Remember this cardinal rule for comments:

✱   **C++ code beginning with double slashes (//) is a comment and is ignored by the C++ compiler to the end of the line.**

Using comments is always optional, although it is a good idea, especially if any humans (including you) are going to ever look at the C++ code.

How It Works

The first statement inside **main** declares variables of type **double**, ctemp and ftemp, which store Celsius temperature and Fahrenheit temperature, respectively.

```
    double  ctemp, ftemp;
```

This gives us two locations at which we can store numbers. Because they have type **double**, they can contain fractional portions. Remember that **double** stands for "double-precision floating point."

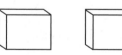

ctemp   ftemp

The next two statements prompt the user and then store input in the variable ctemp. Assume that the user types 10. Then the numeric value 10.0 gets put into ctemp.

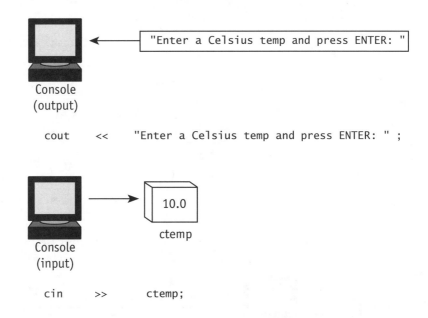

In general, you can use similar statements in your own programs, to print a prompting message and then store the input. The prompt is very helpful—because otherwise the user may not know when they're supposed to do something.

Note ▶ Although the number entered in this case was 10, it is stored as 10.0. In purely mathematical terms, 10 and 10.0 are equivalent—but in C++ terms, the notation 10.0 indicates that the value is stored in floating-point format rather than integer format. This turns out to have important consequences.

The next statement performs the actual conversion, using the value stored in ctemp to calculate the value of ftemp:

```
ftemp = (ctemp * 1.8) + 32;
```

This statement features an *assignment*: the value on the right side of the equal sign (=) is evaluated and then copied to the variable on the left side. This is one of the most common operations in C++.

Again, assuming that 10 was input by the user, this is how data would flow in the program:

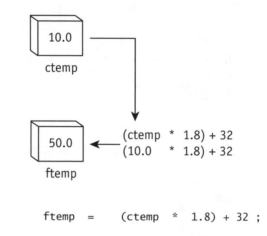

$$\begin{array}{l}(\text{ctemp} \quad * \quad 1.8) + 32 \\ (10.0 \quad * \quad 1.8) + 32\end{array}$$

```
ftemp  =    (ctemp  *  1.8) + 32 ;
```

Finally, the program prints the result—in this case, 50.

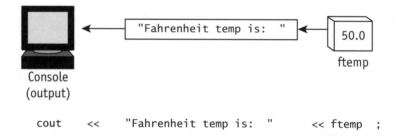

```
cout   <<    "Fahrenheit temp is:  "      << ftemp  ;
```

Optimizing the Program

If you look at the previous example carefully, you might ask yourself, was it really necessary to declare two variables instead of one?

Actually, it wasn't. Welcome to the world of optimization. The following version improves on the first version of the program by getting rid of ftemp and combining the conversion and output steps:

convert3.cpp

```cpp
#include <iostream>
using namespace std;
```

CODE, cont.

```cpp
int main() {

    double  ctemp;    // Celsius temperature

    // Prompt and input value of ctemp.

    cout << "Input a Celsius temp and press ENTER: ";
    cin >> ctemp;


    // Convert ctemp and output results.

    cout << "Fahr. temp is: " << (ctemp * 1.8) + 32;
    cout << endl;

    system("PAUSE");
    return 0;
}
```

Do you detect a pattern by now? With the simplest programs, the pattern is usually as follows:

1 Declare variables.

2 Get input from the user (after printing a prompt).

3 Perform calculations and output results.

For example, the next program does something different but should look familiar. This program prompts for a number and then prints the square. The statements are similar to those in the previous example but use a different variable (n) and a different calculation.

square.cpp

```cpp
#include <iostream>
using namespace std;

int main() {
```

▼ *continued on next page*

CODE, cont.

```
       double  n;

       // Prompt and input value of n.

       cout << "Input a number and press ENTER: ";
       cin >> n;


       // Calculate and output the square.

       cout << "The square is: " << n * n << endl;

       system("PAUSE");
       return 0;
}
```

EXERCISES

Exercise 1.3.1. Rewrite the example so it performs the reverse conversion: Input a value into ftemp (Fahrenheit) and convert to ctemp (Celsius). Then print the results. (Hint: The reverse conversion formula is ctemp = (ftemp − 32) / 1.8.)

Exercise 1.3.2. Write the Fahrenheit-to-Celsius program using only one variable, ftemp. This is an optimization of Exercise 1.3.1.

Exercise 1.3.3. Write a program that inputs a value into a variable n and outputs the cube (n * n * n). Make sure the output statement uses the word *cube* rather than *square*.

Exercise 1.3.4. Rewrite the example square.cpp using the variable name num rather than n. Make sure you change the name everywhere *n* appears.

A Word about Variable Names and Keywords

This chapter has featured the variables ctemp, ftemp, and n. Exercise 1.3.4 suggested that you could replace *n* with *num*, as long as you did the substitution consistently throughout the program. So num is a valid name for a variable as well.

There is an endless variety of variable names I could have used instead. I could, for example, give some variables the names killerRobot or GovernorOf-California.

What variable names are permitted, and what are not? You can use any name you want, as long as you follow these rules.

▶ The first character should be a letter. It cannot be a number. The first character can be an underscore (_), but the C++ library uses that naming convention internally, so it's best to avoid starting a name that way.

▶ The rest of the name can be a letter, a number, or an underscore (_).

▶ You must avoid words that already have a special, predefined meaning in C++, such as the keywords.

It isn't necessary to sit down and memorize all the C++ keywords. You need to know only that if you try using a name that conflicts with one of the C++ keywords, the compiler will respond with an error message. In that case, try a different name.

EXERCISE

Exercise 1.3.5. In the following list, which of the following words are legal variable names in C++, and which are not? Review the rules just mentioned as needed.

```
x
x1
EvilDarkness
PennslyvaniaAve1600
1600PennsylvaniaAve
Bobby_the_Robot
Bobby+the+Robot
whatThe???
amount
count2
count2five
5count
main
main2
```

Chapter 1   *Summary*

Here are the main points of Chapter 1:

▶ Creating a program begins with writing C++ source code. This consists of C++ statements, which bear some resemblance to English. (Machine code, by contrast, is completely incomprehensible unless you look up the meaning of each combination of 1s and 0s.) Before the program can be run, it must be translated into machine code, which is all the computer really understands.

▶ The process of translating C++ statements into machine code is called *compiling*.

▶ After compiling, the program also has to be linked to standard functions stored in the C++ library. This process is called *linking*. After this step is successfully completed, you have an executable program.

▶ If you have a development environment, the process of compiling and linking a program (*building*) is automated so you need only press a function key.

▶ Simple C++ programs have the following general form:

```
#include "iostream"
using namespace std;

int main() {
    Enter_your_statements_here!
    return 0;
}
```

▶ To print output, use the **cout** object. For example:

```
cout << "Never fear, C++ is here!";
```

▶ To print output and advance to the next line, use the **cout** object, and send a newline character (**endl**). For example:

```
cout << "Never fear, C++ is here!" << endl;
```

▶ Almost every C++ statement is terminated by a semicolon (;).

▶ Double slashes (//) indicate a comment; all text to the end of the line is ignored by the compiler itself. But comments can be read by humans who have to maintain the program.

▶ Before using a variable, you must declare it. For example:

```
double x;     // Declare x as a floating-pt variable.
```

▶ Variables that may store a fractional portion should have type **double**. This stands for "double-precision floating point." The single-precision type (**float**) should be used only when storing large amounts of floating-point data on disk.

▶ To get keyboard input into a variable, you can use the **cin** object. For example:

```
cin >> x;
```

▶ You can also put data into a variable by using assignment (=). This operation evaluates the expression on the right side of the equal sign (=) and places the value in the variable on the left side. For example:

```
x = y * 2;  // Multiply y times 2, place result in x.
```

2 Decisions, Decisions

Once you know how to do input, output, and data calculations, you're on your way to writing real programs. But the most useful programs have behavior: the ability to respond to conditions.

Although they don't have human judgment, computers do make simple decisions. That's what this chapter is about. We'll start by looking at short programs. By the end of the chapter, you'll have the tools to write a complete game program!

But First, a Few Words about Data Types

You might think of a variable as a magic box or a bucket to hold data. But it can hold only so much information—information being a precious commodity. It's not infinite.

Chapter 1 developed examples using floating-point data. This chapter uses integer data, which (unlike floating point) cannot hold fractional portions. You might think that you can just use **double**, the floating-point type, for all situations. But it's very inefficient to use **double** when you don't really need it.

Under the covers, integer and floating-point formats look nothing alike. Here's how a value—150—is stored in different formats. I've made a number of simplifying assumptions here: For example, floating-point format uses binary, not decimal, representation (and integer format usually uses something called *two's complement*, which I describe in Appendix B). The sign bit, s, is 0 for positive, and 1 is for negative.

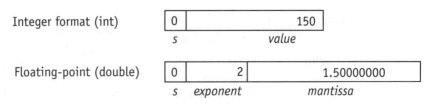

| Integer format (int) | 0 | 150 |
| | s | value |

| Floating-point (double) | 0 | 2 | 1.50000000 |
| | s | exponent | mantissa |

The range of type **double** is much greater than integer; it can also store fractional portions of a number. But its use is more taxing on computer resources. Furthermore, its precision for very high integers is limited, and rounding errors can occur.

So, use the right data type for the job. It is definitely better to use the integer format when you're working with whole numbers only.

Here's the syntax for declaring an **int** (integer) variable:

```
int variable_name;
```

```
int variable_name = initial_value;
```

You can also declare multiple **int** variables together:

```
int variable1, variable2, variable3,...;
```

Each variable (*variable1*, *variable2*, and so on) can be initialized, whether or not the others are. For example:

```
int a = 0, b = 1, c, d, e, f, g = 20;
```

You can assign values between integer and floating-point variables, but if you assign a floating-point value to an integer, the compiler complains about loss of data.

```
int n = 5;
double x = n;   // Ok: convert 5 to floating-pt
n = 3.7;        // Warning: convert from double to int
n = 3.0;        // This also gets a warning.
```

If you assign 3.7 to n, the fractional portion, 0.7, is dropped, so that the value 3 is stored in the variable n. But assigning 3.0 is also problematic, because the presence of a decimal point (.) causes a value to be stored in floating-point (**double**) format.

C++0x ▶ The new C++0x specification includes support for the **long long int** type, which has an incredibly large range. I'll have more to say about **long long int** in Chapter 10. (Note: Some compilers have already been supporting this type for several years.)

Decision Making in Programs

A computer can carry out only those instructions that are clear and precise.

The computer will always do exactly what you say. That's both good and bad news. The problem is that the computer follows instructions even if they are absurd; it has no judgment with which to question anything. Once again, this is one of the cardinal rules of programming...maybe *the* cardinal rule:

A computer can carry out only those instructions that are absolutely clear.

A computer has no such thing as discretion or judgment. It can follow only those rules that are mathematically precise, such as comparing two values to see whether they are equal.

What about Artificial Intelligence (AI)?

"But," I hear you say, "computers are smart! They *can* use judgment. What about that program Big Blue that beat Gary Kasparov, the world's chess champion, in 1997?"

Artificial intelligence (AI) is the exception that proves the rule. It might seem that an AI computer program is exercising judgment...but only because of a complex program made up of thousands, even millions, of individual little decisions, each of which is simple and mathematically clear.

Consider the human brain. The operation of each neuron is simple: Given sufficient stimulus, it fires; otherwise, it doesn't. It's the *network* of billions of neurons, analogous to the millions of lines in a big computer program, that creates a host for consciousness.

Is that so different? This question leads us to Very Big Dilemmas. If a computer can be conscious, is it murder to shut it off or junk it? But if a computer cannot be conscious, then what is it about the brain that's so special? Answering such questions is far outside the scope of this book, but I consider this issue—could robots or computers theoretically become conscious?—the most central problem in philosophy today.

if and if-else

The simplest way to program behavior is to say, "If A is true, then do B." That's what the C++ **if** statement does. Here is the simple form of the **if** statement syntax:

```
if (condition)
    statement
```

There are more complex forms of this statement, which we'll get to soon. But first consider an **if** statement that compares two variables, x and y.

```
if (x == y)
    cout << "x and y are equal.";
```

This is strange. There are two equal signs (==) here instead of one (=). This is not a typo. C++ has two separate operators in this regard: One equal sign means assignment, which copies values into a variable. Two equal signs (==) test for equality.

Note ▶ Using assignment (=) where you meant to use test-for-equality (==) is one of the most common C++ programming errors.

What if, instead of executing one statement in response to a condition, you want to do a series of things? The answer is you can use a *compound statement* (or *block*):

```
if (x == y) {
    cout << "x and y are equal." << endl;
    cout << "Isn't that nice?";
    they_are_equal = true;
}
```

The significance of the block is that either all these statements are executed or none of them is executed. If the condition is not true, the program jumps past the end of the block. A block can be plugged into the **if** statement syntax because of another cardinal rule:

✱ **Anywhere you can use a statement in C++ syntax, you can use a compound statement (or *block*).**

A compound statement is just another kind of statement. The block itself is not terminated by a semicolon (;)—only the statements inside are. This is one of those few exceptions to the semicolon rule.

Here's the **if** statement syntax again:

```
if (condition)
    statement
```

Applying the cardinal rule I just stated, we can insert a block for the *statement*:

```
if (condition) {
    statements
}
```

where *statements* is zero or more statements (there will almost always be at least one).

You can also specify actions to take if the condition is *not* true. This is optional. As you might guess, this variation uses the **else** keyword:

```
if (condition)
    statement1
else
    statement2
```

Either *statement1* or *statement2*, or both, can be a compound statement. Now you have the complete **if** syntax.

Here's a brief example:

```
if (x == y)
    cout << "x and y are equal";
else
    cout << "x and y are NOT equal";
```

This code can be rewritten to use statement-block style:

```
if (x == y) {
    cout << "x and y are equal";
} else {
    cout << "x and y are NOT equal";
}
```

All **if** and **if-else** code can be written this way so that curly braces (also called *set braces*) always appear even when the statement blocks include just one statement each. This is extra work, but many programmers recommend it. The advantage of this approach is that it is clearer and easier to maintain, especially when you go back and add new statements.

Consider a simple **if-else** statement:

```
if (x == y)
    cout << "x and y equal";
else
    cout << "x, y not equal";
```

The following diagram illustrates the flow of control:

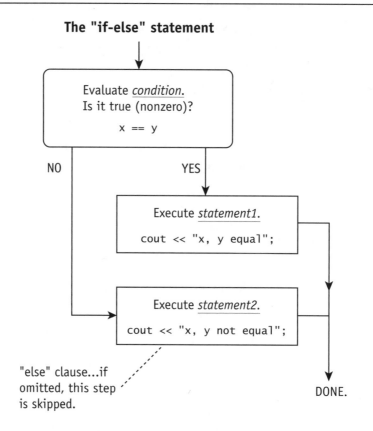

The "if-else" statement

Evaluate *condition*.
Is it true (nonzero)?

x == y

NO   YES

Execute *statement1*.

cout << "x, y equal";

Execute *statement2*.

cout << "x, y not equal";

"else" clause...if
omitted, this step
is skipped.

DONE.

Interlude

Why Two Operators (= and ==)?

If you've used another programming language such as Pascal or Basic, you may wonder why = and == are two separate operators. After all, Basic uses a single equal sign (=) for both assignment and test-for-equality, using context to tell them apart.

In C and C++, the following code is freely permitted. Yet it's almost always wrong.

```
int x, y;
...
if (x = y)                    // ERROR! Assignment!
    cout << "x and y are equal";
```

What this example does is assign the value of y to x and use that value as the test condition. If this value is nonzero, it is considered "true." Conse-

Interlude

▼ *continued*

quently, if y is any value other than zero, the previous condition is "true," and the statement is always executed!

Here is the correct version, which will do what you want:

```
if (x == y)           // CORRECT: test for equality
    cout << "x and y are equal";
```

Here, "x == y" is an operation that tests for equality and evaluates as true or false. The important thing to remember is not to confuse test-for-equality with assignment (x = y).

Why allow this potential source of problems? Well, most expressions in C++ (the main exception being calls to **void** functions) produce a value, and this includes assignment (=), which is an expression with a side effect. So, you can initialize three variables at once by doing this:

```
x = y = z = 0;   // Set all vars to 0.
```

which is equivalent to this:

```
x = (y = (z = 0));   // Set all vars to 0.
```

Each assignment, beginning with the rightmost one (z = 0), produces the value that was assigned (0), which is then used in the next assignment (y = 0). In other words, 0 is passed along three times, each time to a new variable.

C++ treats "x = y" as an expression that produces a value. And there'd be nothing wrong with that, except that *almost any valid numeric expression can be used as a condition.* Therefore, the compiler does not complain if you write this, even though it's usually wrong:

```
if (x = y)
    // Do action... (Probably should have used ==)
```

Example 2.1.   *Odd or Even?*

OK, enough preliminaries. It's time to look at a complete program that uses decision making. This is a simple example, but it introduces a new operator (%) and shows the **if-else** syntax in action.

The program takes a number from the keyboard and reports whether it is odd or even.

```cpp
even1.cpp

#include <iostream>
using namespace std;

int main() {
    int  n, remainder;

    // Get a number from the keyboard.

    cout << "Enter a number and press ENTER: ";
    cin >> n;

    // Get remainder after dividing by 2.

    remainder = n % 2;

    // If remainder is 0, the number input is even.

    if (remainder == 0)
        cout << "The number is even." << endl;
    else
        cout << "The number is odd." << endl;

    system("PAUSE");
    return 0;
}
```

Once again, if you are following along and want to enter this example by hand, the comments—lines beginning with double slashes (//)—are optional.

How It Works

The first statement of the program declares two integer variables, n and remainder:

```cpp
    int  n, remainder;
```

The next thing the program does is get a number and store it in the variable n. This should look familiar by now:

```cpp
    cout << "Enter a number and press ENTER: ";
    cin >> n;
```

Now it's just a matter of performing a test on n to see whether it is odd or even. How do you do that? Answer: You divide the number by 2 and look at the remainder. If the remainder is 0, the number is even (in other words, divisible by 2). Otherwise, it's odd.

That's exactly what's done here. The following statement divides by 2 and gets the remainder. This is called *modulus* or *remainder* division. The result is stored in a variable named (appropriately enough) remainder.

```
int remainder = n % 2;
```

Again, if the remainder is 0, that means n was divided evenly by 2.

The percent sign (%) loses its ordinary meaning in C++ and instead signifies "remainder division." Here are some sample results:

EXAMPLE	REMAINDER FROM DIVISION	REMARKS
3 % 2	1	Odd
4 % 2	0	Even
25 % 2	1	Odd
60 % 2	0	Even
25 % 5	0	Divisible by 5
13 % 5	3	Not divisible by 5

After dividing n by 2 and getting the remainder, we get a result of either 0 (even) or 1 (odd). The **if** statement compares the remainder to 0 and prints the appropriate message.

```
if (remainder == 0)
    cout << "The number is even." << endl;
else
    cout << "The number is odd." << endl;
```

Notice the double equal signs (==) used in this code. As I mentioned earlier, test-for-equality uses double equal signs; a single equal sign (=) would mean assignment. If I'm getting repetitive on this subject, it's because when I was first learning C, I made this mistake too many times myself!

Here is the same code written in statement-compound style:

```
if (remainder == 0) {
    cout << "The number is even." << endl;
} else {
    cout << "The number is odd." << endl;
}
```

Optimizing the Code

The version of the Odd-or-Even program I just introduced is not as efficient as it could be. The remainder variable is not necessary in this case. This version is a little better:

```cpp
#include <iostream>
using namespace std;

int main() {
    int  n;

    // Get a number n from the keyboard.

    cout << "Enter a number and press ENTER: ";
    cin >> n;


    // Get remainder after dividing by 2.
    // If remainder is 0, then n is even.

    if (n % 2 == 0)
        cout << "The number is even.";
    else
        cout << "The number is odd.";

    return 0;
}
```

even2.cpp

This version performs modulus division inside the condition, comparing the result to 0.

EXERCISE

Exercise 2.1.1.   Write a program that reports whether a number input is divisible by 7. (Hint: If a number is divisible by 7, that means you can divide it by 7 and get a remainder of 0.)

Introducing Loops

One of the most powerful concepts in any programming language is that of loops. It's one of the things that enables a program to do far more than perform a simple calculation and quit. In this section, you'll see how a few lines of C++ can set up an operation to be performed—potentially—thousands of times.

When a program is in a loop, it performs an operation over and over as long as a condition is true. The simplest form is the classic **while** statement:

```
while (condition)
    statement
```

As with **if**, you can make replace *statement* with a compound statement, which in turns lets you put as many statements inside the loop as you want.

```
while (condition) {
    statements
}
```

while evaluates the *condition* and executes the *statement* if that condition is true. Then it repeats that operation until *condition* evaluates to false.

About the simplest program example is a loop that prints the numbers 1 to N, where N is a number input at the keyboard. We'll look first at this program in *pseudocode* form. For the next page or so, I use the variable names I and N, because it makes the pseudocode easier to follow. Assume that the variables have already been declared.

Here's how to print the numbers from 1 to N:

1 Get a number from the keyboard and store in N.

2 Set I to 1.

3 While I is less than or equal to N,

> **3A** Output I to the console.

> **3B** Add 1 to I.

The first two steps initialize the variables I and N, which are integers. I is set directly to 1. N is set by keyboard input. Assume that the user inputs 2.

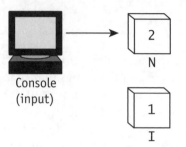

Console
(input)

Step 3 is the interesting one. The program first considers whether I (which is 1) is less than or equal to N (which is 2). Since I *is* less than N, the program carries out steps 3A and 3B. First, it prints the value of I.

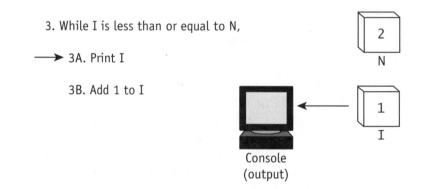

3. While I is less than or equal to N,

⟶ 3A. Print I

3B. Add 1 to I

Console
(output)

Then it increases the value of I by 1. (This is also called *incrementing*.)

3. While I is less than or equal to N,

3A. Print I

⟶ 3B. Add 1 to I

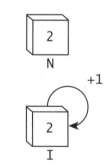

Having carried out these steps, the program performs the comparison again. Because this is a **while** statement, not an **if**, the program continues to perform the steps 3A and 3B until the condition is no longer true.

The condition is still true (because I is still less than or equal to 2), so the program continues.

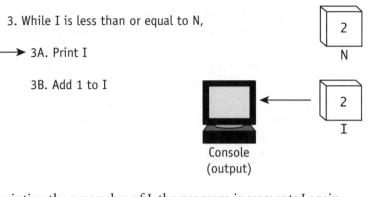

3. While I is less than or equal to N,

→ 3A. Print I

3B. Add 1 to I

2
N

2
I

Console
(output)

After printing the new value of I, the program increments I again.

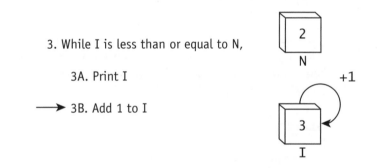

3. While I is less than or equal to N,

3A. Print I

→ 3B. Add 1 to I

2
N

+1

3
I

The program performs the test once more. Because I is now greater than N, the condition (is I less than or equal to N?) is no longer true. The program ends. 3 is never printed. The output of the program, in this case, is as follows:

    1 2

Because the user input 2, the loop executed twice. But with a large input for N (say, 1024), the loop would continue many more times.

Think about it: Here's a program a few steps long that could (depending on the value input for N), print millions of numbers! The theoretical value of N has no limit, except for the maximum integer size; the largest number that can be stored in an **int** variable on a 32-bit system is approximately 2 billion (that is, 2,000 million). But note that the new **long long int type** (mandated in the new C++0x spec) is far larger still.

Interlude

Infinite Loopiness

Can you set the loop condition in such a way that it will *always* be true? And if so, what happens? The answer is yes, and the loop will run until something interrupts it. (One such way is to use the **break** keyword, as you'll see in upcoming material.)

Unless you have a mechanism for escaping from a loop, it's important to make sure it doesn't run forever. Otherwise, the program will seem to reach a state where it sits there and does nothing. It's not doing nothing; it just can't break out of a pointless loop that, left to itself, threatens to go on till the end of time.

Therefore, always make sure there's a way to exit.

Example 2.2.   *Print 1 to N*

Now let's use C++ code to implement the loop described in the last section. This uses a simple **while** loop with compound-statement syntax. Here and in the remainder of the book, I stick to the C++ convention of using lowercase letters for variable names.

```
count1.cpp
   #include <iostream>
   using namespace std;

   int main() {
       int  i, n;

       // Get number from the keyboard and initialize i.

       cout << "Enter a number and press ENTER: ";
       cin >> n;
       i = 1;

       while (i <= n) {  // While i less than or equal n,
           cout << i << " ";   //    Print i,
           i = i + 1;          //    Add 1 to i.
       }
```

CODE, cont.

```
        system("PAUSE");
        return 0;
    }
```

Some of the comments are on the same line as the C++ statements. This works because a comment begins with the double slashes (//) and continues to the end of line. Comments can be on their own lines or to the right of the statements.

The program, when run, counts to the specified number. For example, if the user inputs 6, the program prints the following:

```
    1 2 3 4 5 6
```

How It Works

This example introduces a new operator—although I'm sure you've surmised what it does. This is the less-than-or-equal-to test.

```
    i <= n
```

The less-than-or-equal operator (<=) is one of several relational operators, all of which return true or false.

OPERATOR	MEANING
==	Test for equality
!=	Test for inequality (greater than or less than)
>	Greater than
<	Less than
>=	Greater than or equal to
<=	Less than or equal to

If you followed the logic in the section "Introducing Loops," you know the loop itself is straightforward. The braces ({}) create a statement block so that the **while** loop executes two statements each time through, rather than one.

```
    while (i <= n) {        // While i less than or equal n,
        cout << i << " "; //    Print i,
        i = i + 1;          //    Add 1 to i.
    }
```

If you think about it, you'll see that the last number to be printed is n—which is what we want. As soon as i becomes greater than n, the loop ends, and the output statement never executes for that case. The first statement inside the loop is as follows:

```
cout << i << " ";      //   Print i,
```

This statement adds a space after i is printed. This is so the output is spaced like this:

    1 2 3 4 5

rather than this:

    12345

The loop then adds 1 to i before continuing to the next cycle. This ensures that the loop eventually ends, because i will sooner or later become greater than n (at which point the loop condition will fail).

```
i = i + 1;                   //   Add 1 to i.
```

It may be easier to see how a **while** loop works in the following diagram, which shows the flow of control in the loop.

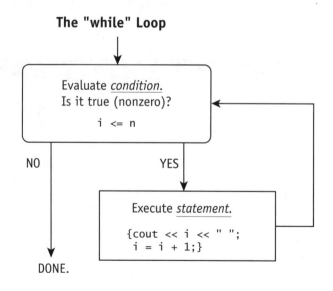

The "while" Loop

Evaluate *condition.*
Is it true (nonzero)?

i <= n

NO   YES

Execute *statement.*

{cout << i << " ";
i = i + 1;}

DONE.

Optimizing the Program

The program can be made more efficient by combining a couple of the statements. You can do this by initialization, in which you assign a value as you declare it. You can use the equal sign (=) to give any numeric or string variable a value when created.

```
int   variable = value;
```

In this revised program, i is initialized so it doesn't need to be assigned a value later.

```cpp
count2.cpp

    #include <iostream>
    using namespace std;

    int main() {
        int  i = 1, n;

        // Get number from the keyboard and initialize i.

        cout << "Enter a number and press ENTER: ";
        cin >> n;


        while (i <= n) {  // While i less than or equal n,
            cout << i << " ";   //    Print i,
            i = i + 1;          //    Add 1 to i.
        }

        return 0;
    }
```

EXERCISES

Exercise 2.2.1.   Write a program to print all the numbers from n1 to n2, where n1 and n2 are two numbers specified by the user. (Hint: You'll need to prompt for two values n1 and n2; then initialize i to n1 and use n2 in the loop condition.)

Exercise 2.2.2.   Alter the example so that it prints all the numbers from n to 1 in reverse order, as in 5 4 3 2 1. (Hint: To decrement a value inside the loop, use the i = i – 1; statement.)

Exercise 2.2.3.   Alter the example so that it prints only even numbers, as in 0, 2, 4. (Hint: One of the things you'll need to do is initialize i to 0.)

Exercise 2.2.4.   Alter the example so that it initializes both i and n in the same line. Initialize n to 0. Although this isn't required in this case, it is good programming practice.

True and False in C++

What exactly are "true" and "false"? Are these values stored in the computer in numeric form, like any other? Yes. Every Boolean (relational) operator returns 1 or 0:

IF THE CONDITION EVALUATED IS...	THE EXPRESSION RETURNS...
true	1
false	0

Also, any nonzero value fed to a condition is interpreted as true. So, in this example, the statements are always executed:

```
if (true) {              // ALWAYS EXECUTED
    // Do some stuff.
}
```

This next case creates an infinite loop: This is normally an error, unless you provide some way to break out of it (such as a **break** or **return** statement):

```
// INFINITE LOOP!

while (true) {
    // Do some stuff.
}
```

Interlude	**The bool Data Type**

Most recent versions of C++ support the **bool** ("Boolean") type, which is similar to the integer type but holds one of two values: true (1) or false (0). Any nonzero numeric input is converted to 1 ("true"). You should use the **bool** type if it is supported.

```
bool  is_less_than;

is_less_than = (i < n);    // Store the value
                           //    true (1) if
                           //    i is less than n.
```

Only very old compilers lack support for the **bool** data type. If your computer lacks it, you'll need to use the **int** type in place of **bool** and use the number 1 in place of **true**.

The Increment Operator (++)

The designers of C—the language on which C++ is based—had an obsession for creating shortcuts. One of their favorites was the increment operator (++), which adds 1 to a variable. For example:

```
n++;        // n = n + 1
```

Consider the loop of the previous section:

```
while (i <= n) {      // While i less than or equal n,
    cout << i << " ";  //    Print i,
    i = i + 1;         //    Add 1 to i.
}
```

The second statement inside the loop can be replaced with a statement using the increment operator, producing the following:

```
while (i <= n) {      // While i less than or equal n,
    cout << i << " ";  //    Print i,
    i++;               //    Add 1 to i.
}
```

So far, this substitution has saved only a few keystrokes. But it gets better. The item i++ is "an expression with a side effect"—meaning it produces a value *and* performs an action. i++ is an expression with the same value as i; but after i++ is evaluated, it adds 1 to i. So, the loop can be shortened to this:

```
while (i <= n) {     // While i less than or equal n,
    cout << i++ << " ";  // Print i, then add 1 to i.
}
```

Do you see what this does? The statement prints out the current value of i and then increments it.

But be forewarned that in a complex statement that features multiple uses of i++, side effects can produce undefined results. ("Undefined" is a polite way of saying "Good luck, for we have no idea what will happen next, but it will probably be very bad.")

Therefore, to be safe, use the increment operator (++) on a given variable no more than once each statement.

You might wonder whether there is a corresponding operator for subtraction. In fact, there are four increment/decrement operators. Here, *var* means any numeric variable: Generally, it should be an integer to work with these operators reliably.

OPERATOR	ACTION
var++	Pass along the current value of *var*; then add 1 to var.
++*var*	Add 1 to *var*; then pass along the result.
var--	Pass along the current value of *var*; then subtract 1 from it.
--*var*	Subtract 1 from *var*; then pass along the result.

Statements vs. Expressions

Until now, I've gone along using the terms *statement* and *expression*. These are fundamental terms in C++, so it's important to clarify them. In general, you recognize a statement by its terminating semicolon (;).

```
cout << i++ << " ";
```

A simple statement such as this is usually one line of a C++ program. But remember that a semicolon terminates a statement, so it's legal (though not especially recommended) to put two statements on a line:

```
cout << i << " ";  i++;
```

Fine, you say—a statement is (usually) one line of a C++ program, terminated with a semicolon. So, what's an expression? An expression usually produces a value (with a few notable exceptions). You terminate an expression to get a simple statement. Here's a sample list of expressions, along with descriptions of what value each produces:

```
x                    // Produces value of x
12                   // Produces 12
x + 12               // Produces x + 12
x == 33              // Test for equality: true or false
x = 33               // Assignment: produces value assigned
++num                // Produces value before incrementing
i = num++ + 2        // Complex expression; produces
                     //    new value of i
```

Because these are expressions, any of these can be used as part of a larger expression, including assignment (=). The last three have *side effects*. x = 33 alters the value of x, and num++ alters the value of num. The last example changes the value of both num and i. Remember, any expression can be turned into a statement by using a semicolon (;).

```
num++;
```

The fact that any expression can be turned into a statement this way makes some strange statements possible. You could, for example, turn a literal constant into a statement, but such a statement would do exactly nothing.

Introducing Boolean (Short-Circuit) Logic

Sometimes you need words like *and*, *or*, and *not* to express a decision. This is just common sense. For example, here (in pseudocode) is a decision that uses "and":

If age > 12 and age < 20

The subject is a teenager

Programmers use *Boolean algebra*, named for nineteenth-century mathematician George Boole, to express such conditions. For example, the subexpressions "age > 12" and "age < 20" are each evaluated, and if both are true, the whole expression is true:

age > 12 and age < 20

The following table summarizes the three logical (Boolean) operators in C++:

SYMBOL	OPERATION	C++ SYNTAX	ACTION
&&	AND	*expr1* **&&** *expr2*	Evaluate *expr1*. If it's true, evaluate *expr2*. Then, if both are true, return true; otherwise, return false.
||	OR	*expr1* **||** *expr2*	Evaluate *expr1*. If false, evaluate *expr2*. Then return true unless both are false.
!	NOT	**!** *expr1*	Evaluate *expr1*. Reverse the true/false value.

So, the earlier example expresses "and" this way in C++:

```
if (age > 12 && age < 20)      // if age>12 AND age<20
    cout << "The subject is a teenager.";
```

Logical operators have lower precedence than the relational operators (<, >, >=, <=, !, and ==), which in turn have lower precedence than arithmetic operators (such as + and *). Consequently, the following statement does what you'd probably expect:

```
if (x + 2 > y && a == b)
    cout << "The data passes the test";
```

This means "If x+ 2 is greater than y and a is equal to b, then print the message." Of course, you can achieve greater clarity by using parentheses:

```
if (((x + 2) > y) && (a == b))
    cout << "The data passes the test";
```

In C++, the "and" and "or" operators (&& and ||) employ short-circuit logic: This means the second operand is evaluated only if it needs to be. For example, with an "and" expression (&&), the first condition is evaluated: If it's false, the value of the entire expression is false, and the second condition is never evaluated. This can make a difference if the second condition has side effects.

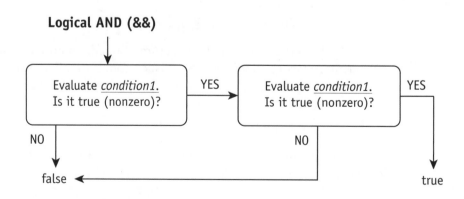

Logical AND (&&)

Note ▶ Don't confuse the logical operators with the C++ bitwise operators (&, |, ^, and ~). The bitwise operators compare each bit in one operand to the corresponding bit in the other. Bitwise operators do not use short-circuit logic, while logical operators do.

2

Interlude

What Is "true"?

The logical operators—&&, ||, and !—can take any expressions as input as long as they are convertible to **bool**, which is a subtype of integer. Any nonzero expression is considered "true." Some programmers take advantage of this behavior to write shortcuts:

```
if (n && b > 2)
    cout << "n is nonzero and b is greater than 2.";
```

Many programmers dislike the use of any conditions other than ones that have obvious true/false values (such as "x > 0" or "x == 0"). However, the following condition, which says "Do as long as n is nonzero," is a shortcut favored by some.

```
if (n--)                        // If n doesn't equal 0.
    cout << n << endl;
```

This fragment is a succinct way of counting down from n to zero. The problem is that if n somehow gets set to a negative value, you're in trouble, because the decrement operator (--) will just keep subtracting the value of n. So, even in this case, it's safer to use this:

```
if (n-- > 0)
    cout << n << endl;
```

Example 2.3. *Testing a Person's Age*

This section demonstrates a simple use of the "and" operator (&&). The program here determines whether a number is in a particular range—in this case, the range of teen numbers, 13 through 19.

```
range.cpp

    #include <iostream>
    using namespace std;

    int main() {
        int  n;

        cout << "Enter an age and press ENTER: ";
        cin >> n;

        if (n > 12 && n < 20)
            cout << "Subject is a teenager." << endl;
        else
            cout << "Subject is not a teenager." << endl;

        system("PAUSE");
        return 0;
    }
```

How It Works

This brief program uses a condition made up of two relational tests:

    n > 12 && n < 20

Because logical "and" (&&) has lower precedence than relational operations (> and <), the "and" operation is performed last. The test performs as if written this way:

    (n > 12) && (n < 20)

Consequently, if the number input is greater than 12 and less than 20, the condition evaluates to true and the program prints the message "Subject is a teenager."

EXERCISE

Exercise 2.3.1.   Write a program to test a number for being in the range 0 to 100, inclusive.

Introducing the Math Library

Until now, I've used the C++ standard library for the support of input-output streams. That enabled the code to use **cout** and **cin**, and it's why the programs had to include the following line:

```
#include <iostream>
```

Now I'm going to introduce one of the math functions. You can use any of the C++ operators (such as +, *, -, /, and %) without library support because operators are intrinsic to the language itself. But to use math functions, you need to include this line:

```
#include <cmath>
```

This **#include** directive brings in declarations for all the math functions, so you don't have to prototype them yourself. C++ supports many math functions (such as the trig and exponential functions), but this chapter uses just one: **sqrt**, which returns a square root.

```
#include <cmath>
//...

double x = sqrt(2.0);  // Assign square root of 2 to x
```

Programmers affectionately refer to this as the "squirt" function. As with most math functions, this function accepts and returns a floating-point result. If you assign the result to an integer, C++ drops the fractional portion (and also issues a warning message).

```
int  n = sqrt(2.0);   // Place the value 1 into n,
                      //   after truncating 1.41421.

double x = sqrt(2);   // Ok: int converted to double.
```

Example 2.4.   *Prime–Number Test*

Now we have enough tools to do something interesting: determine whether a number is prime. A prime number is a number divisible only by itself and 1. It's obvious that 12,000 is not prime (since it's a multiple of 10), but it's not obvious whether 12,001 is. This is a classic math problem to give to a computer program. Here's the code:

prime1.cpp

```cpp
#include <iostream>
#include <cmath>
using namespace std;

int main() {
    int  n;    // Number to test for prime-ness
    int  i;    // Loop counter
    int  is_prime = true;   // Boolean flag...
                            // Assume true for now.

    // Get a number from the keyboard.

    cout << "Enter a number and press ENTER: ";
    cin >> n;

    // Test for prime by checking for divisibility
    //  by all whole numbers from 2 to sqrt(n).

    i = 2;
    while (i <= sqrt(n)) {   // While i is <= sqrt(n),
        if (n % i == 0)      //   If i divides n,
            is_prime = false; //     n is not prime.
        i++;                 //   Add 1 to i.
    }

    // Print results

    if (is_prime)
        cout << "Number is prime." << endl;
    else
        cout << "Number is not prime." << endl;

    system("PAUSE");
    return 0;
}
```

When the program is run, if the user enters 12000, the program will print the following:

```
Number is not prime.
```

To discover what happens with 12001, I'll leave you to run the program for yourself.

Note ▶ When running the program, enter 12000 rather than 12,000. A C++ program doesn't normally expect or permit commas inside numerals. In Chapter 10, I show a way around this limitation.

How It Works

The core of the program is the following loop:

```
while (i <= sqrt(n)) { // While i is <= sqrt(n),
    if (n % i == 0)         //  If i divides n,
        is_prime = false;   //    n is not prime.
    i++;                    //    Add 1 to i.
}
```

Let's look at this a little more closely. Here's a pseudocode version of this loop:

Set i to 2.

While i is less than or equal to the square root of i,

    If n is divisible by the loop counter (i),

        n is not prime.

    Add 1 to i

The loop checks for divisors starting with 2, stopping at the square root of n, because if it was going to find divisors, it would have found them by that point.

The divisibility test uses the modulus operator (%) introduced earlier. This operator performs division and returns the remainder. If the second number, i, perfectly divides the first, the remainder is 0; in that case, n is not prime.

```
if (n % i == 0)
    is_prime = false;
```

The beginning of the program assumes the number is prime (is_prime = true), so if no divisors are found, the result is true. The values **true** and **false** are predefined in C++.

Optimizing the Program

There are several ways this program can be improved, but the most important change is to exit the loop after a divisor is found. There is no reason to continue, since that would waste CPU time. The C++ **break** keyword exits the nearest enclosing loop. Here is the revised code:

```
i = 2;
while (i <= sqrt(n)) {
    if (n % i == 0) {
        is_prime = false;
        break;
    }
    i++;
}
```

Note how braces ({}) are now used to create a statement block for the **if** statement, because two actions must be taken. In this case, the braces are not optional.

EXERCISE

Exercise 2.4.1.   Optimize the program by calculating the square root of n just once, rather than over and over. You'll need to declare another variable and set it to the square root of n. The type should be **double**. You can then use this variable in the **while** condition.

Example 2.5.   *The Subtraction Game (NIM)*

In this final example, we'll use the tools in the chapter to create a simple game...and give the computer a strategy that wins every time unless the player acts correctly.

Welcome to the game of NIM. The simplest version is the Subtraction Game, in which two players take turns subtracting a number from a common total. Each player may subtract either 1 or 2. Whoever first reduces the total to zero or less wins. For example:

1 We agree to start with the number 7, and you go first.

2 You subtract 2 from the total, making it 5.

3 I also subtract 2 from the total, making it 3.

4 You subtract 1 from the total, making it 2.

5 I subtract 2 from the total, making it 0. I win!

This is a simple game, with a simple winning strategy. Consider what happens if the total is 3. Then, regardless of whether you subtract 1 or 2, I can always cause the next subtraction to get to zero, and I win. Therefore, if I make the total 3, I can force a win.

Similarly, if I make the total 6, then whether you subtract 1 or 2, I can make the total 3, which indirectly forces a win for me. I win on the following turn.

The winning strategy, therefore, is for me to always make the total a multiple of 3 if I can. Programmatically, how do I do this? I use our old friend, the remainder-division operator:

SITUATION	BEST RESPONSE
total % 3 produces 2.	Subtract 2; the new total will be an exact multiple of 3.
total % 3 produces 1.	Subtract 1; the new total will be an exact multiple of 3.
total % 3 produces 0.	The total is already a multiple of 3. All I can do is subtract 1 and hope for the best.

The pseudocode version of the program is as follows:

> Print invitation to play, and ask for a starting total.
> While true   // This is an "infinite loop"
> > If total % 3 is 2
> > > Subtract 2 from total and announce move
> > Else
> > > Subtract 1 from total and announce move
> > If total is 0 or less
> > > Announce "I win!" and exit
> > Prompt opponent for move
> > While input is not 1 or 2
> > > Re-prompt for input
> > Adjust total by input amount and announce result
> > If total is 0 or less,
> > > Announce "You win!" and exit

This is the most complex program yet. It creates a complete game, with an optimal computer strategy. The user can win only by selecting each move perfectly.

nim.cpp

```cpp
#include <iostream>

using namespace std;

int main() {
    int total, n;

    cout << "Welcome to NIM. Pick a starting total: ";
    cin >> total;
    while (true) {

        // Pick best response and print results.

        if ((total % 3) == 2) {
            total = total - 2;
            cout << "I am subtracting 2." << endl;
        } else {
            total--;
            cout << "I am subtracting 1." << endl;
        }
        cout << "New total is " << total << endl;
        if (total == 0) {
            cout << "I win!" << endl;
            break;
        }

        // Get user's response; must be 1 or 2.

        cout << "Enter num to subtract (1 or 2): ";
        cin >> n;
        while (n < 1 || n > 2) {
            cout << "Input must be 1 or 2." << endl;
            cout << "Re-enter: ";
            cin >> n;
        }
```

```
            total = total - n;
            cout << "New total is " << total << endl;
            if (total == 0) {
                cout << "You win!" << endl;
                break;
            }
        }
        system("PAUSE");
        return 0;
    }
```

How It Works

The program makes use of the "or" operator (||) introduced earlier. If either condition—n is less than 1 *or* n is greater than 2—is true, the user is prompted for a new value.

```
    while (n < 1 || n > 2) {
        cout << "Input must be 1 or 2." << endl;
        cout << "Re-enter: ";
        cin >> n;
    }
```

Because of short-circuit logic, if the first condition (n < 1) is true, the second condition is not evaluated because it's not necessary.

This program example also uses the **break** keyword, which exits out of the loop.

```
        break;
```

EXERCISES

Exercise 2.5.1.   One problem is that if the initial starting number is less than 1, the program will deal in negative numbers and never end. Revise the program so that it only accepts an initial total greater than 0.

Exercise 2.5.2.   For the more ambitious: Write a version that permits subtracting *any* number from 1 to N, where N is stipulated at the beginning of the game. For example, the user when prompted might say that each player can subtract any number from 1 to 7. Can you create an optimal computer strategy for this general case?

Exercise 2.5.3. Revise the program so that it keeps playing the game until the user wants to quit. (Hint: You'll need to add yet another loop around the existing main loop.)

Chapter 2   *Summary*

Here are the main points of Chapter 2:

▶ Use the right data type for the job. A variable that can have no fractional portion should be given type **int**, unless it exceeds the range of **int** type—more than 2 billion (thousand million).

▶ You can declare integer variables by using the data type's name followed by a variable name and semicolon. You can also declare multiple variables, separating adjacent variable names with a comma.

```
int  variable;
int  variable1, variable2, ...;
```

▶ Constants have **int** or **double** type as appropriate. Any value with a decimal point is automatically considered a floating-point value: 3 is stored as an **int**, but 3.0 is stored as a **double**.

▶ The simplest decision-making structure in C++ is the **if** statement:

```
if (condition)
    statement
```

▶ The **if** statement has an optional **else** clause, so you can use this form:

```
if (condition)
    statement
else
    statement
```

▶ Anywhere you can use a statement, you can use a compound statement (or *block*), consisting of zero or more statements enclosed in braces ({}).

```
if (condition) {
    statements
}
```

▶ Don't confuse assignment (=) with test-for-equality (==). Here's a correct use of the two operators:

```
if (x == y)
    is_equal = true;
```

▶ The **while** keyword executes a statement as long as the condition is true:

```
while (condition)
    statement
```

▶ The modulus operator performs division and then returns the remainder. For example, the result of the following expression is 3:

```
13 % 5
```

▶ An expression is a value formed by a variable, literal, or smaller expressions combined with C++ operators (this can include assignment, =).

▶ Any expression can be turned into a statement by adding a semicolon.

```
num++;
```

▶ The increment operator is convenient shorthand for adding 1 to a number. This creates an expression with a side effect.

```
cout << n++;     // Print n and then add 1 to n.
```

▶ You can use the C++ logical (Boolean) operators "and" (&&), "or" (||), and "not" (!) to create complex conditions. The "and" and "or" operators use short-circuit logic.

▶ The easiest way to get out of a loop is often to use the **break** keyword:

```
break;
```

The Handy, All-Purpose "for" Statement

3

Some tasks are so common that C++ provides special syntax just to represent them with fewer keystrokes: for example, the increment operator (++). Because adding 1 is so common, C++ provides this operator even though you could get away without it.

```
n++;    // Add 1 to n.
```

Another case is the **for** statement. Its only purpose in life is to make certain kinds of **while** loops more concise. But this turns out to be so useful that programmers come to rely on it heavily. I use it throughout the rest of this book.

You'll find that once you use it a few times, the **for** statement will become second nature. But it looks strange the first time you see it.

Loops Used for Counting

As you worked with **while** loops in Chapter 2, you may have noticed the typical use of a loop is to count to a number, performing some action a specific number of times. For example:

```
i = 1;
while(i <= 10) {
    cout << i << " ";
    i++;
}
```

This code basically just prints numbers from 1 to 10. The loop variable gets an initial value of 1 and then is incremented each time through the loop. You can summarize what happens this way:

1 Set i to 1.

2 Perform the loop action.

3 Set i to 2.

4 Perform the loop action.

5 Set i to 3.

6 Perform the loop action.

7 Continue in this manner up to, and including, i being set to 10.

In other words, perform the loop 10 times, each time giving a successively higher value to i. Loops of this kind tend to do the same things over time.

We can identify three such actions: *initialize* the loop counter; test the loop *condition*; and, if true, execute the statement and the *increment*. Then go back to step 2 until the condition is false.

initializer: evaluated just once, before the loop begins

condition

```
i = 1;
while (i <= 10) {
    cout << i << " ";
    i++;
}
```

increment: evaluated after each execution of the loop statement

It would be nice to have a way to express these actions in one succinct statement. Then it would be easy to write a loop that counts to 10.

Introducing the "for" Loop

The **for** statement provides this mechanism, letting you specify the *initializer*, *condition*, and *increment* in one compact line.

initializer: evaluated just once, before the loop begins

condition

increment: evaluated after each execution of the loop statement

```
for (i = 1; i <= 10; i++)
    cout << i << " ";
```

This is obviously more concise. All the settings that control operation of the loop are placed between parentheses. More formally, here is the syntax of the **for** statement, along with the equivalent **while** loop.

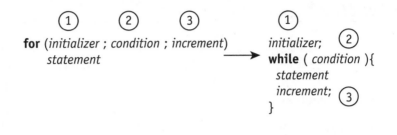

Syntax diagrams are all well and good. But sometimes it's more helpful to look at a flowchart. It's easy to see from the following chart that the *initializer* is evaluated one time, after which the **for** statement sets up an enhanced version of the **while** loop by evaluating *increment* before cycling. Remember, this prints all numbers from 1 to 10:

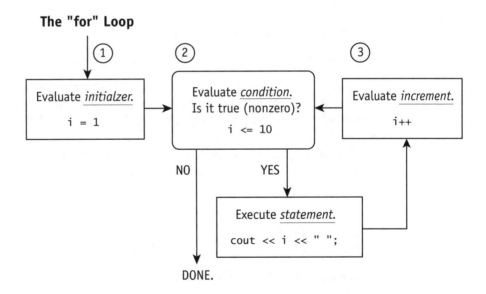

I've found that a structure like **for** can still be fuzzy until you look at a lot of examples. That's the purpose of the next section.

C++0x ▶ The new C++0x specification provides a new version of the **for** keyword that automatically works on all members of a set, similar to "for each" in some other languages. To use this version, however, you need to understand arrays and containers. I present this new version of **for** in Chapter 10.

A Wealth of Examples

Let's start with a slight variation of the example you've already seen. The loop variable, i, is initialized to 1 (i = 1), and the loop continues while the condition (i <= 5) is true. This is the same as the earlier example, except that the loop counts only to 5.

```
for(i = 1; i <= 5; i++)
    cout << i << " ";
```

This produces the following output:

```
1 2 3 4 5
```

The next example runs from 10 to 20 rather than 1 to 5:

```
for(i = 10; i <= 20; i++)
    cout << i << " ";
```

This produces the following output:

```
10 11 12 13 14 15 16 17 18 19 20
```

Here the *initializer* is i = 10, and the *condition* is i <= 20. These expressions determine the initial and terminal settings of the loop. (The condition terminates the loop when it is no longer true; therefore, the highest value of i will be 20 in this case.)

These settings do not have to be constants. In this next example, they are determined by variables. The loop counts from n1 to n2.

```
n1 = 32;
n2 = 38;
for (i = n1; i <= n2; i++)
    cout << i << " ";
```

This produces the following output:

```
32 33 34 35 36 37 38
```

The *increment* expression can be any expression at all; it does not have to be i++. You can just as easily use i--, which causes the **for** loop to count downward. Note the use of greater-than-or-equal-to (>=) in the condition in this example.

```
for(i = 10; i >= 1; i--)
    cout << i << " ";
```

This produces the following output:

```
10 9 8 7 6 5 4 3 2 1
```

The **for** statement is highly flexible. By changing the *increment* expression, you can count by 2 rather than by 1.

```
for(i = 1; i <= 11; i = i + 2)
    cout << i << " ";
```

This produces the following output:

```
1 3 5 7 9 11
```

As a final example, you don't have to use i as the loop variable. Here's an example that uses a loop variable named j:

```
for(j = 1; j <= 5; j++)
    cout << j * 2 << " ";
```

This produces the following output:

```
2 4 6 8 10
```

Note that in this case, the loop statement prints j * 2, which is why this loop prints even numbers.

Interlude

Does "for" Always Behave Like "while"?

I said that a **for** loop is a special case of **while** and performs exactly as the corresponding **while** loop would. That's *almost* true. There is one minor exception, which—for the purposes of this entire book and 99 percent of all the code you will ever write—will likely make no difference. The exception involves the **continue** keyword. You can use this keyword in a loop, placing it in its own statement, to say "Advance immediately to the next cycle of the loop."

```
continue;
```

This is a kind of "Advance directly to Go" statement. It doesn't break out of the loop (which the **break** keyword does); it just speeds things up.

The difference in behavior is this: In a **while** loop, the **continue** statement

▼ *continued on next page*

Interlude

▼ *continued*

neglects to execute the *increment* (i++) before advancing to the next cycle of the loop. In a **for** loop, the **continue** statement does execute the *increment* before advancing. This second behavior would usually be the behavior you'd want, and that provides one more reason why **for** is useful.

Example 3.1.   *Printing 1 to N with "for"*

Now we'll apply the **for** statement in a complete program. This example does the same thing as Example 2.2 on page 46: It prints all the numbers from 1 to n. But this version is more compact.

```cpp
count2.cpp

#include <iostream>
using namespace std;

int main() {
    int  i, n;

    // Get number from the keyboard and initialize i.

    cout << "Enter a number and press ENTER: ";
    cin >> n;

    for (i = 1; i <= n; i++)    //   For i = 1 to n,
        cout << i << " ";       //       Print i.

    system("PAUSE");
    return 0;
}
```

The program, when run, counts to the specified number. For example, if the user inputs 9, the program prints the following:

    1 2 3 4 5 6 7 8 9

How It Works

This example features a simple **for** loop. The loop condition in this example uses n, a number that the program gets from the user.

```
cout << "Enter a number and press ENTER: ";
cin >> n;
```

The loop prints numbers from 1 to n, where n is the number entered.

```
for (i = 1; i <= n; i++)    //   For i = 1 to n,
    cout << i << " ";       //        Print i.
```

To review:

▶ The expression "i = 1" is the *initializer* expression; this is evaluated just once, before the loop is executed. This initial value of i is therefore 1.

▶ The expression "i <= n" is the *condition*. This is checked before each loop cycle to see whether the loop should continue. If, for example, n is 9, the loop terminates when i reaches 10, so the loop is not executed for the case of i equal to 10.

▶ The expression "i++" is the *increment* expression, which is evaluated after each execution of the loop statement. This drives the loop by adding 1 to i each time.

The program logic is therefore as follows:

Set i to 1.

While i is less than or equal to n,

Print i,

Add 1 to i.

EXERCISES

Exercise 3.1.1.   Use the **for** statement in a program that prints all the numbers from n1 to n2, where n1 and n2 are two numbers specified by the user. (Hint: You'll need to prompt for the two values; then, inside the **for** statement, initialize i to n1, and use n2 in the loop condition.)

Exercise 3.1.2.   Rewrite the example so that it prints all the numbers from n to 1 in reverse order. For example, the user enters 4, and the program prints 5 4 3 2 1. (Hint: In the **for** loop, initialize i to n, use the condition i >= 1, and subtract 1 from i in the increment step.)

Exercise 3.1.3.   Write a program that prints all numbers from 1 to n but prints only even numbers or only odd numbers. Each number printed will be 2 higher than the last.

Compound Statements (Blocks) with "for"

Up until now, I've used the following statement in the body of every loop.

```
cout << i << " ";
```

Of course, you don't have to use this statement. You don't have to print the value of i; in fact, you don't have to print out anything at all. I chose this statement for its value in demonstrating what a loop does. You can do a lot of other things in a loop.

As with **if** and **while**, you can use a compound statement with **for**.

```
for (initializer; condition; increment) {
    statements
}
```

As before, this syntax follows from the rule that wherever you can use a statement in C++, you can also use a compound statement.

Here is an example that executes two statements inside a **for** loop:

```
for (i = 1; i <= 10; i++) {
    cout << "The square root of " << i << " is ";
    cout << sqrt(i) << endl;
}
```

This is equivalent to the following:

```
i = 1;
while (i <= 10) {
    cout << "The square root of " << i << " is ";
    cout << sqrt(i) << endl;
    i++;
}
```

Declaring Loop Variables on the Fly

One of the added benefits of the **for** statement is that you can use it to declare a variable that has scope local to the **for** loop itself. The variable is declared "on the fly," for the explicit use of the **for** loop itself. For example:

```
for (int i = 1; i <= n; i++)   // For i = 1 to n,
    cout << i << " ";          // Print i.
```

Here, i is declared inside the *initializer* expression of the **for** statement.

If you use this technique, you don't need to declare i separately from the loop. You could rewrite Example 3.1 this way:

---

count3.cpp

```
#include <iostream>
using namespace std;

int main() {
    int  n;

// Get a number from the keyboard.

    cout << "Enter a number and press ENTER: ";
    cin >> n;

    for (int i = 1; i <= n; i++)   // For i = 1 to n,
        cout << i << " ";          //     Print i.

    system("PAUSE");
    return 0;
}
```

Example 3.2.   *Prime-Number Test with "for"*

Now let's return to the prime-number example of Example 2.3 (page 55), but write that program using a **for** loop rather than **while**. This example determines whether a number input is a prime number. (Remember, a number is prime if it is evenly divisible only by itself and 1.)

The same basic logic is involved as in Example 2.3. Here is pseudocode for a prime-number test:

> Set i to 2.
>
> While i is less than or equal to the square root of n,
>
>> If i divides evenly into n,

> n is not prime.

> Add 1 to i.

The **for**-loop version uses exactly the same approach; when compiled, it carries out the same instructions as the **while** loop. However, because the essential nature of a **for** loop is to perform counting—in this case counting from 2 to the square root of n—we can think of it a little differently. Conceptually, this approach is simpler:

> For all whole numbers from 2 to the square root of n,

>> If i divides evenly into n,

>>> n is not prime.

Here is the complete program for testing whether a number is a prime number. Again, this is a version of the program described in Example 3.2, so most of it should look familiar.

prime2.cpp

```cpp
#include <iostream>
#include <cmath>
using namespace std;

int main() {
    int  n = 0;    // Number to test for prime-ness
    bool is_prime = true; // Boolean flag; assume true
                          //   until proven otherwise

    // Get a number from the keyboard.

    cout << "Enter a number and press ENTER: ";
    cin >> n;

    // Test for prime by checking for divisibility
    //   by all whole numbers from 2 to sqrt(n).

    for (int i = 2; i <= sqrt(n); i++) {
        if (n % i == 0)
            is_prime = false;
    }
```

prime2.cpp, cont.

```
    // Print results

    if (is_prime)
        cout << "Number is prime." << endl;
    else
        cout << "Number is not prime." << endl;

    system("PAUSE");
    return 0;
}
```

When the program is run, if the user enters 23, the program prints the following:

```
Number is prime.
```

How It Works

The beginning of the program uses **#include** directives to enable needed C++-library support. The C++ library is used here, because the program will be calling the **sqrt** function to get the square root of a number.

```
#include <iostream>
#include <cmath>
```

The rest of the program defines **main**—the main (and so far, only) function. The first thing that **main** does is declare the three variables the program will use. (Note: The loop variable i is declared in the **for** loop itself.)

```
int  n = 0;    // Number to test for prime-ness
bool is_prime = true; // Boolean flag; assume
                      //   true until proven
                      //   otherwise
```

The purpose of is_prime is to store a value of true (1) or false (0). If your version of C++ does not support the **bool** type, you need to declare it as an integer:

```
int  is_prime = 1;    // is_prime is assumed TRUE
```

If the program cannot find a divisor for n, it should conclude that the number is prime. Therefore, is_prime gets a default setting of **true**. In other words, if is_prime isn't specifically set to **false**, then it will reflect the fact that the number is prime.

The heart of the program is the **for** loop that performs the prime-number test. As I described in Chapter 2, it's necessary to test for divisors only up to the square root of n. If a divisor is not found by then, the number being tested has no divisors other than itself and 1.

Remember that the expression n%i divides n by i and returns the remainder: If this remainder is ever zero, n is not prime.

```
for (int i = 2; i <= sqrt(n); i++) {
    if (n % i == 0)
        is_prime = false;
}
```

Remember how a **for** loop works: The first expression in parentheses, i = 2, is the *initializer*; the second expression, i <= sqrt(n), is the *condition*; and the last is the *increment*. This **for** loop is therefore equivalent to the following:

```
int i = 2;
while (i <= sqrt(n)) {
    if (n % i == 0)
        is_prime = false;
    i++;
}
```

The **for**-loop version includes only one statement inside the loop—this embedded statement is an **if** statement. The braces ({}) are legal because you can always have a compound statement with only statement between the braces. Yet their only purpose here is clarity. The **for** loop works just as well if you write it this way, without the braces:

```
for (int i = 2; i <= sqrt(n); i++)
    if (n % i == 0)
        is_prime = false;
```

Or, for greater clarity, you can include the braces at each level so that the program is clearer about what is in the **for** loop and what is in the body of the **if** statement:

```
for (int i = 2; i <= sqrt(n); i++){
    if (n % i == 0) {
        is_prime = false;
    }
}
```

Some programmers advise against *ever* writing a **for** or **if** statement without compound statement syntax (that is, use of the braces), even when they are not strictly necessary. In this case, leaving in the braces—at least for the **for** statement—is probably a good idea, because they make the program easier to follow.

EXERCISE

Example 3.2.1.   Revise the example to be more optimal. When you consider the speed of today's microprocessors, it's unlikely you'll see a difference in execution...although if you attempt to test an extremely large number, say, more than a billion, you might see a difference. (By the way, good luck in finding a prime number in that range, if you're just looking for one by chance. Prime numbers become rarer as you get into larger values.)

In any case, the following changes to code make the program more efficient for large numbers:

▶ Calculate the square root of n only once by declaring a variable square_root_of_n and determining its value before entering the **for** loop. This variable should be a **double** variable.

▶ Once a divisor of n is found, you don't need to look for any more divisors. Therefore, in the **if** statement inside the loop, add a **break** statement (breaking out of the loop) after setting is_prime to false.

I described both of these optimizations in Chapter 2. The point of this exercise is to use them with the **for** statement.

Comparative Languages 101: The Basic "For" Statement

If you've programmed in Basic or FORTRAN, you've seen statements something like the C++ **for** statement, whose purpose is to count from one number to another. For example, this Basic loop prints all the whole numbers from 1 to 10:

```
For i = 1 To 10
    Print i
Next i
```

The Basic "For" statement has the advantage of clarity and ease of use. It admittedly takes fewer keystrokes to use than C++'s **for**.

But against that, the advantage of the C++ **for** statement is its flexibility.

One way in which the C++ **for** statement is so much more flexible is that you can use it with any three valid C++ expressions. The condition (the middle expression) does not even have to be a logical expression such as i < n, although using other kinds of expressions is not recommended. For the purposes of evaluating a condition in an **if**, **while**, or **for** statement, remember that any nonzero value is considered "true."

The **for** statement does not require you to use all three expressions (*initializer*, *condition*, and *increment*). If any of these are missing, they are ignored. If the *condition* is omitted, it's considered "true" by default, setting up an infinite loop.

```
for(;;) {
    // Infinite loop!
}
```

An infinite loop can be a bad thing. But if you have some way to break out of it (for example, by using the **break** statement), it may be perfectly OK. In the following example, the user can break out of the loop by entering the value 0:

```
for (;;) {
    // Do some stuff...

    cout << "Enter a number and press ENTER: ";
    cin >> n;
    if (n == 0)
        break;

    // Do some more stuff...
}
```

Chapter 3   *Summary*

Here are the main points of Chapter 3:

▶ The purpose of a **for** statement is usually to repeat an action while counting to a particular value. The statement has this following syntax:

```
for (initializer; condition; increment)
    statement
```

This is equivalent to the following **while** loop:

```
initializer;
while (condition) {
    statement
    increment;
}
```

▶ A **for** loop behaves exactly like its **while**-loop counterpart, with one exception: In a **for** loop, the **continue** statement increments the loop variable before advancing to the top of the next loop cycle.

▶ As with other kinds of control structures, you can always use a compound statement with **for**, by using opening and closing braces ({}):

```
for (initializer; condition; increment) {
    statement
}
```

▶ A variable such as i in the following example is called a *loop variable*:

```
for (i = 1; i <= 10; i++)
    cout << i << " ";
```

▶ In the *initializer* expression, you can declare a variable "on the fly." This declaration gives the variable scope local to the **for** loop itself, meaning that changes to the variable don't affect variables of the same name outside the loop.

```
for (int i = 1; i <= 10; i++)
    cout << i << " ";
```

▶ As with **if** and **while**, the loop condition of a **for** statement can be any valid C++ expression that evaluates to a true/false value or a numeric value; any nonzero value is considered "true."

▶ You can omit any and all of the three expressions inside the parentheses of the **for** statement (*initializer, condition, increment*). If the condition is omitted, the loop is executed unconditionally. (In other words, the loop is infinite.) Remember to use a **break** statement to get out of it.

```
for (;;) {

    // Infinite loop!

}
```

Functions: Many Are Called

The most fundamental building block in the programming toolkit is the function—often known as *procedure* or *subroutine* in other languages. A function is a group of related statements that accomplish a specific task. Once you define a function, you can execute it whenever you need to do so.

Understanding functions is a crucial step to programming in C++: Without functions, it would be a practical impossibility to engage in serious programming projects. Imagine how difficult it would be to write a word processor, for example, without some means of dividing the labor. Functions make this possible.

The Concept of Function

If you've followed the book up until this point, you've already seen use of a function—the **sqrt** function, which takes a single number as input and returns a result.

```
double sqrt_of_n = sqrt(n);
```

This is not far removed from the mathematical concept of function. A function takes zero or more inputs—called *arguments*—and returns an output, called a *return value*. Here's another example. This function takes two inputs and returns their average:

```
cout << avg(1.0, 4.0);
```

Once a function is written, you can call it any number of times. By *calling* a function, you transfer execution of the program to the function-definition code, which runs until it is finished or until it encounters a **return** statement; execution then is transferred back to the caller.

This may sound like a foreign language if you're not used to it. It's easy to see in a conceptual diagram. In the following example, the program 1) runs normally until it calls the function avg, passing the arguments a and b, and 2) as a result, the program transfers execution to avg. (The values of a and b are passed to x and y, respectively.)

① ↓
```
void main() {
    double a = 1.2;
    double b = 2.7;
    cout << "Avg is" << avg(a,b);
    cout << endl;
    cout << endl;
    system("PAUSE");
}                                    ②


double avg(double x, double y) {
    double v = (x + y)/2;
    return v;
}
```

The function runs until it encounters **return**, at which point: 3) execution returns to the caller of the function, which in this case prints the value that was returned. Then, 4) execution resumes normally inside **main**, and the program continues until it ends.

④ ↓
```
void main() {
    double a = 1.2;
    double b = 2.7;
    cout << "Avg is" << avg(a,b);
    cout << endl;
    cout << endl;
    system("PAUSE");
}                                    ③


double avg(double x, double y) {
    double v = (x + y)/2;
    return v;
}
```

Note that only **main** is guaranteed to be executed. Other functions run only as called. But there are many ways a function can be called. For example, main can call a function A, which in turn calls B and C, which in turn calls D.

The Basics of Using Functions

I recommend the following approach for creating and calling user-defined functions:

1 At the beginning of your program, *declare* the function.

2 Somewhere in your program, *define* the function.

3 Other functions can then call the function.

Step 1: Declare (Prototype) the Function

A function declaration (or *prototype*) provides type information only. It has this syntax:

```
return_type   function_name (argument_list);
```

The *return_type* is a data type indicating what kind of value the function returns (what it passes back). If the function does not return a value, use **void**.

The *argument_list* is a list of zero or more argument names—separated by commas if there are more than one—each preceded by the corresponding type. (Technically, you don't need the argument names in a prototype, but it is a good programming practice.) For example, the following statement declares a function named avg, which takes two arguments of type **double** and returns a **double** value.

```
double avg(double x, double y);
```

The *argument_list* may be empty, which indicates that it takes no arguments.

Step 2: Define the Function

The function definition tells what the function does. It uses this syntax:

```
return_type   function_name (argument_list) {
    statements
}
```

Most of this looks like a declaration. The only thing that's different is that the semicolon is replaced by zero or more statements between two braces ({}). The braces are required no matter how few statements you have. For example:

```
double avg(double x, double y) {
    return (x + y) / 2;
}
```

The **return** statement causes immediate exit, and it specifies that the function returns the amount (x + y) / 2. Functions with no return value can still use the **return** statement but only to exit early.

```
return;
```

Step 3: Call the Function

Once a function is declared and defined, it can be used—or rather, *called*—any number of times, from any function. For example:

```
n = avg(9.5, 11.5);
n = avg(5, 25);
n = avg(27, 154.3);
```

A function call is an expression: As long as it returns a value other than **void**, it can be used inside a larger expression. For example:

```
z = x + y + avg(a, b) + 25.3;
```

When the function is called, the values specified in the function call are passed to the function arguments. Here's how a call to the avg function works, with sample values 9.5 and 11.5 as input. These are *passed* to the function, as arguments. When the function returns, the value in this case is assigned to z.

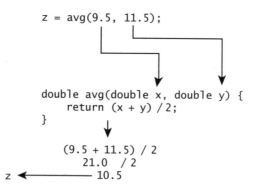

Another call to the function might pass different values—in this case, 6 and 26. (Because these are integer values, they are implicitly converted, or *promoted*, to type **double**.)

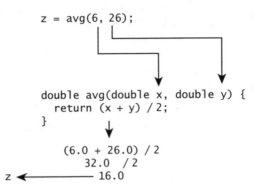

```
z = avg(6, 26);


      double avg(double x, double y) {
         return (x + y) / 2;
      }

            (6.0 + 26.0) / 2
               32.0  / 2
    z ←          16.0
```

Example 4.1.   *The avg() Function*

This section shows a simple function call in the context of a complete program. It demonstrates all three steps: declare a function, define it, and call it.

```cpp
avg.cpp

#include <iostream>
using namespace std;

// Function must be declared before being used.

double avg(double x, double y);

int main() {
    double a = 0.0;
    double b = 0.0;

    cout << "Enter first number and press ENTER: ";
    cin >> a;
    cout << "Enter second number and press ENTER: ";
    cin >> b;

    // Call the function avg().
    cout << "Average is: " << avg(a, b) << endl;
```

▼ *continued on next page*

avg.cpp, cont.

```
        system("PAUSE");
        return 0;
}


// Average-number function definition
//
double avg(double x, double y) {
    return (x + y)/2;
}
```

How It Works

This code is a very simple program, but it demonstrates the three steps I outlined earlier:

1 *Declare* (that is, prototype) the function at the beginning of the program.

2 *Define* the function somewhere in the program.

3 *Call* the function from within another function (in this case, **main**).

Although function declarations (prototypes) can be placed anywhere in a program, you should almost always place them at the beginning. The general rule is that functions must be declared before being called. (They do not, however, have to be defined before being called, which makes it possible for two functions to call each other.)

```
double avg(double x, double y);
```

The function definition for the avg function is extremely simple, containing only one statement. In general, though, function definitions can contain as many statements as you want.

```
double avg(double x, double y) {
    return (x + y)/2;
}
```

The **main** function calls avg as part of a larger expression. The computed value (in this case, the average of the two inputs, a and b) is returned to this statement in **main**, which then prints the result.

```
cout << "Average is: " << avg(a, b) << endl;
```

Function Call a Function!

A program can have any number of functions. For example, you could have two functions in addition to **main**, as in the following version of the program. Lines that are new or changed are in bold.

```
avg2.cpp
```

```cpp
#include <iostream>
using namespace std;

// Functions must be declared before being used.

void print_results(double a, double b);
double avg(double x, double y);

int main() {
    double a = 0.0;
    double b = 0.0;

    cout << "Enter first number and press ENTER: ";
    cin >> a;
    cout << "Enter second number and press ENTER: ";
    cin >> b;

    // Call the function pr_results().
    print_results(a, b);

    system("PAUSE");
    return 0;
}

// print_results function definition
//
void print_results(double a, double b) {
    cout << "Average is: " << avg(a, b) << endl;
}
```

▼ *continued on next page*

avg2.cpp, cont.

```
// Average-number function definition
//
double avg(double x, double y) {
    return (x + y)/2;
}
```

This version is a little less efficient, but it illustrates an important principle: You are not limited to only one or two functions. The program creates a flow of control as follows:

$$\text{main()} \rightarrow \text{print\_results()} \rightarrow \text{avg()}$$

EXERCISES

Exercise 4.1.1. Write a program that defines and tests a factorial function. The factorial of a number is the product of all whole numbers from 1 to N. For example, the factorial of 5 is 1 * 2 * 3 * 4 * 5 = 120. (Hint: Use a **for** loop as described in Chapter 3.)

Exercise 4.1.2. Write a function named print_out that prints all the whole numbers from 1 to N. Test the function by placing it in a program that passes a number n to print_out, where this number is entered from the keyboard. The print_out function should have type **void**; it does not return a value. The function can be called with a simple statement:

```
print_out(n);
```

Example 4.2. *Prime-Number Function*

Chapter 2 included an example that was actually useful: determining whether a specified number was a prime number. We can also write the prime-number test as a function and call it repeatedly.

The following program uses the prime-number example from Chapters 2 and 3 but places the relevant C++ statements into their own function, is_prime.

prime2.cpp

```
#include <iostream>
#include <cmath>
using namespace std;
```

prime2.cpp, cont.

```cpp
// Function must be declared before being used.
bool prime(int n);

int main() {
    int i;

// Set up an infinite loop; break if user enters 0.
// Otherwise, evaluate n from prime-ness.

    while (true) {
      cout << "Enter num (0 = exit) and press ENTER: ";
      cin >> i;
      if (i == 0)                 // If user entered 0, EXIT
        break;
      if (prime(i))                     // Call prime(i)
        cout << i << " is prime" << endl;
      else
        cout << i << " is not prime" << endl;
    }
    system("PAUSE");
    return 0;
}

// Prime-number function. Test divisors from
//   2 to sqrt of n. Return false if a divisor
//   found; otherwise, return true.

bool prime(int n) {
    int i;

    for (i = 2; i <= sqrt(n); i++) {
      if (n % i == 0)         // If i divides n evenly,
        return false;     //   n is not prime.
    }
    return true;    // If no divisor found, n is prime.
}
```

How It Works

As always, the program adheres to the pattern of 1) declaring function type information at the beginning of the program (*prototyping* the function), 2) defining the function somewhere in the program, and 3) calling the function.

The prototype says that the prime function takes an integer argument and returns a **bool** value, which will be either **true** or **false**. (Note: If you have a really old compiler, you may have to use the **int** type instead of **bool**.)

```
bool prime(int n);
```

The function definition is a variation on the prime-number code from Chapter 3, which used a **for** loop. If you compare the code here to Example 3.2 on page 75, you'll see only a few differences.

```
bool prime(int n) {
    int i;

    for (i = 2; i <= sqrt(n); i++) {
        if (n % i == 0)      // If i divides n evenly,
            return false;    //  n is not prime.
    }
    return true;  // If no divisor found, return
                  //  true.
}
```

Another difference is that instead of setting a Boolean variable, is_prime, this version returns a Boolean result. The logic here is as follows:

For all whole numbers from 2 to the square root of n,

If n is evenly divisible by the loop variable (i),

Return the value false immediately.

Remember that the modulus operator (%) carries out division and returns the remainder. If this remainder is 0, that means the second number divides the second evenly—in other words, it is a *divisor* or *factor* of the second number.

The action of the **return** statement here is key. This statement returns immediately—causing program execution to exit from the function and passing control back to **main**. There's no need to use **break** to get out of the loop.

The loop in the main function calls the prime function. The use of a **break** statement here provides an exit mechanism, so the loop isn't really infinite. As soon as the user enters 0, the loop terminates and the program ends. Here I've put the exit lines in bold.

```
while (true) {
  cout << "Enter num (0 = exit) and press ENTER: ";
  cin >> i;
  if (i == 0)                // If user entered 0, EXIT
    break;
  if (prime(i))                      // Call prime(i)
    cout << i << " is prime" << endl;
  else
    cout << i << " is not prime" << endl;
}
```

The rest of the loop calls the prime function and prints the result of the prime-number test. Note that the prime function, in this case, returns a true/false value, and so the call to prime(i) can be used as an if/else condition.

EXERCISES

Exercise 4.2.1.   Optimize the prime-number function by calculating the square root of n only once during each function call. Declare a local variable sqrt_of_n of type **double**. (Hint: A variable is local if it is declared inside the function.) Then use this variable in the loop condition.

Exercise 4.2.2.   Rewrite **main** so that it tests all the numbers from 2 to 20 and prints out the results, each on a separate line. (Hint: Use a **for** loop, with i running from 2 to 20.)

Exercise 4.2.3.   Write a program that finds the first prime number greater than 1 billion (1,000,000,000).

Exercise 4.2.4.   Write a program that lets the user enter any number n and then finds the first prime number larger than n.

Local and Global Variables

Nearly every programming language has a concept of local variable. As long as two functions mind their own data, as it were, they won't interfere with each other.

That's definitely a factor in the previous example (Example 4.2). Both **main** and prime have a local variable named i. If i were not local—that is, if it was shared between functions—then consider what could happen.

First, the **main** function executes prime as part of evaluating the **if** condition. Let's say that i has the value 24.

```
if (prime(i))
    cout << i << " is prime" << endl;
else
    cout << i << " is not prime" << endl;
```

The value 24 is passed to the prime function.

```
// Assume i is not declared here, but is global.

int prime(int n) {

    for (i = 2; i <= sqrt((double) n); i++)
        if (n % i == 0)
            return false;

    return true;  // If no divisor found, n is prime.
}
```

Look what this function does. It sets i to 2 and then tests it for divisibility against the number passed, 24. This test passes—because 2 does divide into 24 evenly—and the function returns. But i is now equal to 2 instead of 24.

Upon returning, the program executes

```
cout << i << " is not prime" << endl;
```

which prints the following:

```
2 is not prime
```

This is not what was wanted, since we were testing the number 24!

So, to avoid this problem, declare variables local unless there is a good reason not to do so. If you look back at Example 2.3, you'll see that i is local; **main** and prime each declare their own version of i.

Is there ever a good reason to not make a variable local? Yes, although if you have a choice, it's better to go local, because you want functions interfering with each other as little as possible.

You can declare global—that is, nonlocal—variables by declaring them outside of any function definition. It's usually best to put all global declarations near the beginning of the program, before the first function. A variable is recognized only from the point it is declared, to the end of the file.

For example, you could declare a global variation named status:

```
#include <iostream>
#include <cmath>
using namespace std;

int status = 0;

void main () {
        //
}
```

Now, the variable named status may be accessed by any function. Because this variable is global, there is only one copy of it; if one function changes the value of status, this reflects the value of status that other functions see.

Interlude

Why Global Variables at All?

For reasons shown in the previous section, global variables can be dangerous. Habitual use of global variables can cause shocks to a program, because changes performed by one function cause unexpected effects in another.

But if they are so dangerous, why use them at all?

Well, they are often necessary, or nearly so. Global variables are often the best way to communicate information *between* functions; otherwise, you might need a long series of argument lists that transfer all the program information back and forth.

Beginning with Chapter 11, we'll work with classes, which provide an alternative, and generally superior, way for closely related functions to share data with each other: Functions of the same class have access to private data that no one else does.

Recursive Functions

So far, I've only shown the use of **main** calling other functions defined in the program, but in fact, any function can call any function. But can a function call itself?

Yes. And as you'll see, it's less crazy than it sounds. The technique of a function calling itself is called *recursion*. The obvious problem is the same one for infinite loops: If a function calls itself, when does it ever stop? The problem is easily solved, however, by putting in some mechanism for stopping.

Remember the factorial function from Exercise 4.1.1 (page 90)? We can rewrite this as a recursive function:

```
int factorial(int n) {
    if (n <= 1)
        return 1;
    else
        return n * factorial(n - 1);  // RECURSION!
}
```

For any number greater than 1, the factorial function issues a call to itself but with a lower number. Eventually, the function factorial(1) is called, and the cycle stops.

There is a literal *stack* of calls made to the function, each with a different argument for n, and now they start returning. The *stack* is a special area of memory maintained by the computer: It is a last-in-first-out (LIFO) mechanism that keeps track of information for all pending function calls. This includes arguments and local variables, if any.

You can picture how to call a factorial(4) this way.

```
factorial(4)
    ↓
    4 * factorial(3)
            ↓
            3 * factorial(2)
                    ↓
                    2 * factorial(1)
                            ↓
                            1
```

Many functions that use a **for** statement can be rewritten so they use recursion instead. But does it always make sense to use that approach?

No. The example here is not an ideal one, because it causes the program to store all the values 1 through n on the stack, rather than totaling them up directly in a loop. This approach is not efficient. The next section makes a better use of recursion.

Example 4.3. *Prime Factorization*

The prime-number examples we've looked at so far are fine, but they have a limitation. They tell you, for example, that a number such as 12,001 is not prime, but they don't tell anything more. Wouldn't it be more useful to know what numbers divide into 12,001?

It'd be more useful to generate the *prime factorization* for any requested number. This would show us exactly what prime numbers divide into that number. For example, if the number 36 was input, we'd get this:

```
2, 2, 3, 3
```

If 99 was input, we'd get this:

```
3, 3, 11
```

And if a prime number was input, the result would be the number itself. For example, if 17 was input, the output would be 17.

We have almost all the programming code to do this already. Only a few changes need to be made to the prime-number code. To get prime-factorization, first get the lowest divisor, and then factor the remaining quotient. To get all the divisors for a number n, do this:

> For all whole numbers from 2 to the square root of n,
>> If n is evenly divisible by the loop variable (i),
>>> Print i followed by a comma, and
>>> Rerun the function on n / i, and
>>>> Exit the current function
>> If no divisors found, print n itself

This logic is a recursive solution, which we can implement in C++ by having the function get_divisors call itself.

prime3.cpp

```cpp
#include <iostream>
#include <cmath>
using namespace std;

void get_divisors(int n);

int main() {
    int n = 0;

    cout << "Enter a number and press ENTER: ";
    cin >> n;
```

▼ *continued on next page*

prime3.cpp, cont.

```
        get_divisors(n);
        cout << endl;
        system("PAUSE");
        return 0;
    }

    // Get divisors function
    //  This function prints all the divisors of n,
    //  by finding the lowest divisor, i, and then
    //  rerunning itself on n/i, the remaining quotient.

    void get_divisors(int n) {
        int i;
        double sqrt_of_n = sqrt(n);

        for (i = 2; i <= sqrt_of_n; i++)
            if (n % i == 0) {    // If i divides n evenly,
                cout << i << ", ";      //    Print i,
                get_divisors(n / i);  //    Factor n/i,
                return;               //    and exit.
            }

        // If no divisor is found, then n is prime;
        //  Print n and make no further calls.

        cout << n;
    }
```

How It Works

As always, the program begins by declaring functions—in this case, there is one function other than **main**. The new function is get_divisors.

Also, the beginning of the program includes iostream and cmath, because the program uses **cout**, **cin**, and **sqrt**. You don't need to declare **sqrt** directly, by the way, because this is done for you in cmath.

```
#include <iostream>
#include <cmath>

void get_divisors(int n);
```

The **main** function just gets a number from the user and calls get_divisors.

```
int main() {
    int n = 0;

    cout << "Enter a number and press ENTER: ";
    cin >> n;

    cout << endl;
    system("PAUSE");
    return 0;
}
```

The get_divisors function is the interesting part of this program. It has a **void** return value, meaning that it doesn't pass back a value. But it still uses the **return** statement to exit early.

```
void get_divisors(int n) {
    int i;
    double sqrt_of_n = sqrt(n);

    for (i = 2; i <= sqrt_of_n; i++)
        if (n % i == 0) {  // If i divides n evenly,
            cout << i << ", ";      //    Print i,
            get_divisors(n / i);  //    Factor n/i,
            return;                 //    and exit.
        }

    // If no divisor is found, then n is prime;
    //  Print n and make no further calls.

    cout << n;
}
```

The heart of this function is a loop that tests numbers from 2 to the square root of n (which has been calculated and placed in the variable sqrt_of_n).

```
    for (i = 2; i <= sqrt_of_n; i++)
        if (n % i == 0) {  // If i divides n evenly,
            cout << i << ", ";      //    Print i,
            get_divisors(n / i);  //    Factor n/i,
            return;                 //    and exit.
        }
```

If the expression n % i == 0 is true, that means the loop variable i divides evenly into n. In that case, the function does several things: It prints out the loop variable, which is a divisor; calls itself recursively; and exits.

The function calls itself with the value n/i. Because the factor i is already accounted for, the function needs to get the prime-number divisors for *the remaining factors* of n, and these are contained in n/i.

If no divisors are found, that means the number being tested is prime. The correct response is to print this number and stop.

```
cout << n;
```

For example, suppose that 30 is input. The function tests to see what the lowest divisor of 30 is. The function prints the number 2 and then reruns itself on the remaining quotient, 15 (because 30 divided by 2 is 15).

During the next call, the function finds the lowest divisor of 15. This is 3, so it prints 3 and then reruns itself on the remaining quotient, 5 (because 15 divided by 3 is 5).

Here's a visual summary. Each call to get_divisors gets the lowest divisor and then makes another call unless the number being tested is prime.

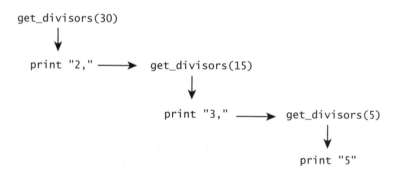

Interlude for Math Junkies

Interlude

A little reflection shows why the lowest divisor is always a prime number. Suppose we test a positive whole number and that A is the lowest divisor *but is not a prime*. Since A is not prime, it must have at least one divisor of its own, B, that is not equal to either 1 or A.

But if B divides evenly into A and A is a divisor of the target number, then B must also be a divisor of the target number. Furthermore, B is less than A. Therefore, the hypothesis that the lowest divisor is not prime results in a contradiction.

Interlude

▼ *continued*

This is easy to see by example. Any number divisible by 4 (a nonprime) is also divisible by 2 (a prime). The prime factors will always be found first, as long as you keep looking for the lowest divisor.

EXERCISES

Exercise 4.3.1.   Rewrite the **main** function for Example 4.3 so that it prints the prompt message "Enter a number (0 = exit) and press ENTER." The program should call get_divisors to show the prime factorization and then prompt the user again, until he or she enters 0. (Hint: If you need to, look at the code for Example 4.2, on page 90.)

Exercise 4.3.2.   Write a program that calculates triangle numbers by using a recursive function. A triangle number is the sum of all whole numbers from 1 to N, in which N is the number specified. For example, triangle(5) = 5 + 4 + 3 + 2 + 1.

Exercise 4.3.3.   Modify Example 4.3 so that it uses a *nonrecursive* solution. You will end up having to write more code. (Hint: To make the job easier, write two functions: get_all_divisors and get_lowest_divisor. The **main** function should call get_all_divisors, which in turn has a loop: get_all_divisors calls get_lowest_divisor repeatedly, each time replacing n with n/i, where i is the divisor that was found. If n itself is returned, then the number is prime, and the loop should stop.)

Example 4.4.   *Euclid's Algorithm for GCF*

In the early grades of school, we're asked to figure out greatest common factors (GCFs). For example, the greatest common factor of 15 and 25 is 5. Your teacher probably lectured you about GCF until you didn't want to hear about it anymore.

Wouldn't it be nice to have a computer figure this out for you? We'll focus just on GCF, because as I'll show in Chapter 11, if you can figure out the CGF of two numbers, you can easily compute the lowest common multiple (LCM).

The technique was worked out almost 2,500 years ago by a Greek mathematician named Euclid, and it's one of the most famous in mathematics.

To get CGF: For whole two numbers A and B:

> If B equals 0,
>
> > The answer is A.

Else

The answer is GCF(B, A%B)

You may remember remainder division (%) from earlier chapters. A%B means this:

Divide A by B and produce the remainder.

For example, 5%2 equals 1, and 4%2 equals 0. A result of 0 means that B divides A evenly.

If B does not equal 0, the algorithm replaces the arguments A, B with the arguments B, A%B and calls itself recursively. This solution works for two reasons:

▶ The terminal case (B equals 0) is valid. The answer is A.

▶ The general case is valid: GCF(A, B) equals CGF(B, A%B), so the function calls itself with new arguments B and A%B.

The terminal case, in which B equals 0, is valid assuming A is nonzero. You can see that A divides evenly into both itself and 0, but nothing larger can divide into A. (Note that 0 can be divided evenly by any whole number except itself.) For example, 997 is the greatest common factor for the pair (997, 0). Nothing larger divides evenly into both.

The general case is valid if the following is true:

The greatest common factor of the pair (B, A%B) is also the greatest common factor of the pair (A, B).

It turns out this *is* true, and because it is, the GCF problem is passed along from the pair (A, B) to the pair (B, A%B). This is the general idea of recursion: Pass the problem along to a simpler case involving smaller numbers.

It can be shown that the pair (B, A%B) involves numbers less than or equal to the pair (A, B). Therefore, during each recursive call, the algorithm uses successively smaller numbers until B is zero.

I save the rest of the proof for an interlude at the end of this section. Here is a complete program for computing greatest common factors:

```
gcf.cpp

    #include <cstdlib>
    #include <iostream>
    using namespace std;
```

```cpp
int gcf(int a, int b);

int main()
{
    int a = 0, b = 0; // Inputs to GCF.

    cout << "Enter a: ";
    cin >> a;
    cout << "Enter b: ";
    cin >> b;
    cout << "GCF = " << gcf(a, b) << endl;

    system("PAUSE");
    return 0;
}

int gcf(int a, int b) {
    if (b == 0)
        return a;
    else
        return gcf(b, a%b);
}
```

How It Works

All that **main** does in this case is to prompt for two input variables a and b, call the greatest-common-factor function (gcf), and print results:

```cpp
    cout << "GCF = " << gcf(a, b) << endl;
```

As for the gcf function, it implements the algorithm discussed earlier:

```cpp
int gcf(int a, int b) {
    if (b == 0)
        return a;
    else
        return gcf(b, a%b);
}
```

The algorithm keeps assigning the old value of B to A and the value A%B to B. The new arguments are equal or less to the old. They get smaller until B equals 0.

For example, if we start with A = 300 and B = 500, the first recursive call switches their order. (This always happens if B is larger.) From that point onward, each call to gcf involves smaller arguments until the terminal case is reached:

VALUE OF A	VALUE OF B	VALUE OF A%B (DIVIDE AND GET REMAINDER)
300	500	300
500	300	200
300	200	100
200	100	0
100	0	Terminal case: answer is 100

When B is 0, the gcf function no longer computes A%B but instead produces the answer.

If the initial value of A is larger than B, the algorithm produces an answer even sooner. For example, suppose A = 35 and B = 25.

VALUE OF A	VALUE OF B	VALUE OF A%B (DIVIDE AND GET REMAINDER)
35	25	10
25	10	5
10	5	0
5	0	Terminal case: answer is 5

Interlude

Who Was Euclid?

Who was this Euclid guy? Wasn't he the Greek who wrote about geometry? (Something like "The shortest distance between two points is a straight line"?)

Indeed he was. Euclid's *Elements* is one of the most famous books in Western civilization. For almost 2,500 years it was used as a standard text-book in schools. In this work he demonstrated for the first time a *tour de force* of deductive logic, proving all that was then known about geometry. In fact, he invented the whole *idea* of proof. It is a great work that has had profound influence on mathematicians and philosophers ever since.

Interlude

▼ *continued*

It was Euclid who (according to legend) said to King Ptolemy of Alexandria, "Sire, there is no royal road to geometry." In other words, you gotta work for it.

Although its focus is on geometry, Euclid's book has results in number theory as well. The algorithm here is the most famous of these results. Euclid expressed the problem geometrically, finding the biggest length commensurable with two sides of a rectangle. He conceived the problem in terms of rectangles, but we can use any two integers.

EXERCISES

Exercise 4.4.1.   Revise the program so that it prints out all the steps involved in the algorithm. Here is a sample output:

```
GCF(500, 300) =>
GCF(300, 200) =>
GCF(200, 100) =>
GCF(100, 0) =>
100
```

Exercise 4.4.2.   For experts: Revise the gcf function so that it uses an iterative (loop-based) approach. Each cycle through the loop should stop if B is zero; otherwise, it should set new values for A and B and then continue. You'll need a temporary variable—temp—to hold the old value of B for a couple of lines: temp=b, b=a%b, and a=temp.

Interlude

Interlude for Math Junkies: Rest of the Proof

Earlier, I worked out some of a proof of Euclid's algorithm. What remains is to show that the greatest common factor of the pair (B, A%B) is also the greatest common factor of the pair (A, B). This is true if we can show the following:

▶ If a number is a factor of both A and B, it is also a factor of A%B.

▶ If a number is a factor of both B and A%B, it is also a factor of A.

▼ *continued on next page*

Interlude

▼ *continued*

If these are true, then all the common factors of one pair are common factors of the other pair. In other words, the set of Common Factors (A, B) is identical to the set of common factors (B, A%B). Since the two sets are identical, they have the *greatest member*—therefore, they share the greatest common factor.

Consider the remainder-division operator (%). It implies the following, where m is a whole number:

```
A = mB + A%B
```

A%B is equal or less than A, so the general tendency of the algorithm is to get progressively smaller numbers. Assume that n, a whole number, is a factor of both A and B (meaning it divides both evenly). In that case:

```
A = cn
B = dn
```

where c and d are whole numbers. Therefore:

```
cn = m(dn) + A%B
A%B = cn - mdn = n(c - md)
```

This demonstrates that if n is a factor of both A and B, it is also a factor of A%B. By similar reasoning, we can show that if n is a factor of both B and A%B, it is also a factor of A.

Because the common factors for the pair (A, B) are identical to the common factors for the pair (B, A%B), it follows that they share the greatest common factor. Therefore, GCF(A, B) equals GCF(B, A%B). QED.

Example 4.5.   *Beautiful Recursion: Tower of Hanoi*

Strictly speaking, the earlier examples don't require recursion. With some effort, they can be revised as iterative (loop-based) functions. But there is a problem that illustrates recursion beautifully, solving a problem that would be very difficult to solve otherwise.

This is the Tower of Hanoi puzzle: You have three stacks of rings. Each ring is smaller than the one it sits on. The challenge is to move all the rings from the first stack to the third, subject to these constraints:

▶ You can move only one ring at a time.

▶ You can place a ring only on top of a larger ring, never a smaller.

It sounds easy, until you try it! Consider a stack four rings high: You start by moving the top ring from the first stack, but where do you move it, and what do you do after that?

To solve the problem, assume we already know how to move a group of N–1 rings. Then, to move N rings from a source stack to a destination stack, do the following:

1 Move N–1 rings from the source stack to the (currently) unused, or "other," stack.

2 Move a single ring from the source stack to the destination stack.

3 Move N–1 rings from the "other" stack to the destination stack.

This is easier to envision graphically. First, the algorithm moves N–1 rings from the source stack to the "other" stack ("other" being the stack that is neither source nor destination for the current move). In this case, N is 4 and N–1 is 3, but these numbers will vary.

1. Move N–1 rings from source to "other."

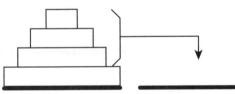

After this recursive move, at least one ring is left at the top of the source stack. This top ring is then moved: This is a simple action, moving one ring from source to destination.

2. Move one ring from source to destination, directly.

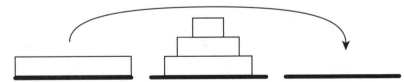

Finally, we perform another recursive move, moving N–1 rings from "other" (the stack that is currently neither source nor destination) to the destination.

3. Move N–1 rings from "other" to destination.

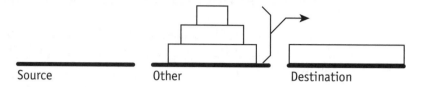

Source   Other   Destination

What permits us to move N–1 rings in steps 1 and 3, when the constraints tell us that we can move only one?

Remember the basic idea of recursion. Assume the problem *has already been solved* for the case N–1, although this may require many steps. All we have to do is tell the program how to solve the Nth case in terms of the N–1 case. The program magically does the rest.

It's important, also, to solve the terminal case, N = 1. But that's trivial. Where one ring is involved, we simply move the ring as desired.

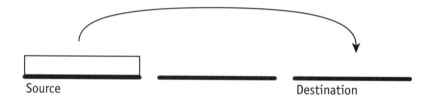

Source   Destination

The following program shows the C++ code that implements this algorithm:

tower.cpp

```
#include <cstdlib>
#include <iostream>

using namespace std;
void move_rings(int n, int src, int dest, int other);

int main()
{
   int n = 3;   // Stack is 3 rings high

   move_rings(n, 1, 3, 2); // Move stack 1 to stack 3
   system("PAUSE");
```

tower.cpp, cont.

```
      return 0;
   }

   void move_rings(int n, int src, int dest, int other) {
      if (n == 1) {
         cout << "Move from " << src << " to " << dest
               << endl;
      } else {
         move_rings(n - 1, src, other, dest);
         cout << "Move from " << src << " to " << dest
               << endl;
         move_rings(n - 1, other, dest, src);
      }
   }
```

How It Works

The program is brief considering what it does. In this example, I've set the stack size to just three rings, although it can be any positive integer:

```
      int n = 3;  // Stack is 3 rings high
```

The call to the move_rings function says that three rings should be moved from stack 1 to stack 3; these are determined by the second and third arguments, respectively. The "other" stack, stack 2, will be used in intermediate steps.

```
      move_rings(n, 1, 3, 2); // Move stack 1 to stack 3
```

This small example—moving only three rings—produces the following output. You can verify the correctness of this solution by using three different coins, all of different sizes.

```
      Move from 1 to 3
      Move from 1 to 2
      Move from 3 to 2
      Move from 1 to 3
      Move from 2 to 1
      Move from 2 to 3
      Move from 1 to 3
```

Try setting n to 4, and you'll get a list of moves more than twice as long.

The core of the move_ring function is the following code, which implements the general solution described earlier. Remember, this recursive approach assumes the N–1 case has already been solved. The function therefore passes along most of the problem to the N–1 case.

```
move_rings(n - 1, src, other, dest);
cout << "Move from " << src << " to " << dest
        << endl;
move_rings(n - 1, other, dest, src);
```

Notice how the functional role of the three stacks is continually switched between *source* (where to move a group of rings from), *destination* (where the group is going), and *other* (the intermediate stack, which is not used now but will be at the next level).

EXERCISES

Exercise 4.5.1. Revise the program so that the user can enter any positive integer value for n. Ideally, you should test the input to see whether it is greater than 0.

Exericse 4.5.2. Instead of printing the "Move" message directly on the screen, have the move_ring function call yet another function, which you give the name exec_move. The exec_move function should take a source and destination stack number as its two arguments. Because this is a separate function, you can use as many lines of code as you need to print a message. You can print a more informative message:

```
Move the top ring from stack 1 to stack 3.
```

Example 4.6. *Random-Number Generator*

OK, we've had enough fun with recursion. It's time to move on to another, highly practical example. This one generates random numbers—a function at the heart of many game programs.

The test program here simulates any number of dice rolls. It does this by calling a function, rand_0toN1, which takes an argument, n, and randomly returns a number from 0 to n – 1. For example, if the user inputs the number 6, this program simulates dice rolls:

```
3 4 6 2 5 3 1 1 6
```

Here is the program code:

```
dice.cpp
```

```cpp
#include <iostream>
#include <cmath>
#include <cstdlib>
#include <ctime>
using namespace std;

int rand_0toN1(int n);

int main() {
    int n, i;
    int r;

    srand(time(NULL)); // Set seed for random numbers.

    cout << "Enter number of dice to roll: ";
    cin >> n;

    for (i = 1; i <= n; i++) {
        r = rand_0toN1(6) + 1; // Get a number 1 to 6
        cout << r << " ";        // Print it
    }
    system("PAUSE");
    return 0;
}


// Random 0-to-N1 Function.
// Generate a random integer from 0 to N-1, with each
//   integer an equal probability.
//
int rand_0toN1(int n) {
    return rand() % n;
}
```

How It Works

The beginning of the program has to include a number of files to support the functions needed for random-number generation:

```
#include <iostream>
#include <cmath>
#include <cstdlib>
#include <ctime>
using namespace std;
```

Make sure you include the last three here—cmath, cstdlib, and ctime—whenever you use random-number generation.

Random-number generation is a difficult problem in computing, because computers follow deterministic rules—which, by definition, are nonrandom. The solution is to generate what's called a *pseudorandom* sequence by taking a number and performing a series of complex transformations on it.

To do this, the program needs a number as random as possible to start off the sequence. So, we're back where we started, aren't we?

Well, fortunately no. You can take the system time and use it as a *seed*: That is the first number in the sequence.

```
srand(time(NULL));
```

NULL is a predefined value that means a data address set to nothing. You don't need to worry about it for now. The effect in this case is simply to get the current time.

C++0x ▶ The C++0x specification provides the **nullptr** keyword, which should be used in preference to NULL if you have a C++0x-compliant compiler.

A program that uses random numbers should call **srand** first. System time changes too quickly for a human to guess its exact value, and even a tiny difference in this number causes big changes in the resulting sequence. This is a practical application of what chaos theorists call the Butterfly Effect.

The rest of **main** prompts for a number and then prints the quantity of random numbers requested. A **for** loop makes repeated calls to rand_0toN1, a function that returns a random number from 0 to $n - 1$:

```
for (i = 1; i <= n; i++) {
    r = rand_0toN1(6) + 1;   // Get num from 1 to 6
    cout << r << " ";        // Print it out
}
```

Here is the function definition for the rand_0toN1 function:

```
int rand_0toN1(int n) {
    return rand() % n;
}
```

This is one of the simplest functions we've seen yet! Calling **rand** produces a number anywhere in the range of the **int** type, which, on 32-bit systems, can be anywhere in the range of roughly plus or minus two billion. But we want much smaller numbers.

The solution is to use your old friend, the remainder-division operator (%), to divide by n and return the remainder. No matter how large the amount being divided, the result must be a number from 0 to n–1, which is exactly what the function is being asked to provide.

In this case, the function is called with the argument 6, so it returns a value from 0 to 5. Adding 1 to the number gives a random value in the range 1 to 6, which is what we want.

EXERCISES

Exercise 4.6.1.   Write a random-number generator that returns a number from 1 to N (rather than 0 to N–1), where N is the integer argument passed to it.

Exercise 4.6.2.   Write a random-number generator that returns a random floating-point number between 0.0 and 1.0. (Hint: Call **rand**, cast the result r to type **double** by using `static_cast<double>(r)`, and then divide by the highest value in the **int** range, RAND_MAX.) Make sure you declare the function with the **double** return type.

Games and More Games

Now that we know how to write functions and generate random numbers, it's possible to enhance some game programs.

The Subtraction Game example at the end of Chapter 2 can be improved. Right now, when the user plays optimal strategy, the computer responds by choosing 1. We can make this more interesting by randomizing the computer's response in these situations. The following program makes the necessary changes, putting altered lines in bold:

nim2.cpp

```
#include <iostream>
#include <cmath>
#include <ctime>
#include <cstdlib>
```

▼ *continued on next page*

```cpp
using namespace std;

int rand_0toN1(int n);

int main() {
    int total, n;

    srand(time(NULL)); // Set seed for random numbers.

    cout << "Welcome to NIM. Pick a starting total: ";
    cin >> total;
    while (true) {

        // Pick best response and print results.

        if ((total % 3) == 2) {
            total = total - 2;
            cout << "I am subtracting 2." << endl;
        } else if ((total % 3) == 1) {
            total--;
            cout << "I am subtracting 1." << endl;
        } else {
            n = 1 + rand_0toN1(2); // n = 1 or 2.
            total = total - n;
            cout << "I am subtracting ";
            cout << n << "." << endl;
        }
        cout << "New total is " << total << endl;
        if (total == 0) {
            cout << "I win!" << endl;
            break;
        }
        // Get user's response; must be 1 or 2.

        cout << "Enter num to subtract (1 or 2): ";
        cin >> n;
        while (n < 1 || n > 2) {
            cout << "Input must be 1 or 2." << endl;
            cout << "Re-enter: ";
            cin >> n;
        }
```

nim2.cpp, cont.

```
            total = total - n;
            cout << "New total is " << total << endl;
            if (total == 0) {
                    cout << "You win!" << endl;
                    break;
            }
    }
    system("PAUSE");
    return 0;
}

int rand_0toN1(int n) {
    return rand() % n;
}
```

Chapter 2 presented an exercise: Alter this program so that it permits any number from 1 to N to be subtracted each time, where N is set at the beginning. That problem is left as an exercise for this version as well. (You can even prompt the end user for this value before the game starts. As always, the computer should win whenever the user does not play perfect strategy.)

The last full example in Chapter 10 presents a game of Rock, Paper, Scissors that can be programmed even with C++ compilers that are not fully C++0x compliant. To use the example in Chapter 10 (Example 10.3) with weak, rather than strong, enumerations, replace this line in Chapter 10:

```
enum class Choice { rock, paper, scissors };
```

with this:

```
enum Choice { rock, paper, scissors };
```

Also, remove the **using** statement:

```
using namespace Choice;
```

Chapter 4 *Summary*

Here are the main points of Chapter 4:

▶ In C++, you can use functions to define a specific task, just as you might use a subroutine or procedure in another language. C++ uses the name function for all such routines, whether they return a value or not.

▶ You need to declare all your functions (other than **main**) at the beginning of the program so that C++ has the type information required. Function declarations, also called *prototypes*, use this syntax:

```
type  function_name (argument_list);
```

▶ You also need to define the function somewhere in the program, to tell what the function does. Function definitions use this syntax:

```
type  function_name (argument_list) {
    statements
}
```

▶ A function runs until it ends or until the **return** statement is executed. A **return** statement that passes a value back to the caller has this form:

```
return expression;
```

▶ A return statement can also be used in a **void** function (function with no return value) just to exit early, in which case it has a simpler form:

```
return;
```

▶ Local variables are declared inside a function definition; global variables are declared outside all function definitions, preferably before **main**. If a variable is local, it is not shared with other functions; two functions can each have a variable named i (for example) without interfering with each other.

▶ Global variables enable functions to share common data, but such sharing provides the possibility of one function interfering with another. It's a good policy not to make a variable global unless there's a clear need to do so.

▶ The addition-assignment operator (+=) provides a concise way to add a value to a variable. For example:

```
n += 50;                    // n = n + 50
```

▶ C++ functions can use recursion—meaning they call themselves. (A variation on this is when two or more functions call each other.) This technique is valid as long as there is a case that terminates the calls. For example:

```
int factorial(int n) {
    if (n <= 1)
        return 1;
    else
        return n * factorial(n - 1);  // RECURSION!
```

Arrays: All in a Row...

Much of the power of computers stems from their ability to work on arbitrarily large amounts of data—*arbitrary* in this case meaning "any number of times you like."

An array is an arbitrarily large collection of data indexed by number. With a few keystrokes you can create array data structures of any size. Then, by using loops, you can process the data structure efficiently, often with just a few lines of code. Loops and arrays go hand in hand. Together, they help make programs not just powerful but useful.

A First Look at C++ Arrays

Suppose you're writing a program to analyze scores given by five judges in an Olympic kite-flying contest. You need to store all five values for a while so you can measure statistical properties: range, average, median, and so on. Also suppose the judges are known by number.

One way to store the information is to declare five variables. Since the scores have a fractional portion (0.1 being the lowest and 9.9 being about the highest), use type **double**.

```
double  scores1, scores2, scores3, scores4, scores5;
```

That's a lot to enter. Wouldn't it be nice to just enter the word *scores* and tell C++ to declare five variables for you?

That's exactly what happens when you declare an array.

```
double  scores[5];
```

This declaration creates five data items of type **double** and places them next to each other in memory. In C++ programs, these items are referred to as

117

scores[0], scores[1], scores[2], scores[3], and scores[4]. The numbers between brackets are *indexes*.

In the rest of the program, you can perform operations on each of these items as if it were an individual variable.

```
scores[0] = 2.7;        // Judge 0 gives a low score.
scores[2] = 9.5;        // Judge 2 gives a high score.
scores[1] = scores[2];  // Judge 1 copies Judge #2.
```

Each of these array elements (scores[0], scores[1], and so on) acts like a variable of type **double**—the difference being that it is referred to, in part, by number. After these operations are performed, the array looks like this:

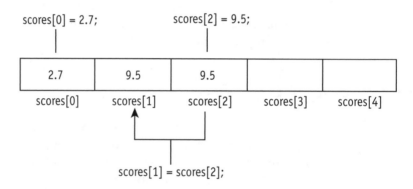

With only five elements, an array can be helpful. But that's nothing compared to the convenience of larger arrays. Look how much labor you save if you have an array with 1,000 elements:

```
int votes[1000];   // Declare array with 1000
elements
```

This declaration creates an array with 1,000 elements, running from votes[0] to votes[999].

To summarize, you can declare variables of int or double (or any other supported data type) by using this syntax:

```
type  array_name[size];
```

As a result, *array_name* is created as an array of the specified *size*. Each element of the array has the indicated *type*.

The element of the array range from *array_name*[0] to *array_name*[size-1].

Initializing Arrays

Referring to a variable you've forgotten to initialize can end up producing garbage (*garbage* being a technical term for a meaningless value). Remember, you can initialize a variable when it's declared, even when you declare more than one on the same line.

```
int  sum = 0, fingers = 10;
```

You can initialize an array with the use of an *aggregate*. This approach uses a simple notation involving brackets and commas:

```
double  scores[5] = {0.0, 0.0, 0.0, 0.0, 0.0};
int  ordinals[10] = {0, 1, 2, 3, 4, 5, 6, 7, 8, 9};
```

Each of these lines is terminated with a closing curly brace (or *set brace*) followed by a semicolon (;). Data declarations and function prototypes always end with a semicolon.

> **Note** ▶ If a variable or an array is global, then by default C++ initializes it to zero. (In the case of arrays, C++ initializes every element to zero.) But local variables not initialized contain random values (garbage).

Zero-Based Indexing

C++ arrays work a little differently from the way you might expect. If you have N items, they are not numbered 1 to N, but from 0 to N–1. Again, for an array declared this way:

```
double  scores[5];
```

the elements are as follows:

```
scores[0]
scores[1]
scores[2]
scores[3]
scores[4]
```

No matter how you declare an array, the highest index number (in this case, 4) will always be *one less than* the size of the array (in this case, 5). This may seem counterintuitive.

But seen from another angle, it makes perfect sense. The index number in a C or C++ array is not an ordinal number (that is, a position) as much as it is an *offset*. That is, the index number of an element is a measure of the distance from the beginning of the array.

And the first element, of course, is zero positions away from the beginning. The index of the first element is therefore 0. This is worth restating as another cardinal rule:

✱ **In a C++ array of size N elements, the indexes run from 0 to N–1.**

Interlude

Why Use Zero-Based Indexes?

Many other languages use 1-based indexing. The declaration ARRAY(5) in FORTRAN creates an array with indexes running from 1 to 5. But all programs, regardless of what language they are written in, must ultimately be translated into machine language, which is what the CPU actually executes.

At the machine level, array indexing is handled through offsets. One register (a memory location on the CPU itself) contains the address of an array—actually, the address of the first element. Another register contains an offset: the distance to the desired element.

What is the offset of the first element? Zero, just as in C++. With a language such as FORTRAN, the 1-based index must first be translated into a 0-based index by subtracting by 1. It is then multiplied by the size of each element. To get the element with index I, do this:

```
address of element I = base address + ((I - 1) *
    size of each element)
```

In a 0-based language such as C++, the subtraction no longer has to be done. This results in a more efficient calculation at runtime.

```
address of element I = base address + (I * size of
    each element)
```

Even though it results in only a slight saving of CPU cycles, it's very much in the spirit of C-based languages to use this approach, because it is closer to what the CPU does.

Example 5.1.   *Print Out Elements*

Let's start by looking at one of the simplest programs possible that uses an array. The rest of the chapter gets into more interesting programming challenges.

```
print_arr.cpp
    #include <iostream>
    using namespace std;

    int main() {
        double scores[5] = {0.5, 1.5, 2.5, 3.5, 4.5};

        for(int i = 0; i < 5; i++) {
            cout << scores[i] << "  ";
        }

        system("PAUSE");
        return 0;
    }
```

The program, when run, prints this:

```
0.5   1.5   2.5   3.5   4.5
```

How It Works

The program uses a **for** loop that sets the loop variable, i, to a series of values—0, 1, 2, 3, 4—corresponding to the range of indexes in the array, scores.

```
        for(int i = 0; i < 5; i++) {
            cout << scores[i] << "  ";
        }
```

This kind of loop is extremely common in C++ code, so you often see these expressions used with **for:** i = 0, i < SIZE_OF_ARRAY, and i++.

The loop cycles five times, each time with a different value for i.

VALUE OF I	ACTION OF THE LOOP	VALUE PRINTED
0	Print scores[0]	0.5
1	Print scores[1]	1.5
2	Print scores[2]	2.5
3	Print scores[3]	3.5
4	Print scores[4]	4.5

You can also understand the action of this loop visually. The following figure demonstrates the action of the first two cycles of the loop.

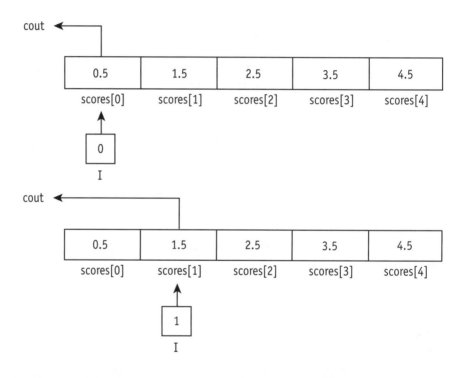

EXERCISES

Exercise 5.1.1. Write a program that initializes an array of eight integers with the values 5, 15, 25, 35, 45, 55, 65, and 75, and then prints each of these out. (Hint: Instead of using the loop condition i < 5, use i < 8, because in this case there are eight elements.)

Exercise 5.1.2. Write a program that initializes an array of six integers with the values 10, 22, 13, 99, 4, and 5. Print each of these out and then print their sum. (Hint: You'll need to keep a running total.)

Exercise 5.1.3. Write a program that prompts the user for each of seven values, stores these in an array, and then prints out each of them, followed by the total. You will need to write two **for** loops for this program: one for collecting data and another for calculating the sum and printing out values.

Example 5.2. ## *How Random Is Random?*

The last example in Chapter 4 introduced a random-number function, rand_0toN1. Randomness—the deliberate *lack* of predictability—is a philosophical paradox. The essence of a computer algorithm is predictability. The best you can do is use the system time and perform a series of complex transformations. True randomness may not be a theoretical possibility.

But is it a *practical* possibility? That is, can a C++ program simulate the results of randomness so well that it becomes a practical impossibility for a user to predict random numbers in advance? If we ask a program to output a series of these numbers, do they behave in a way that has all the qualities we'd expect of a true random sequence?

The rand_0toN1 function outputs an integer from 0 to N–1, where N is the argument to the function. We can use this function to get a series of numbers from 0 to 9, and count how many we get of each digit. What you'd expect to happen is this:

▶ Each of the 10 digits should be produced about one-tenth of the time.

▶ But the digits shouldn't be produced with absolutely equal frequency. Especially with a small number of trials, you should see variation. However, as the number of trials increase, the ratio of actual hits to expected hits for each digit (one-tenth of the total number) ought to get closer and closer to 1.0.

If these conditions can be met, we have a good example of practical randomness, probably good enough for the great majority of game programs.

We can test these conditions by using an array of 10 integers to register the results. When the program is run, it will prompt for a number of trials to run. It will then report the total number of hits for each of the numbers 0 to 9. Here's what sample output for 20,000 trials should look like:

```
Enter number of cases to do: 20000

0: 1950  Accuracy: 0.975
1: 2026  Accuracy: 1.013
2: 1897  Accuracy: 0.9485
```

```
3: 2102   Accuracy: 1.051
4: 2019   Accuracy: 1.0095
5: 1997   Accuracy: 0.9985
6: 1999   Accuracy: 0.9995
7: 1969   Accuracy: 0.9845
8: 2033   Accuracy: 1.0165
9: 2008   Accuracy: 1.004
```

With 20,000 trials, you should get a fast response. Depending on your computer, it may take millions of trials before you see a noticeable delay. I have run this program with as many as 2 billion trials (input: 2000000000). My desktop computer, which is a few years old, takes 28 minutes to respond in that case. But your computer may be faster.

It's interesting to run this program with different values for N. You should find, as I have, that as the number of trials increase, the accuracy (the ratio of expected hits to actual hits) does in fact get closer to 1.0, consistent with math's Law of Large Numbers.

Here's the code for this program:

stats.cpp

```cpp
#include <iostream>
#include <ctime>
#include <cmath>
using namespace std;

int rand_0toN1(int n);

int hits[10];

int main() {
    int n;    // Number of trials; prompt from user
    int i;    // All-purpose loop variable
    int r;    // Holds a random value

    srand(time(NULL));    // Set seed for randomizing.

    cout << "Enter how many trials and press ENTER: ";
    cin >> n;
```

```
    // Run n trials. For each trial, get a num 0 to 9
    //  and then increment the corresponding element
    //  in the hits array.

    for (i = 0; i < n; i++) {
        r = rand_0toN1(10);
        hits[r]++;
    }

    // Print all elements in the hits array, along
    //  with ratio of hits to EXPECTED hits (n / 10).

    for (i = 0; i < 10; i++) {
        cout << i << ": " << hits[i] << "  Accuracy: ";
        double results = hits[i];
        cout << results / (n / 10.0) << endl;
    }
    system("PAUSE");
    return 0;
}

// Random 0-to-N1 Function.
// Generate a random integer from 0 to N-1.
//
int rand_0toN1(int n) {
    return rand() % n;
}
```

How It Works

The program begins with a couple of declarations:

```
int rand_0toN1(int n);
```

```
int hits[10];
```

The rand_0toN1 function is declared here because it is going to be called by **main**. The declaration of hits creates an array of 10 integers, ranging in index from 0 to 9. Because this array is global (declared outside of any function), all its elements are initialized to 0.

Note ▶ Technically, the array is initialized to all-zero values because it has a static storage class. Local variables can also be declared static, causing them to retain values between calls even though they are not visible outside the function.

The main function begins by defining three integer variables—i, n, and r—and by setting the seed for the sequence of random numbers. Remember, this needs to be done in every program that uses random-number generation.

```
srand(time(NULL));    // Set seed for randomizing.
```

The program then prompts for the value of n. This should look familiar by now.

```
cout << "Enter how many trials and press ENTER: ";

cin >> n;
```

The next part of the program is a **for** loop that carries out the requested number of trials (namely, n) and stores results in the hits array.

```
// Run n trials. For each trial, get a num 0 to 9
//   and then increment the corresponding element
//   in the hits array.

for (i = 0; i < n; i++) {
    r = rand_0toN1(10);
    hits[r]++;
}
```

Each time through, the loop gets a random number r between 0 and 9 and then records this as a "hit" for the number chosen by adding 1 to the appropriate array element. At the end of the process, the element hits[0] contains the number of 0s generated, hits[1] contains the number of 1s generated, and so on.

The expression hits[r]++ saves a lot of programming effort. If you weren't using an array, you'd have to write a series of if/else statements like this:

```
if (r == 0)
    hits0++;
else if (r == 1)
    hits1++;
else if (r == 2)
    hits2++;
else if (r == 3)
    hits3++;
// etc.
```

Because we're working with arrays, what would otherwise take 20 lines of code takes only 1! This single statement adds 1 to whatever element is selected by r:

```
hits[r]++;
```

The rest of **main** consists of a loop that prints all the elements of the array. This action reports the results and is run after all the trials have been performed. As before, this code is much more concise than would be the case if we weren't using an array.

```
// Print all the elements in the hits array, along
//  with ratio of hits to EXPECTED hits (n / 10).

for (i = 0; i < 10; i++) {
    cout << i << ": " << hits[i] << "  Accuracy: ";
    double results = hits[i];
    cout << results / (n / 10.0) << endl;
}
```

The middle line of this compound statement may seem odd, but it is necessary. The results are put in a temporary variable of type **double**. Because **double** has a larger range than **int**, the compiler does not complain of information loss.

```
double results = hits[i];
```

This assignment needs to be done to force floating-point division in the statement that follows. Otherwise—as happens when you divide one integer by another—C++ would perform integer division, throwing fractional results away! An alternative would have been to use `static_cast<double>(hits[i])` to cast the data.

The rand_0toN1 function is the same function I introduced at the end of Chapter 2.

```
// Random 0-to-N1 Function.
// Generate a random integer from 0 to N-1.
//
int rand_0toN1(int n) {
    x = rand() % n;
}
```

EXERCISES

Exercise 5.2.1.   Alter Example 5.2 so that it generates not 10 different values but 5: In other words, use the rand_0toN1 function to get a 0, 1, 2, 3, or 4. Then perform the requested number of trials, in which you'd expect each value of the five values to be produced one-fifth of the time.

Exercise 5.2.2. Alter the example so that it can work with any number of values, simply by changing one setting in the program. You can do this with a **#define** directive near the beginning of the code. This directive instructs the compiler to replace all occurrences of a symbolic name (in this case, "VALUES") with the specified text.

For example, to have each random trial generate one of five different values (0 through 4), first put the following directive at the beginning of the code:

```
#define VALUES 5
```

Then use the symbolic name VALUES throughout the program, wherever the program refers to the number of possible values. For example, you'd declare the hits array as follows:

```
int hits[VALUES];
```

From then on, you can control the number of different values by going back and changing one line—the **#define** directive—with a different number and then recompiling. The beauty of this approach is that the behavior of the program can be so easily modified by that one line of code.

Exercise 5.2.3. Rewrite the code in **main** so that it uses a loop similar to the one in Example 4.3 (page 96), allowing the user to keep rerunning sessions of any number of times until he or she enters 0 to terminate the program. Before each session, you need to reinitialize all the elements of the hits array to 0. You can do that either by including a **for** loop that sets each element to 0 or by calling a function that contains this loop.

Strings and Arrays of Strings

To do the examples in the remainder of this chapter, I'm going to have to get a little ahead of the story, to show how to declare arrays of strings. In Chapter 7, we'll return to the subject of strings.

Up until now, I've shown the use of string literals. For example, to print a message, you'd use a line of code like this:

```
cout << "What a good C++ am I.";
```

But you can have string variables, just as you can have integer and floating-point variables. These require a strange-looking **char*** notation. For example, the following code first stores the string in the variable message and then prints it:

```
char *message = "What a good C++ am I";
cout << message;
```

The rest of this chapter uses arrays of strings. The declarations look just like those for arrays of numbers, except that the **char*** notation must be used for the array's data type. For example:

```
char *members[4] =
    {"John", "Paul", "George", "Ringo" };
```

To refer to an individual string in executable code, use array notation. (But you don't use the * operator when printing the string.) For example:

```
cout << "The leader of the band is " << members[0];
```

This prints out the following:

```
The leader of the band is John.
```

Because the names of the members are all stored in the array, we can use a loop to efficiently print all of them out. For example, this code

```
for (i = 0; i < 4; i++)
    cout << members[i] << endl;
```

prints out this list of names:

```
John
Paul
George
Ringo
```

Example 5.3.   *Card Dealer #1*

Now we're ready to have some fun. The example in this section uses two arrays of strings—ranks and suits—to simulate the dealing of a card from a standard deck of 52 playing cards.

This example has one major limitation: The same card may be dealt again before the rest of the deck has been exhausted. The behavior simulated, then, is the act of dealing a card, noting it, and then putting it back and reshuffling before dealing another card. In later sections, I'll develop a technique for preventing a card from being redealt.

This example, at least, shows some of the basic code you need for a card-dealing program, even though in some ways it's not yet complete:

dealer1.cpp

```cpp
#include <iostream>
#include <cstdlib>
#include <ctime>
#include <cmath>
using namespace std;

int rand_0toN1(int n);
void draw_a_card();

char *suits[4] =
        {"hearts", "diamonds", "spades", "clubs"};
char *ranks[13] =
        {"ace", "two", "three", "four", "five",
         "six", "seven", "eight", "nine",
         "ten", "jack", "queen", "king" };

int main() {
    int n, i;

    srand(time(NULL));    // Set seed for randomizing.

    while (1) {
        cout << "Enter no. of cards to draw ";
        cout << "(0 to exit): ";
        cin >> n;
        if (n == 0)
            break;
        for (i = 1; i <= n; i++)
            draw_a_card();
    }
    return 0;
}

// Draw-a-card function
// Perform a card draw by getting a random 0-4 and a
//   random 0-12. Use these to index the strings
//   arrays, ranks and suits.
//
void draw_a_card() {
```

dealer1.cpp, cont.

```cpp
        int r;      // Random index (0 thru 12) into
                    //   ranks array
        int s;      // Random index (0 thru 3) into
                    //   suits array

        r = rand_0toN1(13);
        s = rand_0toN1(4);
        cout << ranks[r] << " of " << suits[s] << endl;
    }


// Random 0-to-N1 Function.
// Generate a random integer from 0 to N-1.
//
int rand_0toN1(int n) {
    return rand() % n;
}
```

How It Works

The key to this example is the use of the two global arrays declared, suits and ranks.

```cpp
char *suits[4] =
        {"hearts", "diamonds", "spades", "clubs"};
char *ranks[13] =
        {"ace", "two", "three", "four", "five",
         "six", "seven", "eight", "nine",
         "ten", "jack", "queen", "king" };
```

Each of these is an array of strings, which can be indexed just like any other array. The suits array has four elements indexed by the numbers 0 to 3. The ranks array has 13 elements, indexed by the numbers 0 to 12.

By happy coincidence, the rand_0toN1 function produces numbers the same way that C++ arrays are indexed: with a number running from 0 to N–1 (where N is the number of elements). This makes the program easier to write.

The draw_a_card function does all the work of drawing a card.

```cpp
void draw_a_card() {
    int r;      // Index (0 thru 12) into ranks array
    int s;      // Index (0 thru 3) into suits array
```

```
        r = rand_0toN1(13);
        s = rand_0toN1(4);
        cout << ranks[r] << " of " << suits[s] << endl;
    }
```

The program calls the rand_0toN1 function, specifying the argument 13. We get back a random integer from 0 to 12: These correspond to all the elements in the ranks array. Therefore, each of the 13 rank values will be selected with equal probability:

```
        r = rand_0toN1(13);
```

The program then calls rand_0toN1, specifying the argument 4. We get back a random integer from 0 to 3, corresponding to all the elements in the suits array:

```
        s = rand_0toN1(4);
```

Now all the function has to do is select two strings and print them, and we're done:

```
        cout << ranks[r] << " of " << suits[s] << endl;
```

EXERCISE

Exercise 5.3.1. Write a program that randomly selects from a bag of eight objects. Each object can be red, blue, orange, or green, and it can be a ball or a cube. Assume that the bag contains one object for each combination (one red ball, one red cube, one orange ball, one orange cube, and so on). Write code similar to Example 5.3, using two string arrays—one to identify colors and the other to identify shapes.

Example 5.4. *Card Dealer #2*

The next step in writing a complete card-dealing program is to select a single number at random and then use this number to get both suit and rank. Such an approach makes it possible later to create an array that tracks the status of each card. The program generates a random number from 0 to 51 and then maps this number to a unique combination of suit and rank.

Each card-draw here is still treated as an independent event. The next section adds the logic to simulate a real deck of cards, in which a card can't be drawn a second time.

In the following code, the new lines (or lines to be changed) are in bold. The rest of the code is identical to that in Example 5.3.

dealer2.cpp

```cpp
#include <iostream>
#include <cstdlib>
#include <ctime>
#include <cmath>
using namespace std;

int rand_0toN1(int n);
void draw_a_card();

char *suits[4] =
        {"hearts", "diamonds", "spades", "clubs"};
char *ranks[13] =
        {"ace", "two", "three", "four", "five",
         "six", "seven", "eight", "nine",
         "ten", "jack", "queen", "king" };

int main() {
    int n, i;

    srand(time(NULL));   // Set seed for randomizing.

    while (1) {
        cout << "Enter no. of cards to draw ";
        cout << "(0 to exit): ";
        cin >> n;
        if (n == 0)
            break;
        for (i = 1; i <= n; i++)
            draw_a_card();
    }
    return 0;
}

// Draw-a-card function
// Perform a card draw by getting a random 0-4 and a
//    random 0-12. Use these to index the strings
//    arrays, ranks and suits.
//
```

▼ *continued on next page*

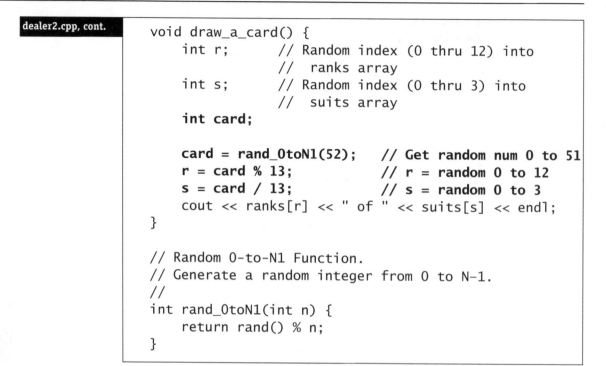

dealer2.cpp, cont.

```cpp
void draw_a_card() {
    int r;          // Random index (0 thru 12) into
                    //   ranks array
    int s;          // Random index (0 thru 3) into
                    //   suits array
    int card;

    card = rand_0toN1(52);   // Get random num 0 to 51
    r = card % 13;            // r = random 0 to 12
    s = card / 13;            // s = random 0 to 3
    cout << ranks[r] << " of " << suits[s] << endl;
}

// Random 0-to-N1 Function.
// Generate a random integer from 0 to N-1.
//
int rand_0toN1(int n) {
    return rand() % n;
}
```

How It Works

There are just four new lines in the program—but I felt these important enough to base an entire example on. These statements are all part of the draw_a_card function.

```cpp
    int card;

    card = rand_0toN1(52);   // Get random num 0 to 51
    r = card % 13;            // r = random 0 to 12
    s = card / 13;            // s = random 0 to 3
```

For each card drawn, this version of the program makes only one call to rand_0toN1. This approach is consistent with the general goal here: to select a single number that corresponds to a unique card.

The card drawn must have a combination of suit and rank that no other card has. Given a number between 0 and 51, the program determines a unique suit and rank combination.

One way to do that would be to create two more arrays:

```
int rank_chooser[52] =
        {0, 1, 2, 3, 4, 5, 6, 7, 8, 9, 10, 11, 12,
         0, 1, 2, 3, 4, 5, 6, 7, 8, 9, 10, 11, 12,
         0, 1, 2, 3, 4, 5, 6, 7, 8, 9, 10, 11, 12,
         0, 1, 2, 3, 4, 5, 6, 7, 8, 9, 10, 11, 12,
};

int suit_chooser[52] =
        {0, 0, 0, 0, 0, 0, 0, 0, 0, 0, 0, 0, 0, 0,
         1, 1, 1, 1, 1, 1, 1, 1, 1, 1, 1, 1, 1, 1,
         2, 2, 2, 2, 2, 2, 2, 2, 2, 2, 2, 2, 2, 2,
         3, 3, 3, 3, 3, 3, 3, 3, 3, 3, 3, 3, 3, 3,
};
```

You could then get r and s values by indexing into these arrays:

```
r = rank_chooser[card];
s = suit_chooser[card];
```

The values generated this way would be unique, as you can see by examining the arrays. For example, a card value of 12 would result in r and s values of 12 and 0, respectively; while a card value of 25 would result in r and s values of 12 and 1.

But indexing into those arrays is exactly equivalent to the following operations:

```
r = card % 13;        // r = random 0 to 12
s = card / 13;        // s = random 0 to 3
```

As you may recall from earlier chapters, the modulus operator (%) performs division between two integers and returns the remainder. The action here is to divide by 13 and produce a number from 0 to 12—the same values as in the rank_chooser array.

Division between two integers returns the quotient, rounded down, and discards the remainder. This produces a number from 0 to 3—the same values as in the suit_chooser array.

So, by using these mathematical operations, you save yourself the trouble of creating the arrays rank_chooser and suits_chooser. The results are the same.

EXERCISE

Exercise 5.4.1. Write a program for the scenario described in Exercise 5.3.1. This exercise features eight objects, each of which had a unique combination of color (red, blue, orange, green) and shape (ball, cube). Use an approach similar to that in Example 5.3, in which you generate one random number for each object picked and then use this number to generate a unique combination of two numbers—one that selects the color and another that selects the shape.

Example 5.5.   *Card Dealer #3*

Now that we know how to use a number from 0 to 51 to represent a deck of cards, we can add the final piece of the puzzle. An accurate card-dealing program must remember which card was drawn and then avoid drawing that card again.

There are two ways to do this. One is to initialize a 52-element array so that each element represents a position in a deck, assign each a card value, and then "shuffle" the deck by doing a series of random swaps.

The approach I adopt here is one that I find a little simpler: I use a 52-element array, in which each element corresponds to a card. The content of an element is a true/false value indicating whether the corresponding card has been selected yet. Once a card is picked, this array is updated to show that the card should be skipped in the future.

Here is the program. As before, only the new lines of code are in bold. All other lines are identical to those in the previous example.

```
dealer3.cpp

    #include <iostream>
    #include <cstdlib>
    #include <ctime>
    #include <cmath>
    using namespace std;

    int rand_0toN1(int n);
    void draw_a_card();
    int select_next_available(int n);

    bool card_drawn[52];
    int cards_remaining = 52;

    char *suits[4] =
            {"hearts", "diamonds", "spades", "clubs"};
```

```
char *ranks[13] =
        {"ace", "two", "three", "four", "five",
         "six", "seven", "eight", "nine",
         "ten", "jack", "queen", "king" };

int main() {
    int n, i;

    srand(time(NULL));    // Set seed for randomizing.

    while (1) {
        cout << "Enter no. of cards to draw ";
        cout << "(0 to exit): ";
        cin >> n;
        if (n == 0)
            break;
        for (i = 1; i <= n; i++)
            draw_a_card();
    }
    return 0;
}

// Draw-a-card function
// Perform a card draw by getting a random 0-4 and a
//    random 0-12. Use these to index the strings
//    arrays, ranks and suits.
//
void draw_a_card() {
    int r;        // Random index (0 thru 12) into
                  //    ranks array
    int s;        // Random index (0 thru 3) into
                  //    suits array
    int n, card;

    n = rand_0toN1(cards_remaining--);
    card = select_next_available(n);
    r = card % 13;            // r = random 0 to 12
    s = card / 13;            // s = random 0 to 3
    cout << ranks[r] << " of " << suits[s] << endl;
}
```

▼ *continued on next page*

dealer3.cpp, cont.

```cpp
// Select-next-available-card function.
// Find the Nth element of card_drawn, skipping over
//  those elements already set to true.
//
int select_next_available(int n) {
    int i = 0;

    // At beginning of deck, skip cards already drawn.

    while (card_drawn[i])
        i++;

    while (n-- > 0) {         // Do the following n times:
        i++;                         // Advance to next card
        while (card_drawn[i]) // Skip past cards
            i++;                     //  already drawn.
    }
    card_drawn[i] = true;     // Note card to be drawn
    return i;                     // Return this number.
}

// Random 0-to-N1 Function.
// Generate a random integer from 0 to N-1.
//
int rand_0toN1(int n) {
    return rand() % n;
}
```

How It Works

The version of the program uses an additional function, select_next_available, to determine what card to draw. It uses a global integer variable, cards_remaining, to remember how many cards are remaining in the deck.

```cpp
int cards_remaining = 52;
```

Every time a card is drawn, this variable is decreased by 1. There is also an array of bool items (each of which holds the value true or false) corresponding to all the cards in the pack.

```cpp
bool card_drawn[52];
```

The draw_a_card function first gets a random integer based on the value of cards_remaining. That integer is then passed to the select_next_available function.

```
n = rand_0toN1(cards_remaining--);
card = select_next_available(n);
```

The job of select_next_available is to count through the array n + 1 times, each time skipping over cards that have already been drawn. These cards are marked by a value of true (1) in the card_drawn array. For example, here's how you'd count ahead three.

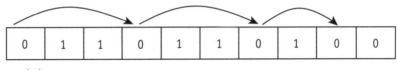

| 0 | 1 | 1 | 0 | 1 | 1 | 0 | 1 | 0 | 0 |

card_drawn array

The code for select_next_available finds the first available card by skipping past all the drawn cards at the beginning of the array.

```
while (card_drawn[i])
    i++;
```

It then counts n more available cards, each time skipping over items already drawn.

```
while (n-- > 0) {      // Do the following n times:
    i++;                       // Advance to next card
    while (card_drawn[i]) // Skip past cards
        i++;                   //  already drawn.
}
```

This loop uses n-- > 0 as the **if** condition: n is compared to zero and then decremented. The effect of the condition is to cycle through the loop n times.

When select_next_available has finally arrived at the card to be drawn, it does two things: It sets the index number to true (1) in the card_drawn array, and then it returns the index to the caller.

```
card_drawn[i] = true;    // Note card to be drawn
return i;                // Return this number.
```

Optimizing the Program

If you're a careful programmer, you may note that this program has a flaw: If the user attempts to deal more than 52 cards, there is no procedure for reshuffling the deck. Instead, the program exceeds the bounds of the card_drawn array. The result can be bad, because the program begins overwriting other areas of memory. It's important to handle this.

An easy fix is to detect this condition at the beginning of the draw_a_card function and then respond by resetting the global array, card_drawn, and the global variable, cards_remaining, to their original values at the start of the program.

```
if (cards_remaining == 0) {
    cout << "Reshuffling." << endl;
    cards_remaining = 52;         // Reset variable.
    for (int i = 0; i < 52; i++)  // Reset all values
        card_drawn[i] = false;    //  in this array.
}
```

There's a second feature of the program that is less than optimal. The select_next_available function performs the same **while** loop (for the "skip ahead" activity) in more than one place. You can fold these together by first incrementing n by 1, so the action is carried out n + 1 times. (An input of 0 counts to the first available item, and input of 1 counts to the second available item, and so on.)

The improved, shorter version is as follows:

```
int select_next_available(int n) {
    int i = -1;

    n++;  // Set up for n + 1 counting operations

    while (n-- > 0) {    // Do the following n times:
        i++;                     // Advance to next card
        while (card_drawn[i]) // Skip past cards
            i++;                 //  already drawn.
    }
    card_drawn[i] = true;    // Note card to draw.
    return i;                // Return this number.
}
```

Note that i is initialized to -1 rather than 0 in this version. That's because picking the first element should increment i to 0, not to 1.

EXERCISE

Exercise 5.5.1. Write a similar program for a bag that contains the eight objects described earlier: Each item has a unique combination of color (red, blue, orange, green) and shape (ball, cube). Every time an object is picked from the bag, it can't be picked again, so the number of possible choices decreases by one. The logic should be identical to that in Example 5.5, but the array settings will differ. You may also want to give your variables different names, such as items_remaining and (for the integer array) items_picked.

A Word to the Wise

While looking at the examples in this chapter, you may have wondered, what happens if you attempt to access an array element that doesn't exist?

C++ is untrustworthy in this regard. For example, you declare an array of size 5 but for some reason attempt to write to an element with index 5. This should not be legal, because the last element has index 4.

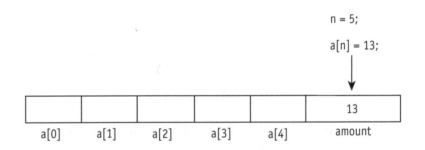

C++ doesn't stop you. Instead, the operation proceeds at the memory location where array[5] would be *if it existed*. The result is that a piece of data outside of the array is overwritten. This can create bugs that are difficult to track down.

C++ and its predecessor, C, were designed with the philosophy that the programmer knows what he or she is doing. C/C++ programs are typically faster and more compact than those created by other languages. The downside is you need to take care that array indexes don't go out of bounds. (But you need to take that care with *any* language that does not perform boundary-checking at runtime.)

2-D Arrays: Into the Matrix

Most computer languages provide the ability not only to create ordinary, one-dimensional arrays, but to create multidimensional arrays as well. C++ is no exception.

Two-dimensional arrays in C++ have this form:

```
type  array_name[size1][size2];
```

The number of elements is size1 * size2, and the indexes in each dimension are 0-based just as in one-dimensional arrays. For example, consider this declaration:

```
int  matrix[10][10];
```

This creates a 10-by-10 array, having 100 elements. Each dimension has index numbers running from 0 to 9. The first element is therefore matrix[0][0], and the last element is matrix[9][9].

To process such an array programmatically, you need to use a nested loop with two loop variables. For example, this code initializes all the members of the array to 0:

```
int i, j;

for (i = 0; i < 10; i++)
    for (j = 0; j < 10; j++)
        matrix[i][j] = 0;
```

The way this works is as follows:

1 i is set to 0, and a complete set of cycles of the inner loop—with j ranging from 0 to 9—is done first.

2 One cycle of the outer loop is then complete; i is incremented to the next higher value, which is 1. Then all the cycles of the inner loop run again, with j (as always) ranging from 0 to 9.

3 The process is repeated until i is incremented past its terminal value, 9.

Consequently, the values of i and j will be (0, 0), (0, 1), (0, 2), ... (0, 9), at which point the inner loop is complete, i is incremented, and the inner loop begins again: (1, 0), (1, 1), (1, 2) .... In all, 100 operations will be performed, because each cycle of the outer loop—which runs 10 times—performs 10 cycles of the inner loop.

In C++ arrays, the index on the right changes the fastest. This means the elements matrix[5][0] and matrix[5][1] are next to each other in memory.

Incidentally, statement-block syntax (which uses braces to explicitly define where a loop begins and ends) can be used here as with all control structures. Here's what this one would look like. It's a little more work, but its meaning is admittedly clearer to a programmer.

```cpp
for (int i = 0; i < 10; i++) {
    for (int j = 0; j < 10; j++) {
        matrix[i][j] = 0;
    }
}
```

Chapter 5 *Summary*

Here are the main points of Chapter 5:

▶ Use bracket notation to declare an array in C++. Declarations have this form:

type   array_name[*number_of_elements*];

▶ For an array of size n, the elements have indexes ranging from 0 to n–1.

▶ You can use loops to efficiently process arrays of any size. For example, assume an array was declared with SIZE_OF ARRAY elements. The following loop initializes every element to 0:

```cpp
for(i = 0; i < SIZE_OF_ARRAY; i++)
    my_array[i] = 0;
```

▶ You can use aggregates—a list of values between set braces—to initialize arrays.

```cpp
double  scores[5] = {6.8, 9.0, 9.0, 8.3, 7.1 };
```

▶ Use the **char*** notation to declare a string variable. For example:

```cpp
char *name = "Joe Bloe";
```

▶ You can declare arrays of strings just as you can declare other kinds of arrays. For example:

```cpp
char *band[4] = {"John", "Paul", "George", "Ringo"};
```

▶ When you print a string or a member of a string array, don't use the * operator.

```cpp
cout << "The leader of the group was " << names[0];
```

▶ C++ does not check array bounds for you at runtime. Therefore, you need to show care that you don't write array-access code that overwrites other areas of memory.

▶ Two-dimensional arrays are declared this way:

```
type   array_name[size1][size2];
```

6 Pointers: Getting a Handle on Data

In interviewing technical writers for Microsoft, I would see on candidates' resumes advanced C and C++ programming listed as accomplished skills. So, I would ask candidates to explain the concept of a pointer to me in their own words. I was interested only in how articulate they could be on a technical subject.

Too often, they'd look at me dumbfounded. They had forgotten an important rule of resume padding: If you claim to know C++, you're supposed to know what a pointer is...or at least make up a good bluff answer.

In this chapter, I'll explain what pointers are and—more importantly—why you should care.

What the Heck Is a Pointer, Anyway?

First, you need to know what an address is. The CPU doesn't understand names or letters: It refers to locations in memory by number, or *address*. You usually don't know what these numbers are, although you can print them out if you want. For example, the computer might store variables a, b, c, at numeric addresses 0x220004, 0x220008, and 0x22000c. These are numbers in hexadecimal notation (that's base 16).

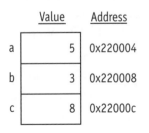

	Value	Address
a	5	0x220004
b	3	0x220008
c	8	0x22000c

There's nothing magic about these particular addresses…they are just numbers I picked at random. Many things can affect what addresses are used at runtime.

Now you're ready to understand what a pointer is.

The Concept of Pointer

A pointer is just a variable that contains an address. While most variables contain useful information (such as 5, 3, and 8 in this example), a pointer contains the numeric location of another variable. A pointer is only useful as a way to get to something else.

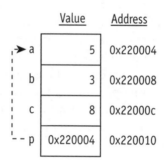

	Value	Address
a	5	0x220004
b	3	0x220008
c	8	0x22000c
p	0x220004	0x220010

Why is this useful? Well, sometimes a function needs to send another function a large amount of data. One way to do this is to copy all that information and pass it along. But another, more efficient way is just to give the address of the data to work on.

Another reason is this: Suppose you want to give a function not just a copy of some data but the ability to change the original value; I want to write a function called double_all_the_values(x, y, z) that doubles all the variables passed to it. In C++, the principal way to do this is to pass a series of pointers. This gives the function the location of the variables and lets the function manipulate the variables themselves, not just copies.

There are other reasons for using pointers. In more advanced programming, pointers enable you to create data structures with links to other data structures, to any level of complexity. So, you can have linked lists and internal networks in memory.

Interlude

What Do Addresses Look Like?

In the previous section, I assumed the variables a, b, and c had the physical addresses 0x220004, 0x220008, and 0x22000c. These are hexadecimal numbers, meaning they use base 16.

There's a good reason for using hexadecimal notation. Because 16 is an exact power of 2 (2 * 2 * 2 * 2 = 16), each hexadecimal digit corresponds to a pattern of exactly four binary digits—no more, no less. Here's how hexadecimal digits work.

HEXADECIMAL DIGIT	EQUIVALENT DECIMAL	EQUIVALENT BINARY
0	0	0000
1	1	0001
2	2	0010
3	3	0011
4	4	0100
5	5	0101
6	6	0110
7	7	0111
8	8	1000
9	9	1001
a	10	1010
b	11	1011
c	12	1100
e	13	1101
e	14	1110
f	15	1111

The advantage of hexadecimal notation is its close relation to binary. For example, the hex numeral 8 is 1000 in binary, and hex numeral f is 1111. Therefore, 88ff is equivalent to 1000 1000 1111 1111.

For computer architects, who need to quickly translate numbers into bit patterns, this is essential. Also, because every hex digit corresponds to four binary digits—no more, no less—you can tell at a glance how wide an address is: 0x8000 has four digits; it therefore corresponds to precisely 16 binary digits.

▼ *continued on next page*

Interlude

▼ *continued*

Every computer architecture uses addresses of some fixed width. It's important to know at a glance whether an address is too large to fit on a certain computer.

At the time of this writing, 32-bit architecture is the universal norm on personal computers, although it will someday give way to 64-bit architecture. With 32-bit addresses, no address can have more than 32 binary digits (eight hexadecimal digits). Technically, all addresses should be expressed in eight hex digits: for example, 0x000080ff. For simplicity's sake, this chapter will use smaller addresses and neglect the leading zeroes, just to make the figures manageable on the page.

Remember that 32-bit addressing supports more than 4 billion locations in memory, although this is even now being exceeded by memory hardware, requiring clever work-arounds on the part of computer and operating-system designers. Someday, 64-bit architecture will support a virtually unlimited number of addresses.

Declaring and Using Pointers

A pointer declaration uses the following syntax:

```
type  *name;
```

For example, you can declare a pointer p, which can point to variables of type **int**:

```
int  *p;
```

At the moment, the pointer is not initialized. All we know is that it can point to data objects of type **int**. But type matters. The base type of a pointer determines how the data it points to is interpreted: p has type **int***, so it should point only to **int** variables.

The next statements declare an integer n, initializes it to 0, and assigns its address to pointer p:

```
int n = 0;
p = &n;               // p now points to n!
```

The ampersand (&) gets the address of its operand. You generally don't care what the address is; all that matters is that p contains the address of n—that is, p *points to* n—and now you can use p to manipulate n.

After p=&n is executed, p contains the address of n. A possible memory layout for the program is shown here.

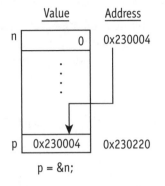

p = &n;

In all these examples, the addresses shown are arbitrary. A program will likely use different addresses every time it is run. The important thing about pointers is the relationships they create.

Here comes the interesting part. Applying the indirection operator (*) says "the thing pointed to." Assigning a value to *p has the same effect as assigning to n, because n is what p points to.

```
*p = 5;     // Assign 5 to the int pointed to by p.
```

So, because of the asterisk (*), this operation changes the thing *that p points to*, not the value of p itself. Now the memory layout looks like this.

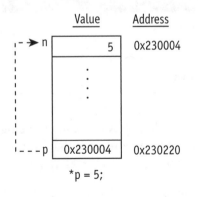

*p = 5;

The effect of the statement, in this case, is the same as n = 5. The computer finds the memory location pointed to by p and puts the value 5 at that location.

You can use a value pointed to by a pointer both to get and to assign data. Here's another example of pointer use:

```
*p = *p + 3;     // Add 3 to the int pointed to by p.
```

The value of n changes yet again—this time from 5 to 8. The effect of this statement is the same as n = n + 3. The computer finds the memory location pointed to by p and adds 3 to the value at that location.

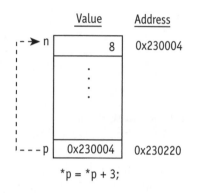

To summarize, when p points to n, referring to *p has the same effect as referring to n. Here are more examples:

WHEN P POINTS TO N, THIS STATEMENT...	HAS THE SAME EFFECT AS THIS STATEMENT...
`*p = 33;`	`n = 33;`
`*p = *p + 2;`	`n = n + 2;`
`cout << *p;`	`cout << n;`
`cin >> *p;`	`cin >> n;`

But if using *p is the same as using n, why bother with *p in the first place? One reason, remember, is that pointers enable a function to change the value of an argument passed to it. Here's how it works in C and C++:

1 The caller of a function passes the address of a variable to be changed. For example, the caller passes &n (the address of n).

2 The function has a pointer argument, such as p, that receives this address value. The function can then use *p to manipulate the value of n.

Example 6.1. *Print Out Addresses*

Before making practical use of pointers, let's print some data and compare pointer values to the standard **int** variables. What's essential here is to understand the difference between a variable's *content* and its *address*.

```cpp
pr_addr.cpp

#include <iostream>
#include <stdlib.h>

using namespace std;

int main() {
    int a = 2, b = 3, c = 4;
    int *pa = &a;
    int *pb = &b;
    int *pc = &c;
    cout << "Value of pointer pa is: " << pa << endl;
    cout << "Value of pointer pb is: " << pb << endl;
    cout << "Value of pointer pc is: " << pc << endl;
    cout << "The values of a, b, and c are: ";
    cout << a << ", " << b << ", " << c << endl;

    system("PAUSE");
    return 0;
}
```

When run, this program should output results similar (but not necessarily identical to) the following, which is what I got:

```
The value of pointer pa is: 0x22ff74
The value of pointer pb is: 0x22ff70
The value of pointer pc is: 0x22ff6b
The values of a, b, and c are: 2, 3, 4
```

This tells us that the values of a, b, and c are 2, 3, and 4. The addresses are expressed as hexadecimal numbers, 0x22ff74, 0x22ff70, and 0x22ff6b, but your results will vary. Physical addresses depend on many things you don't control.

What matters is that once you get a pointer—a variable containing another variable's address—you can use it to manipulate the thing pointed to.

Although a, b, and c were declared in that order, my C++ compiler assigned their addresses in reverse order: c got a lower address than a! There's a lesson here: Except in the case of array elements (which we'll get to in this chapter), and classes (which we'll get to later), never make assumptions about the ordering of variables in memory.

After a, b, and c are declared, the program declares pointers and initializes them to the addresses of a, b, and c. Remember that the ampersand (&) means "Get the address of."

```
int *pa = &a;
int *pb = &b;
int *pc = &c;
```

Example 6.2. *The double_it Function*

Now let's put pointers to use. This program uses a function named double_it, which doubles a variable passed to it—or rather doubles a variable whose address is passed to it.

```
#include <iostream>
using namespace std;

void double_it(int *p);

int main() {
   int a = 5, b = 6;

   cout << "Val. of a before doubling: " << a << endl;
   cout << "Val. of b before doubling: " << b << endl;

   double_it(&a);       // Pass address of a.
   double_it(&b);       // Pass address of b.

   cout << "Val. of a after doubling: " << a << endl;
   cout << "Val. of b after doubling: " << b << endl;

   system("PAUSE");
   return 0;
}
```

```
void double_it(int *p) {
    *p = *p * 2;
}
```

How It Works

This is a straightforward program. All the main function does is the following:

1 Print the values of a and b.

2 Call the double_it function to double the value of a, by passing the address of a (&a).

3 Call the double_it function to double the value of b, by passing the address of b (&b).

4 Print the values of a and b again.

This example needs pointers to work. You could write a version of double_it that took a simple **int** argument, but such a function would do nothing.

```
void double_it(int n) {     // THIS DOESN'T WORK!
    n = n * 2;
}
```

The problem is that when an argument is passed to a function, the function gets a copy of the argument. As soon as the function returns, the copy is thrown away.

Getting a variable passed to you is like getting photocopies of a secret document. You can view the information, but you have no access to the originals. But getting a pointer is like getting the location of the original documents. You not only get to look at them; you can make changes. So to enable a function to change the value of a variable, use pointers.

```
void double_it(int *p);
```

This declaration says that "the thing pointed to by p" has **int** type. Therefore, p itself is a pointer to an **int**. The caller must pass an address, which it does by using the address operator (&).

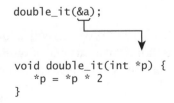

```
double_it(&a);

void double_it(int *p) {
    *p = *p * 2
}
```

Visually, here's the effect in terms of a hypothetical memory layout. The address of a is passed to the function, which then uses it to change the value of a.

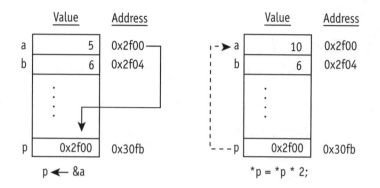

The program then calls the function again, this time passing the address of b. The function now uses this address to change the value of b.

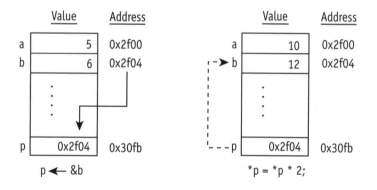

EXERCISES

Exercise 6.2.1.   Write a program that calls a function triple_it that takes the address of an **int** and triples the value pointed to. Test it by passing an argument n, which is initialized to 15. Print out the value of n before and after the function is called. (Hint: The function should look similar to double_it in Example 6. Remember to pass &n.)

Exercise 6.2.2.   Write a program with a function named convert_temp: The function takes the address of a variable of type **double** and applies Centigrade-to-Fahrenheit conversion. A variable that contains a Centigrade temperature should, after the function is called, contain the equivalent Fahrenheit temperature. Test the function. (Hint: The relevant formula is F = (C * 1.8) + 32.)

Swap: Another Function Using Pointers

Suppose you have two **int** variables and you want to swap their values. It's easy to do this with a third variable temp, whose function is to hold a temporary value.

```
temp = a;
a = b;
b = temp;
```

Now, wouldn't this be useful to put into a function that you could call whenever you needed to call? Yes, but as I explained earlier, unless you pass pointers to the variables (that is, addresses), changes to the variables are ignored.

Here's a solution that works, using pointers to enable the function to alter the variables:

```
// Swap function.
// Swap the values pointed to by p1 and p2.
//
void swap(int *p1, int *p2) {
    int temp = *p1;
    *p1 = *p2;
    *p2 = temp;
}
```

The expressions *p1 and *p2 are integers, and you can use them as you would any integer variables. But remember that p1 and p2 are addresses, and the addresses themselves do not change. The data that's altered is the data *pointed to* by p1 and p2. This is easy to see with an example.

Assume that big and little are initialized to 100 and 1, respectively.

```
int big = 100;
int little = 1;
```

The following statement calls the swap function, passing the addresses of these two variables. Note the use of the address operator (&) here.

```
swap(&big, &little);
```

Now if you print these variables, you'll see that the values have been exchanged.

```
cout << "The value of big is now " << big << endl;
cout << "The value of little is now " << little;
```

The values at the addresses in p1 and p2 change, not p1 and p2 themselves. This is why the indirection operator (*) is often called the *at* operator.

Example 6.3.   *Array Sorter*

Now it's time to show the power of this swap function. Pointers are not limited to pointing to simple variables—although I used that terminology to keep things simple. An **int** pointer (for example) can point to any memory location that stores an **int** value. This means it can point to elements of an array as well as pointing to a variable.

For example, here the swap function is used to swap the values of two elements of an array named arr:

```
int arr[5] = {0, 10, 30, 25, 50};

swap(&values[2], &values[3]);
```

Given the right procedure, you can use the swap function to sort the values of an array. Take a look at arr again—this time with the data jumbled around.

30	25	0	50	10
arr[0]	arr[1]	arr[2]	arr[3]	arr[4]

Here's a straightforward solution—the well-known "bubble sort" algorithm:

1 Find the lowest value and put that value in arr[0].

2 Find the *next* lowest value and put that value in arr[1].

3 Continue in this manner until you get to the end.

Here is the solution written out in pseudocode.

For i = 0 to n − 2,
    Find the lowest value in the range a[i] to a[n−1]
    If i is not equal to the index of the lowest value found,
        Swap a[i] and a[index_of_lowest]

That's the plan. The effect will be to put the lowest value in a[0], the next lowest value in a[1], and so on. Note that by

For i = 0 to n − 2,

I mean a **for** loop in which i is set to 0 during the first cycle of the loop, 1 during the next cycle of the loop, and so on, until i is set to n - 2, at which point it completes the last cycle. Each cycle of the loop places the correct element in a[i] and then increments i.

Inside the loop, a[i] is compared to all the *remaining elements* (the range a[i] to a[n−1], which includes all elements on the *right*). By the time every value of i has been processed, the whole array will have been sorted. Here's an example of the first three cycles of the loop, illustrated.

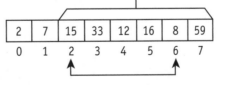

But how do we find the lowest value in the range a[i] to a[n−1]? We need another algorithm.

What the following algorithm does is 1) start by assuming that i is the lowest element and so initialize "low" to i; and 2) whenever a lower element is found, this lower element becomes the new "low" element.

To find the lowest value in the range a[i] to a[n–1], do the following:

Set low to i

For j = i + 1 to n–1,

   If a[j] is less than a[low]

      Set low to j

We then combine the two algorithms. After this, it's an easy matter to write the C++ code.

For i = 0 to n – 2,

   Set low to i

   For j = i + 1 to n–1,

      If a[j] is less than a[low]

         Set low to j

      If i is not equal to low,

         Swap a[i] and a[low]

Here's the complete program that uses this algorithm to sort an array:

sort.cpp

```cpp
#include <iostream>
using namespace std;

void sort(int n);
void swap(int *p1, int *p2);

int a[10];

int main () {
    int i;

    for (i = 0; i < 10; i++) {
        cout << "Enter array element #" << i << ": ";
        cin >> a[i];
    }
    sort(10);

    cout << "Here is the array, sorted:" << endl;
    for (i = 0; i < 10; i++)
```

```cpp
                cout << a[i] << "  ";

        return 0;
}

// Sort function: sort array named a with n elements.
//
void sort (int n) {
    int i, j, lowest;

    for(i = 0; i < n - 1; i++) {

        // This part of the loop finds the lowest
        //   element in the range i to n-1; the index
        //   is set to the variable named low.

        low = i;
        for (j = i + 1; j < n; j++)
            if (a[j] < a[low])
                low = j;

        // This part of the loop performs a swap if
        //   needed.

        if (i != low)
            swap(&a[i], &a[low]);
    }
}

// Swap function.
// Swap the values pointed to by p1 and p2.
//
void swap(int *p1, int *p2) {
    int temp = *p1;
    *p1 = *p2;
    *p2 = temp;
}
```

How It Works

Only two parts of this example are directly relevant to understanding pointers. The first is the call to the swap function, which passes the addresses of a[i] and a[low]:

```
swap(&a[i], &a[low]);
```

An important point here is that you can use the address operator (&) to take the address of array elements, just as you can use it with variables.

The other part of the example that's relevant to pointer use is the function definition for swap, which I described in the previous section.

```
// Swap function.
// Swap the values pointed to by p1 and p2.
//
void swap(int *p1, int *p2) {
    int temp = *p1;
    *p1 = *p2;
    *p2 = temp;
}
```

As for the sort function, the key to understanding it is to note what each part of the main loop does. The main **for** loop successively sets i to 0, 1, 2…up to and including n − 2. Why n − 2? It's because by the time it gets to the last element (n–1), all the sorting will have been done. (There is no need to compare the last element to itself.)

```
for(i = 0; i < n - 1; i++) {
    //...
}
```

The first part of the loop finds the lowest element in the range that includes a[i] and all the elements *to its right.* An inner loop conducts this search using a variable j, initialized to start at i + 1 (one position to the right of i).

```
low = i;
for (j = i + 1; j < n; j++)
    if (a[j] < a[low])
        low = j;
```

This, by the way, is an example of a *nested loop*, and it's completely legal. A **for** statement is just another kind of statement; therefore, it can be put inside another **if, while,** or **for** statement, and so on, to any degree of complexity.

The other part of the loop has an easy job. All it has to do is ask whether i differs from the index of the lowest element (stored in the variable "low"). Remember that the != operator means "not equal." There's no reason to do the swap if a[i] is already the lowest element in the range; that's the reason for the **if** condition here.

```
if (i != low)
        swap(&a[i], &a[low]);
```

EXERCISES

Exercise 6.3.1.   Rewrite the example so that instead of ordering the array from high to low, it sorts the array in reverse order: high to low. This is actually much easier than it may look. It's helpful, for the sake of clarity, if you rename the variable low as "high." Otherwise, you need to change only one statement; this statement involves a comparison.

Exercise 6.3.2.   Rewrite the example so that it sorts an array that has elements of type **double**. It's essential that you rewrite the swap function to work on data of the right type for the example to work correctly. But note that you should not change the type of any variables that serve as loop counters or array indexes—such variables should always have type **int**, regardless of the type of the rest of the data.

Pointer Arithmetic

One of the important uses of pointers is efficiently processing arrays. Suppose you declare this:

```
int arr[5] = {5, 15, 25, 35, 45};
```

The elements arr[0] through arr[4], of course, can all be used like individual integer variables. You can, for example, write statements such as "arr[1] = 10;".

But what is the expression "arr" itself? Can "arr" ever appear by itself?

Yes, "arr" is a constant that translates into an address—specifically, the address of the first element. Because it's a constant, you cannot change the value of "arr" itself. You can, however, use it to assign a value to a pointer variable:

```
int *p;
p = arr;
```

The statement "p = arr" is equivalent to this:

```
p = &arr[0];
```

This is a more concise, cleaner way to initialize a pointer to the address of the first element, arr[0]. Is there a similar technique for the other elements? You betcha. For example, to assign p the address of arr[2], you use this:

```
p = arr + 2;                    // p = &arr[2];
```

C++ interprets all array names as address expressions. `arr[2]` translates into the following:

```
*(arr + 2)
```

If you've been paying attention, you may think this looks wrong. We add 2 to the address of the start of the array, arr. But the element arr[2] is not two, but eight bytes away (four for each integer—assuming you are using a 32-bit system)! Yet this still works. Why?

It's because of *pointer arithmetic*. Only certain arithmetic operations are allowed on pointers and other address expressions (such as arr). These are as follows:

```
address_expression + integer
integer + address_expression
address_expression - integer
address_expression - address_expression
```

When integer and address expressions are added together, the result is another address expression. Before the calculation is completed, however, the integer is automatically *scaled* by the size of the base type. The C++ compiler performs this scaling for you.

```
new_address = old_address + (integer *
size_of_base_type)
```

So, for example, if p has base type **int**, adding 2 to p has the effect of increasing it by 8—because 2 times the size of the base type (4 bytes) yields 8.

Scaling is an extremely convenient feature of C++, because it means that when a pointer p points to an element of an array and it is incremented by 1, this always has the effect of making p point to the next element:

```
p++;       // Point to next element in the array.
```

This is one of the most important things to remember when using pointers:

✱ **When an integer value is added or subtracted from an address expression, the compiler automatically multiplies that integer by the size of the base type.**

Another way of saying this is to say that adding N to a pointer produces an address N elements away from the original pointer value.

Address expressions can also be compared to each other. You should not make assumptions about a memory layout except where array elements are involved. The following expression is always true:

```
&arr[2] < &arr[3]
```

which is another way of saying that the following is always true, just as you'd expect:

```
arr + 2 < arr + 3
```

Pointers and Array Processing

Because pointer arithmetic works the way it does, functions can access elements through pointer references rather than array indexing. The result is the same, but the pointer version (as I'll show) executes slightly faster.

In these days of incredibly fast CPUs, such minor speed increases make little difference for most programs. CPU efficiency was far more important in the 1970s and 1980s, with their slow processors. CPU time was often at a premium.

But for a certain class of programs, the superior efficiency gained from C and C++ can still be useful. C and C++ are the languages of choice for people who write operating systems, and subroutines in an operating system or device driver may be called upon to execute thousands or even millions of times a second. In such cases, the small efficiencies due to pointer usage can actually matter.

Here's a function that uses pointer reference to zero out an array with n elements:

```
void zero_out_array(int *p, int n) {
    while (n-- > 0) {   // Do n times:
        *p = 0;         //  Assign 0 to element pointed
                        //    to by p.
        p++;            //  Point to next element.
    }
}
```

This is a remarkably compact function, which would appear more compact still without the comments. (But remember that comments have no effect on a program at runtime.) Here's another version of the function, using code that may look more familiar:

```
void zero_out_array2(int *arr, int n) {
    for (int i = 0; i < n; i++) {
```

```
        arr[i] = 0;
    }
}
```

But this version, while nearly as compact, may run a bit slower (depending on the ability of the compiler to optimize the runtime code). The value of i must be scaled and added to arr each and every time through the loop to get the location of the array element arr[i].

```
arr[i] = 0;
```

This in turn is equivalent to the following:

```
*(arr + i) = 0;
```

It's actually worse than that, because the scaling effect has to be done at runtime; so at the level of machine code, the calculation is as follows:

```
*(arr + (i * 4)) = 0;
```

The problem is that the address has to be recalculated over and over again. In the pointer version, the address arr is figured in only once. The loop statement does less work:

```
*p = 0;
```

Of course, p has to be incremented each time through the loop, but both versions have a loop variable to update. Incrementing p is no more work than incrementing i.

Conceptually, here's how the pointer version works. Each time through the loop, *p is set to 0, and then p itself is incremented to the next element. (Because of scaling, p is actually increased by 4 each time through the loop, but that's an easy operation.)

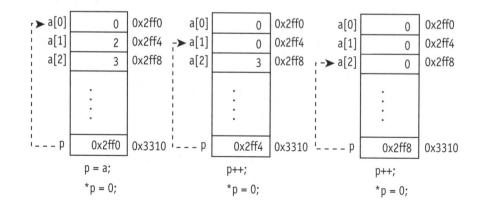

Example 6.4. *Zero Out an Array*

Here's the zero_out_array function in the context of a complete example. All this program does is initialize an array, call the function, and then print the elements so that you can see it worked.

```cpp
zero_out.cpp

#include <iostream>
using namespace std;

void zero_out_array(int *arr, int n);

int a[10] = {1, 2, 3, 4, 5, 6, 7, 8, 9, 10};

int main() {
    int i;

    zero_out_array(a, 10);

    // Print out all the elements of the array.
    for (i = 0; i < 10; i++)
        cout << a[i] << "   ";

    system("PAUSE");
    return 0;
}

// Zero-out-array function.
// Assign 0 to all elements of an int array of size n.
//
void zero_out_array(int *p, int n) {
    while (n-- > 0) {   // Do n times:
        *p = 0;         //   Assign 0 to element pointed
                        //     to by p.
        p++;            //   Point to next element.
    }
}
```

9

How It Works

The key to understanding the zero_out function is to remember that adding 1 to a pointer makes it point to the next element of an array:

```
p++;
```

This example demonstrates how to pass an array in C++. The first argument shown here, a, translates into the address of the first element:

```
zero_out_array(a, 10);
```

To pass an array, therefore, just use the array name. The function gets the address of the first element and should treat this as a pointer value.

Writing More Compact Code

In Example 6.3, the **while** loop in the zero_out_array function does two things: It zeros out an element and then increments the pointer so it points to the next element:

```
while (n-- > 0) {
    *p = 0;
    p++;
}
```

If you recall from past chapters, p++ is just an expression, and expressions can always be used within larger expressions. That means we can combine the pointer-access and increment operations to produce this:

```
while (n-- > 0)
    *p++ = 0;
```

To properly interpret *p++, I have to introduce two aspects of expression evaluation: precedence and associativity. Operators such as assignment (=) and test-for-equality (==) have low precedence, meaning that they are applied after other operations are resolved.

The pointer-indirection (*) and increment (++) operators have the same level of precedence as each other, but (unlike most operators) they associate right-to-left. Therefore, the statement *p++ = 0; is evaluated as if it were written this way:

```
*(p++) = 0;
```

This means: Increment pointer p, but only after using its value in this operation:

```
*p = 0;
```

Incidentally, using parentheses differently would produce an expression that is legal, but not, in this case, useful.

```
(*p)++ = 0;  // Assign 0 to *p and then increment *p.
```

The effect of this statement would be to set the first array element to 0 and then to 1, over and over; p itself would never get incremented, and you'd fail to process most of the array. The expression (*p)++ says, "Increment the thing p points to," not p itself.

Whew! That's a lot of analysis required to understand a tiny piece of code. You're to be forgiven if you swear never to write such cryptic statements yourself.

Note ▶ Appendix A summarizes precedence and association for all C++ operators.

EXERCISES

Exercise 6.4.1.   Rewrite the program to use direct-pointer reference for the loop that prints out the values of the array. Declare a pointer p and initialize it to start the array. The loop condition should be p < a + 10.

Exercise 6.4.2.   Write and test a copy_array function that copies the contents of one int array to another array of the same size. The function should take two pointer arguments. The operation inside the loop should be as follows:

```
*p1 = *p2;
p1++;
p2++;
```

If you want to write more compact but cryptic code, you can use this statement:

```
*(p1++) = *(p2++);
```

or even the following, which means the same thing:

```
*p1++ = *p2++;
```

Chapter 6 *Summary*

Here are the main points of Chapter 6:

▶ A pointer is a variable that can contain a numeric memory address. You can declare a pointer by using the following syntax:

```
type *p;
```

▶ You can initialize a pointer by using the address operator (&):

```
p = &n;              // Assign address of n to p.
```

▶ Once a pointer is initialized, you can use the indirection operator (*) to manipulate data pointed to by the pointer.

```
p = &n;
*p = 5;              // Assign 5 to n.
```

▶ To enable a function to manipulate data (pass by reference), pass an address.

```
double_it(&n);
```

▶ To receive an address, declare an argument having pointer type.

```
void double_it(int *p);
```

▶ An array name is a constant that translates into the address of its first element. A reference to an array element a[n] is translated into the pointer reference, *(a + n).

▶ When an integer value is added to an address expression, C++ performs scaling, multiplying the integer by the size of the expression's base type.

```
new_address = address_expression + (integer *
size_of_base_type)
```

▶ The unary operators * and ++ operators associate right-to-left. Consequently, this expression:

```
*p++ = 0;
```

does the same thing as the following expression, which sets *p to 0 *and then* increments the pointer p to point to the next element:

```
*(p++) = 0;
```

Strings: Analyzing the Text

Most computer programs, at some point in their lives, have to communicate with a human being. The standard way to do this is to use text strings; that's especially true for the console-based applications in this book.

Using text strings to print simple messages is easy enough. Text strings get more interesting when you pick apart, combine, or analyze them. That's what this chapter is all about.

Text Storage on the Computer

In Chapter 1, I said the computer stores text numerically, just like any other kind of data. But with text data, each byte uses a special code that corresponds to a particular character: This is called ASCII code. Suppose I declared the following string:

```
char *str = "Hello!";
```

C++ allocates exactly seven bytes—one byte for each character and one for a terminating null byte. Here's what the string data looks like in memory.

Actual data:	72	101	108	108	111	33	0
ASCII code for:	'H'	'e'	'l'	'l'	'o'	'!'	(null)

You can turn to Appendix D and see the ASCII code for every character. In reality, the computer doesn't actually store alphanumeric characters; it stores only numbers. When and how, then, do the numeric values get translated into text characters?

This translation happens at least two times: when data is typed at the keyboard and when it's displayed on the monitor. When you press H on the keyboard, a series of actions happen at a low level that result in the ASCII code for H (72) getting read into your program, which then stores that value as data.

The rest of the time, a text string is just a series of numbers—or more specifically, as a series of bytes ranging in value from 0 to 255. But as programmers, we can think of C++ storing text characters in memory, one byte per character. (Exception: The international standard, Unicode, uses more than one byte per character.)

Interlude

How Does the Computer Translate Programs?

Programming books sometimes point out that the CPU doesn't understand the C++ language. All the C++ statements must be translated into machine code before they can be executed. But who does the translation?

Oh, that's no mystery, they say; the translation is done by the compiler—which itself is a computer program. But in that case, the computer is doing the translation.

When I was first learning how to program, this seemed to me an insolvable paradox. The CPU (the "brain" at the heart of the computer) doesn't understand a word of C++, yet it performs the translation between C++ and its own internal language. Isn't that a contradiction?

A large part of the answer is this: C++ source code is stored in a text file, just as you might store an essay or a memo. But text characters, as I've pointed out, are stored in numeric form. When the compiler works on this data, therefore, it's doing another form of number crunching, evaluating data and making decisions according to precise rules.

In case that doesn't clear things up, imagine this: You have the task of reading letters from a person who knows Japanese but no English. You, meanwhile, know English but not one word of Japanese. (My apologies to philosopher John Searle, who originated this idea with his "Chinese Room" thought experiment.)

Interlude

▼ *continued*

But suppose you have an instruction book that tells you how to translate Japanese characters into their English-language equivalent. The instruction book itself is written in English, so you have no problem using it.

So, even though you don't understand Japanese, you're able to translate all the Japanese you want, by carefully following instructions.

That's what a computer program is, really: an instruction book read by the CPU. A computer program is an inert thing—a sequence of instructions and data—yet the "knowledge" inside a computer arises from its programs. Programs enable a computer to do all kinds of clever things—including translating a text file containing C++.

A compiler, of course, is a very special program, but what it does is not at all strange or impossible. As a computer program, it's an "instruction book," as described. What it tells how to do is to read a text file containing C++ source code and output another instruction book: This output is your C++ program in executable form.

The very first compilers had to be written in machine code. Later, old compilers could be used to write new compilers...so, through a bootstrap process, even skilled programmers could rely on writing machine code less and less.

It Don't Mean a Thing If It Ain't Got That String

If you read Chapter 5, you may have already guessed what a string is: an array. More specifically, a string is an array of base type **char**.

Technically, **char** is an integer type, one byte wide, large enough to store 256 different values (ranging from 0 to 255). This is more than enough to contain all the different ASCII codes for the standard set of characters, including uppercase and lowercase letters, as well as numerals and punctuation marks.

You can, if you want, create a **char** array of a definite size but no initial values:

```
char str[10];
```

This creates a string that can hold up to 10 bytes but has yet to be initialized. More often, programmers give a string initial values when they declare it, like this:

```
char str[10] = "Hello!";
```

This declaration creates the array of **char** shown and equates the name str to the starting address of this array. (Remember that the name of an array always translates into its starting address.) This figure omits showing the ASCII codes and shows only the characters represented—but underneath, it's all numbers.

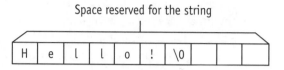

Space reserved for the string

The character \0 is C++ notation for a null character: It means the actual value 0 is stored in this byte (as opposed to value 48, the ASCII code for the digit 0). A C++ string terminates with a null byte, which indicates where the string data ends.

If you don't specify a definite size but initialize the string anyway, C++ allocates just enough space needed for the string (including its null-terminator byte).

```
char s[] = "Hello!";
char *p  = "Hello!";
```

The effect of these two statements is roughly the same, but there is a difference: s is an array name and is therefore a constant that cannot change, but p can be reassigned to point to other locations. In either case, C++ allocates just enough space in the data segment and assigns the starting address to s or p:

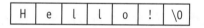

String-Manipulation Functions

Just as it provides math functions to crunch numbers, C++ provides functions to manipulate strings. These functions take pointer arguments—that is, they get the addresses of the strings—but they work on the string data pointed to.

Here are some of the most commonly used string functions:

FUNCTION	DESCRIPTION
strcpy($s1, s2$)	Copy contents of s2 to destination string s1.
strcat($s1, s2$)	Concatenate (join) contents of s2 onto the end of s1.
strlen(s)	Return length of string s (not counting terminating null.).
strncpy($s1, s2, n$)	Copy s2 to s1, but copy no more than n characters (not counting the null).
strncat($s1, s2, n$)	Concatenate contents of s2 onto the end of s1, copying no more than n characters (not counting the null).

Possibly the most common are **strcpy** ("string copy") and **strcat**, which stands for "string concatenation." Here's an example of their use:

```
char s[80];
strcpy(s, "One");
strcat(s, "Two");
strcat(s, "Three ");
cout << s;
```

This produces the following output:

```
OneTwoThree
```

This example illustrates some important points:

▶ The string variable, s, must be declared with enough space to hold all the characters in the resulting string. C++ does nothing to ensure that there is space enough to hold all the string data necessary; this is your responsibility.

▶ Although the string is not initialized, 80 bytes are reserved for it. This example assumes that storing 80 characters (including the null) will be sufficient.

▶ The string literals "One" and "Two" and "Three" are arguments. When a string literal appears in code, C++ allocates space for the string and returns the address of the data: That is, in the C++ code, a string name evaluates to an address. Therefore, "Two" and "Three" are interpreted as address arguments.

The action of the statement:

```
strcat(s, "Two");
```

looks like this.

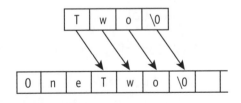

There's a risk with these string functions, as you can see: How do you guarantee that the first string is large enough for the existing string data along with the new? One approach is to make the target string so large you don't think it will ever be exceeded.

A more secure technique is to use the **strncat** and **strncpy** functions. Each of these functions avoids copying more than N characters, not including the terminating null. For example, the following operation cannot exceed the memory allocated for s1:

```
char s1[20];
// . . .
strncpy(s1, s2, 19);
strncat(s1, s3, 19 - strlen(s1));
```

The limit of characters to copy is 19, not 20. It's necessary to leave one extra byte for the terminating null.

Example 7.1.   *Building Strings*

Let's start with a simple string operation: building a string out of smaller strings. The following program gets a couple of strings from the user (by calling the **getline** function, described later), builds a larger string, and then prints the results:

```
buildstr.cpp

#include <iostream>
#include <cstring>
using namespace std;

int main() {
    char str[600];
    char name[100];
    char addr[200];
    char work[200];

    // Get three strings from the user.

    cout << "Enter name and press ENTER: ";
    cin.getline(name, 99);
    cout << "Enter address and press ENTER: ";
    cin.getline(addr, 199);
    cout << "Enter workplace and press ENTER: ",
    cin.getline(work, 199);

    // Build the output string, and then print it.
```

buildstr.cpp, cont.

```
        strcpy(str, "\nMy name is ");
        strcat(str, name);
        strcat(str, ", I live at ");
        strcat(str, addr);
        strcat(str, ",\nand I work at ");
        strcat(str, work);
        strcat(str, ".");

        cout << str << endl;

        system("PAUSE");
        return 0;
    }
```

Here's a sample session using this program:

```
Enter name and press ENTER: Niles Cavendish
Enter address and press ENTER: 123 May Street
Enter work and press ENTER: Bozo's Carnival of Fun

My name is Niles Cavendish, I live at 123 May Street,
and I work at Bozo's Carnival of Fun.
```

How It Works

This example starts with a new include-file directive:

```
#include <cstring>
```

This is needed because it brings in declarations for the **strcpy** and **strcat** functions. As a general rule, using any standard-library function that begins with the three letters *str* requires you to include <cstring>.

The first thing that the main function does is to declare a series of strings to hold data. The program assumes these strings are sufficiently large that they won't be exceeded:

```
        char str[600];
        char name[100];
        char addr[200];
        char work[200];
```

It seems absurd that you'd ever want to enter a name longer than 100 characters, so these limits are probably sufficient, especially if you're writing the program for your own use.

But of course any such limits *can* be exceeded, and if you write programs for large numbers of other people, it's wise to assume that users are going to test every limit they can at some point. (This problem is addressed in Exercise 7.1.1.)

The other part of the example that's new is the use of the **getline** function:

```
cin.getline(name, 99);
```

The **getline** function gets an entire line of input: All the characters input before the user pressed ENTER. The first argument (in this case, name) specifies the destination string. The second argument specifies the maximum number of characters to copy; this should never be more than N–1, where N is the number of bytes allocated for the string.

After putting input into the three strings—name, addr, and work—the program builds the string. The first call is to **strcpy**, which copies string data to the beginning of str. (Calling **strcat** wouldn't produce correct results in this case, unless you knew that the first byte of str was a null—not a safe assumption here.)

```
strcpy(str, "\nMy name is ");
```

The characters \n are a C++ *escape sequence*: They are not intended literally but instead represent a special character. In this case, \n denotes a newline character.

The program builds the rest of the string by calling **strcat** repeatedly.

```
strcat(str, name);
strcat(str, ", I live at");
strcat(str, addr);
strcat(str, ",\nand I work at ");
strcat(str, work);
strcat(str, ".");
```

EXERCISES

Exercise 7.1.1.   Rewrite the example so that it cannot exceed the limits of str. For example, you'd replace the statement

```
strcat(str, addr);
```

with the following statement:

```
strncat(str, addr, 599 - strlen(str));
```

Exercise 7.1.2.   After completing Exercise 7.1.1, test it by experimenting with different limitations for the str string. It helps if you replace the number 600 with the symbolic constant STRMAX, putting the following **#define** directive at the beginning of the program. During preprocessing, this directive causes the compiler to replace occurrences of STRMAX in the source code with the indicated text (599).

```
#define STRMAX 599
```

You can then use STRMAX+1 to declare the length of str

```
char str[STRMAX+1];
```

and then use STRMAX to determine how many bytes to copy:

```
strncpy(str, "\nMy name is ", STRMAX);
strncat(str, name, STRMAX - strlen(str));
```

The beauty of this approach is that if you need to change the maximum string size, you need to change only one line of code (the line contain the **#define** directive) and then recompile.

Interlude

What about Escape Sequences?

Escape sequences can create some odd-looking code, if you're not used to them. Consider this statement:

```
cout << "\nand I live at";
```

This has the same effect as the following:

```
cout << endl << "and I live at";
```

The key to understanding a strange-looking string such as \nand is to remember this rule:

✱ In C++ source code, when the compiler reads a backslash (\), the very next character is interpreted as having a special meaning.

In addition to \n, which represents a newline, other escape sequences include \t (tab) and \b (backspace).

Now, if you have an inquiring mind, you may be asking this: How do I print an actual backslash? The answer is simple. Two backslashes in a row (\\) represent a single backslash. For example, consider this statement:

```
cout << "\\nand I live at";
```

▼ *continued on next page*

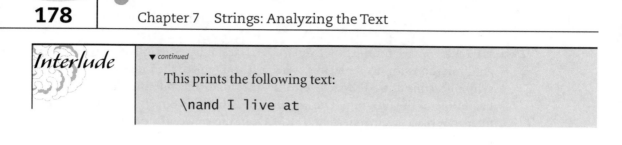

▼ *continued*

This prints the following text:

```
\nand I live at
```

Reading String Input

So far, I've been treating data input in a simplistic way. In previous examples, I assumed that the user types a number—for example, 15—and that this value gets directly entered into the program. Actually, there's more to it than that.

All the data entered at a keyboard is initially text data: This means ASCII codes. So, when you're a user and you press 1 and 5 on the keyboard, the first thing that happens is that these characters get put into the input stream.

Input stream:

	Actual data:	· · ·	32	49	53	32	· · ·
	ASCII code for:		(sp)	'1'	'5'	(sp)	

The **cin** object, which has been told to get a number, analyzes this text input and produces a single integer value, in this case the value 15. That number gets assigned to an integer variable in a statement such as this one:

```
cin >> n;
```

If the type of n were different (say, if it had type **double**), a different conversion would be called for. Floating-point format requires a different kind of value to be produced. Normally, the stream-input operator (>>) handles all this for you.

The previous section introduced the **getline** function, which has some strange-looking syntax:

```
cin.getline(name, 99);
```

This is our first look at member functions. The dot (.) is necessary to show that **getline** is a member of the object **cin**. Admittedly, there's some new terminology here.

I'll explain a lot more about objects starting in Chapter 11. For now, think of an object as a data structure that comes with built-in knowledge of how to do certain things. The way you call upon an object's abilities is to call a member function:

```
object.function(arguments)
```

The *object* is what the function applies to—in this case, **cin**. The *function* in this case is **getline**. (For the record, file-input objects, introduced in Chapter 8, also support this function.) Calling **cin.getline** is an alternative to getting input by using the stream operator (>>):

```
cin >> var;
```

We've seen this kind of statement used to get **int** and **double** data. Can you use it with strings? Yes.

```
cin >> name;
```

The problem with this statement is that it doesn't do what you might expect. Instead of getting an entire line of input—that is, all the data that the user types before pressing ENTER—it gets data up to the first white space ("white space" being programmer-ese for a blank space, tab, or newline). So, given this line of input:

```
Niles Cavendish
```

the effect of "cin >> name" would be to copy the letters "Niles" into the string variable, name, while "Cavendish" would remain in the input stream to be picked up by the next input operation.

So, assume the user types in the following and then presses ENTER.

```
50 3.141592 Joe Bloe
```

This works fine if you're expecting two numbers and two strings separated by a blank space. Here's the statement that would successfully read the input:

```
cin >> n >> pi >> first_name >> last_name;
```

But in general, the use of the stream input operator gives you a lack of control. I avoid it myself, except for simple test programs. One of the limitations of this operator is that it doesn't allow you to set a default value. Suppose you prompt for a number:

```
cout << "Enter number: ";
cin >> n;
```

If the user presses ENTER without typing anything, nothing happens. The computer just sits there, waiting for the user to type a number and press ENTER again. If the user keeps pressing ENTER, the program will wait forever, like a stubborn child.

Personally, I think it's much better to have the program support the behavior implied by the following prompt:

```
Enter a number (or press ENTER to specify 0):
```

Wouldn't you find it convenient to have 0 (or whatever number you choose) as a default value? But how do you implement this behavior? This next example demonstrates how.

Note ▶ If you use the **getline** function at all, you may find that further operations using the stream input operator (>>) do not work correctly. This is because the **getline** function and the stream-input operator make different assumptions about when a newline character is "consumed." It's a good idea to stick to one approach or the other.

Example 7.2. *Get a Number*

The following program gets numbers and prints their square roots, until the user either presses 0 or presses ENTER directly after the prompt:

```
get_num.cpp

#include <iostream>
#include <cstring>
#include <cmath>
#include <cstdlib>
using namespace std;

double get_number();

int main() {
    double x;

    while(true) {
        cout << "Enter a num (press ENTER to exit): ";
        x = get_number();
        if (x == 0.0)
            break;
```

```
                        cout << "Square root of x is: " << sqrt(x);
                        cout << endl;
            }
        system("PAUSE");
        return 0;
}


// Get-number function.
// Get number input by the user, taking only the first
//  numeric input entered. If user presses ENTER with
//  no input, then return a default value of 0.0.
//
double get_number() {
        char s[100];

        cin.getline(s, 100);
        if (strlen(s) == 0)
            return 0.0;
        return atof(s);
}
```

You can use this same function (get_number) in all your programs as a better way of getting numeric input.

How It Works

The program begins by including <cstring> and <cmath>, which bring in type information for string functions and math functions; also, <cstdlib> brings in the declaration of the **atof** function used in this example. The program also declares the get_number function up front:

```
#include <iostream>
#include <cstring>
#include <cmath>
#include <cstdlib>
using namespace std;

double get_number();
```

What the main function does should be familiar by now. It performs an infinite loop, which is terminated when 0 is returned by the get_number function. When any value other than zero is entered, the program calculates a square root and prints the results.

```
while (true) {
    cout << "Enter a num (press ENTER to exit): ";
    x = get_number();
    if (x == 0.0)
        break;
    cout << "Square root of x is: " << sqrt(x);
    cout << endl;
}
```

What's new here is the get_number function itself. When this function calls **getline**, it gets an entire line of input up to n–1 characters. Since the n argument in this case is 100, it will read at most 99 characters, leaving one byte for the terminating null. If the user presses ENTER directly after the prompt, **getline** returns an empty string.

```
double get_number() {
    char s[100];

    cin.getline(s, 100);
    if (strlen(s) == 0)
        return 0.0;
    return atof(s);
}
```

Once the input line is stored in the local string, s, it's a trivial matter to return 0 if the string is empty.

```
if (strlen(s) == 0)
    return 0.0;
```

The literal 0.0 is equal to 0 but is stored in **double** format. Remember that every literal containing a decimal point is considered a floating-point number by C++.

If the length of string s is not 0, data in the string needs to be converted. Because we're not relying on the stream operator (>>), the get_number function must take responsibility for interpreting data itself. It therefore needs to examine the characters read—the ASCII codes sent from the keyboard—and produce a **double** value.

Fortunately, the C++ standard library supplies a handy function—**atof**—for doing just that, and we can make use of it here. The **atof** function takes string input and produces a floating-point (**double**) value, just as its cousin **atoi** produces an **int** value.

```
return atof(s);
```

This function has a sibling, **atoi**, that does the same thing for integers:

```
return atoi(s);        // Return an int value.
```

EXERCISE

Exercise 7.2.1.   Rewrite Example 7.2 so that it accepts only integer input. (Hint: You'll want to change all types directly affected, from **double** to **int** format—including constants.)

Example 7.3.   *Convert to Uppercase*

In Example 7.5, I'm going to do some fancy string manipulation by referring to individual characters. First, however, I'll show a simple example that accesses individual characters.

```
upper.cpp
    #include <iostream>
    #include <cstring>
    #include <cctype>
    using namespace std;

    void convert_to_upper(char *s);

    int main() {
        char s[100];

        cout << "Enter string to convert & press ENTER: ";
        cin.getline(s, 100);

        convert_to_upper(s);
        cout << "The converted string is:" << endl;
        cout << s << endl;
```

▼ *continued on next page*

upper.cpp, cont.

```
        system("PAUSE");
        return 0;
    }

    void convert_to_upper(char *s) {
        int length = strlen(s);

        for (int i = 0; i < length; i++)
            s[i] = toupper(s[i]);
    }
```

How It Works

The main purpose of this example is to show that you can manipulate individual characters of a string. To pass a string to a function, pass its address. To do that, of course, you just give the name of the string. (This is the standard procedure to pass any kind of array.)

```
    convert_to_upper(s);
```

The function uses the argument passed—which, after all, is an address—to index into the string data.

```
    void convert_to_upper(char *s) {
        int length = strlen(s);

        for (int i = 0; i < length; i++)
            s[i] = toupper(s[i]);
    }
```

This example introduces a new function, **toupper**. The two functions, **toupper** and **tolower**, operate on individual characters:

FUNCTION	DESCRIPTION
toupper(*c*)	If c is a lowercase letter, return the uppercase equivalent; otherwise, return c as is.
tolower(*c*)	If c is an uppercase letter, return the lowercase equivalent; otherwise, return c as is.

The following statement therefore converts a character to uppercase (if it is a lowercase letter) and replaces the original character with the result.

```
s[i] = toupper(s[i]);
```

Again, note that to use these functions, you must include <cctype>:

```
#include <cctype>
```

EXERCISES

Exercise 7.3.1. Write a program that is similar to Example 7.3 but converts the string input to all lowercase. (Hint: Use the **tolower** function from the C++ library.)

Exercise 7.3.2. Rewrite Example 7.3 so that it uses direct pointer reference—described at the end of Chapter 6—rather than array indexing. If you have reached the end of the string, the value of the current character is a null-terminator, so you can test for the end-of-string condition by using *p == '\0'. You can also use *p itself as the condition, because it is nonzero if it's not pointing to a zero (or null) value.

```
while (*p++)
    // Do some stuff...
```

Individual Characters vs. Strings

C++ makes a distinction between individual characters and strings. A lot depends on whether you use single or double quotation marks.

The expression 'A' represents a single character. During compilation, C++ replaces this expression with the ASCII value for a letter 'A', which happens to be 65 decimal.

On the other hand, expression "A" represents a string of length 1. When C++ sees this expression, it places two bytes in the data area:

▶ The ASCII code for the letter 'A', as shown earlier.

▶ A null-terminating byte.

The C++ compiler then replaces the expression "A" *with the address* of this two-byte array. 'A' and "A" are different because one is converted to an integer value, whereas the other represents a string and so is converted to an address.

This may seem like a lot to digest, but just remember to pay close attention to the quotation marks. The following code provides an example of how they can be intermixed correctly:

```
char s[] = "A";
if (s[0] == 'A')
    cout << "The first letter of the string is 'A'. ";
```

This produces a correct result. But this next comparison is an error, because it tries to compare a character to an address:

```
if (s[0] == "A")                        // WRONG!
    //...
```

This fragment attempts to compare an element of the string array s with an *address expression*, "A". The cardinal rules are as follows:

✱ **Expressions in single quotation marks (such as 'A') are treated as numeric values after translation into ASCII codes. They are not arrays.**

✱ **Expressions in double quotation marks (such as "A") are arrays of char and as such are translated into addresses.**

Example 7.4. *Breaking Up Input with Strtok*

When you read in a line of text (for example, with the **getline** function), you'll often find you need to break it into smaller strings. For example, consider this text input:

```
Me, myself, and I.
```

Suppose you want to break this into the individual substrings separated by commas and spaces (*delimiters*). As a test, you might print each of the substrings on its own line:

```
Me
Myself
and
I
```

You can do this yourself through a combination of searching for delimiter characters and then indexing the string to select the substrings you find. But it's easier to use the **strtok** function (string token) from the C++ standard library.

In this context, the word *token* means a substring containing a single word. There are two ways to use this function.

FUNCTION USAGE	DESCRIPTION
strtok(source_string, delims)	Return the first token from source string, using the delimiters found in *delims*.
strtok(NULL, *delims*)	Using the source string already specified (during an earlier call to **strtok**), get the next token. Use the delimiters found in *delims*.

The first time you use **strtok**, specify both the source string and the delimiter characters; **strtok** returns a pointer to the first substring (that is, token) it finds. For example:

```
p = strtok(the_string, ", ");
```

Thereafter, call **strtok** specifying NULL for the first argument; **strtok** returns the next token from this same source string. The function remembers what source string it was working on and where it was in that string.

```
p = strtok(NULL, ", ");
```

If instead you specify *source_string* again, **strtok** starts over and returns the first token.

The return value from the function is usually a pointer to a token; but if there are no further tokens (substrings) left to read, **strtok** returns NULL.

C++0x ▶ The new C++0x specification provides a new keyword, **nullptr**, that can and should be used in place of NULL if you have a C++0x-compliant compiler.

Here is a simple program that interprets spaces and commas as delimiters (that is to say, separator characters) and prints each substring—that is, each token—on its own line:

tokenize.cpp

```cpp
#include <iostream>
#include <cstring>

using namespace std;

int main() {
    char the_string[81], *p;
```

▼ continued on next page

```
        cout << "Input a string to parse: ";
        cin.getline(the_string, 81);
        p = strtok(the_string, ", ");
        while (p != NULL) {
                cout << p << endl;
                p = strtok(NULL, ", ");
        }
        system("PAUSE");
        return 0;
    }
```

How It Works

This program is a simple demonstration of **strtok**. It begins with **#include** directives.

```
#include <iostream>
#include <cstring>
```

Before going into the **while** loop, the program calls **strtok** and specifies the input string. It finds the first token (substring), if any, and returns a pointer to it.

```
p = strtok(the_string, ", ");
```

This is the only place that `the_string` is specified. After that, the loop calls **strtok** with a NULL first argument, which means "Keep working on the same input string, and return the next token (substring) within it."

```
while (p != NULL) {
        cout << p << endl;
        p = strtok(NULL, ", ");
}
```

A NULL return value means "There are no tokens left to read."

EXERCISES

Exercise 7.4.1. Revise the example so that in addition to printing out tokens (substrings) one to a line, it also prints a statement telling you how many tokens it found.

Exercise 7.4.2. Put all the tokens back together but separated by ampersands (&). Print the result.

Exercise 7.4.3. Use an ampersand (&) as a delimiter.

The New C++ String Type

Null-terminated strings used in C and C++ are often referred to as *C-strings*. They are a little more difficult to use than, say, the strings that Visual Basic maintains. Basic has a special string type that hides the details from you and frees you from having to worry about such messy issues as string length.

Recent versions of C++ also have such a type, declared not as **char*** but rather as **string**. This type is a class provided by the Standard Template Library (STL) that all but the oldest versions of C++ now support. If your compiler doesn't support STL, you'll have to stick to using C-strings. (But note that Chapter 16 explains how to define your own String class, which has many of the features presented here.)

Include String-Class Support

To use the new string type, the first thing you need to do is turn on support for it by using an **#include <string>** directive. This is not the same directive that enables C-string support in the function library. They look similar.

```
#include <string>     // Support new string class
```

But C-string support, remember, uses "cstring" rather than "string":

```
#include <cstring>    // Support old-style string
                       //   functions
```

What a difference the "c" makes! By the way, you can turn on support for both. Including "cstring" is not necessary if all you want to do is use string literals; it is only needed to support old-style functions such as **strcpy**.

As with **cin** and **cout**, the name **string** must be qualified with the **std** prefix unless you include the using statement at the beginning of your programs:

```
using namespace std;
```

Declare and Initialize Variables of Type string

Once you have turned on support for the string type, it's easy to use it to declare variables.

```
string a, b, c;
```

This creates three variables having string type. Notice how easy this is: You don't have to worry about how much space might be needed for each string. You can initialize the strings in a number of ways. For example:

```
string a("Here is a string."), b("Here's another.");
```

You can also use the assignment operator (=) for this purpose.

```
string a, b;
a = "Here is a string."
b = "Here's another."
```

You can even use the operator for initialization, combining the two steps:

```
string a = "Here is a string.";
```

Working with Variables of Type string

The standard-library **string** class works as you'd probably expect. Unlike C-strings, **string** objects can be copied and compared without calling library functions.

For example, suppose you have the following strings:

```
string cat = "Persian";
string dog = "Dane";
```

You can assign new data without worrying about capacity. For example, dog—which had four characters—"automagically" grows to store seven characters:

```
string dog = "Persian";
```

You can compare these strings by using the test-for-equality operator (==). This does what you'd expect: return **true** if the contents are identical. (To perform this comparison with C-strings, you'd need to call **strcmp**.)

```
if (cat == dog)
   cout << "cat and dog have the same name";
```

To copy from one string variable to another, use the assignment operator (=). Again, this does what you'd expect: It copies string contents, not a pointer value.

```
string country = dog;
```

As in Basic, you can concatenate (join) strings by using a plus sign (+):

```
string new_str = a + b;
```

You can even embed string literals in this operation:

```
string str = a + " " + b;
```

However, the following statement does not compile:

```
string str = "The dog" + " is my friend"; // ERROR!
```

The problem is that although the plus sign (+) is supported as a concatenation operator between two **string** variables or between a **string** variable and a C-string, it is not supported between two C-strings…and string literals are still C-strings.

Input and Output

Variables of type **string** work with **cin** and **cout** just as you'd expect.

```
string prompt = "Enter your name: ";
string name;
cout << prompt;
cin >> name;
```

Use of the stream-input operator (>>) has the same drawback that it does with C-strings: Characters are returned from the keyboard up until the first white-space character.

But you can use the **getline** function to put an entire line of input into a string variable. This version doesn't require you to enter a maximum number of characters to read, because the string variable will store data of any size.

```
getline(cin, name);
```

Example 7.5. *Building Strings with the string Type*

This example performs the same action as Example 7.1, except that it uses string variables:

---

buildstr2.cpp

```cpp
#include <iostream>
#include <cstring>
using namespace std;

int main() {
    string str, name, addr, work;

    // Get three strings from the user.

    cout << "Enter name and press ENTER: ";
    getline(cin, name);
```

▼ *continued on next page*

```
        cout << "Enter address and press ENTER: ";
        getline(cin, addr);
        cout << "Enter workplace and press ENTER: ";
        getline(cin, work);

        // Build the output string, and then print it.

        str = "\nMy name is " + name + ", " +
              "I live at " + addr +
              ",\nand I work at " + work + ".\n";

        cout << str << endl;

        system("PAUSE");
        return 0;
    }
```

How It Works

If anything, this version of the program is easier to write than the version in Exercise 7.1. The first difference is the **include** directive, which must refer to <string>, not <cstring>.

```
#include <string>
using namespace std;
```

The using namespace statement, as usual, enables you to refer to **std** symbols (such as **cin**, **cout**, and also **string**) without a **std** prefix.

Then things get easier. This version of the program declares four string variables without worrying about how much space to reserve for each.

```
string str, name, addr, work;
```

The program then calls the **getline** function without needing to specify maximum number of characters to read.

```
        cout << "Enter name and press ENTER: ";
        getline(cin, name);
        cout << "Enter address and press ENTER: ";
        getline(cin, addr);
        cout << "Enter workplace and press ENTER: ";
        getline(cin, work);
```

Finally, the program builds the string. The addition operator (+) provides a concise way to represent string concatenation.

```
str = "\nMy name is " + name + ", " +
      "I live at " + addr +
      ",\nand I work at " + work + ".\n";
```

Then it's an easy matter to print the resulting string.

```
cout << str;
```

EXERCISES

Exercise 7.5.1.   Get three pieces of information from the user: a dog's name, its breed, and its age. Then print a sentence combining all this information.

Exercise 7.5.2.   Rewrite one of the Card-Dealing programs in Chapter 5 by using the **string** class. (Hint: To declare an array of string, treat it just like an array of any other fundamental data type. You'll still need to allocate enough space for array members, but each string is treated as a unit. No pointer syntax is required. Treat an array of string like an array of simple data types.)

Other Operations on the string Type

You can access individual characters in a **string** object with the same syntax used to access characters inside C-strings.

```
string[index]
```

For example, the following code prints out individual characters of a string, one to a line:

```
#include <string>
using namespace std;
//...
string dog = "Mac";
for (int i = 0; i < dog.size(); i++)
    cout << dog[i] << endl;
```

When run, this code prints the following:

```
M
a
c
```

As with C-strings, or any array in C, **string** variables use zero-based indexing. This is why the initial setting for i is 0.

The loop condition depends on the length of the string. To find this length with a C-string, you'd use the **strlen** function. With a string object, use the **size** member function.

```
int length = dog.size();
```

Chapter 7   *Summary*

Here are the main points of Chapter 7:

▶ Text characters are stored in the computer according to their ASCII codes. For examples, the string "Hello!" is represented by the byte values 72, 101, 108, 108, 111, 33, and 0 (for the terminating null).

▶ The traditional "C-string" type uses a terminating null—a 0 byte value. This enables string-handling functions to determine where the string ends. When you declare a string literal such as "Hello!", C++ automatically allocates space for this terminating null along with the other characters.

▶ The current length of a string (determined by searching for the terminating null) is not the same as the amount of total storage reserved for the string. The following declaration reserves 10 bytes of storage for str but initializes it so that its current length is only six. The string will have three unused bytes as a result, enabling it to grow later if needed.

```
char str[10] = "Hello!";
```

▶ Library functions such as **strcpy** (string copy) and **strcat** (string concatenation) can alter the length of an existing string. When you perform these operations, it's important that the string have enough space reserved to accommodate the new string length.

▶ The **strlen** function gets the current length of the string.

▶ Include the string.h file to provide type information for string-handling functions.

```
#include <cstring>
```

▶ If you try to increase the length of a string without having the necessary space reserved, you'll overwrite another variable's data area, creating hard-to-find bugs.

```
char str[] = "Hello!";
strcat(str, " So happy to see you.");   // ERROR!!!!
```

▶ To ensure that you don't copy too many characters to a string, you can use the **strncat** and **strncpy** functions.

```
char str[100];
strncpy(str, s2, 99);
strncat(str, s2, 99 - strlen(str));
```

▶ The stream operator (>>), used with the **cin** object, provides only limited control over input. When you use it to send data to a string address, it gets the characters only up to the first white space (blank, tab, or newline).

▶ To get a full line of input, use the **cin.getline** function. The second argument specifies the maximum number of characters to copy to the string (not counting the terminating null).

```
cin.getline(input_string, max);
```

▶ An expression such as 'A' represents a single integer value (after translation into ASCII code); an expression such as "A" represents an array of **char** and is therefore translated into an address.

▶ The STL **string** class lets you to create, copy contents (=), test for equality of contents (==), and concatenate (+) strings without having to worry about size issues.

Files: Electronic Storage

8

Most practical applications (reservation systems, database systems, spreadsheets, and even games) store and retrieve persistent information. This is data that hangs around after the program ends and even after the computer is turned off.

Main memory (RAM) is not persistent. As soon as the computer is turned off, data in memory is lost forever. But even if main memory were more permanent—even if it didn't zero out when the computer shuts down—main memory is too precious a resource to be dedicated to long-term record storage.

So when you need a place to put data for later use, put it in a disk file.

Introducing File-Stream Objects

In using **cin** and **cout** (console input and output), you've already made use of objects. Now it's time to introduce some new objects. C++ provides file streams that support the same set of function calls and operators that **cin** and **cout** do.

C++ programmers often talk about *streams*. A stream is something to which you can read or write data. The term evokes the image of data flowing like water in a river—flowing from some source (for example, the console) or toward some destination (for example, a file). Although data streams are not always as endless as a river, it's a useful image.

Writing to a text file involves a few simple steps. The first step is to enable support for file-stream operations by using an `#include <fstream>` directive. This implicitly brings in declarations for file-stream operations.

```
#include <fstream>
```

The second step is to create a file-stream object and associate it with a disk file. (I've chosen the name fout, but you could choose any name you want: MyGoofyFile, RoundFile, Trash, or whatever.) Also, I've specified a file named output.txt.

```
ofstream fout("output.txt");  // Open file output.txt
```

Now the object fout is associated with the file output.txt and has type **ofstream**. When you open a file stream, you can use any of the following types:

▶ **ofstream**, for file-output streams

▶ **ifstream**, for file-input streams

▶ **fstream**, a generic file stream (to which you have to specify input, output, or both when you open it—more on that later)

The third step is as follows: After the object is successfully created, you can write to it just as you would write to **cout**. This sends data to the associated file—in this case, output.txt.

```
fout << "This is a line of text.";
```

As a variation on an example from Chapter 1, you could use the following code to write to the disk file output.txt:

```
#include <fstream>
// ...
ofstream fout("output.txt");  // Open file output.txt

fout << "I am Blaxxon," << endl;
fout << "the cosmic computer.";
```

The object fout provides access to the disk file. In object-oriented terms, we can say that fout *encapsulates* the file, in terms of its ability to receive output. First, fout is declared, associating it with a particular disk file (output.txt in this example). Afterward, writing to fout results in sending data to this same file.

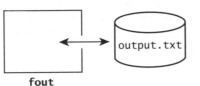

ofstream   fout("output.txt");

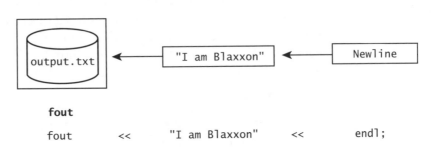

fout   <<   "I am Blaxxon"   <<   endl;

You can have multiple file-stream objects open at the same time—one for each file you want to interact with.

```
ofstream  out_file_1("memo.txt");
ofstream  out_file_2("messages.txt");
```

When done reading or writing to a file, you should call the **close** function. This causes the program to give up ownership of the file so that some other process can access it. C++ closes the file for you when the program exits successfully, but it's a good idea to close files as soon as you no longer need them.

```
out_file_1.close();
out_file_2.close();
```

How to Refer to Disk Files

In the previous section, I showed how you can create a file object by specifying the file's name. If successful, this declaration opens the file for output, giving you exclusive access.

```
ofstream fout("output.txt");
```

By default, the file referred to is in the current directory—the directory from which you run the program. (Or, to use Windows or Macintosh lingo, this is the current *folder.*) But you can, if you want, specify a complete path name, option-ally including a drive letter. This is all part of the complete filename—or more precisely, the file specification.

For example, you can open a file in the root directory of C: drive.

```
ofstream fout("c:\\output.txt");
```

The string literal here uses the C++ backslash notation. In the previous chap-ter, I explained that the backslash character has a special meaning in C++ pro-grams: For example, \n represents a newline, and \t represents a tab. To represent the backslash itself, use two in a row. So, c:\\output.txt in a C++ program code names this file:

```
c:\output.txt
```

When you enter c:\\output.txt, C++ interprets \\ in program code as a single backslash, just as it interprets \n to mean a newline.

As another example, the following statement creates a file-stream output object located in the c:\programs\text directory:

```
ofstream fout("c:\\programs\\text\\output.txt");
```

This opens this file:

```
c:\programs\text\output.txt
```

Example 8.1. *Write Text to a File*

The example in this section does about the simplest thing you can do with a text file: open it, write a couple of lines of text, close, and exit.

The program prompts the user for the name of a file to write to. As a user, you enter the exact filename, including drive letter and complete path if desired. Do *not* use two backslashes to represent one: That is a notational convention within C++ program code only and has no effect on the user or on how strings are stored generally.

For example, as the user you might enter this

```
c:\documents\output.txt
```

and if the file is successfully opened, text gets written to this file.

Note ▶ This program will replace whatever file you specify, destroying its old con-tents. Therefore, when you run it, be careful not to enter the name of an existing file unless you don't mind losing that file's contents.

```
writetxt.cpp

#include <iostream>
#include <fstream>
using namespace std;

int main() {
    char filename[MAX_PATH + 1];

    cout << "Enter a file name and press ENTER: ";
    cin.getline(filename, MAX_PATH);
    ofstream file_out(filename);
    if (! file_out) {
        cout << filename << " could not be opened.";
        cout << endl;
        system("PAUSE");
        return -1;
    }
    cout << filename << " was opened." << endl;
    file_out << "I read the" << endl;
    file_out << "news today," << endl;
    file_out << "ooh boy.";
    file_out.close();
    system("PAUSE");
    return 0;
}
```

After running this program, you'll probably want to view its contents to verify that the program wrote the text successfully. You can use any text editor or word processor to do that. (Or, if you are inside an MS-DOS command shell, you can use the TYPE command.)

How It Works

The beginning of the program begins by enabling support for the iostream and fstream portions of the C++ library.

```
#include <iostream>
#include <fstream>
using namespace std;
```

There is only one function, **main**. The first thing it does is to prompt for a file-name:

```
char filename[MAX_PATH + 1];

cout << "Enter a file name and press ENTER: ";
cin.getline(filename, MAX_PATH);
```

This last line refers to MAX_PATH, a predefined constant. MAX_PATH contains the maximum length for filenames (including the path) supported on the system. Allocating MAX_PATH + 1 characters guarantees the string named "filename" will be big enough to hold any valid filename plus one extra byte for the terminating null.

The next thing that the main function does is create a file object, file_out.

```
ofstream file_out(filename);
```

This statement attempts to open the named file. If the attempt to open the file is unsuccessful, a null value is placed in file_out. This value can this be tested in an **if** statement: A null value equates to false in this context.

If the file was not successfully opened, the program prints an error message and exits. The logical negation operator (!) reverses the true/false value, so in effect this is a test to see whether file_out is null, indicating failure to open the file.

```
if (! file_out) {
    cout << filename << " could not be opened.";
    cout << endl;
    system("PAUSE");
    return -1;
}
```

There are a couple reasons the file open could fail. The user may have not entered a valid file specification. Or, the user attempted to open a file that has been given read-only privileges by the operating system and cannot be overwritten.

If the file was successfully opened, the program writes confirmation on the console, writes text to the file, and then closes the file stream.

```
cout << filename << " was opened." << endl;
file_out << "I read the" << endl;
file_out << "news today," << endl;
file_out << "ooh boy.";
file_out.close();
system("PAUSE");
return 0;
```

EXERCISES

Exercise 8.1.1.   Rewrite Example 8.1 so it prompts for directory location and file-name separately. (Hint: Use two strings and use the **strcat** function to join them.)

Exercise 8.1.2.   Write a program that lets the user enter any number of lines of text, one at a time. In effect, this creates a primitive editor, which permits text entry but no editing of a line of text after it's been entered. Set up a loop that doesn't terminate until the user presses ENTER without typing any text (a zero-length string).

Alternatively, you can recognize a special code (for example, @@@) to terminate the session. You can then use the **strcmp** ("string compare") function to detect this string.

```
if (strcmp(input_line, "@@@"))
    break;
```

Remember to print a short prompt before each line of text, such as the following:

```
Enter (@@@ to exit)>>
```

Example 8.2. ## *Display a Text File*

After you write to a file, you'll want to view it. Writing a complete text editor is beyond the scope of this book. But the examples in this chapter cover some of the basic elements. The main thing a word processor or text editor does is open a file, read lines of text, let the user manipulate those lines of text, and then write out the changes.

This example displays 24 lines of text at a time, asking the user whether to continue. The user can print another 24 lines or quit. I picked this number as typical of number of vertical lines in a window less one to interact with the user.

This example opens a stream as an **ifstream**...this assumes text and input modes: The file will not be successfully opened unless you name a file that already exists.

---

readtxt.cpp

```cpp
#include <iostream>
#include <fstream>
using namespace std;
#define COL_WIDTH  80
```

▼ *continued on next page*

readtxt.cpp, cont.

```cpp
int main() {
    int c;    // input character
    int i;    // loop counter
    char filename[MAX_PATH + 1];
    char input_line[COL_WIDTH + 1];

    cout << "Enter a file name and press ENTER: ";
    cin.getline(filename, MAX_PATH);

    ifstream file_in(filename);

    if (! file_in) {
        cout << filename << " could not be opened.";
        cout << endl;
        system("PAUSE");
        return -1;
    }

    while (true) {
        for (i = 1; i <= 24 && ! file_in.eof(); i++) {
            file_in.getline(input_line, COL_WIDTH);
            cout << input_line << endl;
        }
        if (file_in.eof())
            break;
        cout << "More? (Press 'Q' and ENTER to quit)";
        cin.getline(input_line, COL_WIDTH);
        c = input_line[0];
        if (c == 'Q' || c == 'q')
            break;
    }
    system("PAUSE");
    return 0;
}
```

How It Works

This example is similar to Example 8.1 but checks a couple of different conditions to determine whether it should keep reading more lines.

After determining whether the file stream was successfully opened, the program sets up an infinite loop that exits when either of the following conditions is true:

▶ The end of the file is reached.

▶ The user indicates that he or she does not want to continue.

Here's the main loop in skeletal form:

```
while (true) {
    // ...
}
```

Within the loop, the program reads up to 24 lines—less, if the end of file is reached first. The easy way to implement this is to use a **for** loop with a complex condition:

```
for (i = 1; i <= 24 && ! file_in.eof(); i++) {
    file_in.getline(input_line, MAX_PATH);
    cout << input_line << endl;
}
```

The loop continues only as long as i is less than or equal to 24 and the end-of-file condition is not detected. The expression

```
file_in.eof()
```

returns true if the end of the file has been reached. Logical "not" (!) reverses this condition, so that "! file_in.eof()" returns true only as long as there is more data to read.

The rest of the main loop checks to see whether it should continue; if not, it breaks out of the loop and the program ends.

```
if (file_in.eof())
    break;
cout << "More? (Press 'Q' and ENTER to quit)";
cin.getline(input_line, 1);
c = input_line[0];
if (c == 'Q' || c == 'q')
    break;
```

EXERCISES

Exercise 8.2.1. Alter the example so the user can optionally enter a number in response to the "More?" prompt. The number determines how many lines to print at a time instead of 24. (Hint: Use the **atoi** library function to convert string input to integer; if the value entered is greater than 0, modify the numbers of lines to read.)

Exercise 8.2.2.   Alter the example so that it prints the contents of the file in all-uppercase letters. You may find it helpful to copy some of the code from Exercise 7.3 on page 185.

Text Files vs. "Binary" Files

So far, we've used text files; these are treated as streams of text, which you read and write to these files as you would the console. If you view the file with a text editor—or print the file on the console—you'll see the contents in human-readable form.

For example, when you write the number 255 to a text file, the program writes the ASCII character codes for 2, 5, and 5.

```
file_out << 255;
```

But there's another way to store data. Instead of writing the ASCII character codes for 255, you write the value 255 directly. If you then tried to view the file with a text editor, you wouldn't see the numerals 255. Instead, the text editor would try to show you ASCII code 255, which is not a regular printable character.

Programming manuals talk about two kinds of files:

▶ Text files, which you read and write to as you would the console. Usually, every byte written to a text file is the ASCII code for a printable character.

▶ So-called binary files, which you read and write using the actual numeric values of the data. With this approach, ASCII translation is not involved.

This second technique may sound simpler, but it's not. To view such a file in a meaningful way, you need an application that understands what the fields of the file are supposed to be and how to interpret them. Are a group of bytes to be interpreted as integer, floating-point, or string data? And where does one group of bytes start and another begin?

When you create a file-stream object, you can specify text mode (the default) or binary mode. The mode setting itself changes one important detail:

✱   In text mode, each newline character (ASCII 10) is translated into a carriage return–linefeed pair during a write operation—and during a read, a carriage return–linefeed pair is translated back into a newline.

Let's consider why the translation is necessary for text mode. Early in the book, the examples used newline characters. These can be printed separately or embedded in the strings themselves.

```
char *msg_string = "Hello\nYou\n";
```

Strings embed a single byte (ASCII code 10) to indicate a newline. But printing to the console requires two actions: printing a carriage return (ASCII code 13), which moves the cursor to the beginning of the line, and printing a linefeed (ASCII code 10).

When a string is written to the console, each newline in memory is translated into a carriage return–linefeed pair. For example, here's what the string "Hello\nYou\n" looks like when stored in main memory and what it looks like when written to the console.

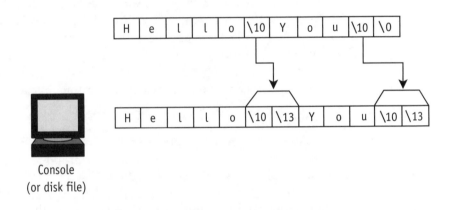

Console
(or disk file)

OK, you say. So, this translation must be done when printing strings on the console. But is it necessary for text files as well?

Yes. Data sent to a text file must have the same format as data sent to the console. This allows C++ to treat all streams of text (whether console or on disk) the same way.

But with a binary file, no such translation should ever be performed. The value 10 may occur in the middle of a numeric field, and it must not be interpreted as a newline. If you translated this value, you'd likely create a great many errors.

There's another difference—probably the most important—between text-mode and binary-mode operations. It concerns the choices you make as a programmer.

▶ If a file is opened in text mode, you should use the same operations used for communicating with the console; these involve the stream operators (<<, >>) and the **getline** function.

▶ If a file is opened in binary mode, you should transfer data only by using the **read** and **write** member functions. These are direct read/write operations.

In the next section, I discuss these two functions.

Interlude

Are "Binary Files" Really More Binary?

The reason people use the term *binary file* is because with such a file, if you write the byte value 255, you're actually writing the binary value of 255 directly.

11111111

The use of the term *binary* is in some ways misleading. If you write 255 as text, you're *still* writing binary data—except that now each of these binary values is an ASCII character code. Conceptually, programmers tend to think of this as "text" format as opposed to "binary," because a text editor displays a file as text.

Incidentally, here's how 255 is actually written in text mode:

00110010   00110101   00110101

This binary sequence represents the numbers 50, 53, and 53, which in turn are the ASCII codes for the numerals 2, 5, and 5. When this data is sent to the console, you see the string of digits 255.

But the important point here is this: This is text mode as opposed to binary mode because while working in text mode, you don't care about the underlying binary representation. All you care about is that the file is seen as a stream of text characters. So, even though ultimately *everything* is binary, you should just think of this mode as "text mode."

Throughout this chapter, I adopt the standard term *binary file* to mean a file in which data isn't necessarily interpreted as ASCII character codes. With a text file, everything is assumed to be readable as text, given the right text-file reader. Files in which this is not true are called *binary*.

Introducing Binary Operations

When working with binary files, you read and write data directly to the file rather than translating data into text representations. Suppose you have the following data declarations. These variables occupy 4, 8, and 16 bytes, respectively.

```
int n = 1;
double x = 215.3
char *str[16] = "It's C++!"
```

The following statements write the values of the three variables (n, amount, and str) directly to the file. Assume that binfil is a file-stream object successfully opened in binary mode.

```
binfil.write((char*)(&n), sizeof(n));
binfil.write((char*)(&x), sizeof(x));
binfil.write(str, sizeof(str));
```

By the way, in this chapter (and Chapter 10) I am using the old-fashioned C-language type cast:

(type**)** data_item

Normally, use of the **reinterpret_cast** operator (which recasts pointers) would be preferred here. But frankly, I just didn't have space to get all that in...and while the C++ specification committee doesn't like old-style casts, it has decided to live with them. You will not get an error message using the shorter—and frankly more convenient—older style. (For information on all the newer, preferred casts, see Appendix A.)

Here's what the data looks like after being written. (The actual binary representations use strings of 1s and 0s, but I've translated these to make them more readable.)

4 bytes	8 bytes	16 bytes
3	215.3	"It's C++!"

To properly read this file, you need to know how to read these three fields. In reality, the lines between different fields are invisible; in fact, they don't even exist, except in the mind of the programmer. (Remember, data on a computer—including disk files—is nothing but a series of bytes containing binary numbers.)

There is nothing in the file itself that tells you where one field begins and another starts. With a text file, you can always read a field by reading to the next newline or white space, but you can't do that with a binary file.

Therefore, when you read a binary file, you have to know what kind of data to expect. In the example just shown, data had this structure: an **int**, a **double**, and a 16-byte array of **char**, in that order. You could therefore read the data by following this procedure:

1 Read four bytes directly into an integer variable.

2 Read eight bytes directly into a **double** variable.

3 Read 16 bytes into a string.

That's exactly what the following lines of code do:

```
binfil.read((char*)(&n), sizeof(n));
binfil.read((char*)(&x), sizeof(x));
binfil.read(str, 20);
```

The order in which these reads are done is critical. If, for example, you tried to read the **double** (floating-point) field first, the results would be garbage—because integer data and floating-point have incompatible formats.

Binary reads require a lot more precision than reading streams of text. With text input, a string of digits such as "12000" can be read as either integer or floating-point, because the text-to-numeric conversion functions know exactly how to interpret such a string. But a direct binary read performs no conversions of any kind. Copying an eight-byte double directly to a four-byte integer would create a really unfortunate situation.

The moral: Know your data formats precisely before proceeding with binary I/O.

You perform input/output to a binary file by using the **read** and **write** member functions. These functions each take two arguments: a data address and a number of bytes.

fstream.**read**(*addr, number_of_bytes*); // Read data into addr

fstream.**write**(*addr, number_of_bytes*); // Write data from addr

The first argument is a data address in memory: In the case of the **read** function, this is a destination to read the file data into. In the case of the **write** function, this is a source address telling where to get the data to write to the file.

In either case, this first argument must have the type **char***, so you need to pass an address expression (a pointer, an array name, or an address obtained with &). You also need to change the type by using a **char*** type cast, unless the type is already **char***.

```
binfil.write((char*)(&n), sizeof(n));
```

In the case of string data, you don't need to use the **char*** cast, because strings already have that type.

```
binfil.write(str, sizeof(str));
```

The **sizeof** operator is helpful here for specifying the second argument. It returns the size of the specified type, the variable, or the array.

Example 8.3.   *Random–Access Write*

This next example writes binary data to a file. Again, observing a strict format is critical. Data fields are differentiated not by a newline or whitespace (as in a text file) but by program behavior.

The programs in this section and the next view a file as a series of fixed-length records, in which each record stores two pieces of data:

▶ A string field 20 bytes in length (19 characters maximum, plus one byte for a terminating null)

▶ An integer

This next example supports *random access*. The user can go directly to any record, specified by number. Data does not have to read data sequentially, starting at the beginning of the file and reading or writing each record in sequence.

If the user writes to an existing record number, that record is overwritten. If the user writes to a record number beyond the current length of the file, the file is automatically extended in length as needed.

```
writebin.cpp

   #include <iostream>
   #include <fstream>
   using namespace std;

   int get_int(int default_value);

   int main() {
       char filename[MAX_PATH + 1];
       int n = 0;
       char name[20];
       int age = 0;
       int recsize = sizeof(name) + sizeof(int);

       cout << "Enter file name: ";
       cin.getline(filename, MAX_PATH);
```

▼ *continued on next page*

```cpp
    // Open file for binary write.

    fstream  fbin(filename, ios::binary | ios::out);
    if (!fbin) {
        cout << "Could not open " << filename << endl;
        system("PAUSE");
        return -1;
    }

    //  Get record number to write to.

    cout << "Enter file record number: ";
    n = get_int(0);

    // Get data from end user.

    cout << "Enter name: ";
    cin.getline(name, sizeof(name) - 1);
    cout << "Enter age: ";
    age = get_int(0);

    // Write data to the file.

    fbin.seekp(n * recsize);
    fbin.write(name, sizeof(name) - 1);
    fbin.write((char*)(&age), sizeof(int));
    fbin.close();
    system("PAUSE");
    return 0;
}

#define COL_WIDTH 80  // 80 is typical column width

// Get integer function
// Get an integer from keyboard; return default
//  value if user enters 0-length string.
//
int get_int(int default_value) {
    char s[COL_WIDTH+1];
```

```
cin.getline(s, COL_WIDTH);
if (strlen(s) == 0)
        return default_value;
return atoi(s);
}
```

How It Works

The concept of *record* is at the heart of this example. A record is a data format repeated throughout a file, giving uniformity to a file's structure. No matter how long the file grows, it remains easy to find a record by using its record number.

Note ▶ Whenever you use records in an array or a binary file, the more natural way to implement them is to use a C structure or C++ class. I spend a lot of time on classes starting in Chapter 11.

One of the first things the program does is calculate this record length:

```
int recsize = sizeof(name) + sizeof(int);
```

You can use this length information to go to any record. For example, record number 0 is at offset 0 in the file, record number 1 is at offset 24, record number 2 is at offset 48, record number 3 is at offset 72, and so on.

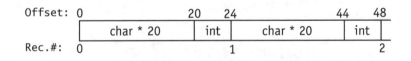

Offset: 0		20 24		44 48
	char * 20	int	char * 20	int
Rec.#: 0		1		2

The program opens the file by specifying two flags: **ios::binary** and **ios::out**. Opening in **ios::out** mode enables a file to be opened for writing; but be careful, because this will destroy old contents of existing files. It also lets you open new files.

```
fstream  fbin(filename, ios::binary | ios::out);
```

If the file was opened successfully, the program gets a record number from the user.

```
cout << "Enter file record number: ";
n = get_int(0);
```

∞

The get_int function uses a technique for getting an integer, described in the previous chapter. The program then gets new data from the user.

```
cout << "Enter name: ";
cin.getline(name, sizeof(name) - 1);
cout << "Enter age: ";
age = get_int(0);
```

Moving to the location of the specified record is just a matter of multiplying the number by the record size (recsize, equal to 24) and then moving to that off-set. The **seekp** member function performs this move.

```
fbin.seekp(n * recsize);
```

The program then writes the data and closes the file.

```
fbin.write(name, sizeof(name) - 1);
fbin.write((char*)(&age), sizeof(int));
fbin.close();
```

EXERCISES

Exercise 8.3.1.　Write a program similar to Example 8.3 that writes records to a file, in which each contains the following information: model, a 20-byte string; make, another 20-byte string; year, a five-byte string; and mileage, an integer.

Exercise 8.3.2.　Revise Example 8.3 so that it prompts the user for a record number and then prompts the user for the rest of the data and repeats. To exit, the user enters -1.

Example 8.4.　*Random–Access Read*

Of course, the program in Example 8.3 isn't very useful unless you have a way of reading the data placed there. The program here reads data using the same record format used in the previous section: a 20-byte string followed by a four-byte integer. The code is similar to that of Example 8.3, except for a few key statements.

In this case, the file is opened with flags **ios::bin** and **ios::in**; the latter requires the file to already exist to be successfully opened.

readbin.cpp

```cpp
#include <iostream>
#include <fstream>
using namespace std;

int get_int(int default_value);

int main() {
    char filename[MAX_PATH + 1];
    int n = 0;
    char name[20];
    int age = 0;
    int recsize =  sizeof(name) + sizeof(int);


    cout << "Enter file name: ";
    cin.getline(filename, MAX_PATH);

    // Open file for binary read-write access.

    fstream  fbin(filename, ios::binary | ios::in);
    if (!fbin) {
        cout << "Could not open " << filename << endl;
        system("PAUSE");
        return -1;
    }

    // Get record number and go to record.

    cout << "Enter file record number: ";
    n = get_int(0);
    fbin.seekp(n * recsize);

    // Read data from the file.

    fbin.read(name, sizeof(name) - 1);
    fbin.read((char*)(&age), sizeof(int));

    // Display the data and close.
```

▼ *continued on next page*

```
        cout << "The name is: " << name << endl;
        cout << "The age is: " << age << endl;
        fbin.close();
        system("PAUSE");
        return 0;
    }


    // Get integer function
    // Get an integer from keyboard; return default
    //   value if user enters 0-length string.
    //
    int get_int(int default_value) {
        char s[81];

        cin.getline(s, 80);
        if (strlen(s) == 0)
            return default_value;
        return atoi(s);
    }
```

How It Works

Most of this program does the same thing as Example 8.3, although because this program reads input from the file, it must be opened in **ios::in** mode (and that requires that it already exists). As before, the program gets a record number and moves to the appropriate offset, after multiplying by recsize:

```
        fbin.seekp(n * recsize);
```

The statements that differ from those in Example 8.3 read data from the file into the variables name and age. These are nearly the same as corresponding **write** statements in the other example; in fact, the arguments are the same.

```
        fbin.read(name, sizeof(name) - 1);
        fbin.read(((char*)(&age), sizeof(int));
```

Once data is read into the two variables—name and age—the program prints the data, closes the file, and it's done.

```
        cout << "The name is: " << name << endl;
        cout << "The age is: " << age << endl;
        fbin.close();
```

EXERCISES

Exercise 8.4.1.   Write a program similar to Example 8.4 that reads records from a file, in which each contains the following information: model, a 20-byte string; make, another 20-byte string; year, a five-byte string; and mileage, an integer.

Exercise 8.4.2.   Revise Example 8.4 so that it prompts the user for a record number and then prints the data at that record and repeats. To exit, the user enters -1.

Exercise 8.4.3.   Revise the example further so that it performs both random-access read *and* write. Once this is completed, you'll have one program that can handle all input/output operations for files observing this format. The file should open with the flags **ios:binary | ios::out | ios::in.** The latter requires the file to exist before being opened.

You'll need to present a command to the user by printing a menu of options:

1 Write a record.

2 Read a record.

3 Exit.

The general loop of the program should do the following: print the menu, carry out a command, and exit if option 3 is chosen. Then repeat.

Chapter 8   *Summary*

Here are the main points of Chapter 8:

▶ To switch on file-stream support from the C++ standard library, use this **#include** statement, which brings in prototypes and declarations as needed.

```
#include <fstream>
```

▶ File-stream objects provide a way to communicate with files. To create a file-output stream, use an **ofstream** type declaration. For example:

```
ofstream fout(filename);
```

▶ You can then write to the stream as you'd write to **cout**:

```
fout << "Hello, human." << endl;
```

▶ To create a file-input stream, use an **ifstream** declaration. A file-input stream supports the same operations that **cin** does, including the **getline** function.

```
ifstream fin(filename);

char input_string[MAX_PATH + 1];
fin.getline(input_string, MAX_PATH);
```

▶ If the file can't be opened, the file-stream object gets set to a null (zero). You can test the object in a condition; if the value is zero, there was an error, and the program should react as appropriate.

```
if (! file_in) {
    cout << "File " << filename;
    cout << " could not be opened.";
    return -1;
}
```

▶ After you're done working with a file-stream operator (regardless of mode), it is good programming practice to close it. This frees up the file so that it can be accessed by other programs.

```
fout.close();
```

▶ Files can be opened in either text mode or binary mode. In text mode, you read and write to a file just as you would the console. In binary mode, you use member functions to read and write data directly. To open a file stream in binary, random-access mode, use the flags **ios::out** and **ios::binary** or **ios::in** and **ios::binary**.

▶ Random-access mode enables you to go directly to any position in the file. You can read any portion of the file and overwrite any existing portions without affecting the rest. If the file pointer is moved beyond the file's current length, the file is automatically extended as needed.

▶ Use the **seekp** member function to move the file pointer. The function takes an argument giving an offset (in bytes) from the beginning of the file.

```
fbin.seekp(offset);
```

▶ The **read** and **write** functions each take two arguments: a data address and the number of bytes to copy.

```
fstream.read(addr, number_of_bytes);
fstream.write(addr, number_of_bytes);
```

▶ With the **read** function, the address argument specifies a destination; the function reads data from the file into this location. With the **write** function, the address argument specifies a source; the function reads data from that source into the file.

▶ Because the type of the address argument is **char***, you need to apply a cast if it is not a string. Use the **sizeof** operator to determine the number of bytes to read or write.

```
binfil.write((char*)(&n), sizeof(n));
binfil.write((char*)(&x), sizeof(x));
binfil.write(str, sizeof(str));
```

Some Advanced Programming Techniques

9

With the ability to process data, print and analyze strings, and access disk files, you already have the tools to write some serious C++ programs. But there are some other tricks to point out before we leave the basics and focus on C++0x and object orientation.

We start with the topic of command-line arguments, a feature that can be used to improve the programs in Chapter 8.

Command–Line Arguments

All the programs in Chapter 8 operate on files. The first thing each of these programs does (after declaring variables) is prompt the user for a filename.

```
cout << "Enter a file name and press ENTER: ";
cin.getline(filename, 80);
```

This works, but it's not always the ideal solution. People using the DOS command line—or another command-line–based system—would usually prefer to enter the filename directly. For example:

```
readtxt  output.txt
```

You can implement this behavior by using the *command-line argument* feature of C++. The first thing you do is to define **main** differently. If you're using the Dev-C++ environment, it already provides these arguments for you.

```
int main(int argc, char *agrv[]) {
   // ...
}
```

The two arguments to **main** supply information as follows:

▶ **argc** gives the total number of command-line arguments entered by the user, including the program name. So, for the following command line, argc returns the value 2.

```
readtxt  output.txt
```

▶ **argv** is an array of strings that contains all arguments on the command line, starting with the program name. In this example, argv[0] points to readtxt, and argv[1] points to output.txt.

You can treat the members of argv as you would any strings, except that they should be considered read-only: But you can freely print them or copy them.

For example, to print the first two command-line arguments (including, remember, the program name), you could use this code:

```
cout << argv[0] << endl;
cout << argv[1] << endl;
cout << "argc is equal to " << argc;
```

which, in the example just mentioned, would produce the following:

```
readtxt
output.txt
argc is equal to 2
```

As another example, consider this command line for a program named copyfile:

```
copyfile  file1.txt  file2.txt
```

Here's how argc and argv would work in this case:

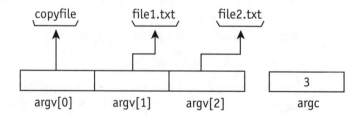

So, you could do the following:

```
cout << argv[0] << endl;    // Print "copyfile"
cout << argv[1] << endl;    // Print "file1.txt"
cout << argv[2] << endl;    // Print "file2.txt"
cout << argc << endl;       // Print "3"
```

Example 9.1. *Display File from Command Line*

This example is a variation on Example 8.2 that uses the filename if it is specified on the command line; otherwise, it prompts for a filename as Example 8.2 does. In the code that follows, the lines are bold when they differ from Example 8.2. The rest of the code is the same.

readfile2.cpp

```cpp
#include <iostream>
#include <fstream>
#include <cstring>
using namespace std;

int main(int argc, char *argv[]) {
    int c;   // input character
    int i;   // loop counter
    char filename[MAX_PATH + 1];
    char input_line[MAX_PATH + 1];

    if (argc > 1)
        strncpy(filename, argv[1], MAX_PATH);
    else {
        cout << "Enter a file name and press ENTER: ";
        cin.getline(filename, MAX_PATH);
    }

    ifstream file_in(filename);

    if (! file_in) {
        cout << filename << " could not be opened.";
        return -1;
    }

    while (true) {
        for (i = 1; i <= 24 && ! file_in.eof(); i++) {
            file_in.getline(input_line, MAX_PATH);
            cout << input_line << endl;
        }
```

▼ *continued on next page*

readfile2.cpp, cont.

```
            if (file_in.eof())
                break;
            cout << endl;
            cout << "More? (Press 'Q' & ENTER to quit.)";
            cin.getline(input_line, MAX_PATH);
            c = input_line[0];
            if (c == 'Q' || c == 'q')
                break;
        }
        system("PAUSE");
        return 0;
    }
```

With this version of the program, you can use the command line to enter commands like this:

```
readfile2  output.txt
```

Alternatively, you can just enter the name of the program and let the program prompt you for the name of the file to display.

```
readfile2
```

How It Works

The heading of the program includes both <fstream> and <cstring>, to enable string-handling functions. You'll see in a moment why this is necessary.

```
#include <fstream>
#include <cstring>
```

Another difference is the argument list for **main**, which is not empty:

```
int main(int argc, char *argv[]) {
```

The program has one other difference from Example 8.2. The first thing the program does is check the value of argc. If argc is greater than 1, that means the user provided a command-line argument (beyond the program name), so the program copies that argument to the filename string. Any further command-line arguments are ignored.

```
        if (argc > 1)
            strncpy(filename, argv[1], MAX_PATH);
```

If argc is not greater than 1, that means the user did not enter a filename on the command line. The program therefore prompts for the filename as in Example 8.2.

```
else {
    cout << "Enter a filename and press ENTER: ");
    cin.getline(filename, MAX_PATH);
}
```

Note that the predefined constant MAX_PATH is used here as it is in Chapter 8, to denote the maximum file-specification length supported by the system.

Improving the Program

In one of loops of the program, I used 24. Why did I choose this number?

```
for (i = 1; i <= 24 && ! file_in.eof(); i++) {
    file_in.getline(input_line, MAX_PATH);
    cout << input_line << endl;
}
```

The purpose of this block of code is to print only as many lines as will fit on the screen. In the case of a console application inside Windows, this number is about 24.

But that reason might not be obvious to someone else who looks at this program and has to maintain it or fix it. Twenty-four is an example of a "magic number," which is a derogatory term in this context. Most places that employ programmers strongly encourage them to use predefined constants, which are symbols with meaningful names but fixed values.

In C++, the #**define** directive lets you place these in the program...usually, you'll want to place them at the beginning, just after #**include** directives.

```
#define  symbol_name  value
```

For example, we could define the name SCR_LINES to be 24:

```
#define  SCR_LINES  24
```

Then SCR_LINES could be used in the program code in preference to 24:

```
for (i = 1; i <= SCR_LINES && ! file_in.eof(); i++) {
    file_in.getline(input_line, MAX_PATH);
    cout << input_line << endl;
}
```

The #**define** directive (technically not a keyword, by the way) is versatile and can be used in several ways. See Appendix B for more information.

Interlude

The Virtue of Predefined Constants

As a beginning programmer, you'll probably want to enter numbers in a program and not worry about defining constants. But the further you move up the ladder of professional programming, the more you'll be urged, even required, to use predefined constants.

```
#define  NUMBER_OF_ROWS  20
```

Why is this so important? As I mentioned earlier, a number like 20 that appears in a program for no apparent reason is seen as a "magic number." The purpose of such a number is not at all evident; it seems like some obscure bit of magic dreamed up by the programmer.

Programmers by their nature tend to be people who love order and hate mysteries. Reading other people's programs is a task that's challenging enough without having to decipher what the numbers mean. So, in most programming "shops," programmers are encouraged to define all their constants, just as they are encouraged to use comments.

This reminds me of an accelerated course in higher math taken by some freshmen at Yale. The course critique commented wryly, "At least half the semester went by before anyone saw any numbers." This is the way professional programmers are: They want to see symbols more than numbers.

EXERCISES

Exercise 9.1.1. Revise Example 9.1 so that it uses the predefined constant SCR_LINES (screen lines) as just described.

Exercise 9.1.2. Alter Exercise 9.1 so that it requires the user to enter the filename on the command line. In other words, the syntax of the program requires the following:

```
readtxt3 filename
```

If the user enters more or fewer command-line arguments, print an error message and exit.

Exercise 9.1.3. Write a program that does nothing except print all the command-line arguments, each on a separate line.

Function Overloading

Natural languages—particularly English—often employ a word to mean different things depending on the context. Think of how many meanings there are for the word *fair*. You can go *to* the fair, enjoy fair weather, and notice which fair-haired people are playing fair.

In computer-programming terminology, we could say this is an example of *overloading*—loading a word with multiple meanings.

C++ uses overloading as well. But rather than being a source of confusion, overloading in C++ is precise: You can reuse a function name to work with different types of data.

Consider the swap function. As with all C++ functions, swap must be declared with definite type information.

```
void swap(int *p1, int *p2);
```

The swap function is defined to work on one type of data, in this case, pointers to **int**. But you might want swap to work on other kinds of data.

One solution—the solution you'd have to use with C, Basic, and most non-object-oriented languages—is to write a different version of the function for each type of data, adopting a naming convention so that you never reuse the exact same name.

```
void swap_int(int *p1, int *p2);
void swap_dbl(double *p1, double *p2);
void swap_ptrs(char **p1, char **p2);
```

This solution works, but it's clumsy. C++ lets you reuse the one name—swap—with different kinds of data, relying on the type information in the argument list to keep the versions separate. The name swap is reused—that is to say, *overloaded*—for programmer convenience.

```
void swap(int *p1, int *p2);
void swap(double *p1, double *p2);
void swap(char **p1, char **p2);
```

Note ▶ The version of swap shown here for the **char*** types does not transfer string data; it swaps only the values of two **char*** pointers themselves. For example, p1 and p2 point to two strings. After calling swap(&p1, &p2), p1 points to the string that p2 formerly pointed to, and vice versa.

How does the C++ compiler keep all these functions straight? Simple, it looks at arguments involved in a function call.

6

Again, for each version of the function, there must be a separate declaration and a separate definition. Here are two definitions for swap:

```
void swap(int *p1, int *p2) {
    int temp = *p1;
    *p1 = *p21;
    *p2 = temp;
}

void swap(double *p1, double *p2);
    double temp = *p1;
    *p1 = *p21;
    *p2 = temp;
}
```

Interlude

Overloading and Object Orientation

Function overloading is related to one of the deepest ideas in object orientation: the idea that a data type dictates how a function or operator behaves.

A related idea is that of *operator overloading.* An operator (such as + or -) can be applied to different data types, and the operator will do the correct thing for the types involved. Chapter 13 describes how to write operator functions for your own types.

You can see operator overloading in the core language. Adding two integers and adding two floating-point numbers require different machine instructions. The C++ compiler executes different low-level routines depending on the types in an expression:

```
a + b
```

If the types of the arguments change, the compiler generates different instructions. Once again, the idea is one deeply ingrained in object orientation: *The type of the data involved dictates the behavior of the function.*

Yet overloading is not a full implementation of this idea. Type information may be known imperfectly at compile time. That's where polymorphism comes into play. I'll have more to say about this concept in Chapter 18.

Example 9.2.   *Printing Different Types of Arrays*

Here's a simple example that uses function overloading. The program prints three kinds of arrays, each time calling a function named print_array.

print_arrs.cpp

```cpp
#include <iostream>
using namespace std;

void print_arr(int *arr, int n);
void print_arr(double *arr, int n);
void print_arr(char **arr, int n);

int a[] = {1, 1, 2, 3, 5, 8, 13};
double b[] = {1.4142, 3.141592 };
char *c[] = {"Inken, Blinken, Nod" };


int main() {
    print_arr(a, 7);
    print_arr(b, 2);
    print_arr(c, 3);
    system("PAUSE");
    return 0;
}

void print_arr(int *arr, int n) {
    for (int i = 0; i < n; i++)
        cout << arr[i] << " ";
    cout << endl;
}

void print_arr(double *arr, int n) {
    for (int i = 0; i < n; i++)
        cout << arr[i] << " ";
    cout << endl;
}

void print_arr(char **arr, int n) {
    for (int i = 0; i < n; i++)
        cout << arr[i] << endl;
}
```

6

How It Works

This example is a straightforward use of function overloading. The first thing it does (after the **#include** directives) is declare the different versions of the function, print_arr.

```
print_arr(int *arr, int n);
print_arr(double *arr, int n);
print_arr(char **arr, int n);
```

The program then declares three arrays:

```
int a[] = {1, 1, 2, 3, 5, 8, 13};
double b[] = {1.4142, 3.141592 };
char *c[] = {"Inken, Blinken, Nod" );
```

From within **main**, the program then uses the same function name—print_arr—to print all these arrays.

```
print_arr(a, 7);
print_arr(b, 2);
print_arr(c, 3);
```

EXERCISE

Exercise 9.2.1. Write two versions of a generic get_number function so that get_number can be used to get either an integer or floating-point number, as desired. As with the get_int and get_dbl examples in this book, the function should take a numeric argument that specifies the default value. Use the argument to determine what kind of data to return. For example, given this call

```
get_number(0)
```

the function should return an integer value, whereas this call

```
get_number(0.0)
```

should return a value of type **double**. Remember that C++ notation recognizes any constant expression with a decimal point as a floating-point expression with **double** type.

The do-while Loop

Here are the control structures I've introduced so far. There are three of them (or four, if you consider that the **if** statement has two versions).

```
if (condition)
    statement
```

```
if (condition)
    statement
else
    statement
```

```
while (condition)
    statement
```

```
for (initializer; condition; increment)
    statement
```

Remember, any instance of *statement* in any of these structures can be replaced with a statement block, consisting of one or more statements between a pair of braces ({}).

```
{ statements }
```

In addition to these statements, you can also use the **break** or **return** statement to transfer control out of a loop or function. With this syntax, you have all the tools you need to control C++ programs. These are sufficient for creating any kind of program flow-of-control you're ever likely to need.

But there are also a couple of other control structures, which, while not strictly necessary, are often helpful. One of these is the **do-while** statement, which has this syntax:

```
do statement
while (condition);
```

This control structure is similar to the ordinary **while** statement. The difference is that with this version of **while**, the statement is guaranteed to be executed at least once, before the condition is ever evaluated.

I've already shown an example where this would have been helpful. Example 5.5 used the following code inside a larger loop:

```
i++;                    // Advance to next card
while (card_drawn[i])   // Skip past cards
    i++;                //  already drawn.
```

Clearly, in this fragment, the statement i++; is executed at least once, and then it may be executed again. This makes the code fragment a perfect candidate for the use of **do-while**. You can rewrite the code this way:

```
do i++;                  // Advance to next card
while (card_drawn[i]);   //  while current card drawn
```

This code fragment, while more compact, tends to be more difficult to read. It's customary to use the statement-block version of **do-while**, substituting { *statements* } for the single *statement*.

```
do {
    i++;                  // Advance to next card
} while (card_drawn[i]); //  while current card drawn
```

This is more readable, don't you think?

Here's a flow-chart representation of **do-while**.

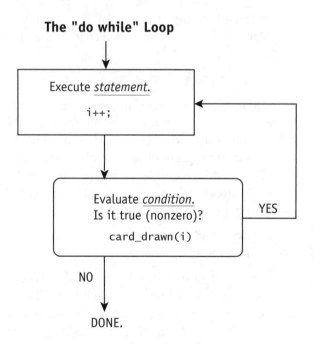

The "do while" Loop

Execute *statement*.

i++;

Evaluate *condition*.
Is it true (nonzero)?

card_drawn(i)

YES

NO

DONE.

The switch-case Statement

Another important control structure in C++ is the **switch** statement. As with the **do-while** statement, the **switch** statement is not strictly necessary, but it can in some cases make for more concise and readable code.

One of the most common patterns you see in programming is a series of if-else statements that test a value against a series of target values. For example, the following code fragment prints "one" or "two" or "three" depending on the value of x:

```
if (x == 1)
    cout << "one";
else if (x == 2)
    cout << "two";
else if (x == 3)
    cout << "three";
```

You can write this as a **switch** statement, which is somewhat more readable:

```
switch(x) {
    case 1:
        cout << "one";
        break;
    case 2:
        cout << "two";
        break;
    case 3:
        cout << "three";
        break;
}
```

Technically, the **switch** statement has a simple syntax.

```
switch (value) {
    statements
}
```

But to make the statements useful, you need to include labeled statements. Labels can have either of these special forms within a **switch** statement:

```
case target_value: statement
```

```
default: statement
```

Here's how the **switch** statement works:

1 The *value* expression, immediately after the **switch** keyword, is evaluated.

2 If there is a **case** statement label that matches this value, then control is transferred to the labeled statement.

3 If no **case** statement label matches the value and there is a **default** label, then control is transferred to the statement labeled by **default**.

Once control is transferred to a labeled statement, it continues to proceed in a forward direction as normal, unless a **break** statement is encountered, in which case control is transferred to the end of the **switch** statement. This is why each **case** statement block needs to be terminated by **break**, unless you want control to fall through to the next case.

```
case 1:
    cout << "one";
    break;
```

Multiple Modules

In Chapter 4, I mentioned that the use of functions in your program enables you to adopt a division-of-labor approach, making large projects more doable. This is true any time you use functions, but it's especially true when you put those functions into multiple modules.

What do I mean by *module*? Well, consider the way all the programs have been created in this book: There is one source file (a .cpp file), which is translated into one object file containing machine code (a .o file) and then linked into an executable (an .exe file).

But you can use more than one source-code module. A single function cannot span more than one source file. You can, however, place individual functions into different files.

Here's a simple example. This program has four functions: **main**, calc, get_int, and get dbl. These could all be put in one source file, but for the sake of illustration, I've put the function definitions into two separate files, mod1.cpp and mod2.cpp.

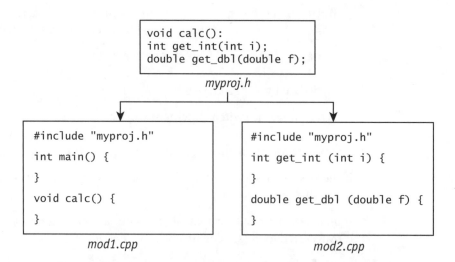

Each of the two source files (.cpp files) is a separate module.

This example also illustrates the use of an include file, myproj.h. (In fact, this is a good illustration of why include files are useful in general.) Assume that any of the three functions other than **main**—these are, remember, calc, get_int, and get_dbl—may be called by a function in another module. To enable such calls, you need to put function declarations at the beginning of each source file.

For example:

```
void calc();
int get_int(int);
double get_dbl(double);
```

This can get a little confusing, so remember these rules:

1 Each function is defined in exactly one place—that is, in one source file. For instance, in the current example, the function calc is defined in mod1.cpp.

2 But every source file needs a declaration (a prototype) of a function before the function can be called.

The C++ compiler will look for the definition of each prototyped function in the source file, but if it cannot find the definition, the compiler will assume the function is defined in another module.

When a function is going to be shared between modules, the best practice is to place all such function declarations (prototypes) in a central file—an include file—and then use an #**include** directive to make sure that each module gets those prototypes automatically.

You can share data variables in the same way, but variables are assumed to be private to the module in which they're created—unless an **extern** declaration is added to each file (or to the include file). For example, the following declaration states that variables a, b, and c are declared somewhere in the program, possibly (though not necessarily) in another module.

```
extern int a, b, c;
```

Each of these variables has to be created in one and only one module—just as each function has to be defined in only one module. You create a variable by using a standard variable declaration, optionally with initialization.

```
int a = 0, b = 0, c = 1;
```

I don't use multiple modules in this book for the most part, because the examples are short. But for large software projects, using multiple modules offers big advantages:

▶ Probably the biggest single advantage is that multiple modules support multiple programmers. Each programmer can work on their own module.

▶ The multimodule approach provides yet another way to logically subdivide the program. Functions that specialize in number crunching can be placed in one module, while another specializes in user-interface functions.

▶ You can control the degree of communication between modules.

This last advantage has a connection to object-oriented programming. In older languages, such as C, the use of separate modules is the only way to create groups of symbols in which some are private and some are public (that is, shared).

This is useful for large, complex projects. A programmer has responsibility for implementing public items, but the programmer can also write his or her own support functions, not intended to be used by anyone else. The private portion of the module is protected from the outside so that the programmer never need worry about other programmers calling these private functions (or referring to private data) and in the process making all kinds of assumptions about how they work.

The public/private distinction is a way of achieving *encapsulation*—something I'll explore in upcoming chapters because it is one of the benefits of C++ classes.

Once you've written all the code, each of the modules can be compiled and linked together. If you set up a project correctly from within your development environment, then this process of compiling and linking is automated for you.

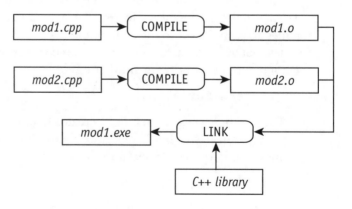

Exception Handling: I Take Exception to That!

Exception handling is the best way to recover from errors cropping up in the middle of complex programs, and in commercial applications, it's often a necessity. But in general, this feature will be most useful only after you start developing large programs.

With that in mind, let's look at C++ exception handling.

Say Hello to Exceptions

So far, we've discussed two major kinds of errors:

▶ *Syntax errors*, which require you to fix your program code before you can successfully compile your program.

▶ *Program-logic errors*, which you discover only after compiling the program, running, and testing it.

There's also a third kind of error—although it can be considered a special case of the second category. This third kind consists of runtime errors, also called *exceptions*.

The term refers to an occurrence at runtime that is "exceptional" because it interrupts the normal flow of the program. The program must respond to the situation, exit, or both. Examples include the following:

▶ Attempt to divide by zero.

▶ Use of a null pointer in an expression that requires a valid address.

▶ Failure to allocate requested memory (if, for example, memory is full).

▶ Arithmetic overflow during a calculation.

An exception is usually, but not always, an error. It may be a program's way of sending a signal to itself. But in any case, an exception must be handled or the program terminates.

The point of exception handling is to respond to the situation smoothly and reasonably. Even if you decide to terminate the program, you want to do so only after shutting down your resources and printing a helpful message to the user, explaining what is going on. The alternative—just quitting abruptly—is not only bad programming but just plain rude.

6

Handling Exceptions: A First Attempt

In a small program—one that involves only a few function calls—you can check for error conditions and handle them where you find them. For example, suppose you have a function that opens a file for reading after getting the name of the file from the user. Here's how it might look:

```
ifstream input_file;

int open_a_file(
    string file_name;

    cout << "Enter a file name: ";
    getline(cin, file_name);
    input_file.open(file_name);
    if (!input_file) {
        cout << "File could not be opened!";
        return -1;
    }
    else
        return 0;
}
```

In this case, the program tests for the error condition and responds directly. An error code of -1 is generated; but for this to be useful, the rest of the program must be able to recognize and respond to this value intelligently.

And there's a bigger problem. In a complex program, this error value must be propagated upward, possibly through many functions, up to the level of code that interacts with the user. In a big program, writing such code can be a headache.

Introducing try-catch Exception Handling

All but the oldest versions of C++ now support the **try**, **catch**, and **throw** keywords for handling exceptions. Exception handling centralizes error handling in your program so that no matter where an exception occurs, control "pops up" to the right handler.

In the simple case (shown here), there is just one **catch** block:

```
try {
    try_statements
}
catch (exception_type  [arguments] ) {
```

```
            catch_statements
    }
```

When this structure is encountered, the *try_statements* are executed unconditionally; that is, the *try_statements* are always executed, unless and until an exception is raised.

If an exception is raised, either by the *try_statements* themselves or by a function called during execution of these statements, such an exception may be caught and handled by the **catch** block, subject to the following conditions.

The action of the **catch** block is as follows: If the type of the exception raised matches the specified *type*, then control is transferred to the **catch** block. If the type does not match, then the argument of the next **catch** block is checked, and so on, until the list of **catch** blocks is exhausted. If no block of code catches the exception, the program terminates.

The items in parentheses following catch may include *type argument* or *type* by itself. The *argument* is optional.

Assume the program has these statements:

```
try {
    open_files();
    read_files();
    process_data();
}
catch (int err ) {
    error_handler_1();
}
catch (double err) {
    error_handler_2();
}
```

The program executes the three statements inside the **try** block unconditionally, calling three functions: open_files, read_files, and process_data. If no exception occurs, the program runs normally.

But if—during the execution of any of these functions—an exception is raised, the type of that exception is checked. If the exception has type **int**, error_handler_1 is executed. If it has type **double**, error_handler_2 is executed.

Interestingly enough, an exception can have any type. When you raise an exception by using the **throw** keyword, you determine its type.

throw *exception_object*;

For example, the following statement raises an exception of type **int**:

```
throw 12;
```

Many types of exceptions are raised automatically by the system, and these are all derived from the **exception** class. The following code catches all such exceptions and prints a description:

```
try {
//...
}
catch(exception &e) {
    cout << "EXCEPTION RAISED: " << e.what() << endl;
}
```

Note that to turn on file-error exceptions (such as "file not found"), you call the **exceptions** function of an **ifstream** object.

```
ifstream in_file;
in_file.exceptions(ifstream::eofbit
                 | ifstream::failbit
                 | ifstream::badbit );
```

Chapter 9 *Summary*

Here are the main points of Chapter 9:

▶ To access command-line arguments, declare **main** with two arguments of its own, arc and argv:

```
int main(int argc, char *argv[]) {
// ...
}
```

▶ argc contains the number of command-line arguments entered by the user, including the program name itself.

▶ argv is an array of pointers to strings, in which each string contains a command-line argument, starting with the program name. For example:

```
cout << argv[0];    // Print program name.
cout << argv[1];    // Print next item on cmd line.
cout << argv[2];    // Print next item after that.
```

▶ Function overloading lets you write multiple versions of the same function, using the type of arguments to differentiate between them. For example, you can have different versions of the swap function:

```
void swap(int *p1, int *p2) {
    int temp = *p1;
    *p1 = *p21;
    *p2 = temp;
}

void swap(double *p1, double *p2);
    double temp = *p1;
    *p1 = *p21;
    *p2 = temp;
}
```

▶ The compiler determines exactly what function to call by checking the type of the arguments at compile time. In this example, the types of a and b determine which version of swap to use.

```
swap(a, b);
```

▶ Although by definition function overloading reuses a function name, it has the effect of creating distinct functions. Each of these functions requires a separate declaration and definition. Despite their sharing of a name—and the fact they may do similar things—the functions are really separate from each other.

▶ The **do-while** loop has the following syntax. This control structure is similar to while, except that the statement is guaranteed to be performed at least once, before the condition is evaluated.

```
do statement
while (condition);
```

▶ Use of the statement-block syntax is particularly helpful with the **do-while** statement. For example:

```
do {
    i++;
} while (card_drawn[i]);
```

▶ As long as you have more than one function or global data declaration, you can subdivide your program into multiple source files. Each of these source files is a *module*.

▶ Among other advantages, the use of multiple modules enables you to have more than one programmer at a time working on a large programming project.

▶ A function can call a function defined in another module, but only if the called function is prototyped. For this reason, the common practice is to place prototypes for all the common functions at the beginning of each and every module. For example:

```
void calc();
int get_int(int);
double get_dbl(double);
```

▶ A convenient approach to managing the prototypes for common functions is to put them into a single file, called an *include* file. That file can then be read into each source file with the help of the #**include** directive.

```
#include "myproj.h"
```

▶ Variables to be shared throughout the program need to be given an **extern** declaration in each module. In addition to the **extern** declarations, the variable also needs to be defined—in one and only module—by using a standard variable declaration.

10 New Features of C++0x

The C++ language has gone through many improvements since it was created by Bjarne Strousup. But more than most changes, the new C++0x specification is a landmark, adding many flexible and time-saving features programmers had requested for years. C++0x is the new standard that major vendors are expected to implement in coming years if not already.

Later in the book, I present C++0x features specific to classes and object-oriented programming. For now, let's look at the features you can start using right away.

Overview of C++0x Features

C++0x ▶ This chapter is for readers who have C++0x-complaint compilers, although some features (notably the **long long int** type) have been supported by some compilers for years.

The new C++0x-specific features described in this chapter include the following:

▶ *The **long long int** type.* This new data type stores values far beyond the limit of the **long int** type, which is only plus or minus 2 billion (thousand million). The **long long int** type is a 64-bit number that can store astronomical values far in excess of a billion...but with absolute precision, unlike **double**.

▶ *Ranged-base for ("for each").* This syntax is a variation on the C++ **for** keyword. Instead of setting begin and end points explicitly in a loop, you just say, "Process each item in the group." It's simpler, easier, and less error-prone.

▶ *The **auto** and **decltype** keywords.* These can be convenient when working with complex, exotic types.

▶ *The **nullptr** keyword*. This is the new way to set null pointers. Although not strictly required, it may someday be needed to write fully correct programs.

▶ *Strongly typed enumerations*. You can use this feature to refer to meaningful symbolic names rather than arbitrary numbers; it's another way to get rid of "magic numbers." This is an existing feature in recent C++ specs but greatly strengthened in C++0x. Both weak and strong **enum** types are now supported.

▶ *Raw string literals*. This feature lets you enter string literals without having to use escape characters for " and \.

   In later chapters, I describe C++0x features that help you mainly when you write classes or use templates, introducing these along with the related topics:

▶ Initializing data members within a class (Chapter 12)

▶ Delegating constructors (Chapter 12)

▶ Consistent initialization (Chapter 12)

▶ Creating user-defined literals (Chapter 13)

▶ Smart pointers (Chapter 15)

▶ Correct interpretation of right-angle brackets (Chapter 16)

▶ Inheriting base-class constructors (Chapter 17)

▶ Requiring explicit override of virtual functions (Chapter 18)

The long long Type (not long long long)

George Harrison, while he was with the Beatles, wrote a song called "Long, Long, Long." Don't start humming it yet. The new C++ type has only two "longs."

   In the PC environment, the C and C++ languages have generally supported 16-bit integers as **short** and 32-bit as **long**. 16 bits was standard for computers back in the Dark Ages, but 16 bits can't store numbers larger than 64KB, a huge limitation. It was necessary to have a **long** integer type, which (at 32 bits wide) ranges over 4 billion numbers.

   But it's not hard to go beyond even this limit. One alternative is to switch to floating point, which—because of scientific notation—can store astronomically big and tiny values. But floating-point data cannot store big numbers with absolute precision.

Sixty-four bits is the future of computing and is the natural size for integers to migrate to, but the **long** type is already taken (32 bits). For that reason, two "longs" are needed.

TYPE	TYPICAL MEANING (SUPPORTED ON NEARLY ALL PCs)	C++0x SPECIFICATION
char	8 bits, large enough to hold an ASCII character	Enough size to hold a standard character
short int	16 bits, limit of 64KB	Size equal to or greater than **char** in size; no larger than **int**
long int	32 bits, limit of approximately 4 billion (plus or minus 2 billion)	Size equal to or greater than **int** in size
long long int	64 bits, limit of 4 billion *squared*	Size greater than **long**

There is also a generic **int** type, which I use a great deal in this book. The **int**, or "natural integer" type, is intended to match the processor size of the architecture on which the program runs, so it naturally results in more efficient programs. On current, 32-bit systems, **int** is equivalent to **long**. (More on this in the Interlude.)

Each of these types has an unsigned version, such as **unsigned short** and **unsigned long**. Unsigned values do not store negative values but instead store twice as many positive values. So, what you lose in the negative range, you gain back by having a bigger positive range. Signed integers (the default) store both positive and negative values.

The syntax for declaring **long long** integers is similar to that for any type. Integer types have a quirk. Except with the **int** type itself, the keyword **int** is optional.

```
long long variables;

long long int variables;    // int is optional
```

And there is also the unsigned version, which doesn't store negative values:

```
unsigned long long variables;

unsigned long long int variables;  // int is optional
```

For example:

```
long long i;         // i is uninitialized 64-bit int
long long i = 0;     // i initialized to 0.
long long i, j, k;   // i, j, and k all 64-bit ints.
```

Interlude

Why a "Natural" Integer?

I use the **int** type throughout this book. For the current PC environment, **int** is equivalent to **long**, the 32-bit type. As the "natural" integer, **int** is intended to correspond to the processor size of the target environment so that programs run efficiently.

There is one downside: If you ever port your code to a smaller architecture (16 bits), programs that run beautifully on 32-bit architecture can break without warning. It's possible your **int** variables hold values larger than 64KB; if so, when ported to a 16-bit architecture, your programs will encounter serious bugs.

The upshot is that you are safe using **int** in programs for your own use only. But...

Code developed professionally at Microsoft avoids this approach. The **int** type is never used in serious commercial projects. Microsoft developers conscientiously stick to types with fixed sizes with names like INT32, controlled and defined in header files. This is because they are developing software for many platforms to be used all over the world. For a beginner, such an approach is overkill. But keep these issues in mind if you ever intend to write commercial (widely distributed) software or port to different platforms.

Working with 64-Bit Literals (Constants)

For the most part, using the 64-bit type is as easy as declaring variables as **long long**. But there is a little more to it: You typically need to initialize variables.

Fortunately, the following works just fine, even though the numeric literal, 0, has **int** type and n has **long long int** type:

```
long long n = 0;
```

This is OK, because C++ automatically promotes a smaller type, like **int**, into a larger type such as **long long** and does so without complaint. But what if you need to initialize n with a larger value?

```
long long n = 123000123000456;   // ERROR
```

The problem is that the literal in this example is too large to be stored as a standard **int**, so you will likely get an error message. To ensure that such a large number (larger than 2 billion or so) can be stored, use the new "LL" suffix, which stands for **long long**, of course:

```
long long n = 123000123000456LL;  // LL used; no error
```

You can also use the "ULL" prefix for **unsigned long long**:

```
long long n = 123000123000456ULL;  // ULL used; OK.
```

Accepting long long Input

Earlier, I used the **atoi** function to convert strings to integers. C++ compilers that support **long long** also provide a useful support function, **atoll**, to convert **char*** strings (C strings) to **long long** integers:

```
char *input_string[MAX_WIDTH + 1];
cin.get(input_string, MAX_WIDTH);

long long n = atoll(input_string);
```

The **long long** type presents another challenge: When numbers get to be this big, they are difficult for an end user to type in or read. For example, suppose you have a program that tests a number for being prime, but you want to use it on very large numbers. The first thing you'd do is replace all the **int** declarations with **long long**.

But that's not all. To be practical and user-friendly, you should permit the end user to enter numbers with group separators. (In America and the United Kingdom, this separator is a comma; in France, it is a blank space; still other nationalities use a dot (.).)

```
123,000,123,000,446,001
```

The issue is that you want an easy way to let the user enter numbers with digit-group separators. Fortunately, there's an easy solution: You can strip away these characters before converting to a number. The following function performs this task, and I invite you to use it in your own programs. You're welcome.

Note ▶ To support the **atoll** function used here, you'll need to include <cstdlib>.

```
#define GROUP_SEP ','

long long read_formatted_input(string s) {
```

```
for (int i = 0; i < s.size(); i++) {
    if (s[i] == GROUP_SEP)
        s.erase(i, 1);
}
return atoll(s.c_str());
}
```

The function merely strips instances of the separator character, converts to a null-terminated C-string, and calls the **atoll** function to convert the string to a **long long**. (You can write a version of this that works with a C-string argument, and it is even simpler, by the way.)

Formatting long long Numbers

Printing formatted numbers with the proper digit-group separators is more of a challenge, because the program has to make intelligent decisions about where to put those characters.

Fortunately, the programming is made easier if you use the STL **substream** class, which treats strings as output streams: You can write to a string as you would write to the console or a file. Make sure you include both these files:

```
#include <string>
#include <sstream>
```

Now you can create and use a "string stream." You can write to the following object, s_out, just as you would write to **cout**. After you are done writing to the stream object, you convert it to an actual string by using the **str** member function.

```
stringstream s_out;
s_out << "The value of i answer is" << i << endl;
string s = s_out.str()
```

We now have enough techniques to write a function that takes a **long long** as input and returns a formatted string. This version does not support negative values, with their minus-sign prefix (-)...but you can modify the code to handle that if you choose.

```
#define GROUP_SEP      ','
#define GROUP_SIZE     3

string output_formatted_string(long long num) {

    // Read data into string s.
```

```
stringstream temp, out;
temp << num;
string s = temp.str();

// Write first characters, in front of
//  first separator (GROUP_SEP).

int n = s.size() % GROUP_SIZE;
int i = 0;
if (n > 0 && s.size() > GROUP_SIZE) {
    out << s.substr(i, n) << GROUP_SEP;
    i += n;
}

// Handle all the remaining groups.

n = s.size() / GROUP_SIZE - 1;
while (n-- > 0) {
    out << s.substr(i, GROUP_SIZE) << GROUP_SEP;
    i += GROUP_SIZE;
}
out << s.substr(i); // Write the rest of digits.
return out.str();   // Convert stream -> string.
}
```

Again, I invite you to steal this code to use freely in your own programs. Once more, you're welcome.

The function is as long as it is because I've provided comments for readability. As always, if you are trying to type it in fast, the comments are optional on your part.

This example uses **substr**, an important function of the **string** class. Its first argument is a starting position (0-based, remember), and the second argument is the number of characters to select from that position onward. The **substr** function returns the indicated substring. When the second argument is omitted, it returns the substring from the indicated position forward to the end of the string.

The function takes numeric input such as 88123000567001LL and returns a string formatted with group separators, making it far more readable for the end user. You can then print the resulting string on the console.

```
88,123,000,567,001
```

10

Example 10.1. *Fibonacci: A 64-Bit Example*

OK, enough preliminaries! Here's a practical example: Suppose you want to know what the 50th Fibonacci number is. It turns out that the answer is well outside the range of a standard **int** or **long** (32 bits) and is a perfect application for **long long.**

First, a quick refresher on Fibonacci numbers. This is a famous set of numbers, in which each member (after the first two) is equal to the total of the two numbers preceding it. So, the first few numbers in the series are as follows:

    1 1 2 3 8 13 21 34 55 89 144

This set of numbers has a formal mathematical definition:

    F(0) = 1
    F(1) = 1
    F(n) = F(n-1) + F(n-2)

At first glance, this is a perfect candidate for recursion. This formal definition translates smoothly into C++ code. (You'll notice my use of **long long**, which is needed here because Fibonacci numbers get large so quickly.)

```
long long Fibo(long long n) {
    if (n < 2)
        return 1;
    else
        return Fibo(n - 1) + Fibo(n - 2);
}
```

But as beautiful as this version is, it is incredibly inefficient. You won't notice a problem running it on low values, say up to Fibo(30). But once you get around Fibo(40) or so, the delay becomes unacceptably long...even in this era of fast processors. This is because every increase in n geometrically increases the number of function calls.

The iterative version requires a few more lines of code. But unlike the recursive version, it can handle Fibo(50) at (what seems like) instantaneous speed instead of taking hours!

```
long long Fibo(int n) {
    if (n < 2)
        return 1;
    long long temp1 = 1;
    long long temp2 = 1;
    long long total = 0;
```

```
        while (n-- > 1) {
            total = temp1 + temp2;
            temp2 = temp1;
            temp1 = total;
        }
        return total;
    }
```

With this version, the issue is not processor time but the ability to hold large numbers. That's why **long long** is needed here...but note that even this huge range is exceeded before you reach Fibo(100).

Here is the complete program that prompts for a number and calculates Fibo(n), the Nth Fibonacci number:

fibo.cpp

```cpp
#include <iostream>
#include <string>
#include <sstream>

using namespace std;

int long long Fibo(int n);
string output_formatted_string(long long num);

int main() {
    int n = 0;
    cout << "Enter a number: ";
    cin >> n;
    string s = output_formatted_string(Fibo(n));
    cout << "Fibo(" << n << ") = " << s << endl;
    system("PAUSE");
    return 0;
}

long long Fibo(int n) {
    if (n < 2)
        return 1;
    long long temp1 = 1;
    long long temp2 = 1;
```

▼ *continued on next page*

10

fibo.cpp, cont.

```cpp
        long long total = 0;
        while (n-- > 1) {
            total = temp1 + temp2;
            temp2 = temp1;
            temp1 = total;
        }
        return total;
}

#define GROUP_SEP      ','
#define GROUP_SIZE     3

string output_formatted_string(long long num) {

    // Read data into string s.

    stringstream temp, out;
    temp << num;
    string s = temp.str();

    // Write first characters, in front of
    //  first separator (GROUP_SEP).

    int n = s.size() % GROUP_SIZE;
    int i = 0;
    if (n > 0 && s.size() > GROUP_SIZE) {
        out << s.substr(i, n) << GROUP_SEP;
        i += n;
    }

    // Handle all the remaining groups.

    n = s.size() / GROUP_SIZE - 1;
    while (n-- > 0) {
        out << s.substr(i, GROUP_SIZE) << GROUP_SEP;
        i += GROUP_SIZE;
    }
    out << s.substr(i); // Write the rest of digits.
    return out.str();   // Convert stream -> string.
}
```

For example, if the end user inputs 70, the program prints this result:

```
Fibo(70) = 308,061,521,170,129
```

How It Works

All that **main** does is get a number from the console and pass it to a function, Fibo. The resulting **long long** integer result is passed to the print_formatted_ string function, which produces a nicely formatted string result. This string is then printed:

```
string s = output_formatted_string(Fibo(n));
cout << "Fibo(" << n << ") = " << s << endl;
```

The rest of the code then works as described earlier. The program uses the iterative version of the Fibo function, which—although not as elegant as the recursive version—is infinitely more practical: It produces instantaneous results even for high numbers. The recursive version would take hours to calculate Fibo(50) if it didn't bring down the system first.

I included the comments for output_formatted_string, which explain how the function works. If you are typing code by hand, you can enter it with or without comments, of course. Without the comments, the function is more concise.

```
#define GROUP_SEP      ','
#define GROUP_SIZE     3

string output_formatted_string(long long num) {
   stringstream temp, out;
   temp << num;
   string s = temp.str();
   int n = s.size() % GROUP_SIZE;
   int i = 0;
   if (n > 0 && s.size() > GROUP_SIZE) {
      out << s.substr(i, n) << GROUP_SEP;
      i += n;
   }
   n = s.size() / GROUP_SIZE - 1;
   while (n-- > 0) {
      out << s.substr(i, GROUP_SIZE) << GROUP_SEP;
      i += GROUP_SIZE;
   }
   out << s.substr(i);
   return out.str();
}
```

EXERCISES

Exercise 10.1.1.   Write a version of the program that maintains an array of 70 integers of type **long long**. Then fill up this array with the first 70 Fibonacci numbers. (Careful: In our nomenclature, we've dubbed the first number F(0), not F(1).) Instead of using the Fibo(0) function from Example 10.1, set F(0) and F(1) directly. Then write a loop to calculate each remaining array element (F(2) to F(70)) by adding the values of the two preceding array elements. If anything, this code should be even simpler than Example 10.1. Print the array with calls to output_formatted_string, which shouldn't change.

Exercise 10.1.2.   Write a program that prompts for a number, which you then store as a **long long**. Permit user to enter the number using optional digit separators. Then determine the first prime number bigger than the number entered and print this print number. If needed, refer to prime-number-testing code in Chapters 2, 3, and 4.

Localizing Numbers

In Chapter 7, I introduced the **#define** preprocessor directive. This directive is useful in minimizing the appearance of "magic numbers" (numbers whose use appears to be entirely arbitrary) from your program.

The syntax for the simple use of **#define** is as follows:

```
#define   symbol_name   replacement_text
```

The result is that the C++ preprocessor replaces each occurrence of *symbol_name* it finds in the rest of the source file (outside of comments and printed strings) with the *replacement_text*.

#define has an especially important use here. If you want to compile the program to work correctly for end users in other countries, you may need to pay attention to formats. Large numbers have one format for Americans and British and another for France and many other European countries. Still other countries use a dot (.), reserving the comma (,) as a decimal-point (radix) indicator.

```
1,235,070,556    // American/UK format
1 235 070 556    // Continental format
1.235.070.556    // Alternative European format
```

I wrote the program in this chapter to provide the easiest possible control. The format used by the print_formatted_string function is determined by the two **#define** directives. You never need to change more than one or two lines.

```
#define GROUP_SEP       ','
#define GROUP_SIZE      3
```

GROUP_SEP specifies the group separator: a comma, blank space, apostrophe, or dot, as appropriate; GROUP_SIZE sets the number of digits grouped together. China and Japan often use groupings of four; most countries use three.

Interlude

Who Was Fibonacci?

Fibonacci did not invent Fibonacci numbers; yet we can thank him for computers. He brought decimal numbers to Europe, and if we didn't understand the decimal system, we wouldn't understand binary numbers. Without binary numbers, no computers.

This great visionary was a man named Leonardo Bonacci, whose nickname was "son of Bonacci"—or in Italian, "Fibonacci." Born in 1170, he is considered the greatest European mathematician in the Middle Ages.

His most famous work, *Liber Abaci* (meaning "Book of Calculation"), introduced Europe to the decimal-number system devised in India and used by Arabs (hence, "Arabic numerals"). It also introduced Europe to a fascinating problem that Hindu mathematicians had asked and answered back in the sixth century: Was there a series of numbers, they wondered, that described the population growth of a pair of rabbits in an ideal environment, free of famine and predators? Their answer was a series of numbers: 1, 1, 2, 3, 5, 8, 13, and so on, later dubbed "Fibonacci numbers" in the West.

Did the ancient Hindus realize the secrets of Nature that lay hidden in this deceptively simple series? It turns out the ratio of two consecutive such numbers converge toward a mysterious transcendental number, approximately 1.618, which the Greeks called the Golden Ratio. The Parthenon is designed on this ratio...and 2,000 years later, Leonardo da Vinci's famous "Vitruvian Man" would diagram how thoroughly the Golden Ratio matches the ratios of the human form: the length of a leg to the torso, for example, and the torso to the body.

When we see so much of nature described this way, does that mean someone is trying to tell us something? All we know for sure is that there's something in the nature of existence that responds to the beauty of mathematics.

10

Range-Based "for" (For Each)

One of the most easy-to-use and programmer-friendly features of C++0x is called *range-based for*. In simple terms, this is a technique for writing less code—and getting fewer errors—when you use a **for** loop to process an array or other container.

Some other languages have had this feature for years. It says, "Process every item in the group (or list or array or STL string)" without having to worry about where you begin or end: C++ automates all the details of beginning and ending.

This approach has two benefits:

▶ It saves programming effort, because it frees you from worrying about how to initialize the beginning and ending conditions in a **for** loop.

▶ More importantly, it frees you from one of the most common sources of bugs in C++ programs: incorrectly setting loop conditions. Even the most experienced programmers commit this sin when tired, overworked, or stressed. But you can't go wrong when beginning and end points are handled automatically.

Here is the general syntax. It comes in two forms.

```
for(base_type&  variable : container)    // Reference
       statement

for(base_type  variable : container)    // By value
       statement
```

In either case, *statement* can, as always, be a compound statement: a series of zero or more statements enclosed in curly braces ({}). The *variable* has scope limited to the *statement* or compound statement, as the case may be.

In the first version of this syntax, the *variable* is a reference type, which means it has the ability to manipulate the data. (No other special syntax is needed.) If you want to set new values to items in the container, use this version. The second version of the syntax provides access only to copies of the values in container. Chapter 12 provides more in-depth information on reference types.

For now, just remember to use the ampersand (&) if you want to alter values inside the container (an array, in this case); otherwise, leave the ampersand off. It's that simple.

Let's look at a practical example using an array. This code fragment sets every member of my_array to 0:

```
int my_array[10];

for(int& i : my_array)
    i = 0;
```

This next example sets every member of my_array to 5:

```
for(int& i : my_array)
    i = 5;
```

Remember, if you don't intend to change any values, you can protect the data by dropping the ampersand (&). For example, to print all the elements of my_array, use this:

```
for(int i : my_array)
    cout << i << endl;
```

Here's an example that prints all the values of an array of type **double**:

```
double float_pt_nums[100];

for(double d : float_pt_nums)
    cout << d << endl;
```

Or, to set all the floating point values to 0.0 (notice the ampersand, &, brought back for this operation because it alters values), use this:

```
for(double& d : float_pt_nums)
    d = 0.0;
```

The amazing thing about this new **for** syntax in C++0x is its flexibility. The *container* can be any of the following:

▶ Any kind of array.

▶ An STL **string** object. (Individual items within a string object correspond to individual characters.) The base type is **char**.

▶ Instances of STL classes that define an iterator, such as **list**. You'll learn more about iterators and lists in Chapter 16.

▶ Instances of any class that supports a **begin**() function and an **end**() function returning iterators. These two functions should work as described in Chapter 16 for list templates.

▶ Initialized lists (see the example immediately following).

10

The range-based **for** syntax supports initialized lists using curly braces (which C++0x endows with the status of a container object). For example, the following code fragment prints the first 12 Fibonacci numbers, one to a line. This is the simplest way to print a lot of numbers.

```
for(const int n : {1,1,2,3,5,8,13,21,34,55,89,144})
    cout << n << endl;
```

(In this case, the **const** keyword assures the compiler that n will not be used to attempt to change any of these values.)

Although the ranged-base **for** is usually more convenient than the standard **for** statement, it does have one limitation: Because range-based **for** cycles through a container without explicit index numbers, pointers, or iterators, it can be harder to do certain things. Every element tends to get treated the same way.

For example, what if you want to set an array to {0, 1, 2, 3, 4}? Using a standard **for** statement, you'd write something like this:

```
for(int i = 0; i < 5; i++)
    array[i] = i;
```

Fortunately, with a little extra programming, this is still doable with range-based **for**:

```
int j = 0;
for (int& i : array)
    i = j++;
```

Example 10.2. *Setting an Array with Range-Based "for"*

The example in this section doesn't do anything novel; it just sets some array values, prints them out, sets new values, and prints them out again. The point of this example is mainly to show the range-based **for** syntax in a variety of contexts.

```
ranged_base_for.cpp

    #include <iostream>
    #include <cstdlib>

    using namespace std;

    #define SIZE_OF_ARRAY 5
```

ranged_base_for.cpp, cont.

```cpp
int main() {
    int arr[SIZE_OF_ARRAY];
    int total = 0;

    // For each element, prompt for a value,
    //   store, and add to total.
    //
    for (int& n : arr) {
        cout << "Enter array value: ":
        cin >> n;
        total += n;
    }
    cout << "Here are the values: ";

    // Print each element.
    //
    for (int n : arr)
        cout << n << endl;

    cout << "Total is: " << total << endl;
    cout << "Now, I'm going to zero out ";
    cout << "the values. " << endl;

    // Set each element to 0.
    //
    for (int& n : arr)
        n = 0;

    cout << "Here are the values: ";
    for (int n : arr)
        cout << n << endl;
    system("PAUSE");
    return 0;
}
```

How It Works

There's nothing new in this example other than the use of the C++0x range-based **for** syntax. It's useful to compare what the statements would look like without it. For example, to print every element of the array, arr, you'd normally write this:

```
for (int i = 0; i < SIZE_OF_ARRAY; i++)
    cout << arr[i] << endl;
```

Not bad, but look how much more succinct the C++0x version is, using range-based **for**:

```
for (int n : arr)
    cout << n << endl;
```

This is a nice savings of programmer effort. It's also simpler to read, once you get used to the syntax. The newer form just says this: "Do this for each and every member of arr."

I used a different integer variable here—n rather than i—to make a point: In the traditional use of for, i is an index into an array; but with the range-based for, n is not an index number but an actual reference (or copy) of an element of the array.

Remember, you can use any type, but the type of the variable and the base type of the container must match. For example, if arr_floating_pt is an array of elements of type **double**, you'd use a reference to (or rather a copy of) a **double**, not **int**:

```
for (double x : arr_floating_pt)
    cout << x << endl;
```

Don't forget that to alter values within the container, you need the ampersand (&).

```
for (int& n : arr)
    n = 0;
```

EXERCISES

Exercise 10.2.1.   Instead of prompting the user with the direction "Enter array value," prompt the user by printing "Enter array value #X of 5: " where X is the current array index. Do this while still using range-based **for**. (Hint: You'll need to set another variable, such as j, to 0 and then increment it.)

Exercise 10.2.2.   Initialize an array to {1, 2, 3, 4, 5}. Then use range-based **for** to double each element of the array. Print out the results to confirm that the statements worked as expected. (Hint: Don't forget to include the ampersand (&).)

The auto and decltype Keywords

For beginners, the **auto** keyword is only a minor convenience, but when you start to write more complicated programs with exotic data types, you mind find it saves you significant work.

Note ▶   The **auto** keyword has another use, which is mostly obsolete: to indicate automatic (that is, stack-based) storage class. Local variables are given this storage class anyway. The compiler differentiates according to context. The old use of **auto** precedes another type name; the new use of **auto** is used in place of a type.

When a variable is declared with the **auto** keyword, its type is determined by context—specifically, by the thing that initializes it. Once fixed, the variable's type does not change. **auto** is not a variable-data type.

For example:

```
auto x1 = 5;        // x1 is an int.
auto x2 = 3.1415    // x2 has type double
auto x3 = "Hello";  // x3 has type char*
```

You may wonder, at first, what the point of the keyword is...given that it's hardly saved any keystrokes...and in the case of **int** actually requires one additional keystroke.

Advanced C++ programmers sometimes use some exotic types. Consider a function return_pp_Fraction that returns a pointer to a pointer to a Fraction object. (You'll learn how to create Fraction objects in the next chapter.) In that case, you could declare and initialize x by writing this:

```
Fraction **x = return_pp_Fraction;
```

But with the new keyword, you could instead write this:

```
auto x = return_pp_Fraction;
```

Even better is the use of the **auto** keyword within range-based **for**. Suppose weirdContainer is an array of pointers to pointers to Fraction objects. In that case, you could write the following:

```
for (Fraction& **x : weirdContainer) ...
```

10

or you could just write this:

```
for (auto& x : weirdContainer) ...
```

auto is so useful in this context that we can state it as part of an alternative syntax with range-based **for:**

```
for(auto& variable : container)       // Reference
     statement
```

```
for(auto variable : container)        // By value
     statement
```

The **auto** keyword is related to another C++0x keyword, **decltype**, which returns the type of its argument.

```
decltype(x)  y;    // Declare y to have same type as x.
```

Of course, you may well ask, when is it that a programmer ever uses a variable without already knowing its type? This situation most often occurs when someone is writing their own templates—one of a very few C++ topics so advanced I don't cover it in this book except briefly in Chapter 16.

The nullptr Keyword

The **nullptr** keyword provides the new preferred way to initialize a pointer to be a null pointer, meaning it "points nowhere." This is not at all unreasonable: programmatically, its uses are important. For example, consider the **strtok** function that I introduced in Chapter 7: calling the function with a null value in the first argument is a major way of using the function.

Traditionally, the technique for making a pointer hold a null value is to set it to 0 or the predefined constant NULL:

```
int *p = 0;      // p points "nowhere" for now
int *p2 = NULL;  //  so does p2.
```

For now, these still work, and they may be supported for a long time to come for the sake of backward compatibility, so rest assured that your code will not break if you use a C++0x-compliant compiler.

But using 0 to initialize or set pointers is bad form because the same value can be used to set ordinary (scalar) variables, which should not be the case.

```
int i = 0;       // 0 also used with pointers
```

The virtue of **nullptr** is that it is, and forever will be, specific to pointers. NULL can also be defined to have pointer type, but it is dependent on a header file setting it correctly. With C++0x, the **nullptr** keyword becomes part of the core language and is guaranteed to work correctly for all C++ code in which it is appropriate (assuming, of course, that your compiler is C++0x compliant). You can use it to initialize or assign null value to a pointer of any type.

There is some possibility that in the future, setting a null pointer without the **nullptr** keyword may be *deprecated*, meaning the compiler will issue a warning, advisory message.

If your compiler supports **nullptr**, then whenever convenient you should start using it in place of NULL, which I have used in a number of examples in this book. Here's the **strtok** example from Chapter 7:

```
p = strtok(the_string, ", ");
while (p != NULL) {
        cout << p << endl;
        p = strtok(NULL, ", ");
}
```

If your compiler is fully C++0x, you ought to replace each of the two occurrences of NULL with **nullptr**:

```
p = strtok(the_string, ", ");
while (p != nullptr) {
        cout << p << endl;
        p = strtok(nullptr, ", ");
}
```

nullptr is not merely a convenient setting for the **strtok** function: Its uses go far beyond that. When any pointer is set to null (that is **nullptr**), it is equivalent to **false** when it is tested directly as a condition. So this conditional test

```
while (p != nullptr) {   // While p is not false
...
}
```

is equivalent to the following:

```
while (p) {             // While p is true (not null)
...
}
```

Strongly Typed Enumerations

The more you program computers, the more you want to get rid of "magic numbers," which are numeric literals that appear in the program for no apparent reason. It's much better to use meaningful symbolic names.

In the next section, we're going to build the game of Rock, Paper, Scissors, in which two players secretly pick one of three choices—rock, paper, or scissors—and then reveal them. Such a program needs a way to store a player's choice.

As a first approach, one might assign the numbers 1, 2, and 3 to the choices. Most of the time, the values don't matter. The most important thing (at least for now) is that the three numbers are used consistently to indicate the choices.

```cpp
cout << "Enter Rock, Paper, or Scissors: "
cin >> input_str;
int c = input_str[0];

if (c == 'R' || c == 'r')
    player_choice = 1;                    // 1 = rock
else if (c == 'P' || c == 'p')
    player_choice = 2;                    // 2 = paper
else if (c == 'S' || c == 's')
    player_choice = 3;                    // 3 = scissors
```

The programmer has to remember that 1 means rock, 2 means paper, and 3 means scissors. Without comments, this kind of program code is nearly incomprehensible. We need to get rid of the "magic numbers" and replace them with meaningful names.

Our next attempt at trying to store this information is to use a series of **#define** directives.

```cpp
#define ROCK      1
#define PAPER     2
#define SCISSORS  3
```

Now we represent ROCK as 1, PAPER as 2, and SCISSORS as 3. The code is instantly more readable.

```cpp
if (comp == ROCK && player == SCISSORS)
    cout << "Rock smashes scissors. I WIN! " << endl;
```

This is a big improvement, but wouldn't it be nice to automate the assignment of these numbers? C++ allows you to do just that, with the **enum** keyword:

```cpp
enum {rock, paper, scissors };
```

The effect of this declaration is to create rock, paper, and scissors as symbolic constants assigned values of three consecutive integers: 0, 1, and 2. (By default they start at 0.) You can then assign values of this class and test them as appropriate.

```
if (c == 'R' || c == 'r') me = rock;
...
if (comp == rock && player == scissors)
    cout << "Rock smashes scissors. I WIN! " << endl;
```

In traditional C++, you can optionally declare an enumerated type by using a type name after **enum**. This is a *weak type*: You can assign enumerated values to integers but not the other way around. C++0x continues to support this weak typing.

```
enum Choice {rock, paper, scissors };

Choice your_pick = paper, my_pick = rock;
int i = my_pick;              // Ok.
my_pick = 1;                  // Error! Requires cast.
my_pick = static_cast<Choice>(1);   // Ok.
```

enum Classes in C++0x

C++0x supports a new way of using the **enum** keyword. By combining **enum** with **class**, you create not just symbolic names but a whole new type—and this is a stronger type than the one just shown for old C++.

```
enum class Choice {rock, paper, scissors };
```

You can now declare variables of type Choice. Such variables can be set or initialized only to Choice values, namely, rock, paper, or scissors. The advantage is you can never accidentally assign a value that isn't from the group or accidentally mistake an enumerated value for an integer. Conversion between a strong **enum** value to an integer, or vice versa, requires a **static_cast** conversion.

```
Choice comp = Choice::rock;
Choice player = Choice::paper;
Choice x = 0;   // Error - 0 not in class Choice!
Choice y = 1;   // Error - 1 not in class Choice!
Choice me = static_cast<Choice>(0)  // Ok, cast used
int i = Choice::rock;  // Error -- requires cast.
```

The first thing you'll notice about the **enum class** syntax is that it creates a separate namespace. This eliminates a potential source of name conflicts, but it does mean that references to the names must be qualified using the scope operator (::).

10

```
Choice my_move = Choice::rock;
...
my_move = Choice::paper;   // This is fine.
my_move = rock;            // Error--rock out of scope.
```

If you want, you can remove the need for the scope operator with a **using** statement.

```
enum class Choice {rock, paper, scissors };
using namespace Choice;

Choice my_move = paper;   // Now this is Ok.
```

The simple version of the **enum class** syntax is as follows:

```
enum class type_name {
  symbols
};
```

Here, *symbols* is a list of symbolic names separated by commas. After this declaration, *type_name* can be used just like any C++ type.

Extended enum Syntax: Controlling Storage

The syntax in the previous section is probably sufficient for nearly all use of **class name** declarations, but occasionally you may need more control over storage. The full syntax is as follows:

```
enum class enumeration_type : storage_type {
    symbols
};
```

For example, you can specify that your symbols should be implemented by the C++ as unsigned long integers:

```
enum class Choice : unsigned long {
    rock, paper, scissors
};
```

Another flexibility of the syntax is that you can optionally specify values for the symbols, as follows:

```
enum class Numbers {
    zero,
    ten = 10;
    eleven,
```

```
        twelve,
        hundred = 100,
        hundred_and_one
    };
```

By default, enumerations start at 0. Otherwise, if not explicitly assigned a value, each symbol is assigned the value of the previous symbol plus 1. Therefore, in the example just shown, the symbols have the values you'd expect.

```
    Numbers oceans = Numbers::eleven;   // Assign oceans 11
```

Example 10.3. *Rock, Paper, Scissors Game*

Considering what a simple game Rock, Paper, Scissors is, you might think this program would be shorter. However, it has to handle all possible interactions between the computer and user, including behaving with a reasonable computer strategy.

The game may not seem that interesting now, but in the next few sections, we'll develop it into a more interesting game.

```
rps1.cpp

    #include <iostream>
    #include <string>
    #include <ctime>
    using namespace std;

    enum class Choice { rock, paper, scissors };
    using namespace Choice;

    Choice player_choice;      // Holds user's move
    Choice computer_choice;    // Holds computer move

    string words[3] = {"rock", "paper", "scissors" };

    Choice get_computer_choice();
    void decide_winner();
    string get_msg(Choice winner);
    int rand0toN1(int n);
```

▼ *continued on next page*

10

```
int main(int argc, char *argv[])
{
    srand(time(NULL));  // Set seed for randomization.
    string input_str;
    int c;
    while (true) {
        cout<<"Enter Rock, Paper, Scissors, or Exit: ";
        getline(cin, input_str);
        if (input_str.size() < 1) {
            cout << "Invalid input." << endl;
            continue;
        }
        c = input_str[0];
        if (c == 'R' || c == 'r')
            player_choice = rock;
        else if (c == 'P' || c == 'p')
            player_choice = paper;
        else if (c == 'S' || c == 's')
            player_choice = scissors;
        else if (c == 'E' || c == 'e')
            break;
        else {
            cout << "Invalid input." << endl;
            continue;
        }
        computer_choice = get_computer_choice();
        int p = (int) player_choice;
        int c = (int) computer_choice;
        cout << "You chose " << words[p];
        cout << "," << endl;
        cout << "I chose " << words[c];
        cout << "," << endl;
        decide_winner();
    }
    return EXIT_SUCCESS;
}

Choice get_computer_choice() {
    int n = rand0toN1(3);
    if (n == 0) return rock;
```

▼ *continued on next page*

```
        if (n == 1) return paper;
        return scissors;
    }

    void decide_winner() {
        if (player_choice == computer_choice) {
            cout << "Result is a tie." << endl << endl;
            return;
        }
        int p = static_cast<int>(player_choice);
        int c = static_cast<int>(computer_choice);
        if (p - c == 1 || p - c == -2) {
            cout << get_msg(player_choice);
            cout << "YOU WIN!" << endl;
        } else {
            cout << get_msg(computer_choice);
            cout << "I WIN!" << endl;
        }
        cout << endl;
    }

    string get_msg(Choice winner) {
        if (winner == rock)
            return string("Rock smashes scissors...  ");
        else if (winner == paper)
            return string("Paper covers rock...  ");
        else
            return string("Scissors cuts paper...  ");
    }

    int rand0toN1(int n) {
        return rand() % n;
    }
```

How It Works

As long as this program is, most of it is straightforward and easy to understand if
you've been paying attention to my discussion of the **enum** keyword. The program uses the C++0x version of the syntax, which uses **enum class** to effectively
create a new type.

```
enum class Choice { rock, paper, scissors };
```

The name Choice creates a new namespace as well so that normally the symbolic names rock, paper, and scissors would have to be referred to as follows:

```
Choice::rock
Choice::paper
Choice::scissors
```

And in fact, in much longer projects, it might be best to continue to limit scope this way, preventing name conflicts. But for the purposes of this program, it's better to lift the restriction so that rock, paper, and scissors can be referred to directly.

```
using namespace Choice;
```

Choice effectively becomes a new type. The program declares two variables of this class, each of which can hold the value rock, paper, or scissors but is prevented from containing other values.

```
Choice player_choice;     // Holds user's move
Choice computer_choice;   // Holds computer move
```

Remember that rock, paper, and scissors are not text strings, so they can't be printed directly as "rock," "paper," or "scissors." But they can be printed by using them as indexes into a string array.

```
string words[3] = {"rock", "paper", "scissors" };
```

This works because player_choice and computer_choice are both variables of type Choice, which contains the underlying value 0, 1, or 2. However, because *strongly typed* **enum** is in use, conversion to integer type requires a cast.

```
int p = (int) player_choice;
int c = (int) computer_choice;
cout << "You chose " << words[p];
cout << "," << endl;
cout << "I choose " << words[c];
cout << "," << endl;
```

Ideally, symbolic constants such as rock, paper, and scissors should be used only as distinct values and not as "normal" integers. To save programming effort, however, the program cheats a bit, not only using Choice values as indexes into an array (as we've just seen) but also to provide a shortcut for determining the winner.

If you look at the order of the symbols—rock, paper, scissors—you should see that the winning situation is to be one position later in this order than the computer player or else two behind: rock smashes scissors, paper covers rock, and scissors cuts paper. So...1 beats 0, 2 beats 1, and 0 beats 2. By casting Choice values into their integer equivalents (0, 1, 2), we can determine the winner:

```
int p = static_cast<int>(player_choice);
int c = static_cast<int>(computer_choice);
if (p - c == 1 || p - c == -2) {
    cout << get_msg(player_choice);
    cout << "YOU WIN!" << endl;
} else {
    cout << get_msg(computer_choice);
    cout << "I WIN!" << endl;
}
```

A More Interesting Game

Modern game theory says the optimal strategy for this game is the one the computer is already following: randomly picking between rock, paper, and scissors with equal probability. But this quickly becomes boring.

We can make the game much more interesting by giving the computer player a personality quirk. At the beginning of the game, we randomly pick a favorite choice for the computer and then have the computer pick this choice 55 percent of the time. By observation, then, the human player should be able to do significantly better than a 50/50 win/loss record.

To implement this, declare three global variables at the beginning of the program (but after the declaration of the Choice class), as well as a function declaration, set_favorites. Put all this just before the main function.

```
Choice favorite;
Choice second_favorite;
Choice third_favorite;
void set_favorites();
```

In **main**, make a call to set_favorites before doing anything else:

```
set_favorites();
```

Somewhere in the program, define set_favorites:

```
void set_favorite() {
    int n = rand0toN1(3);
    favorite = static_cast<Choice>(n);
    int m = rand0toN1(2);    // m will be 0 or 1
    if (m == 0) {
```

```
          second_favorite = static_cast<Choice>((n+1)%3);
          third_favorite = static_cast<Choice>((n+2)%3);
     } else {
          second_favorite = static_cast<Choice>((n+2)%3);
          third_favorite = static_cast<Choice>((n+1)%3);
     }
}
```

Again, the program takes advantage of the fact that rock, paper, and scissors are implemented as integers 0, 1, and 2. But to assign an integer value to a Choice variable, it's necessary to use a cast.

Finally, revise the get_computer_choice function as follows. As a result, the computer selects favorite 55 percent of the time, second_favorite 30 percent of the time, and third_favorite 15 percent of the time.

```
Choice get_computer_choice() {
     int n = rand0toN1(20);
     if (n >= 0 && n <= 10)
          return favorite;
     if (n >= 11 && n <= 16)
          return second_favorite;
     return third_favorite;
}
```

EXERCISES

Exercise 10.3.1.   Declare two global integer values, player_wins and computer_wins. After each round of the game, increment one or the other as appropriate. Then (again, after each round), print a running score of total player computer victories.

Exercise 10.3.2.   Implement the computer "personality quirk" as described in the previous section, as well as the player/computer winnings display described in Exercise 10.3.1. An observant player should be able to consistently win more often than the computer.

Exercise 10.3.3.   For experts: At periodic intervals (this is best if done randomly, say an average of once in 10 turns), have the computer analyze the player's move and change strategy accordingly. For example, if the computer determines that the player's most frequent choice is rock, the computer should reset its favorite choice to be paper (paper covers rock) and its second favorite to be rock. This should make for a very interesting, competitive game; the player must always stay alert to changing strategies on the part of the computer. The challenge is to outplay the computer (getting better than a 50/50 win-loss record).

Raw String Literals

The string literal conventions introduced in Chapter 7 create a standard C-string of type **char***. (C++ also supports a **wchar_t*** format for wide-character strings often used in international applications.)

The standard convention for string literals supports special characters such as tab and newline, but it also forces certain ordinary characters—notably \ and "—to be "escaped" by means of the backslash. For example, to represent this string data in traditional C++

```
The "file" is c:\docs\a.txt.
```

you have to use this representation:

```
char s[] = "The \"file\" is c:\\docs\\a.txt.";
```

This at least has the virtue of being unambiguous to the compiler. But the C++0x specification supports a new "raw string" convention, whereby everything between " (and) " is considered part of the string and no characters need to be "escaped." Everything really *is* taken literally.

```
char s[] = R"(The "file" is c:\docs\a.txt.)";
```

The R prefix signals a C++ raw-string literal. This is more readable, don't you think? In general, the syntax is as follows:

```
R"(raw-string-text)"
```

Instead of using " (and) " to enclose the string, you can add another character (or string of characters, up to 16 in length) to further delimit the string. This example uses "* (and) *":

```
char s[] = R"*(The "file" is c:\docs\a.txt.)*";
```

The delimiter character—in this case, *—takes on its special meaning only in the special contexts shown. Otherwise, it can be used literally within the string, as can every character.

Chapter 10 *Summary*

Here are the main points of Chapter 10:

▶ C++0x adds support for the **long long int**, a 64-bit integer. There is also a corresponding **unsigned long long int** type. In declaring variables of either type, the **int** keyword is optional.

```
long long x = 0;
unsigned long long y = 0;
```

▶ For numeric literals outside the range of long integers, C++0x provides new numeric literal prefixes: LL for **long long** and ULL for **unsigned long long**.

```
long long x = 1230004560012LL;
```

▶ The **atoll** function takes string input and returns a **long long** (64-bit) integer.

▶ Range-based **for** is a new syntax that says, "Do this statement for each member of specified container." The container can be an array, STL **string** object, or any STL class that supports a **begin** and **end** function, such as the **list** template.

▶ This **for** syntax is simplest if you don't need to alter contents of the container during the loop.

```
for(int n : my_array)      // Print each member of
    cout << n << endl;     //    my_array
```

▶ Use an ampersand (&) in the variable declaration if you want to enable change of values.

```
for(int& n : my_array)     // Set each member of
    n = 0;                 //    my_array to 0
```

▶ The **auto** keyword declares a data item in which the type is determined by context. (But once declared, the type is fixed.) For example:

```
int my_int_array[NUM_ITEMS];

for (auto x : my_int_array)
    cout << x << endl;       // x has int type
```

▶ The **decltype** keyword returns the type of its argument.

▶ Use the **nullptr** keyword to initialize a pointer that "points nowhere."

```
int *p = nullptr;
```

▶ C++0x supports both weak and strong **enum** (enumerated types). Use of **enum class** (see the following example) creates a strongly typed set of enumerated values in which a separate namespace is created and values cannot be assigned to or from another integer type without a cast.

```
enum class type_name { symbols };
```

▶ When using this version (strongly typed), remember the symbols listed are in a separate namespace and have to be referred to with class scope, unless you have a **using namespace** statement. For example:

```
enum class Choice { rock, paper, scissors };

Choice player = Choice::rock;

using namespace Choice;
Choice comp = scissors;    // Now this is ok.
```

▶ The R prefix is used in C++0x complaint compilers to permit raw string literals in which no character needs to be escaped, not even quote marks (") and back-slashes (\). The sequences "(and)" delimit the string. Here is the general syntax:

```
R"(raw-string-text)"
```

Introducing Classes: The Fraction Class

It's time to turn toward a new vista: the world of classes and objects. Up until now, you've read about features that are either already in the old C language or represent small refinements to that language.

The major feature of C++ is that it adds this new capability—classes—to the C language. (There's also another big feature called *templates* we'll get to in Chapter 16.) And to understand what classes are all about, we'll develop a class that's particularly useful and not too difficult to write: the Fraction class.

Object Orientation: Quasi-Intelligent Data Types

Before embarking on the journey of creating a Fraction class, let me say a few words as to why the journey is necessary. In other words, what are objects and classes all about?

In traditional programming, code and data are separate. Object-oriented programming (OOP) alters this relationship. It enables you to package code and data together into something called a *class*. The important thing to know about classes is this:

✱ **A class creates a data type that has both state (values) and behavior.**

Once a class is declared, you can use it to create individual data items: *objects*, each of which has its own values but shares the behavior programmed into the class. For example, you can write code like the following. Here the Fraction objects know how to respond to the addition operator (+) as well as how to print themselves.

```
Fraction a(1,2), b(1,3);  // Declare Fraction objects.
Fraction c = a + b;

cout << "The total of 1/2 and 1/3 is " << c;
```

277

OOP has a couple of immediate practical advantages: First, each class defines its own namespace. So, for example, every class can have its own size function:

```
aString.size()
aList.size()
aStack.size()
```

This is better than having to declare tring_size, list_size, stack_size, and so on, to differentiate function names according to what kind of data they operate on.

Second, it's more efficient to package code and data together because otherwise, to get the same functionality, functions would have to pass an additional argument pointing to a structure. Because of OOP, the Structured Template Library lets you write elegant expressions like this:

```
myFractionList.push_back(fr)
```

instead of this:

```
list_push_back<Fraction>(&myFractionListStruct, fr);
```

The OOP version is more succinct, but it's not just the gain in brevity that's significant. It's the gain in comprehensibility. The OOP version says I have an object, myFractionList, with a built-in ability, push_back. This version is easier to read and understand.

The most advanced feature of OOP involves polymorphism, which has important uses in graphical, event-based, and network programming. In simplest terms, it means the following:

> **The knowledge of how to respond to a function is built into the object itself.**

Objects, then, are quasi-intelligent data items. They contain the "knowledge," as it were, of how to respond to requests in the form of function calls and operators.

How and why this matters is something I'll return to in Chapter 18. For now, let's get to the basics of classes and objects.

Interlude

OOP...Is It Worth It?

Object orientation goes at least as far back as the 1960s with the Simula language, along with other attempts to make programming more data-centric. It got a boost in the 1970s when the Xerox PARC group (the same people who developed graphical user interface) invented Smalltalk, a language built on the idea of independent objects sending messages to each other. By the 1980s, the concepts began to be widely evangelized.

Interlude

▼ *continued*

In the early 1990s OOP became the standard it is today. Bjarne Strousup married OOP to the popular C language, creating C++. Pascal and Basic also got object-oriented extensions. Thereafter, new languages followed such as C# and Java. Today, you can't get away from it.

But do OOP concepts actually help you program more efficiently? There has been some backlash to the great push for everyone to become object-oriented. Detractors argue that you end up writing the same amount of code and data anyway.

Yet a couple of points are undeniable:

▶ Graphical-user interface (GUI) systems have come to dominate the world. Although you don't *have* to use an OOP language to write for such systems, they are well matched. Conceptually, they are highly compatible ideas, both developed at PARC.

▶ More and more, code and data are packaged into OOP form. If you want to take advantage of libraries such as Microsoft Foundation Classes (for Windows) or the C++ Standard Template Library (STL), you have no choice but to master the basics of object-oriented syntax.

Clearly, then, OOP is here to stay. And when you use the Structured Template Library, as I'll show in Chapter 16, you'll reap big benefits.

Point: A Simple Class

Here is the general syntax of the C++ class keyword:

```
class class_name {
    declarations
};
```

Except when you write a subclass (also called a *derived class*), the syntax is no more complicated than this. The declarations can include data declarations, function declarations, or both. Here's a simple example that involves only data declarations:

```
class Point {
    int x, y;        // private -- may not be accessed
};
```

But members are private by default, which means they cannot be accessed. This first attempt at declaring a Point class is therefore not useful. To be of any use at all, the class needs to have at least one public member.

```
class Point {
public:
    int x, y;
};
```

This is better. Now the class can actually be used. Given a class declaration for Point, you can declare individual Point objects, such as pt1, pt2, and pt3.

```
Point pt1, pt2, pt3;
```

You can then assign values to individual data fields (called *data members*):

```
pt1.x = 1;
pt1.y = -2;
pt2.x = 0;
pt2.y = 100;
```

In this example, which includes no function members, you can think of the Point class as just a collection of two data fields. Each item declared with Point type has an x and y member, and you can use these members just as you would any integer variable.

```
cout << pt1.y + 4;      // Print sum of two integers.
```

Before we leave the simple version of the Point class, there's an aspect of syntax worth commenting on. A class declaration ends with a semicolon.

```
class Point {
public:
    int x, y;
};
```

When you're starting to write C++ code, the semicolon is an easy thing to get tripped up on. A class declaration *requires* a semicolon after the closing brace (}), whereas a function definition *rejects* that same use of a semicolon. (In other words, you'd get a syntax error.)

Keep in mind this cardinal rule:

A class or data declaration always ends with a semicolon.

So, class declarations place a semicolon after the closing brace, whereas function definitions do not.

Interlude

Interlude for C Programmers: Structures and Classes

11

In C++, the **struct** and **class** keywords are equivalent, except that members of a **struct** are public by default. Both keywords create classes in C++. This means that the general term *class* and the keyword **class** are not precisely co-extensive.

In C, when you declare a structure, you have to reuse the **struct** keyword wherever the new type name appears—for example, when creating individual data items.

```
struct Point pt1, pt2, pt3;
```

This is not necessary in C++. Once you declare a class (with either the **struct** or **class** keyword), you can use the name in all contexts involving a type. So after you port C-language code to C++, you can replace the previous data declaration with this:

```
Point pt1, pt2, pt3;
```

The support of **struct** in C++ arises from the need for backward compatibility. C code often uses the **struct** keyword.

```
struct Point {
    int x, y;
};
```

The C language has no **public** or **private** keyword, and the user of a **struct** type must be able to access all members. For backward compatibility with C, therefore, types declared with **struct** had to have members public by default.

Does C++ really even need a **class** keyword? Technically, no. But the **class** keyword performs a self-documenting function, because the purpose of a class is usually to add function members. Moreover, **class** members are private by design. In object orientation, making a member public ought to happen only as a deliberate choice.

Private: Members Only (Protecting the Data)

In the previous section, the Point class permitted direct access to its data members because they were declared public.

But what if you want to control access to data members? You might, for example, want to ensure that the data is in a particular range. The way to do that is to make the members private and provide access through public functions.

The following version of Point prevents direct access to x and y from outside the class:

```
class Point {
private:              // Data members (private)
    int x, y;
public:              // Member functions
    void set(int new_x, int new_y);
    int get_x();
    int get_y();
};
```

This class declaration is still simple. It declares three public *member functions*—set, get_x, and get_y—as well as two private data members. Now, after declaring Point objects, the object's user can manipulate values only by calling one of the functions:

```
Point point1;
point1.set(10, 20);
cout << point1.get_x() << ", " << point1.get_y();
```

This prints the following:

```
10, 20
```

What is this new syntax used with get_x and get_y? Actually, it's not new; we've seen it before with other objects, such as string objects and **cin**. The dot (.) syntax says that a certain function (in this case, get_x) applies specifically to a particular object:

```
point1.get_x()
```

This function call returns the x value stored in point1. If you instead try to access a private data member directly, the compiler flags that attempt as an error:

```
point1.x = 10;       // ERROR! The x member is private!
```

Of course you have to define the member functions. The function definitions can go anywhere, as long as the class is declared first. You don't have to separately prototype these functions; in effect, the class declaration itself provides the prototypes.

The Point:: prefix clarifies the scope of these definitions so that the compiler knows they apply to the Point class. This is important, because other classes could have their own functions with these same names.

```
void Point::set(int new_x, int new_y) {
    x = new_x;
```

```
        y = new_y;
}

int Point::get_x() {
    return x;
}

int Point::get_y() {
    return y;
}
```

The Point:: scope prefix is applied to the function name. The return type (**void** or **int**, as the case may be) still appears where it would be with a standard function definition—at the very beginning.

The syntax for member-function definitions can be summarized as follows:

```
type  class_name::function_name (argument_list) {
    statements
}
```

Given these functions, you have control over the data. You can, for example, rewrite the Point::set function so that negative input values are converted to positive.

```
void Point::set(int new_x, int new_y) {
    if (new_x < 0)
        new_x *= -1;
    if (new_y < 0)
        new_y *= -1;
    x = new_x;
    y = new_y;
}
```

Here, I'm using the multiplication-assignment operator (*=); "new_x *= -1" that has the same effect that "new_x = new_x * -1" does. (You could also use the **abs** function for this purpose.)

Although function code *outside the class* cannot refer to private data members x and y, function definitions *within* the class can refer to class members whether private or not.

You can visualize the Point class this way. Every Point object (that is, variable declared with the Point class name) shares this same structure.

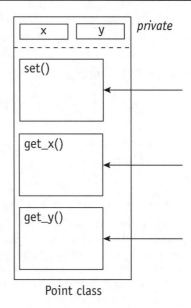

Point class

Remember that the class declaration describes the general characteristic for the type (Point). But each Point object stores its own values of the data members. For example, the value printed here is the value of x in the object pt1, not pt2 or pt3:

```
Point p1, p2, p3;
...
cout << pt1.get_x();  // Print value of x in pt1.
```

The relationship between classes, objects, and members can be summarized as follows:

```
class_name    object_name;    // Create (declare) object
object_name.member            // Data member access
object_name.member(args)      // Member function access
```

Exmple 11.1.   *Testing the Point Class*

Once you create the Point class, you can use the name "Point" just as you would any standard type name—**int, float, double**, and so on. There is no need to qualify references to Point with any other keyword.

The following program performs some simple tests on the Point class, using it to set and get some data. Code that's new is in bold; the rest is existing code from the chapter.

Point.cpp

```cpp
#include <iostream>
using namespace std;

class Point {
private:                    // Data members (private)
    int x, y;
public:                     // Member functions
    void set(int new_x, int new_y);
    int get_x();
    int get_y();
};

int main() {
    Point pt1, pt2;    // Create two Point objects.

    pt1.set(10, 20);
    cout << "pt1 is " << pt1.get_x();
    cout << ", " << pt1.get_y() << endl;
    pt2.set(-5, -25);
    cout << "pt2 is " << pt2.get_x();
    cout << ", " << pt2.get_y() << endl;
    system("PAUSE");
    return 0;
}

void Point::set(int new_x, int new_y) {
    if (new_x < 0)
        new_x *= -1;
    if (new_y < 0)
        new_y *= -1;
    x = new_x;
    y = new_y;
}

int Point::get_x() {
    return x;
}

int Point::get_y() {
    return y;
}
```

How It Works

This is a simple example. The Point class must be declared first so that it can be used by **main**. Given this declaration, **main** can create two objects, pt1 and pt2, with Point type:

```
Point pt1, pt2;   // Create two Point objects.
```

The set, get_x, and get_y member functions can then be applied to any Point objects. For example, the following three statements call Point functions through the Point object p1, thereby accessing p1's data:

```
pt1.set(10, 20);
cout << "pt1 is " << pt1.get_x();
cout << ", " << pt1.get_y() << endl;
```

These next statements call Point functions through the p2, thereby accessing p2's data:

```
pt2.set(-5, -25);
cout << "pt2 is " << pt2.get_x();
cout << ", " << pt2.get_y() << endl;
```

EXERCISES

Exercise 11.1.1.   Revise the set function so that it establishes an upper limit of 100 for values of x and y; if a value greater than 100 is entered, it is reduced to 100. Revise **main** to test this behavior.

Exercise 11.1.2.   Write two new functions for the Point class: set_x and set_y, which set the individual values x and y. Remember to reverse the negative sign, if any, as is done in the set function.

Introducing the Fraction Class

One of the best ways to think about object orientation is to consider it a way to define useful new data types. A class becomes an extension to the language itself. A perfect example is a Fraction class (which could also be called a "rational number" class) that stores two numbers representing a numerator and denominator.

The Fraction class is useful if you ever need to store numbers such as 1/3 or 2/7 and need to store them precisely. You also even use the class to store dollar-and-cents figures, such as $1.57.

In creating the Fraction class, it becomes especially important to restrict access to the data members, for several reasons. For one thing, you should never allow a 0 denominator, because the ratio 1/0 is not a legal operation.

And even with legal operations, it's important to simplify ratios so that there's a unique expression of every rational number. For example, 3/3 and 1/1 specify the same quantity, as do 2/4 and 1/2.

In the next few sections, we'll develop functions that automatically handle all this work. Users of the class will be able to create any number of Fraction objects, and operations such as the following will do the right thing "automagically."

```
Fraction a(1, 6);      // a = 1/6
Fraction b(1, 3);      // b = 1/3

if (a + b == Fraction(1, 2))
    cout << "1/6 + 1/3 equals 1/2" << endl;
```

This full version of the Fraction class will take a few chapters to develop. Let's start with the simplest possible version.

```
class Fraction {
private:
    int num, den;          // Numerator and denominator.
public:
    void set(n, d);
    int get_num();
    int get_den();
private:
    void normalize();      // Convert to standard form.
    int gcf();             // Greatest Common Factor.
    int lcm();             // Lowest Common Denominator.
};
```

This class declaration has three parts:

▶ Private data members num and den, which store numerator and denominator. In the fraction 1/3, for example, 1 is the numerator and 3 is the denominator.

▶ Public function members. These provide access to class data.

▶ Private function members. These are support functions we'll make use of later in the chapter. For now, they just return zero values.

With these functions declared, you can use the class for simple operations such as these:

```
Fraction fract;
fract.set(1, 2);
cout << fract.get_num();
cout << "/";
cout << fract.get_den();
```

So far, this isn't very interesting, because the class does nothing more sophisticated than the Point class. But it's a place to start. You can visualize the Fraction class this way.

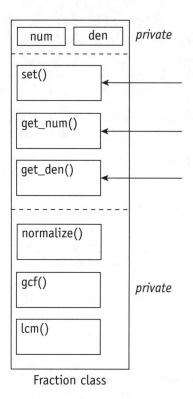

Fraction class

As always, functions declared in the class—whether public or private—have to be defined somewhere. Remember, the class declaration provides the function prototypes.

```
void Fraction::set(int n, int d) {
    num = n;
    den = d;
}
```

```
int Fraction::get_num(){
    return n;
}

int Fraction::get_den(){
    return d;
}

// TO BE DONE...
// The remaining functions are syntactically correct,
//   but don't do anything useful yet.
//   We'll fill them in later.

void Fraction::normalize(){
    return;
}

int Fraction::gcf(int a, int b){
    return 0;
}

int Fraction::lcm(int a, int b){
    return 0;
}
```

Inline Functions

Three of the functions in the Fraction class do simple things: set or get data. They are good candidates for *inlining*.

When a function is inlined, the program does not transfer control to a separate block of code. Instead, the compiler replaces the function call with the body of the function. For example, suppose that the set function is inlined, as follows:

```
void set() {num = n; den = d;}
```

Now, whenever the following statement is encountered in program code

```
fract.set(1, 2);
```

the compiler inserts the machine instructions for the "set" function. The result is essentially the same as if the following C++ code were inserted into the program:

```
{fract.num = 1; fract.den = 2;}
```

And if the get_num function is inlined, the expression

```
fract.get_num()
```

is replaced with a machine instruction or two that gets the value of fract.num.

You can make functions inline by placing their function definitions in the class declaration itself. These function definitions do not need to be followed by semicolons (;) even though they are member declarations.

The altered lines in the following example are in bold:

```
class Fraction {
private:
    int num, den;        // Numerator and denominator.
public:
    void set(int n, int d)
        {num = n; den = d; normalize();}
    int get_num()   {return num;}
    int get_den()   {return den;}
private:
    void normalize();    // Convert to standard form.
    int gcf(int a, int b)  // Greatest Common Factor.
    int lcm(int a, int b)  // Lowest Common Denom.
};
```

Because the three private functions are not inlined, their function definitions still need to be included separately in the code:

```
void Fraction::normalize(){
    return;
}

int Fraction::gcf(int a, int b){
    return 0;
}

int Fraction::lcm(int a, int b){
    return 0;
}
```

If the action of the function amounts to only a few actions, you improve efficiency by writing it as an inline function. A true function call involves overhead, and when the action of the function amounts to less work than this overhead, it ought to be inlined.

But functions that have more than a few simple statements should not be inlined. If such an inline function is called often, the program ends up taking up more space than it needs. Inline functions also have some additional restrictions. They cannot call themselves recursively, for example.

The three support functions—normalize, gcf, and lcm—are going to get longer, so we won't make those inline.

Find the Greatest Common Factor

The actions inside the Fraction class rest on two concepts in number theory: greatest common factor and lowest common multiple. Fortunately, in Chapter 4 we used an ingenious little recursive algorithm, thanks to the ancient Greek scientist Euclid and saw that it worked beautifully.

Remember, the greatest common factor is the largest number that evenly divides two other numbers. For example:

NUMBERS	GREATEST COMMON FACTOR
12, 18	6
12, 10	2
25, 50	25
50, 25	25

Here is Euclid's algorithm from Chapter 4, written as a recursive C++ function:

```
int gcf(int a, int b) {
    if (b == 0)
        return a;
    else
        return gcf(b, a%b);
}
```

Now, to rewrite this as a member function, we just add the Fraction:: prefix to give it Fraction-class scope:

```
int Fraction::gcf(int a, int b) {
    if (b == 0)
        return a;
    else
        return gcf(b, a%b);
}
```

We're almost done. But one concern is that strange things happen if negative numbers are passed to the GCF function: It still produces correct results—gcf(35, -25) produces 5—but the resulting sign becomes difficult to predict. To remove this problem, we can use the **abs** (absolute value) function to ensure only positive values are returned. (This function, by the way, requires an `#include <cstdlib>` directive, although this gets automatically included with <iostream>.)

Here, the changes to the original version of gcf are in bold:

```
int Fraction::gcf(int a, int b) {
    if (b == 0)
        return abs(a);
    else
        return gcf(b, a%b);
}
```

Find the Lowest Common Denominator

Another support function that will come in handy is getting the lowest common multiple (LCM). But with the gcf function at hand, this will be an easy task.

The LCM is the lowest number that is a multiple of both of two inputs. This is the converse of the greatest common factor (GCF). So, for example, the LCM of 200 and 300 is 600. The greatest common factor, meanwhile, is 100.

The trick in finding the LCM is to isolate the greatest common factor and multiply by this factor only once. In multiplying A and B, you implicitly include the same factor twice. The common factor must therefore be removed from A and from B. The formula is

$n = GCF(a, b)$

$LCM(A, B) = n * (a / n) * (b / n)$

which simplifies to the following:

$LCM(A, B) = a / n * b$

The LCM function is now easy to write:

```
int Fraction::lcm(int a, int b) {
    int n = gcf(a, b);
    return a / n * b;
}
```

Example 11.2. *Fraction Support Functions*

Now that we know how to write the gfc and lcm functions, it's an easy matter to add that code to the Fraction class. Here is a first working version of the class. I've also added code for the normalize function, which simplifies fractions after each operation.

Code that is new or altered from earlier versions is in bold.

Fract1.cpp

```cpp
#include <cstdlib>

class Fraction {
private:
    int num, den;        // Numerator and denominator.
public:
    void set(int n, int d)
        {num = n; den = d; normalize();}
    int get_num()   {return num;}
    int get_den()   {return den;}
private:
    void normalize();    // Convert to standard form.
    int gcf(int a, int b);  // Greatest Common Factor.
    int lcm(int a, int b);  // Lowest Common Denom.
};

// Normalize: put fraction into standard form, unique
//   for each mathematically different value.
//
void Fraction::normalize(){

    // Handle cases involving 0

    if (den == 0 || num == 0) {
        num = 0;
        den = 1;
    }

    // Put neg. sign in numerator only.
```

▼ *continued on next page*

Fract1.cpp, cont.

```cpp
        if (den < 0) {
            num *= -1;
            den *= -1;
        }

        // Factor out GCF from numerator and denominator.

        int n = gcf(num, den);
        num = num / n;
        den = den / n;
    }

// Greatest Common Factor
//
int Fraction::gcf(int a, int b){
    if (b == 0)
        return abs(a);
    else
        return gcf(b, a%b);
}

// Lowest Common Multiple
//
int Fraction::lcm(int a, int b){
    int n = gcf(a, b);
    return a / n * b;
}
```

How It Works

When the gcf function calls itself in the recursive function call

```cpp
gcf(a/i, b/i)
```

it's not necessary to use the Fraction:: prefix. That's because, inside a class function, class scope is assumed. Similarly, when the Fraction::lcm function calls gcf,
class scope is again assumed.

```cpp
int Fraction::lcm(int a, int b){
    int n = gcf(a, b);
```

```
        return a / n * b;
    }
```

In general, each time the C++ compiler comes across a variable or function name, it looks for the declaration of that name in this order:

▶ It looks within the same function (in the case of local variables).

▶ It looks within the same class.

▶ If no declaration is found at the function or class level, the compiler looks for a global declaration.

The normalize function is the only new code here. The first thing the function does is to handle cases involving zero. A denominator equal to 0 is invalid, so the fraction is changed to 0/1. In addition, all values with numerators equal to 0 are equivalent:

    0/1   0/2   0/5   0/-1   0/25

These are all put in standard form 0/1.

One of the main goals of the Fraction class is to ensure that equal values are represented the same way. This will make it easy to implement the test-for-equality operator. One problem is posed by negative numbers. These two expressions represent the same value:

    -2/3   2/-3

As do these:

    4/5   -4/-5

The easiest solution is to test the denominator: If it's less than 0, reverse the sign of both the numerator and denominator. This takes care of both of the problematic cases shown earlier.

```
        if (den < 0) {
            num *= -1;
            den *= -1;
        }
```

The rest of the function is straightforward: Find the greatest common factor and then divide both the numerator and denominator by this amount.

```
        int n = gcf(num, den);
        num = num / n;
        den = den / n;
```

For example, take the fraction 30/50. The greatest common factor is 10. The normalize function executes the necessary division and produces 3/5.

The normalize function is important because it ensures equivalent values are expressed the same way. Also, when we start crunching numbers with the Fraction class, large numbers can accumulate for the numerator and denominator. To avoid overflow errors at runtime, it's important to reduce Fraction expressions at every opportunity.

EXERCISES

Exercise 11.2.1. Rewrite the normalize function so that it uses the division-assignment operator (\=). Remember that this operation

```
a \= b
```

is equivalent to the following:

```
a = a \ b
```

Exercise 11.2.2. Inline every class function in which it would be reasonable to do so. (Hint: gcf can't be inlined because it is recursive, and normalize is too long.)

Example 11.3. *Testing the Fraction Class*

Once you have completed a class declaration, you need to test it by creating and using objects. The following code prompts for input values and displays values after simplifying the fractions:

```cpp
Fract2.cpp

#include <iostream>
#include <string>
using namespace std;

class Fraction {
private:
    int num, den;        // Numerator and denominator.
public:
    void set(int n, int d)
        {num = n; den = d; normalize();}
    int get_num()   {return num;}
```

Fract2.cpp, cont.

```cpp
        int get_den()   {return den;}
    private:
        void normalize();   // Convert to standard form.
        int gcf(int a, int b);  // Greatest Common Factor.
        int lcm(int a, int b);   // Lowest Common Denom.
    };

    int main() {
        int a, b;
        string str;
        Fraction fract;
        while (true) {
            cout << "Enter numerator: ";
            cin >> a;
            cout << "Enter denominator: ";
            cin >> b;
            fract.set(a, b);
            cout << "Numerator is   " << fract.get_num()
                << endl;
            cout << "Denominator is " << fract.get_den()
                << endl;
            cout << "Do again? (Y or N) ";
            cin >> str;
            if (!(str[0] == 'Y' || str[0] == 'y'))
                break;
        }
        system("PAUSE");
        return 0;
    }

    // -------------------------------------------------
    // FRACTION CLASS FUNCTIONS

    // Normalize: put fraction into standard form, unique
    //  for each mathematically different value.
    //
    void Fraction::normalize(){

        // Handle cases involving 0
```

▼ *continued on next page*

```
        if (den == 0 || num == 0) {
            num = 0;
            den = 1;
        }

        // Put neg. sign in numerator only.

        if (den < 0) {
            num *= -1;
            den *= -1;
        }

        // Factor out GCF from numerator and denominator.

        int n = gcf(num, den);
        num = num / n;
        den = den / n;
    }

// Greatest Common Factor
//
int Fraction::gcf(int a, int b) {
    if (b == 0)
        return abs(a);
    else
        return gcf(b, a%b);
}

// Lowest Common Multiple
//
int Fraction::lcm(int a, int b){
    int n = gcf(a, b);
    return a / n * b;
}
```

How It Works

A common practice is to put class declarations, along with any other needed declarations and directives, into a header file. Assuming that the name of this header file was Fraction.h, you'd need to add the following to a program that used the Fraction class:

```
#include "Fraction.h"
```

Function definitions that are not inlined must be placed somewhere in the program, or else they must be separately compiled and linked into the project.

The third line of **main** creates an uninitialized Fraction object:

```
Fraction fract;
```

Other statements in **main** then set the Fraction and print its value. Note that the call to the "set" function assigns values, but it also calls the normalize function, which causes the fraction to be simplified as appropriate.

```
fract.set(a, b);
cout << "Numerator is   " << fract.get_num()
        << endl;
cout << "Denominator is " << fract.get_den()
        << endl;
```

A New Kind of #include?

In the previous example, you may notice I introduced new syntax for the **#include** directive. Remember that to turn on support for an area of the C++ library, the preferred method is to use angle brackets:

```
#include <iostream>
```

But to include declarations from your own project files, you need to use quotation marks:

```
#include "Fraction.h"
```

The two forms of the **#include** directive do almost the same thing, but with the quote-mark syntax, the C++ compiler is directed to first look in the current directory and then only after look in the standard include-file directory (which is usually set by an environment variable or environment setting of the operating system).

▼ *continued on next page*

Interlude

▼ *continued*

Depending on what C++ compiler you have, you could probably get away with using the quote-mark syntax for both library files and project files. But the standard practice is to use angle brackets to turn on features of the standard library, as I follow in this book.

EXERCISE

Exercise 11.3.1.   Write a program that uses the Fraction class by setting a series of values by calling the "set" function: 2/2, 4/8, -9/-9, 10/50, 100/25. Have the program print out the results and verify that each fraction was correctly simplified.

Example 11.4.   *Fraction Arithmetic: add and mult*

The next step in creating a Fraction class is to add some arithmetic functions, add and mult. In Chapter 13, we'll create operator functions that call these arithmetic functions.

Addition is the hardest, but you may recall the technique from grade school. Consider addition of two fractions:

```
A/B + C/D
```

The trick is to first find the lowest common denominator—which is the same as the lowest common multiple (lcm) between B and D:

```
LCD = LCM(B, D).
```

Fortunately, we have a convenient utility function, lcm, to do just that. Then A/B has to be converted to a fraction that uses this lowest common denominator (LCD):

```
A    *    LCD/B
--        -----
B    *    LCD/B
```

We then get a fraction in which the denominator is LCD. It's similar for C/D:

```
C    *    LCD/D
--        -----
D    *    LCD/D
```

After these multiplications are done, the two fractions will have a common denominator (LCD), and they can be added together. The resulting fraction is as follows:

```
(A * LCD/B)  + (C * LCD/D)
--------------------------
            LCD
```

The algorithm is therefore as follows:

Calculate LCD from LCM(B, D)

Set Quotient1 to LCD/B

Set Quotient2 to LCD/D

Set numerator for the new fraction to A * Quotient1 + C * Quotient2

Set denominator for the new fraction to LCD

Multiplication is easier:

Set numerator for the new fraction to A * C

Set denominator for the new fraction to B * D

With these algorithms in hand, we can now write code that declares and implements the two new functions, as well as tests the class. As before, the lines that are bold represent new or altered lines; everything else is the same as in the previous example.

Fract3.cpp

```cpp
#include <iostream>
using namespace std;

class Fraction {
private:
    int num, den;       // Numerator and denominator.
public:
    void set(int n, int d)
        {num = n; den = d; normalize();}
    int get_num()  {return num;}
    int get_den()  {return den;}
    Fraction add(Fraction other);
    Fraction mult(Fraction other);
```

▼ *continued on next page*

```cpp
    private:
        void normalize();    // Convert to standard form.
        int gcf(int a, int b);  // Greatest Common Factor.
        int lcm(int a, int b);  // Lowest Common Denom.
};

int main() {
    Fraction fract1, fract2, fract3;

    fract1.set(1, 2);
    fract2.set(1, 3);
    fract3 = fract1.add(fract2);
    cout << "1/2 plus 1/3 = ";
    cout << fract3.get_num() << "/" << fract3.get_den()
        << endl;
    system("PAUSE");
    return 0;
}


// -----------------------------------------------------
// FRACTION CLASS FUNCTIONS

// Normalize: put fraction into standard form, unique
//   for each mathematically different value.
//
void Fraction::normalize(){

    // Handle cases involving 0

    if (den == 0 || num == 0) {
        num = 0;
        den = 1;
    }

    // Put neg. sign in numerator only.

    if (den < 0) {
        num *= -1;
        den *= -1;
    }
```

Fract3.cpp, cont.

```cpp
        // Factor out GCF from numerator and denominator.

        int n = gcf(num, den);
        num = num / n;
        den = den / n;
    }

    // Greatest Common Factor
    //
    int Fraction::gcf(int a, int b) {
        if (b == 0)
            return abs(a);
        else
            return gcf(b, a%b);
    }


    // Lowest Common Denominator
    //
    int Fraction::lcm(int a, int b){
        int n = gcf(a, b);
        return a / n * b;
    }

    Fraction Fraction::add(Fraction other) {
        Fraction fract;
        int lcd = lcm(den, other.den);
        int quot1 = lcd/den;
        int quot2 = lcd/other.den;
        fract.set(num * quot1 + other.num * quot2, lcd);
        return fract;
    }

    Fraction Fraction::mult(Fraction other) {
        Fraction fract;
        fract.set(num * other.num, den * other.den);
        return fract;
    }
```

How It Works

The add and mult functions apply the algorithms that I described earlier. They also use a new type signature: Each of these functions takes an argument of type Fraction and also returns a value of type Fraction. Consider the type declaration of the add function.

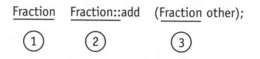

Each occurrence of Fraction in this declaration has a different purpose.

▶ The use of Fraction at the beginning of the declaration indicates that the function returns an object of type Fraction.

▶ The name prefix Fraction:: indicates that the add function is declared within the Fraction class.

▶ Within the parentheses, Fraction indicates that there is one argument, named other, which has type Fraction.

Each of these uses is distinct. For example, you could have a function that takes an argument of type **int** and returns a Fraction object, but is not declared within the Fraction class. The declaration would look like this:

```
Fraction my_func(int n);
```

Because the Fraction::add function returns an object of type Fraction, it must first create a new object:

```
Fraction fract;
```

The function then applies the algorithm I described earlier:

```
int lcd = lcm(den, other.den);
int quot1 = lcd/other.den;
int quot2 = lcd/den;
```

Finally, after setting the values for the new Fraction object (fract), the function returns this object:

```
return fact;
```

EXERCISES

Exercise 11.4.1. Rewrite **main** so that it adds any two fractions input and prints the results.

Exercise 11.4.2. Rewrite **main** so that it multiplies any two fractions input and prints the results.

Exercise 11.4.3. Write an add function for the Point class introduced earlier. The function should add the x values to get the new value of x, and it should add the y values to get the new value of y.

Exercise 11.4.4. Write sub and div functions for the Fraction class, along with code in **main** to test these functions. (The algorithm for sub is similar to that for add, although you can write an even simpler function by multiplying the numerator of the argument by -1 and then just calling the add function.)

Chapter 11 *Summary*

Here are the main points of Chapter 11:

▶ A class declaration has this form:

```
class class_name {
    declarations
};
```

▶ In C++, the **struct** keyword is equivalent to the **class** keyword, except that in classes declared with **struct**, members are public by default.

▶ Because members of a class declared with the **class** keyword are private by default, you need to declare at least one member public.

```
class Fraction {
private:
    int num, den;
public:
    void set(n, d);
    int get_num();
    int get_den();
private:
    void normalize();
```

```
        int gcf();
        int lcm();
};
```

▶ Class and data declarations end with a semicolon; function definitions do not.

▶ Once a class is declared, you can use it as a type name, just as you would **int**, **float**, **double**, and so on. For example, you can declare a series of objects:

```
Fraction a, b, c, my_fraction, fract1;
```

▶ Functions of a class can refer to other members within that same class (whether private or not) without use of the scope operator (::).

▶ To place a member-function definition outside its class's declaration, use this syntax:

```
type  class_name::function_name (argument_list)
    statements
}
```

▶ If you place a member-function definition inside the class declaration, the function is inline. When the function is called, machine instructions that implement the function are placed into the body of the program.

▶ When you inline a function, no semicolon is needed after the closing brace:

```
void set(n, d) {num = n; den = d;}
```

▶ The class declaration must precede all uses of the class. The function definitions can be placed anywhere in the program (or even in a separate module), but they must follow the class declaration.

▶ If a function has a class for its return type, it must return an object of that type. One way to do this is to first declare such an object as a local variable.

Constructors: If You Build It...

One of the themes in this book is that object orientation is a way to create fundamental new data types—types that, if useful enough, can be reused in multiple programs.

The promise that you can make classes as convenient as standard data types has yet to be fulfilled. One of the most important features of types such as **int**, **float**, **double**, and so on, is that you can initialize them as you declare them.

But you're about to see how to do that with classes. Welcome to the craft of C++ construction.

Introducing Constructors

The term *constructor* is C++-speak for an initialization function, specifically, I mean functions that tell the compiler how to interpret declarations like this:

```
Fraction a(1, 2);    // a = 1/2
```

Given what you've seen of the Fraction class, you'd probably guess that what this declaration *ought* to do is have the same effect as the following statements:

```
Fraction a;
a.set(1, 2);
```

And in fact, in this chapter, we're going to make the class behave precisely that way. But the computer has no way of guessing this is what you want to do. You have to tell the computer how to carry out initializations. This is what constructors are for.

A constructor is a special member function (and as such, it must be declared inside the class). It has this syntax:

```
class_name(argument_list)
```

This makes for an odd-looking function. There is no return type—not even **void**! The class name, in a sense, is the return type. Here's an example:

```
Fraction(int n, int d);
```

Within the context of the class, the declaration looks like this:

```
class Fraction {
public:
// ...
    Fraction(int n, int d);
// ...
};
```

This is only a declaration, of course. Like any function, the constructor needs to be defined somewhere. You can place the definition outside the class declaration, if you choose, in which case you have to use a Fraction:: prefix to clarify scope:

```
Fraction::Fraction(int n, int d) {
    set(n, d);
}
```

A constructor defined outside of the declaration has this syntax:

```
class_name::class_name(argument_list) {
    statements;
}
```

The first use of *class_name* is in the name prefix (*class_name*::), which states that this is a member function of the specified class. The second use says this is a constructor.

Confused yet? Just remember the name of a constructor is always the name of the class. Therefore, the first use of *class_name* defines the scope; the second use names the function itself.

You can also inline the constructor. Because most constructors are short, they are often good candidates for inlining.

```
class Fraction {
public:
// ...
    Fraction(int n, int d) {set(n, d);}
// ...
};
```

Now, with this constructor in place, you can initialize Fraction objects as you declare them:

```
Fraction one(1, 0), two(2, 0), half(1, 2);
```

Multiple Constructors (Overloading)

Chapter 9 pointed out that you can reuse a name to create different functions, relying on different argument lists to differentiate them. This extends to constructors.

For example, you can declare several different constructors for the Fraction class—one with no arguments, another with two, and a third with just one argument. At compile time, the compiler looks at the argument list to see which constructor to call.

```
class Fraction {
public:
// ...
    Fraction();
    Fraction(int n, int d);
    Fraction(int n);
// ...
};
```

Any or all of these can be inlined.

C++0x Only: Initializing Members within a Class

C++0x ▶ This section applies to C++0x-compliant compilers only.

C++0x compilers provide a new way to specify default initial values for data members. This technique might sound like it conflicts with writing constructors or makes them unnecessary. Actually, it doesn't; the two techniques work together.

With the Point class, it's reasonable for an object to default to zero values. C++0x enables you to do this by initializing members within the class declaration itself.

```
class Point {
    public:
```

```
        int x = 0;
        int y = 0;
};
```

Now an uninitialized Point object takes on zero values even if it is local (remember, uninitialized local variables contain garbage).

```
int main() {
    Point silly_point;
    cout << silly_point.x;  // This prints 0.
```

For the Fraction class, you'd want to assign 1 to the denominator, not 0, because 0/0 is not a legitimate fraction!

```
class Fraction {
    private:
        int num = 0;
        int den = 1;
    ...
```

When you use C++0x to initialize values this way, every constructor assigns the specified value (in this case, 0 and 1) for each data member you choose to initialize, except where the constructor overrides that setting with values of its own.

If you write no constructors at all, this approach provides an alternative way to initialize objects to reasonable default values. But regardless of what version of C++ you have, heed the warning in the next section!

The Default Constructor—and a Warning

Every time you write a class, you should usually write a default constructor—that's the constructor with no arguments—unless you want to strictly require the user of the class to initialize every object as soon as he or she declares it. This is because

✱ **If you write no constructors, the compiler automatically supplies a default constructor for you (which is a "no-op"). But if you write any constructors at all, the compiler does not supply a default constructor.**

OK, that's an odd but critical point. Let me go over it again. Let's say you define a class with no constructors.

```
class Point {
private:
```

```
    int x, y;
public:
    set(int new_x, int new_y);
    int get_x();
    int get_y();
};
```

Because you wrote a class with no constructors, the compiler obliges you by supplying one: a default constructor. That's the constructor with no arguments. Because this constructor is supplied for you, you can go ahead and use the class to declare objects. (By the way, this constructor is a brain-dead no-op that performs no initialization.)

```
Point a, b, c;
```

So far, so good: If you write *no* constructors, one is supplied for you so the user of the class can declare objects. But look what happens as soon as you do define a constructor:

```
class Point {
private:
    int x, y;
public:
    Point(int new_x, int new_y) {set(new_x, new_y);}
    set(int new_x, int new_y);
    int get_x();
    int get_y();
};
```

Given this constructor, you can now declare objects this way:

```
Point a(1, 2), b(10, -20);
```

But now, you get an error if you try to declare objects with no arguments!

```
Point c;      // ERROR! No more default constructor
```

What happened? The problem is the behavior I mentioned earlier. If you define *any constructors at all*, the compiler does not supply a default constructor for you. The automatic default constructor, which you had been relying upon, is rudely yanked away!

When you first start writing classes, this behavior can take you by surprise. You use a class without writing constructors, letting users of the class declare objects this way:

```
Point a, b, c;
```

But this innocent-looking code breaks as soon as you write a constructor other than the default constructor.

In some cases, you might not want a default constructor at all: You might want to *force* the user of the class to initialize objects. In that case, this behavior is fine.

More often, you probably do want the objects to default to some reasonable value, such as all-zero values for data members. But here's another warning: The default constructor supplied by the compiler does not do that for you. It is a no-op. And objects, remember, are like other data items. If they are local and uninitialized, they are guaranteed to contain garbage.

C++0x ▶   If you initialize individual data members as described earlier, your objects will, of course, get those initial values...even if you rely on the compiler-supplied default constructor, which is otherwise a no-op.

Interlude

Is C++ Out to Trick You with the Default Constructor?

It may seem strange that C++ operates this way: lulling you into a false sense of security by supplying a default constructor (again, that's the constructor with no arguments) and then yanking it away from you as soon as you write any other constructor.

Admittedly, this is weird behavior. It's one of the quirks that C++ has because it has to be both an object-oriented language and a language designed to be relatively backwardly compatible with C. (Actually, it is not 100 percent backward compatible, but it comes close.)

The **struct** keyword, in particular, causes some issues. C++ treats a **struct** type as a class (as I've mentioned), but it also has to work so that C code, such as the following, still compiles successfully in C++:

```
struct Point {
    int x, y;
};

struct Point a;
a.x = 1;
```

The C language has no **public** or **private** keyword, so this code can compile only if **struct** classes have members that are public by default. Another problem is that the C language has no concept of a constructor; so if this code is to compile in C++, then the C++ compiler *must* supply a default constructor, enabling statements like this to compile:

Interlude

▼ *continued*

```
struct Point a;
```

By the way, C++ supports this usage but also allows you to drop *struct* in this context:

```
Point a;     // "struct" not necessary
```

So for backward compatibility, C++ had to supply an automatic default constructor. However, if you write any constructor at all, it's assumed that you are writing original code in C++ and that, therefore, you know all about member functions and constructors.

In that case, your excuse—that you don't know about constructors—is gone, and C++ assumes you ought to write everything you need, including the default constructor. C++ also gives you the choice of not writing a default constructor in order to force the class user to initialize objects explicitly. In some cases, you might want that.

C++0x Only: Delegating Constructors

C++0x ▶ This section applies only to compilers that are C++0x compliant.

Once you've written a constructor for a given class, it would be nice to be able to reuse it in other constructors. C++0x lets you do this. Suppose you have this simple declaration of the Point class:

```
Class Point {
private:
    int x, y;
public:
    Point(int new_x, int new_y) {x = new_x; y = new_y;}
};
```

It would be nice to be able to write a default constructor by reusing the existing constructor. Here's how to do that with C++0x compilers:

```
Class Point {
private:
    int x, y;
public:
```

```
    Point(int new_x, int new_y) {x = new_x; y = new_y;}
    Point() : Point(0, 0) {}
};
```

Look again at that new line of code:

```
    Point() : Point(0, 0) {}
```

This declares a default constructor, but it delegates the work to the other constructor: It calls the constructor with two integer arguments and passes the arguments 0, 0. With the C++0x specification, still another way to achieve this result is to initialize individual data members within the class.

```
Class Point {
private:
    int x = 0;
    int y = 0;
public:
    Point(int new_x, int new_y) {x = new_x; y = new_y;}
    Point(){}
};
```

In either case, though, the default constructor needs to be declared somewhere—unless you make a deliberate decision to restrict the class user from using a default constructor (that is, to restrict the user from declaring objects without explicit initialization).

C++0x Only: Consistent Initialization

C++0x ▶ This section applies only to compilers that are C++0x compliant.

Traditional C++ (that is, versions of the language prior to the C++0x specification) handles initialization of different kinds of data in an inconsistent way. Consider how arrays and objects are initialized.

```
int int_array[] = {1, 2, 3, 4, 5};
string beats[] = {"John", "Paul", "George", "Ringo"};

Point pt1;
Point pt2(3, 4);
Point pt3 = Point(1, 2);
```

To improve consistency, the C++ standard supports use of braces ({}) in all situations involving initialization. For the sake of backward compatibility, the statements just shown are still supported. You can still use "function style" (which uses parentheses) for initializing data. But the following use of braces is also supported:

```
Point p1{};
Point pt2{3, 4};
Point pt3 = Point{1, 2};
Point pt4 = {0, 1};
```

In Chapter 14, you'll learn how to use the **new** keyword to dynamically allocate objects from memory. Traditional C++ uses this syntax with **new**:

```
Point *p = new Point(1, 3);
```

With C++0x, you can use braces instead of the functional-style initialization (which uses parentheses):

```
Point *p = new Point{1, 3};
```

Example 12.1. *Point Class Constructors*

This example revisits the Point class from the previous chapter and adds a couple of simple constructors—the default constructor and a constructor taking two arguments. It then tests these in a simple program.

```
Point2.cpp

#include <iostream>
using namespace std;

class Point {
private:              // Data members (private)
    int x, y;
public:              // Constructors
    Point() {x = 0; y = 0;}
    Point(int new_x, int new_y) {set(new_x, new_y);}

// Other member functions

    void set(int new_x, int new_y);
    int get_x();
    int get_y();
```

Point2.cpp, cont.

```cpp
};

int main() {
    Point pt1, pt2;
    Point pt3(5, 10);

    cout << "The value of pt1 is ";
    cout << pt1.get_x() << ", ";
    cout << pt1.get_y() << endl;

    cout << "The value of pt3 is ";
    cout << pt3.get_x() << ", ";
    cout << pt3.get_y() << endl;
    system("PAUSE");
    return 0;
}

void Point::set(int new_x, int new_y) {
    if (new_x < 0)
        new_x *= -1;
    if (new_y < 0)
        new_y *= -1;
    x = new_x;
    y = new_y;
}

int Point::get_x() {
    return x;
}

int Point::get_y() {
    return y;
}
```

How It Works

Two lines in the class declaration add the constructors. Because these are provided as inline functions, no other external function definitions need to be added.

```
public:              // Constructors
    Point() {x = 0; y = 0;}
    Point(int new_x, int new y) {set(new_x, new_y);}
```

Note that the two constructors are declared in the public section of the class. If they were declared private, they wouldn't be accessible to users of the Point class, and so the whole point (as it were) would be lost.

The default constructor sets Point members to zero—useful behavior if the user of the class forgets to initialize them explicitly.

```
Point() {x = 0; y = 0;}
```

The code in **main** uses the default constructor twice (for pt1 and pt2), and it uses the second constructor once (for pt3).

```
Point pt1, pt2;
Point pt3(5, 10);
```

EXERCISES

Exercise 12.1.1.   Add code to the two constructors of the Point class to report their use. The default constructor should print "Using default constructor," and the other should print "Using (int, int) constructor." (Tip: If you want to keep these functions inline, you can have the function definitions span multiple lines if you need to do so.)

Exercise 12.1.2.   Add a third constructor that takes just one integer argument. This constructor should set x to the argument specified and set y to 0.

Exercise 12.1.3.   If you have a C++0x-compliant compiler, use individual member initialization (described a few sections earlier) to create a default value of 0 for both x and y. Then write a default constructor that does nothing and a constructor that assigns a value to x but not y. Then test the combinations. You should find that 0 is an effective default for x and y but that one or both can be overridden in the constructors.

Example 12.2.   *Fraction Class Constructors*

This example features a default constructor that sets the fraction to 0/1. Remember that this is different from the Point class constructor, which assigns zero to both members. As always, code that is bold represents lines that are new or altered. Everything else is unchanged from the previous version of the Fraction class, in Chapter 11.

Fract4.cpp

```cpp
#include <iostream>
using namespace std;

class Fraction {
private:
    int num, den;        // Numerator and denominator.
public:
    Fraction() {set(0, 1);}
    Fraction(int n, int d) {set(n, d);}

    void set(int n, int d)
        {num = n; den = d; normalize();}
    int get_num()  {return num;}
    int get_den()  {return den;}
    Fraction add(Fraction other);
    Fraction mult(Fraction other);
private:
    void normalize();   // Convert to standard form.
    int gcf(int a, int b);  // Greatest Common Factor.
    int lcm(int a, int b);  // Lowest Common Denomin.
};

int main() {
    Fraction f1, f2;
    Fraction f3(1, 2);

    cout << "The value of f1 is ";
    cout << f1.get_num() << "/";
    cout << f1.get_den() << endl;

    cout << "The value of f3 is ";
    cout << f3.get_num() << "/";
    cout << f3.get_den() << endl;
    system("PAUSE");
    return 0;
}

// -----------------------------------------------------
// FRACTION CLASS FUNCTIONS
```

12

```cpp
// Normalize: put fraction into standard form, unique
//   for each mathematically different value.
//
void Fraction::normalize(){

    // Handle cases involving 0

    if (den == 0 || num == 0) {
        num = 0;
        den = 1;
    }

    // Put neg. sign in numerator only.

    if (den < 0) {
        num *= -1;
        den *= -1;
    }

    // Factor out GCF from numerator and denominator.

    int n = gcf(num, den);
    num = num / n;
    den = den / n;
}

// Greatest Common Factor
//
int Fraction::gcf(int a, int b){
    if (b == 0)
        return abs(a);
    else
        return gcf(b, a%b);
}

// Lowest Common Multiple
//
int Fraction::lcm(int a, int b){
    int n = gcf(a, b);
```

▼ *continued on next page*

Fract4.cpp, cont.

```
        return a / n * b;
    }

    Fraction Fraction::add(Fraction other) {
        Fraction fract;
        int lcd = lcm(den, other.den);
        int quot1 = lcd/den;
        int quot2 = lcd/other.den;
        fract.set(num * quot1 + other.num * quot2, lcd);
        return fract;
    }

    Fraction Fraction::mult(Fraction other) {
        Fraction fract;
        fract.set(num * other.num, den * other.den);
        return fract;
    }
```

How It Works

If you followed Example 12.1, this example is straightforward. The twist is that the default constructor needs to set the denominator value to 1 rather than 0.

```
Fraction() {set(0, 1);}
```

The code in **main** uses constructors three times. The first two variable declarations (f1, f2) invoke the default constructor. The declaration of f3 invokes the other constructor.

EXERCISES

Exercise 12.2.1.   Rewrite the default constructor so that instead of calling set(0, 1), it sets the data members, num and den, directly. Is this more or less efficient? Is it necessary to call the normalize function?

Exercise 12.2.2.   Write a third constructor that takes just one **int** argument. Respond by setting num to this argument and by setting den to 1. Do you need to call normalize?

Reference Variables and Arguments (&)

Before you proceed to learn about the other special constructor (called the *copy constructor*), it's necessary to take a detour to learn about C++ references.

Simply stated, a reference in C++ provides the behavior of a pointer without the pointer syntax. That's an important point, so let me state it again.

✳ **A reference variable, argument, or return value provides behavior very much like a pointer, but it does not have pointer syntax.**

The simplest way to manipulate a variable, of course, is to do so directly:

```
int n;
n = 5;
```

The next way to manipulate a variable—as you should recall from Chapter 6—is to use a pointer.

```
int n, *p;
p = &n;        // Let p point to n.
*p = 5;        // Set the THING p POINTS TO, to 5.
```

Here, p points to n, so setting *p to 5 has the same effect as setting n to 5.

The important point here (and I'll resist the temptation to employ puns) is that there is one copy of n, but you can have any number of pointers to it. Getting a pointer to n does not create a new integer, just another way to manipulate n.

A reference does much the same thing, although it avoids the pointer syntax. It involves declaring a variable and then a reference variable.

```
int n;
int &r = n;
```

You may notice ampersand (&) is exactly the same character used for the address operator. The difference is that this ampersand is being used in a data declaration. Given this context, it creates a reference variable that refers to the variable n. This means that changes to r (the reference variable) cause changes to n:

```
r = 5;          // This has the effect of setting n to
5.
```

This operation has essentially the same effect of using pointer p to set the value of n, but with reference variable r, no "at" operator (*) is involved because it is with pointer indirection.

```
*p = 5;
```

The crucial thing that references and pointers have in common here is that they just create another way to refer to an existing data item...they do not allocate new data. For example, I can create many references to n:

```
int n;
int &r1 = n;
int &r2 = n;
int &r3 = n;

r1 = 5;   // n is now 5.
r2 = 25;  // n is now 25.
cout << "New value of n is " << r3;  // Print n.
```

Now, changes to *any* of the reference variables—r1, r2, and r3—all cause changes to n.

But unlike pointer variables, a reference variable can be set to refer to something just once—during initialization. At no other time can you ever make it refer to anything else. (Not unless it goes out of scope and becomes, in effect, a different variable.)

```
int &r = n;   // For the rest of time, r refers to n.
```

But ordinary reference variables like this are little used in C++. Much more useful are reference arguments. Remember the swap function from Chapter 6, which required pointers? You can create the same behavior by using reference arguments.

```
void swap_ref(int &a, int &b) {
    int temp = a;
    a = b;
    b = temp;
}
```

This example may seem to violate what I said in Chapter 6—about how such an example requires pointers—but actually it doesn't, because reference arguments behave very much *like* pointers. (In fact, the compiler almost certainly implements reference arguments by using pointers under the cover.)

Remember that in this example, the swap function does not get copies of a and b but references to them. This enables swap to make permanent changes to the arguments.

When you use references, pointer and address syntax is eliminated. So, you pass integers rather than pointers to integers.

```
int big = 100;
int little = 1;
swap_ref(big, little);    // swap big and little
```

When the compiler implements this code, it almost certainly passes addresses under the cover. But that fact is hidden. It looks like you're passing ordinary integers. The pointer version, in contrast, requires you to explicitly pass addresses:

```
int big = 100;
int little = 1;
swap_ptr(&big, &little);  // swap big and little
```

The Copy Constructor

Earlier I introduced a special constructor: the default constructor. Another other special constructor is the *copy constructor*.

The copy constructor is special for two reasons. First, this constructor gets called in a number of common situations, whether you're aware of its existence or not.

Second, if you don't write one, the compiler automatically supplies one for you. The compiler is somewhat more forgiving than it is with the default constructor. It doesn't yank the automatic copy constructor away just because you decided to write constructors of your own. There will always be a copy constructor, whether you supply one or not.

The copy constructor is automatically called in these circumstances:

▶ When the return value of a function has class type. (We've already seen this in the case of the add and mult functions from Chapter 11.) The function creates a copy of the object and hands this back to the caller.

▶ When an argument has class type. A copy of the argument is made and then passed to the function.

▶ When you use one object to initialize another. For example:

```
Fraction a(1, 2);
Fraction b(a);
```

The copy constructor is not called when a pointer to an object is passed. That's why it's called the *copy* constructor. It's called only when a new copy of an existing object needs to be made.

The syntax for the copy constructor declaration is as follows:

```
class_name(class_name const &source)
```

The **const** keyword is new here. This keyword ensures that the argument cannot be altered by the function (which makes sense, because making a copy of something should never corrupt the original). The C++ compiler requires this use of **const** in the copy-constructor declaration.

The other thing that's new about this syntax is the use of a reference argument. The function gets a reference to the *source* object, not a new copy of it. It's as if the constructor gets a pointer to *source*, but using reference rather than pointer syntax.

Here's an example for the Point class. First, the copy constructor has to be declared within the class declaration.

```
class Point {
//...
public:                    // Constructors
    Point(Point const &src);
//...
};
```

Because this function definition was not inlined, the definition has to be included separately. Outside of the class declaration, Point must occur three times, the first time to define the scope.

```
Point::Point(Point const &src) {
    x = src.x;
    y = src.y;
}
```

A short function like this can be inlined.

Why write a copy constructor at all, if the compiler supplies one? In this case—and also in the case of the Fraction class—it isn't necessary. The compiler-supplied copy constructor performs a simple member-by-member copy operation, which is sufficient.

In Chapter 14, I show an example of a class, String, that definitely needs to have a programmer-defined copy constructor to work correctly.

Interlude	## The Copy Constructor and References

One of the main reasons C++ needs to support references is so that you can write copy constructors. Without this syntax, it would be impossible. Consider, for example, what would happen if you declared a copy constructor this way:

```
Point(Point const src)
```

The compiler doesn't allow this, and a little reflection shows why. When an argument is passed to a function, a copy of that object must be placed on the stack (the area of memory used to store function arguments and addresses). But this would mean for the copy constructor to work, it would have to make a copy of that same kind of object first; therefore, it would have to call itself! This would be an infinite regress.

What if the copy constructor were declared this way?

```
Point(Point const *src)
```

There's nothing syntactically wrong with such a declaration, and in fact it's a valid constructor. But it can't be used as a *copy* constructor. This syntax indicates that a pointer, not an object, is the argument...and so it could only be used with addresses of Point objects, not with Point objects themselves.

Happily, the difficulty is not insurmountable, because it's basically a problem in syntax.

Using a reference enables the function to work as a copy constructor. Syntactically, the argument is an object, not a pointer. However, because the *implementation* of the call (most likely) involves pointers under the cover, no infinite regress occurs. The function does not have to copy an object as part of the process of copying an object!

```
Point(Point const &src)
```

Example 12.3. *Fraction Class Copy Constructor*

Here is the Fraction class, revised to include a programmer-defined copy constructor, which prints a message every time it is called. As always, code in bold represents lines new or altered from previous versions of the Fraction class.

Fract5.cpp

```cpp
#include <iostream>
using namespace std;

class Fraction {
private:
    int num, den;        // Numerator and denominator.
public:
    Fraction() {set(0, 1);}
    Fraction(int n, int d) {set(n, d);}
    Fraction(Fraction const &src);

    void set(int n, int d)
        {num = n; den = d; normalize();}
    int get_num()  {return num;}
    int get_den()  {return den;}
    Fraction add(Fraction other);
    Fraction mult(Fraction other);
private:
    void normalize();   // Convet to standard form.
    int gcf(int a, int b);  // Greatest Common Factor.
    int lcm(int a, int b);  // Lowest Common Denomin.
};

int main() {
    Fraction f1(3, 4);
    Fraction f2(f1);

    Fraction f3 = f1.add(f2);

    cout << "The value of f3 is ";
    cout << f3.get_num() << "/";
    cout << f3.get_den() << endl;
    system("PAUSE");
    return 0;
}

// --------------------------------------------------
// FRACTION CLASS FUNCTIONS
```

Fract5.cpp, cont.

```cpp
Fraction::Fraction(Fraction const &src) {
    cout << "Now calling copy constructor." << endl;
    num = src.num;
    den = src.den;
}

// Normalize: put fraction into standard form, unique
//  for each mathematically different value.
//
void Fraction::normalize(){

    // Handle cases involving 0

    if (den == 0 || num == 0) {
        num = 0;
        den = 1;
    }

    // Put neg. sign in numerator only.

    if (den < 0) {
        num *= -1;
        den *= -1;
    }

    // Factor out GCF from numerator and denominator.

    int n = gcf(num, den);
    num = num / n;
    den = den / n;
}

// Greatest Common Factor
//
int Fraction::gcf(int a, int b){
    if (b == 0)
        return abs(a);
    else
        return gcf(b, a%b);
}
```

▼ *continued on next page*

Fract5.cpp, cont.

```
// Lowest Common Multiple
//
int Fraction::lcm(int a, int b){
    int n = gcf(a, b);
    return a / n * b;
}

Fraction Fraction::add(Fraction other) {
    Fraction fract;
    int lcd = lcm(den, other.den);
    int quot1 = lcd/den;
    int quot2 = lcd/other.den;
    fract.set(num * quot1 + other.num * quot2, lcd);
    return fract;
}

Fraction Fraction::mult(Fraction other) {
    Fraction fract;
    fract.set(num * other.num, den * other.den);
    return fract;
}
```

How It Works

There's little that's new in this example. All it does is print a message when the copy constructor is called.

```
Fraction::Fraction(Fraction const &src) {
    cout << "Now calling copy constructor." << endl;
    num = src.num;
    den = src.den;
}
```

When you run the program, you'll see that it makes repeated calls to the copy constructor. The following statement, obviously, results in one call to this constructor:

```
Fraction f2(f1);
```

But this next statement results in three calls to the copy constructor: once when the object f2 is passed as an argument, once when the new object is passed back as a return value, and once again when that object is copied to f3.

```
Fraction f3 = f1.add(f2);
```

That's a lot of copying—probably more than you expected. Some of the copying can be eliminated by making the add function take a reference argument. That's a task we'll take up in the next chapter.

EXERCISES

Exercise 12.3.1.   Rewrite the Fraction copy constructor as an inline function. Do not include the statement that prints a message.

Exercise 12.3.2.   Instead of setting num and den separately, make a call to the "set" function. Is this more or less efficient? Explain why.

A Constructor from String to Fract

Wouldn't it be nice to initialize a Fraction object from a string? For example:

```
Fraction a = "1/2", b = "1/3";
```

This is possible if we write a constructor that takes a **char*** string as its one argument. With this constructor, it becomes easier to initialize arrays of Fraction objects.

```
Fraction arr_of_fract[4] = {"1/2", "1/3", "3/4"};
```

Of course, it would be nice to do away with the quotation marks. But that won't do. Without the use of a **char*** string (necessitating the quote marks), C++ would actually carry out the integer division 1/3 and then round it down to 0.

```
Fraction a = 1/3;        // This won't do what we want!
```

So, let's accept the quotation marks. First, we're going to need to access C-string functions, so that mandates an **include** directive:

```
#include <cstring>
```

Next, the constructor has to be declared within the Fraction class declaration:

```
Fraction(char *s);
```

OK, that was easy. Writing the function definition is more involved, but don't worry: We'll deconstruct the code and see how it works.

```
Fraction::Fraction(char *s) {
    int n = 0;
    int d = 1;
```

```
    char *p1 = strtok(s, "/, ");
    char *p2 = strtok(NULL, "/, ");
    if (p1 != NULL)
        n = atoi(p1);
    if (p2 != NULL)
        d = atoi(p2);
    set(n, d);
}
```

The first thing this function does is declare two integer variables and give them reasonable defaults: This is essential because we can't assume the string argument has any characters at all, or if it does, we don't know if we can get two substrings out of it.

```
    int n = 0;
    int d = 1;
```

The default value of d (which will be assigned to the denominator) is 1. This will enable the user of the class to initialize Fraction objects this way:

```
    Fraction a = "5";   // Initialize a to 5/1.
```

The next two statements extract two substrings separated by the divide sign (/) or, optionally, a comma (,).

```
    char *p1 = strtok(s, "/, ");
    char *p2 = strtok(NULL, "/, ");
```

Remember that if the **strtok** function (explained in Chapter 6) can't get another substring from the input string, it returns a null pointer. Therefore, the code must test to see whether p1 and/or p2 are null pointers before passing them to the **atoi** function and finally calling **set**.

```
    if (p1 != NULL)
        n = atoi(p1);
    if (p2 != NULL)
        d = atoi(p2);
    set(n, d);
```

Putting this code into the Fraction class and testing it is left as an exercise for the reader.

C++0x ▶ For C++0x-compliant compilers, the end of the next chapter builds on the code you've just seen to implement one of the slickest (and most requested) features of C++0x: user-defined literals. You can customize your program so that when C++ sees an expression such as 2_3r in the program's source code, it converts it to a Fraction object (in this case, 2/3).

Chapter 12 *Summary*

Here are the main points of Chapter 12:

▶ A constructor is an initialization function for a class. It has this form:

```
class_name(argument_list)
```

▶ If a constructor is not inlined, the constructor's function definition has this form:

```
class_name::class_name(argument_list) {
    statements
}
```

▶ You can have any number of different constructors. They have the same function name (which is the name of the class). But each constructor must be uniquely identified by number or type of arguments.

▶ The default constructor is the constructor with no arguments at all. It has this declaration:

```
class_name()
```

▶ The default constructor is called when an object is declared with no argument list. For example:

```
Point a;
```

▶ If you declare no constructors, the compiler automatically supplies a default constructor for you. This automatic constructor does nothing; it is a no-op. However, if you write any constructors at all, the compiler does not supply a default constructor for you.

▶ So, to program defensively, you will usually want to write a default constructor. It can include zero statements, if you want. For example:

```
Point a() {};
```

▶ In C++, a reference is a variable or argument declared with the ampersand (&). The result is (almost always) that a pointer is passed under the covers, but no pointer syntax is involved. The program appears to be passing a value, even though it's probably passing a pointer.

▶ A class's copy constructor is called whenever an object needs to be copied. This includes situations in which an object is passed to a function or the function returns an object as its return value.

▶ The copy constructor uses a reference argument, as well as the **const** keyword, which prevents changes to an argument. The copy constructor has this syntax:

class_name(*class_name* **const** *&source*)

▶ If you don't write a copy constructor, the compiler supplies one for you. It carries out a simple member-by-member copy.

Operator Functions: Doing It with Class

After reading Chapter 12, you know how to write classes (object types) that work just like standard data types, right?

Well, almost. One of the most important features of a standard data type such as **int**, **float**, **double**, and even **char** is that you can perform operations on them. Without these operators, it would be difficult to perform any calculations in C++ at all.

C++ lets you define how to perform these same operations (such as +, -, *, and /) on objects of your own classes. You can also define how a test-for-equality is carried out, helping you determine whether two quantities are equal, as in this fragment of code:

```
Fraction a(1, 2), b(1, 3);
if (a + b == Fraction(5, 6))
    cout << "1/2 + 1/3 equals 5/6";
```

Introducing Class Operator Functions

The basic syntax for writing class-operator functions is fairly simple.

return_type **operator@(***argument_list***)**

In this syntax, replace the symbol @ with a valid C++ operator, such as +, -, *, or /. Any operator symbol supported for C++ standard types can be used. Normal precedence rules are enforced, as appropriate, for the symbol. (See Appendix A.)

You can define an operator function as either a member function or a global (that is, nonmember) function.

▶ If you declare an operator function as a member function, then the object through which the function is called corresponds to the left operand.

▶ If you declare an operator function as a global function, then each operand corresponds to a function argument.

Here's how the + and - operator functions are declared inside the Point class:

```
class Point {
//...
public:

    Point operator+(Point pt);
    Point operator-(Point pt);
};
```

Given these declarations, you can apply operators to a Point object:

```
Point point1, point2, point3;
point1 = point2 + point3;
```

The compiler interprets this statement by calling the operator+ function through the left operand—point2 in this case. The right operand—point3 in this case—becomes the argument to the function. You can visualize the relationship this way.

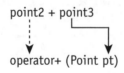

What happens to point2? Is its value ignored? No. The function treats point2 as "this object," so that unqualified use to x and y refer to *point2's* copy of x and y. You can see how this works in the function definition:

```
Point Point::operator+(Point pt) {
    Point new_pt;
    new_pt.x = x + pt.x;
    new_pt.y = y + pt.y;
    return new_pt;
}
```

Unqualified use of data members x and y refer to values in the left operand (point2 in this case). The expressions pt.x and pt.y refer to values in the right operand (point3 in this case).

The operator function is declared with Point return type, which means it returns a Point object. This makes sense: If you add two points together, you should get another point, and if you subtract a point from another, you should get another point. But C++ allows you to specify any valid type for the return-value type.

If there is a Point(int, int) constructor, you can write the function more succinctly as follows:

```
Point Point::operator+(Point pt) {
    return Point(x + pt.x, y + pt.y);
}
```

The argument list can contain any type. Overloading is permitted here: You can declare an operator function that interacts with the **int** type, another that interacts with the **float** type, and so on.

In the case of the Point class, it might make sense to permit multiplication by an integer. The declaration of the corresponding operator function (within the class) would look like this:

```
Point operator*(int n);
```

The function definition might reasonably look like this:

```
Point Point::operator*(int n) {
    Point new_pt;
    new_pt.x = x * n;
    new_pt.y = y * n;
    return new_pt;
}
```

Again, the function returns a Point object, although you could return anything you choose.

As a contrasting example, you could create an operator function that calculates the distance between two points and returns a floating-point (**double**) result. For this example, I've chosen the % operator, but you can choose any other binary operator defined in C++. The important thing here is that you can choose any return type that would be appropriate for the operation you're performing.

```
#include <cmath>

double Point::operator%(Point pt) {
    int d1 = pt.x - x;
    int d2 = pt.y - y;
```

```
    return sqrt(d1 * d1 + d2 * d2);
}
```

Given this function definition, the following code would correctly print out the distance between points (20, 20) and (24, 23) as 5.0:

```
Point pt1(20, 20);
Point pt2(24, 23);
cout << "Distance between points is :" << pt1%pt2;
```

Operator Functions as Global Functions

In the previous section, I stated that you can declare operator functions as global functions. There is a disadvantage to doing things this way: You no longer have all the relevant functions centered in the class declaration. But in one case (which I'll discuss in a moment) it turns out to be necessary to use this approach.

A global operator function is declared outside of any class. The types in the argument list determine what kinds of operands the function applies to. For example, the Point class addition-operator function can be rewritten as a global function. Here's the declaration (prototype), which should appear before the function is called:

```
Point operator+(Point pt1, Point pt2);
```

Here's the function definition:

```
Point operator+(Point pt1, Point pt2) {
    Point new_pt;
    new_pt.x = pt1.x + pt2.x;
    new_pt.y = pt1.y + pt2.y;
    return new_pt;
}
```

You can visualize a call to this function this way.

point2 + point3

operator+ (Point pt1, Point pt2)

Now both operands are interpreted as function arguments. The left operand (point2 in this case) gives its value to the first argument, pt1. There is no concept of "this object," and all references to Point data members must be qualified.

That can create a problem. If the data members are not public, this function cannot access them. One solution is to use function calls, if available, to get access to the data.

```
Point operator+(Point pt1, Point pt2) {
    Point new_pt;
    int a = pt1.get_x() + pt2.get_x();
    int b = pt1.get_y() + pt2.get_y();
    new_pt.set(a, b);
    return new_pt;
}
```

· But that's not a pretty solution, and with some classes, it may not even work. (For example, you might have a class in which the private data members are completely inaccessible, but you still want to be able to write operator functions.) A better solution is to declare a function as a *friend* function, which means that the function is global, but it has access to private members.

```
class Point {
//...
public:

    friend Point operator+(Point pt1, Point pt2);
};
```

Sometimes it's necessary to write an operator functions as a global function. In a member function, the left operand is interpreted as "this object" in the function definition. But what if the left operand does not have an object type? What if you want to support an operation like this?

```
point1 = 3 * point2;
```

The problem here is that the left operand has **int** type, not Point type. The only way to support such an operation is to write a global function.

```
Point operator*(int n, Point pt) {
    Point new_pt;
    new_pt.x = pt.x * n;
    new_pt.y = pt.y * n;
    return new_pt;
}
```

To gain access to private data members, the function may need to be made a friend of the class:

```
class Point {
//...
public:

    friend Point operator*(int n, Point pt);
};
```

You can visualize the call to this function this way.

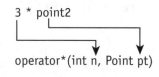

Improve Efficiency with References

As Chapter 12 pointed out, every time an object is passed or returned as a value, a call to the copy constructor is issued and memory must be allocated. You can make your programs more efficient by writing classes in such a way they minimize object creation. There's an easy way to do that: Use reference types.

Here's a Point-class add function, along with an addition-operator (+) function that calls it, written without use of reference types:

```
class Point {
//...
public:

    Point add(Point pt);
    Point operator+(Point pt);
};

Point Point::add(Point pt) {
    Point new_pt;
    new_pt.x = x + pt.x;
    new_pt.y = y + pt.y;
    return new_pt;
}

Point Point::operator+(Point pt) {
    return add(pt);
}
```

This is the obvious way to write these functions, but look how much an expression such as "pt1 + pt2" results in the creation of new objects:

▶ The right operand is passed to the operator+ function. A copy of pt2 is made and passed to the function.

▶ The operator+ function calls the add function. Now *another* copy of pt2 must be made and passed along to this function.

▶ The add function creates a new object, new_pt. This calls the default constructor. When that function returns, the program makes a copy of new_pt and passes it back to its caller (the operator+ function).

▶ The operator+ function returns the object to *its* caller, requiring yet another copy of new_pt to be made.

That's a lot of copying! Five new objects are created, involving one call to the default constructor and four calls to the copy constructor. This is extremely inefficient behavior.

Note ▶ In these days of super-fast CPUs, it may seem efficiency is not a factor. With a class as simple as Point, it may take many thousands of repeated operations to experience any noticeable time delay when you do something inefficiently. However, you can never be sure of how a class will be used. When there's an easy way to make your code more efficient, you ought to take advantage of it.

You can eliminate two of these copy operations by using reference arguments. Here is the revised version, with altered lines in bold:

```
class Point {
//...
public:

    Point add(const Point &pt);
    Point operator+(const Point &pt);
};

Point Point::add(const Point &pt) {
    Point new_pt;
    new_pt.x = x + pt.x;
    new_pt.y = y + pt.y;
    return new_pt;
}
```

```
Point Point::operator+(const Point &pt)
    return add(pt);
}
```

One of the benefits of using reference types, such as Point&, is that the implementation of the function calls change, but no other change is required in the source code. Remember, when you pass a reference, the function gets a reference to the original data—but without pointer syntax.

I also use the **const** keyword here; this keyword prevents changes to the argument being passed. When the function got its own copy of the argument, it couldn't alter the value of the original copy, no matter what it did. The **const** keyword preserves data protection, so that you can't even accidentally alter the value of one of the operands.

The change eliminates two instances of object copying. But each time one of these functions returns, it makes a copy of an object. You can cut down on this copying by making one or both of the functions inline. The operator+ function, which does nothing more than call the add function, is a good candidate for inlining.

```
class Point {
//...
public:

    Point operator+(const Point &pt) {return add(pt);}
};
```

When the operator+ function is inlined in this manner, operations such as "pt1 + pt2" are translated directly into calls to the add function. This saves another copy operation. Now most of the copying has been eliminated.

Example 13.1.   *Point Class Operators*

You now have all the tools you need to write efficient, useful operator functions for the Point class. The following code shows a complete declaration of the Point class, along with code that tests it by operating on objects.

Code brought over from Chapter 12 is left in normal font. New or altered lines are in bold.

point3.cpp

```cpp
#include <iostream>
using namespace std;

class Point {
private:                     // Data members (private)
    int x, y;
public:                      // Constructors
    Point() {set(0,0);}
    Point(int new_x, int new_y) {set(new_x, new_y);}
    Point(const Point &src) {set(src.x, src.y);}

// Operations

    Point add(const Point &pt);
    Point sub(const Point &pt);
    Point operator+(const Point &pt) {return add(pt);}
    Point operator-(const Point &pt) {return sub(pt);}

// Other member functions

    void set(int new_x, int new_y);
    int get_x() const {return x;}
    int get_y() const {return y;}
};

int main() {

    Point point1(20, 20);
    Point point2(0, 5);
    Point point3(-10, 25);
    Point point4 = point1 + point2 + point3;

    cout << "The point is " << point4.get_x();
    cout << ", " << point4.get_y() << "." << endl;

    system("PAUSE");
    return 0;
}
```

▼ *continued on next page*

13

point3.cpp, cont.

```cpp
void Point::set(int new_x, int new_y) {
    if (new_x < 0)
        new_x *= -1;
    if (new_y < 0)
        new_y *= -1;
    x = new_x;
    y = new_y;
}

Point Point::add(const Point &pt) {
    Point new_pt;
    new_pt.x = x + pt.x;
    new_pt.y = y + pt.y;
    return new_pt;
}

Point Point::sub(const Point &pt) {
    Point new_pt;
    new_pt.x = x - pt.x;
    new_pt.y = y - pt.y;
    return new_pt;
}
```

How It Works

This example adds a series of operator functions to the Point class:

```cpp
Point add(const Point &pt);
Point sub(const Point &pt);
Point operator+(const Point &pt) {return add(pt);}
Point operator-(const Point &pt) {return sub(pt);}
```

To review, the add and sub functions carry out point addition and subtraction operations so that you can write statements like this:

```cpp
Point point1 = point2.add(point3);
```

This statement adds point2 and point3 together to produce a new Point object. The operator+ function is an inline function that translates expressions such as the following into calls to the add function:

```cpp
Point point1 = point2 + point3;
```

Because this function is inline and because it uses a reference argument (const Point &), there is minimum overhead involved. The expression "point2 + point3" is translated into a call to the operator+ function, which in turn calls the add function.

The add function, in turn, creates a new point and initializes it by adding the coordinates of "this object" (point2 in this example) to the coordinates of the argument (point3).

```
point2.add(point3);
```

The operator- and sub functions work in a similar manner.

This example also adds the **const** keyword to the declarations of the get_x and get_y functions. In this context, the **const** keyword says, "The function agrees not to change any data member or call any function other than another const function."

```
int get_x() const {return x;}
int get_y() const {return y;}
```

This is a useful change. It prevents accidental changes to data members, it allows the functions to be called by other **const** functions, and it allows the functions to be called by functions that have agreed not to alter a Fraction object (because they have a **const** Fraction argument).

EXERCISES

Exercise 13.1.1. Write a test to see how many times the default constructor and the copy constructor are called. (Hint: Insert statements that send output to **cout**; you can span multiple lines if needed, as long as the function definitions are syntactically correct.) Then run the program with and without the reference arguments (const Point &) changed back to ordinary arguments (Point). How much more efficient is the former approach?

Exercise 13.1.2. Write and test an expanded Point class that supports multiplication of a Point object by an integer. Use global functions, aided by **friend** declarations, as described in the previous section.

Exercise 13.1.3. Write a similar class but for a three-dimensional point (Point3D).

Example 13.2. *Fraction Class Operators*

This example uses techniques similar to those in Example 13.1 to extend basic operator support to the Fraction class. As before, the code uses reference arguments (const Fraction &) for efficiency.

Fract6.cpp

```cpp
#include <iostream>
using namespace std;

class Fraction {
private:
    int num, den;        // Numerator and denominator.
public:
    Fraction()  {set(0, 1);}
    Fraction(int n, int d)   {set(n, d);}
    Fraction(const Fraction &src);

    void set(int n, int d)
        {num = n; den = d; normalize();}
    int get_num() const  {return num;}
    int get_den() const  {return den;}
    Fraction add(const Fraction &other);
    Fraction mult(const Fraction &other);
    Fraction operator+(const Fraction &other)
        {return add(other);}
    Fraction operator*(const Fraction &other)
        {return mult(other);}

private:
    void normalize();   // Convert to standard form.
    int gcf(int a, int b);  // Greatest Common Factor.
    int lcm(int a, int b);  // Lowest Common Denom.
};

int main() {
    Fraction f1(1, 2);
    Fraction f2(1, 3);

    Fraction f3 = f1 + f2;

    cout << "1/2 + 1/3 = ";
    cout << f3.get_num() << "/";
    cout << f3.get_den() << "." << endl;
    system("PAUSE");
    return 0;
}
```

Fract6.cpp, cont.

```cpp
// ----------------------------------------------------
// FRACTION CLASS FUNCTIONS

Fraction::Fraction(Fraction const &src) {
    num = src.num;
    den = src.den;
}

// Normalize: put fraction into standard form, unique
//   for each mathematically different value.
//
void Fraction::normalize(){

    // Handle cases involving 0

    if (den == 0 || num == 0) {
        num = 0;
        den = 1;
    }

    // Put neg. sign in numerator only.

    if (den < 0) {
        num *= -1;
        den *= -1;
    }

    // Factor out GCF from numerator and denominator.

    int n = gcf(num, den);
    num = num / n;
    den = den / n;
}

// Greatest Common Factor
//
int Fraction::gcf(int a, int b){
    if (b == 0)
        return abs(a);
```

▼ *continued on next page*

13

Fract6.cpp, cont.

```
        else
            return gcf(b, a%b);
    }

    // Lowest Common Multiple
    //
    int Fraction::lcm(int a, int b){
        int n = gcf(a, b);
        return a / n * b;
    }

    Fraction Fraction::add(const Fraction &other) {
        Fraction fract;
        int lcd = lcm(den, other.den);
        int quot1 = lcd/other.den;
        int quot2 = lcd/den;
        fract.set(num * quot1 + other.num * quot2, lcd);
        return fract;
    }

    Fraction Fraction::mult(const Fraction &other) {
        Fraction fract;
        fract.set(num * other.num, den * other.den);
        return fract;
    }
```

How It Works

The add and mult functions are taken from previously existing code in the Fraction class. All I've done is change the type of the argument so that each of these functions uses reference arguments, providing a more efficient implementation.

```
Fraction add(const Fraction &other);
Fraction mult(const Fraction &other);
```

When the declarations of these functions change, the function definitions must change as well, to reflect the altered argument type. But this change affects only the function heading (shown in bold). The rest of the definitions stay the same.

```
Fraction Fraction::add(const Fraction &other) {
    Fraction fract;
    int lcd = lcm(den, other.den);
    int quot1 = lcd/den;
    int quot2 = lcd/other.den;
    fract.set(num * quot1 + other.num * quot2, lcd);
    return fract;
}

Fraction Fraction::mult(const Fraction &other) {
    Fraction fract;
    fract.set(num * other.num, den * other.den);
    return fract;
}
```

The operator functions do nothing more than call the appropriate member function (add or mult) and return the value. For example, when the compiler sees the expression

```
f1 + f2
```

it translates this expression by making the following function call:

```
f1.operator+(f2)
```

Because of how the operator+ function is written, the call is translated, finally, as follows:

```
f1.add(f2)
```

The statements in the main function test the operator-function code by declaring fractions, adding them, and printing the results.

Optimizing the Code

Beginning in Chapter 12, the Fraction class has had a very useful Fraction(int, int) constructor. You can take advantage of this constructor, revising the add and mult functions to be more succinct. Although the versions of add and mult previously shown will run just fine, the following code is more optimal. The constructor automatically allocates the Fraction object to be returned and calls the set function, which in turn sets the data members and calls the normalize function for you.

```
Fraction Fraction::add(const Fraction &other) {
    int lcd = lcm(den, other.den);
```

```
        int quot1 = lcd/den;
        int quot2 = lcd/other.den;
        return Fraction(num * quot1 + other.num * quot2,
           lcd);
    }

    Fraction Fraction::mult(const Fraction &other) {
        return Fraction(num * other.num, den * other.den);
    }
```

EXERCISES

Exercise 13.2.1. Revise the main function in Example 13.1 so it prompts for a series of fraction values, exiting the input loop when 0 is entered for a denominator. Make the program track the sum of all the fractions entered and print the result.

Exercise 13.2.2. Write an operator- function (subtraction) for the Fraction class.

Exercise 13.2.3. Write an operator/ function (division) for the Fraction class.

Working with Other Types

Thanks to overloading, you can write many different functions for each operator, in which each function works on different types. For example, you can write several versions of operator+ that deal with the Fraction class:

```
class Fraction {
//...
public:
    operator+(const Fraction &other);
    friend operator+(int n, const Fraction &fr);
    friend operator+(const Fraction &fr, int n);
}
```

Each of these functions deals with a different combination of **int** and Fraction operands, enabling you to support expressions like this:

```
Fraction  fract1;
fract1 = 1 + Fraction(1, 2) + Fraction(3, 4) + 4;
```

But there's a much easier way to support operations with integers. All you really need is a function that converts integers to Fraction objects. If such an operation were in place, you'd only need to write one version of the operator+

function. In an expression such as the following, the compiler would convert the number 1 into Fraction format and then call the Fraction::operator+ function to add two fractions.

```
Fraction fract1 = 1 + Fraction(1, 2);
```

It turns out that such a conversion function is easy to write—it's supplied by the Fraction constructor that takes a single **int** argument! This is a simple constructor, and it can be made an inline function for efficiency.

```
Fraction(int n)   {set(n, 1);}
```

The Class Assignment Function (=)

When you write a class, the C++ compiler is friendly enough to automatically supply three special member functions for you. I've introduced two of these so far.

▶ The default constructor. The compiler version initializes nothing. Also, the compiler yanks this constructor away if you write any constructors of your own. To be safe, you should usually write your own default constructor.

▶ The copy constructor. The behavior of the automatic version is to perform a simple member-by-member copy of the source object.

▶ The assignment operator function (=). This is the new one.

The compiler supplies an assignment-operator function if you don't. That's why you've been able to do operations such as this one:

```
f1 = f2 + f3;
```

The compiler-supplied operator= function is similar to the compiler-supplied copy constructor: It performs a simple member-by-member copy. But remember that the copy constructor creates a new object, so they are not identical.

To write your own assignment operator function, use the following syntax:

class_name **&operator=(const** *class_name* **&source_arg)**

This declaration has an interesting twist: It is similar to the copy constructor, but the operator= function should return a reference to an object of the class. It should not create a new object. Here's what the operator= function might look like for the Fraction class:

```
class Fraction {
//...
```

```
public:
    Fraction &operator=(const Fraction &src) {
        set(src.num, src.den);
        return *this;
    }
};
```

This code involves the use of a new keyword, **this**. I explain the use of the **this** keyword, and other mysteries of the assignment-operator function, in the next chapter.

But for now it's enough to know that for a class like this one, you don't need to write an assignment-operator function at all. The default behavior is adequate here, and the compiler always supplies this operator function if you don't.

The Test-for-Equality Function (==)

The test-for-equality operator is another matter. The compiler does not automatically supply an operator== function for your class. The following code does not work if you don't write the required function:

```
Fraction f1(2, 3);
Fraction f2(4, 6);

if (f1 == f2)
    cout << "The fractions are equal.";
else
    cout << "The fractions are not equal.";
```

What this ought to do, of course, is print a message stating that the fractions are equal, even though different numbers (2/3 vs. 4/6) were entered.

Thanks to the normalize function, which is always called by the set function, this comparison ought to work correctly, if we can just get it to happen! If the numerators and denominators are both equal, then the fractions are equal. Therefore, the operator= function can be written as follows:

```
bool Fraction::operator==(const Fraction &other) {
    if (num == other.num && den == other.den)
        return true;
    else
        return false;
}
```

This function definition can be made even more concise:

```
bool Fraction::operator==(const Fraction &other) {
    return (num == other.num && den == other.den);
}
```

The function definition is now short enough that inlining is appropriate.

```
class Fraction {
//...
public:
    int operator==(const Fraction &other) {
        return (num == other.num && den == other.den);
    }
};
```

A Class "Print" Function

It's a real bother to have to keep writing essentially the same lines of code every time we want to print the contents of a fraction:

```
cout << f3.get_num() << "/";
cout << f3.get_den() << "." << endl;
```

The obvious way to handle this is to write a function. But since each class has its own data format, each should ideally have its own "print" function. You can even name a member function "print," because it is not a reserved word in C++.

```
void Fraction::print() {
    cout << num << "/";
    cout << den;
};
```

But as good as this solution is, it is far from being the best. A more object-oriented solution takes advantage of the fact that **cout** is an object. The ideal "print" function would interact with **cout** and all objects of the same class.

This is what you ought to be able to do:

```
cout << fract;
```

The way to support such statements is to write an operator<< function that interacts with **cout**'s parent class, **ostream**. The function must be a global function, because the left operand is an object of **ostream** class, and we don't have access to updating or altering **ostream** code.

The function should be declared as a friend of the Fraction class so that it has access to private members.

```
class Fraction {
//...
public:
    friend ostream &operator<<(ostream &os, Fraction &fr);
};
```

Notice that the function returns a reference to an **ostream** object. This is necessary so that statements such as the following work correctly:

```
cout << "The fraction's value is " << fract << endl;
```

Finally, here is a working definition for the operator<< function:

```
ostream &operator<<(ostream &os, Fraction &fr) {
    os << fr.num << "/" << fr.den;
    return os;
}
```

This solution directs the Fraction output to be sent to any **ostream** object specified. For example, if outfile is a text-file output object, you can use it to print a fraction to the file.

```
outfile << fract;
cout << "The object " << fract;
cout << " was printed to a file." << endl;
```

Example 13.3. *The Completed Fraction Class*

Although you can add many more extensions to the Fraction class (especially support for subtraction and division, which were specified earlier as an exercise), the class is getting reasonably complete.

Here is the (more or less) complete version of the Fraction class, along with code to test it. As before, only code that is new is shown in bold here.

Fract7.cpp

```
#include <iostream>
using namespace std;

class Fraction {
private:
```

Fract7.cpp, cont.

```
        int num, den;        // Numerator and denominator.
    public:
        Fraction() {set(0, 1);}
        Fraction(int n, int d)  {set(n, d);}
        Fraction(int n)  {set(n, 1);}
        Fraction(const Fraction &src);

        void set(int n, int d)
            {num = n; den = d; normalize();}
        int get_num() const {return num;}
        int get_den() const {return den;}
        Fraction add(const Fraction &other);
        Fraction mult(const Fraction &other);
        Fraction operator+(const Fraction &other)
            {return add(other);}
        Fraction operator*(const Fraction &other)
            {return mult(other);}
        bool operator==(const Fraction &other);
    friend ostream &operator<<(ostream &os, Fraction &fr);

    private:
        void normalize();   // Convert to standard form.
        int gcf(int a, int b);  // Greatest Common Factor.
        int lcm(int a, int b);  // Lowest Common Denom.
    };

    int main() {
        Fraction f1(1, 2);
        Fraction f2(1, 3);

        Fraction f3 = f1 + f2 + 1;

        cout << "1/2 + 1/3 + 1 = " << f3 << endl;
        system("PAUSE");
        return 0;
    }

    // ------------------------------------------------
    // FRACTION CLASS FUNCTIONS
```

▼ continued on next page

```cpp
Fraction::Fraction(Fraction const &src) {
    num = src.num;
    den = src.den;
}

// Normalize: put fraction into standard form, unique
//   for each mathematically different value.
//
void Fraction::normalize(){

    // Handle cases involving 0

    if (den == 0 || num == 0) {
        num = 0;
        den = 1;
    }

    // Put neg. sign in numerator only.

    if (den < 0) {
        num *= -1;
        den *= -1;
    }

    // Factor out GCF from numerator and denominator.

    int n = gcf(num, den);
    num = num / n;
    den = den / n;
}

// Greatest Common Factor
//
int Fraction::gcf(int a, int b){
    if (b == 0)
        return abs(a);
    else
        return gcf(b, a%b);
}
```

Fract7.cpp, cont.

```cpp
// Lowest Common Multiple
//
int Fraction::lcm(int a, int b){
    int n = gcf(a, b);
    return a / n * b;
}

Fraction Fraction::add(const Fraction &other) {
    int lcd = lcm(den, other.den);
    int quot1 = lcd/den;
    int quot2 = lcd/other.den;
    return Fraction(num * quot1 + other.num * quot2,
      lcd);
}

Fraction Fraction::mult(const Fraction &other) {
  return Fraction(num * other.num, den * other.den);
}

bool Fraction::operator==(const Fraction &other) {
    return (num == other.num && den == other.den);
}

// -----------------------------------------------
// FRACTION CLASS FRIEND FUNCTION

ostream &operator<<(ostream &os, Fraction &fr) {
    os << fr.num << "/" << fr.den;
    return os;
}
```

How It Works

This example adds just a few more capabilities to the Fraction class:

▶ A constructor that takes a single **int** argument

▶ An operator function that supports the test-for-equality operator (==)

▶ A global function that supports printing Fraction objects to an **ostream** object such as **cout**

This example adds another constructor; this one takes a single integer as argument. As a benefit of having this constructor, the program automatically converts integers to Fraction objects as needed.

```
Fraction(int n) {set(n, 1);};
```

The action of this function is to use whatever number is specified as numerator and use 1 for the denominator. This means that 1 is converted to 1/1, 2 is converted to 2/1, 5 is converted to 5/1, and so on.

That action suits the mathematics of the situation perfectly. When the integer 5 is converted into 5/1, for example, it retains the same value but is in Fraction format.

The other new extensions to the Fraction class incorporate code introduced in previous sections. First, the class declaration is expanded so that it declares two new functions:

```
int operator==(const Fraction &other);
friend ostream &operator<<(ostream &os, Fraction &fr);
```

The operator== function is a function of the Fraction class. It is identified outside the class as "Fraction::operator==".

```
int Fraction::operator==(const Fraction &other) {
    return (num == other.num && den == other.den);
}
```

Remember, unqualified references to num and den refer to members of "this object"—in other words, the left operand. The expressions other.num and other.den refer to values of the right operand.

The operator<< function is a global function but is also a friend of the Fraction class. It can therefore access private data (specifically, num and den).

```
ostream &operator<<(ostream &os, Fraction &fr) {
    os << fr.num << "/" << fr.den;
    return os;
}
```

EXERCISES

Exercise 13.3.1.   Alter the operator<< function of Exercise 13.4 so that it prints numbers in the format "(n, d)", where n and d are the numerator and denominator (num and den members), respectively.

Exercise 13.3.2.   Write greater-than (>) and less-than (<) functions, and revise the main function of Exercise 13.4 to test these functions. For example, test whether

1/2 + 1/3 is greater than 5/9. (Hint: Remember that A/B is greater than C/D if A * D > B * C.)

Exercise 13.3.3.   Write an `operator<<` function for sending the contents of a Point object to an **ostream** object (such as **cout**). Assume the function has been declared as a friend function of the Point class. Write the function definition.

C++0x Only: User-Defined Literals

C++0x ▶   This section applies only to C++0x-compliant compilers.

The C++0x specification was developed in response to requests over the years by C++ programmers. One of the most widely requested features was user-defined literals.

A literal—as opposed to a variable or symbol—is something that specifies a fixed value as soon as it is read by the compiler. The following are all standard literals in C++:

```
100
0xffff108e
-25
3.1415
```

C++ has built-in hexadecimal, octal, floating-point, and decimal literals (as well as string literals), but it doesn't have everything programmers would like. It would be nice, for example, to be able to write binary numbers such as

```
111100001100B
```

in which the "B" suffix indicates that this is a binary number. It would also be nice to be able to write complex numbers with imaginary-number quantities, such as the following:

```
2i
```

The C++0x specification lets you extend the language to create new literal formats like these so you can use them in your programs. This is amazing flexibility.

Since we're working with the Fraction class, we'll create a format for Fraction literals. It would be nice to write an expression like $3/7r$ ("r" standing for "rational"), but unfortunately that won't work because the slash (/) is an operator; C++ would interpret 3 as a separate number and carry out integer division, rounding down. So we must pick out some other separator, such as the underscore (_).

```
1_2r            //  One half (1/2)
2_3r            //  Two thirds (2/3)
13_50r          //  13/50
```

Defining a Raw-String Literal

One way to define a literal is to read the string data and process that data directly. This approach uses the following syntax:

type **operator** *"suffix"* **(const char** **str***)**

In this syntax, *type* is the type of object you want to produce: In our case, it will be Fraction. The *suffix* consists of the character or characters that indicate the format: When this *suffix* appears at the end of a literal, this function is invoked. (Only suffixes are supported, not prefixes.)

We can build on the code at the end of Chapter 12 to create a function defining literals for the Fraction class, using the "r" suffix. (Note that this function takes advantage of a constructor to create a Fraction object "on the fly" and return it.)

```
#include <cstring>
#include <cstdlib>
...
Fraction operator "r" (const char *s){
     int n = 0;
     int d = 1;
     char *p1 = strtok(s, "_");
     char *p2 = strtok(nullptr, "_");
     if (p1)
          n = atoi(p1);
     if (p2)
          d = atoi(p2);
     return Fraction(n, d);
}
```

Again, note that the underscore is used as a separator here, because it does not conflict with any C++ operator.

Once this function is defined, you can write code like this:

```
Fraction a = 11_12r;          // Assign 11/12.
Fraction b = 1_2r + 1_3r;     // Assign 5/6.
```

Defining a Cooked Literal

Upon hearing about "cooked" literals, you might visualize Julia Child working away in her kitchen, following a complex recipe, burning the flambé, and dropping the soufflé.

But don't worry. The cooked-literal approach is actually easier to work with than raw-string literals. Cooked literals use an existing data format, usually **int** or **double**.

For floating-point data (**double**), the syntax is as follows:

type **operator** "*suffix*" (**double** *data*)

The characters in front of the suffix are assumed to form a number in **double** format (or integer format, which is automatically promoted to **double**); this number is then passed as a numeric argument. For example, assume you've declared your own Complex number class:

```
class Complex {
  public:
    double real;
    double imag;
    Complex(double r)
      (real = r; imag = 0; }
    Complex(double r, double i)
      {real = r; imag = i; }
    ...
};
```

It's easy, then, to create an "i" suffix for notating imaginary numbers:

```
Complex operator "i" (double x) {
    return Complex(0, x);
}
```

With this definition in place, you can write expressions like this:

```
Complex number = 52.7i;
Complex y = 1.5 + 2i;    // Assuming there is an
                         // operator+ fnct. defined
```

Chapter 13 *Summary*

Here are the main points of Chapter 13:

▶ An operator function for a class has the following declaration, in which @ stands for any valid C++ operator.

> *return_type* **operator@(***argument_list***)**

▶ An operator function may be declared as a member function or a global function. If it is a member function, then (for a binary operator) there is one argument. For example, the operator+ argument for the Point class could have this declaration and definition:

```
class Point {
//...
public:
    Point operator+(Point pt);
};

Point Point::operator+(Point pt) {
    Point new_pt;
    new_pt.x = x + pt.x;
    new_pt.y = y + pt.y;
    return new_pt;
}
```

▶ Given this code, the compiler now knows how to interpret the addition sign when applied to two objects of the class.

```
point1 + point2
```

▶ When an operator function is used this way, the left operand becomes the object through which the function is called, and the right operand is passed as an argument. Thus, in the operator+ definition shown earlier, unqualified references to x and y refer to the values of the left operand.

▶ Operator functions can also be declared as global functions. For a binary operator, the function has two arguments. For example:

```
Point operator+(Point pt1, Point pt2) {
    Point new_pt;
    new_pt.x = pt1.x + pt2.x;
    new_pt.y = pt1.y + pt2.y;
    return new_pt;
}
```

▶ One drawback of writing the operator function this way is that it loses access to private members. To overcome this limitation, declare the global function as a friend of the class. For example:

```
class Point {
//...
public:
    friend Point operator+(Point pt1, Point pt2);
};
```

▶ If an argument takes an object but does not need to alter it, you can often improve the efficiency of a function by revising it to use a reference argument—for example, changing an argument of type "Point" to type "const Point&."

▶ A constructor with one argument provides a conversion function. For example, the following constructor enables automatic conversion of integer data into Fraction-class format:

```
Fraction(int n) {set(n, 1);};
```

▶ If you don't write an assignment operator function (=), the compiler automatically supplies one for you. The behavior of the compiler-supplied version is to perform a simple member-by-member copy.

▶ The compiler does not supply a test-for-equality function (==), so you need to write your own if you want to be able to compare objects. It's a good idea to use the **bool** return type, if your compiler supports it; otherwise, use **int** return type for this function.

▶ To write a "print" function for a class, write a global **operator<<** function: The first argument should have **ostream** type, so that the stream operator (<<) is supported for **cout** and other output-stream classes. You should first declare this function as a friend to your class. For example:

```
class Point {
//...
public:
   friend ostream &operator<<(ostream &os, Fraction
&fr);
};
```

▶ In the function definition, the statements should write data from the right operand (fr in this case) to the ostream argument. Then the function should return the ostream argument itself. For example:

```
ostream &operator<<(ostream &os, Fraction &fr) {
    os << fr.num << "/" << fr.den;
```

13

```
        return os;
    }
```

▶ C++0x supports the creation of user-defined literals by writing a function called **operator** *suffix*. The raw-string version uses this syntax:

```
    Fraction operator "r" (const char *str) {
    ...
    }
```

Dynamic Memory and the String Class

If you have a C++ compiler created in the past 5 or 10 years, you almost certainly have support for the Standard Template Library (STL), and that includes support for the automatic new **string** class described in Chapter 7—in addition to old-fashioned C-strings (arrays of **char**).

But in this chapter, we're going to write our own version of the string class, calling it String. Why go to this trouble? Because the String class, even though it's already provided for you, provides a perfect demonstration of many things you need to consider when writing your own classes, including the use of the **new**, **delete**, and **this** keywords.

And if by some chance you don't have a compiler that supports STL, you can always use the String class presented in this chapter.

Dynamic Memory: The "new" Keyword

As you become more experienced with C++, you'll find you need *dynamic memory allocation*. This big phrase means you can create new data items "on the fly," in response to the needs of the moment. Dynamic memory gives you much more direct control over when data is allocated. It's also an aspect of C++ in which there is a rich use for pointers.

Up till now, I've described pointer operations in two familiar steps: Allocate data by declaring a variable, and then assign its address to a pointer. For example:

```
int n;
int *p = &n;
```

This procedure is perfectly fine for simple programs. But such statements create either static data (which is created just once, at the beginning of the program) or automatic (local variables). Automatic variables are allocated in response to a function call.

With dynamic memory allocation, which is more flexible, C++ uses the **new** keyword.

```
new type
```

This syntax is an expression that produces a pointer to the specified type. The *type* can be any C++ standard type or a class. For example:

```
int *p;
p = new int;
```

You can combine these two statements into one:

```
int *p = new int;
```

The effect of this statement is to create an unnamed integer variable, accessible only through a pointer, p.

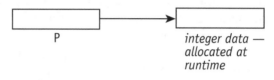

```
int *p = new int;
```

By using the pointer, you can (as usual) manipulate the value of the integer and use it in expressions.

```
*p = 5;
*p = *p + 1;
cout << "The value of the integer is " << *p;
```

This approach gives you control over when the memory is allocated. Each use of **new** causes memory allocation at runtime. You can therefore control memory allocation, creating new items in response to runtime conditions.

The operator has a counterpart, an operator that gives back the memory that **new** requested. This is the **delete** operator, which has the following syntax:

```
delete pointer;
```

This syntax describes a statement in which *pointer* is an address expression. The effect of the statement is to destroy the item pointed to by *pointer*, giving back the memory used.

The following example code does these three things: creates an integer on the fly, uses a pointer to manipulate the integer, and releases the memory occupied by that integer back to the operating system.

```
int *p = new int;
*p = 5;
*p = *p + 3;
cout << "The value of the integer is " << *p;
delete p;
```

Objects and "new"

So far, I've said little about an important concept in object orientation: *pointers to objects*. This concept turns out to be critical in the more advanced concepts in object orientation.

When a program interacts with other programs in a graphical user interface or network environment, it typically passes or receives pointers to objects. Passing pointers is usually far more efficient than creating new copies.

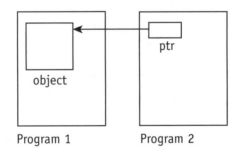

Remember that **new** and **delete** work with classes as well as other data types. For example, you can allocate a Fraction object and get a pointer to it.

```
Fraction *pFract = new Fraction;
```

This statement creates a Fraction object and calls the default constructor because no arguments are specified. But you can specify arguments if you choose.

```
Fraction *pFract = new Fraction(1, 2);   // Init to 1/2
```

The syntax for using **new** to allocate an object with an argument list is as follows:

```
new class_name(argument_list)
```

This expression allocates an object of the specified class, calls the appropriate constructor (determined by *argument_list*), and returns the address of the object.

Once you have a pointer to an object, how do you use it? How do you refer to the object's members? The obvious way is to dereference the pointer and then access a member. For example:

```
Fraction *pFract = new Fraction(1, 2);
cout << "The numerator is " << (*pFract).get_num();
```

This operation—dereferencing a pointer and then accessing members of the object pointed to—is so common that C++ supplies a special operator just to make it easier to write. Here's the syntax of this expression, which access a class member:

```
pointer->member
pointer->member()
```

These expressions are equivalent to the following:

```
(*pointer).member
(*pointer).member()
```

The example shown earlier, using a pointer to call get_num, can be rewritten as follows:

```
cout << "The numerator is " << pFract->get_num();
```

Here's another example, which calls the object's set function to assign new values to the fraction:

```
pFract->set(2, 5);      // Set fraction pointed to,
                        //  assigning the value 2/5.
```

Allocating Multiple Data

So far, I've shown how to dynamically allocate memory at runtime—to ask for more memory than the program originally required. This sounds good, but when is it of value? Actually, in advanced applications, it's used all the time.

A simple, and rather common, case is this: What if you need to allocate space for an array, but you don't know ahead of time how big to make the array? One obvious solution is just to use arrays so big that you don't think they'll be exceeded and hope that nothing goes wrong. But this clearly isn't the best solution.

C++ enables you to declare a memory block of arbitrarily large size by using new—subject only to the physical limits of the computer and the operating system.

```
new type[size]
```

This expression allocates *size* elements, in which element has the specified *type*; then it returns the address of the first element. The *type* can be either a standard type (**int**, **double**, **char**, and so on) or a class. *size* is an integer value.

This version produces the same kind of expression—a pointer to the specified type—produced by other uses of **new**. You can use an index with it as you would an array name.

```
double *p = new double[50];
p[0] = 3.1415;
p[20] = -25.7;
```

The specified size need not be a constant. You can determine how many elements are needed at runtime. For example:

```
int n;
cout << "How many elements?";
cint >> n;
int *p = new int[n];
```

Remember that this use of **new** produces the same kind of expression as the single-item version: a pointer to the requested *type*. You can allocate multiple Fraction objects, for example, getting back a pointer of type Fraction*.

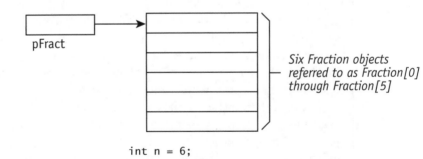

pFract

Six Fraction objects referred to as Fraction[0] through Fraction[5]

```
int n = 6;

Fraction *pFract = new pFract[n];
```

By the end of the program, you should use the **delete** operator to destroy any new memory objects you've created. If you have allocated a memory block using the syntax in this section, release that block by using this form of **delete**:

delete [] *pointer*;

This syntax describes a complete statement.

Interlude   Dealing with Problems in Memory Allocation

When you use the **new** operator, the program makes a request to the operating system, asking for memory. The system responds by checking available memory and seeing whether there is space available.

With today's modern computer platforms, large amounts of memory are available. Unless you're making exceptionally large memory requests, you can generally expect to always get the memory you need. Still, it is possible that the memory may not be available. Commercial (that is, widely sold) programs need to plan for this possibility.

If the memory requested is not available, the **new** operator returns a null pointer. You can test for this possibility and take the appropriate action.

```
int *p = new int[1000];
if (!p) {
    cout << "Insufficient memory.";
    exit(-1);
}
```

Another problem that can occur is due to *memory leaks*. When you successfully request memory with **new**, the operating system reserves the memory block until it is released with **delete**. If you then end the program without releasing all your dynamically allocated memory blocks, then the system loses some memory every time you run the program. Eventually, your computer has a great deal less usable memory.

The computer isn't losing physical memory, of course, and rebooting restores memory completely. But users hate to do that.

To avoid that problem, make sure you use **delete** to release any dynamically allocated memory before the program ends. Some programming systems—such as Java and Microsoft Visual Basic—have a process called a garbage collector, which runs in the background, finding memory blocks no longer in use and deleting them. Old versions of C++ do not have such a feature, but the new C++0x specification supports "smart pointers," introduced in Chapter 15, which automate memory clean-up.

Example 14.1.   *Dynamic Memory in Action*

This example allocates an array of any size requested. The array is then used to hold values input by the user, print them, total them, and print out the average.

new1.cpp

```cpp
#include <iostream>
using namespace std;

int main() {
    int sum = 0;
    int n = 0;

    cout << "Enter number of items: ";
    cin >> n;

    int *p = new int[n];       // Allocate n integers.

    for (int i = 0; i < n; i++) {
        cout << "Enter item #" << i << ": ";
        cin >> p[i];
        sum += p[i];
    }
    cout << "Here are the items: ";
    for (int i = 0; i < n; i++)
        cout << p[i] << ", ";
    cout << endl;
    cout << "The total is: " << sum << endl;
    cout << "The average is: " << (double) sum / n
        << endl;

    delete [] p;        // Release n integers.

    system("PAUSE");
    return 0;
}
```

How It Works

The most interesting feature of this example is that it uses the **new** operator to dynamically request memory. First, the program prompts the user for a number:

```cpp
cout << "Enter number of items: ";
cin >> n;
```

Having gotten a value for n, the program then allocates space for n elements.

```
int *p = new int[n];      // Allocate n integers
```

The pointer p now contains the address of the first element. You can use it as a base address for indexing, just as you'd use an array name. The rest of the code proceeds to do just that, up until the final statement, which uses **delete** [] to release all the elements allocated with **new**.

```
delete [] p;         // Release n integers.
```

Note that the brackets ([]) are required here because **new** was used to create multiple elements pointed to by p. Otherwise, the simpler form of **delete** would suffice.

EXERCISE

Exercise 14.1.1.   Revise Exercise 14.1 so that it creates an array of floating-point numbers (type **double**). Note that most variables should change to use base type **double**, although n should still be an integer.

Introducing Class Destructors

In the next section, we'll write a simple version of your own String class, which automates the basic tasks of creation and destruction. Before that, however, I need to introduce a new piece of syntax, the destructor. This is a member function that has the following declaration:

```
~class_name()
```

In other words, the destructor for a class has a syntax similar to that for a constructor, except for the tilde (~) at the beginning of the name—and the fact that the argument list must be blank.

For example, the Fraction class might have a destructor declared as follows:

```
class Fraction {
//...
public:
    ~Fraction();
};
```

The purpose of a class's destructor is to clean up resources just before an object is destroyed. This happens whenever an object is explicitly destroyed by **delete**:

```
Fraction *pF = new Fraction;
//...
delete pF;        // Destroy object pointed to by pF.
```

An object is also destroyed when it's declared as a variable and then goes out of scope.

```
void aFunction() {
//...
    Fraction fract1(1, 2);  // Object fract1 created.
    cout << fract1 + 1;
}                           // Object destroyed.
```

So, what happens when an object is destroyed? Often, nothing happens. The memory occupied by the object is released and thereby made available for other data items. Just before that happens, the class destructor, if any, is called.

With the Fraction class, for example, there's nothing to do. Upon destruction, Fraction data members—specifically, num and den—simply go away. There are no system resources that have to be closed or released.

But the String class is different. The String class needs to contain a single data member—a pointer to string data.

```
class String {
private:
    ptr;
//...
};
```

All the String constructors, as you'll see, allocate the actual string data—which the data member, ptr, merely points to. The destructor (of which, by the way, there can be only one) has to release this data.

```
~String() {delete [] ptr;};
```

Without this destructor, use of the String class would cause continual memory leaks…which might not seem like a problem at first, but any program foolish enough to use such class would chip away at memory, until after a while the user found that he or she didn't have enough memory to do anything and must reboot. Poorly written classes equal unhappy end users. That's not a happy equation.

Example 14.2. *A Simple String Class*

Now, let's write our own String class. This version has enough functionality to be useful. It has two constructors, one destructor, and a test-for-equality (==) operator function.

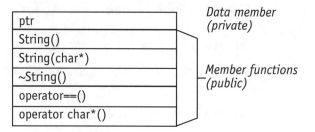

String class

Here is the code that implements and tests this class:

```cpp
string1.cpp

#include <iostream>
#include <cstring>
using namespace std;

class String {
private:
    char *ptr;
public:
    String();
    String(char *s);
    ~String();

    operator char*()  {return ptr; }
    int operator==(const String &other);
};

int main() {
    String a("STRING 1");
    String b("STRING 2");
    cout << "The value of a is: " << endl;
    cout << a << endl;
    cout << "The value of b is: " << endl;
    cout << b << endl;
    system("PAUSE");
    return 0;
}
```

```cpp
// -----------------------------------
// STRING CLASS FUNCTIONS

String::String() {
    ptr = new char[1];
    ptr[0] = '\0';
}

String::String(char *s) {
    int n = strlen(s);
    ptr = new char[n + 1];
    strcpy(ptr, s);
}

String::~String() {
    delete [] ptr;
}

int String:: operator==(const String &other) {
    return (strcmp(ptr, other.ptr) == 0);
}
```

How It Works

The class is actually pretty simple. It only contains one data member, ptr.

```cpp
private:
    char *ptr;
```

This member is made private because it will be set and reset by class functions that allocate memory blocks. It's important that code outside the class not touch this pointer.

All the complexity of the class stems from its behavior. Every time string data is copied to a String object, memory must be allocated, and ptr must be assigned the address of this memory block.

This is true even if an empty string is assigned to a String object. This is why the default constructor must allocate one byte of string data and copy a null terminator.

```cpp
String::String() {
    ptr = new char[1];
```

```
        ptr[0] = '\0';
}
```

Assigning NULL (address = 0) to ptr would be inadequate here. A null pointer is effectively an invalid pointer; it contains no address at all. Instead, we need a valid pointer to a memory block one byte long, and that byte contains a null character.

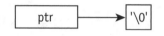

The `String(char*)` constructor is less mysterious: It must copy string data from a **char*** argument. The constructor allocates enough bytes to hold all the string data; this length is determined by using the **strlen** function. The constructor allocates enough bytes for this data, plus one for a terminating null.

```
String::String(char *s) {
    int n = strlen(s);
    ptr = new char[n + 1];
    strcpy(ptr, s);
}
```

The destructor simply releases the memory through a single use of **delete** [].

```
String::~String() {
    delete [] ptr;
}
```

The test-for-equality operator function (==) is tricky. You might be tempted to write this:

```
// INCORRECT VERSION - TOO RESTRICTIVE!

int String:: operator==(const String &other) {
    return (ptr == other.ptr);
}
```

But this version of **operator==** returns true only if the objects being tested point to the *same block of memory*. That's too restrictive. Suppose two string objects each point to a string "cat" but that each has its own copy of that string. That's the case here:

```
String str1("cat");
String str2("cat");
```

You'd want a comparison to these two objects to return true even though each has its own string "cat," and therefore each copy of ptr points to a different area in memory.

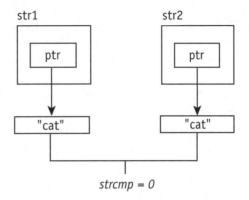

$strcmp = 0$

The solution is to call the **strcmp** library function. This function takes two string addresses and performs a comparison between the two strings pointed to. It returns 0 if the two strings have the same contents. That's precisely what you want in this case.

```
int String:: operator==(const String &other) {
    return (strcmp(ptr, other.ptr) == 0);
}
```

The main function performs a simple test of String functions.

```
int main() {
    String a("STRING 1");
    String b("STRING 2");
    cout << "The value of a is: " << endl;
    cout << a << endl;
    cout << "The value of b is: " << endl;
    cout << b;
    system("PAUSE");
    return 0;
}
```

Note that the string objects (a and b) are "printable"—that is, they can be given to **cout** as output by using the stream operator, <<.

And you can do this marvelous action because the String class declares a **char*** conversion function. With this function declared, you can use a String object wherever data of type **char*** is expected.

```
operator char*()   {return ptr; }
```

The conversion function responds just by returning the address of the string data, which is of course contained in the data member, ptr.

EXERCISES

Exercise 14.2.1.   Rewrite the main function in Example 14.2 so that it uses and tests the default constructor for the String class.

Exercise 14.2.2.   Write `operator>` and `operator<` functions for the String class. (Hint: The **strcmp** function returns a value greater than or less than zero, respectively, if the first string comes later or earlier in alphabetical sequence. Thus, the string "abc" is "less than" the string "xyz.")

"Deep" Copying and the Copy Constructor

So far, the String class works, but frankly, it's a little dull. The class will become more useful when we can start using it to copy one String object to another. This is where things get interesting.

The obvious way to copy one object to another is just to do what the automatic (compiler-supplied) copy constructor does: perform a simple member-by-member copy. This is called *shallow copying*.

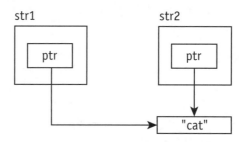

This works fine in some cases, but there is at least one major problem: What if something happens to the string data that str2 points to? In particular, if str2 subsequently goes out of scope or is deleted for some reason, the object str1 becomes invalid as well.

The following figure shows what happens if str1 gets a shallow copy of str2 but then str2 is deleted.

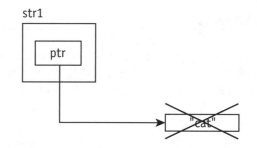

Do you see the problem? When str2 was deleted, the memory block that str2 pointed to was released and given back to the system, to be used for other purposes. Now, str1 still has an address stored in its ptr member…but it is a pointer to an invalid address!

So, to avoid this problem, use a *deep copy*. This is an approach to copying an object that reconstructs its *contents* rather than simply copying a pointer value. In the case of the String class, this means giving the destination object its own copy of the string data.

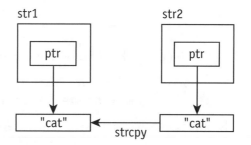

So, the copy constructor must utilize the deep-copy technique. The code here makes use of the **strlen** library function (which gets the current length of a string, up to but not including its null terminator) and the **strcpy** function (which copies string data from one area of memory to another).

```
String::String(const String &src) {
    int n = strlen(src.ptr);
    ptr = new char[n + 1];
    strcpy(ptr, src.ptr);
}
```

A correctly written assignment operator function uses similar code. First, however, you need to understand another C++ keyword: **this.**

The "this" Keyword

The **this** keyword is a pointer to the current object. When a member function is called, the C++ compiler passes a hidden argument, which is—you guessed it—the **this** pointer. Consider the following call to a Fraction class member function:

```
fract1.set(1, 3);
```

Although this is not reflected in the source code, the function call is translated into this form:

```
Fraction::set(&fract1, 1, 3);
```

In other words, a pointer to fract1 is passed as the hidden first argument. That argument is accessible within the member function as **this**.

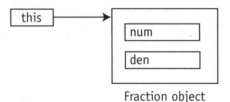

Fraction object

Once again, here's the definition of the Fraction class set function:

```
void set(int n, int d)
     {num = n; den = d; normalize();}
```

The function behaves *as if* it were written this way:

```
void set(int n, int d)
     {this->num = n; this->den = d; normalize();}
```

In fact, you *can* write the function that way. It's not necessary, because unqualified references to a data member are assumed to be references to the current object. In most cases, using the **this** pointer to refer to data members, even though legal, is unnecessary.

Incidentally, the call to normalize passes a hidden **this** pointer, although (once again) the hidden argument is not reflected in source code.

```
normalize(this);
```

That's actually not a legal statement, because the **this** pointer, though passed as an argument, must remain hidden. It *is* legal to write the call in the following way, although (as with the data members) this usage is unnecessary.

```
this->normalize();
```

Revisiting the Assignment Operator

Now, remember how assignments work in C++. The assignment operator (=) produces an expression just like any other and must return a value, although it has an important side effect: that of setting the value of the left operand.

The value returned by an assignment expression (for example, "X = Y") returns the value that was assigned—in other words, the new value of the left operand. This value can then be reused in a larger expression. For example, consider this expression:

```
x = y = 0;
```

This statement is equivalent to the following, in which the expression "y = 0" returns the new value of y (which is 0) and passes it along:

```
x = (y = 0);
```

The statement therefore assigns 0 to both x and y.

In C++, assignment-operator functions must therefore return a value, and the value you want to return is that of the left operand. In a class operator function (you'll recall), the left operand is the object through which the function was called.

But how does an object return itself? That's right; it uses the **this** pointer. By applying the indirection operator (*) to **this**, you get not a pointer to the current object but the object itself.

In other words, this statement

```
return *this;
```

says, "Return myself!"

This may be a complex train of logic, but all you really have to do is remember one cardinal rule:

✱   In the definition of any assignment-operator function (=), the last statement should be the "return *this;" statement.

That's all you really have to remember about the **this** keyword. The keyword can also be useful, upon occasion, when an object needs to call a global function and explicitly pass a pointer to itself. But mostly, you'll use it in assignment-operator functions.

To simplify matters, let's first create a cpy function that copies string data from a **char*** argument.

```
void String::cpy(char *s) {
    delete [] ptr;
```

```
        int n = strlen(s);
        ptr = new char[n + 1];
        strcpy(ptr, s);
    }
```

Now it's an easy matter to write an assignment-operator function.

```
    String& String::operator=(const String &src) {
        cpy(src.ptr);
        return *this;
    }
```

Notice that the function returns a *reference* to a String object (type "String&"), rather than a String object itself. This return type prevents an unnecessary use of the copy constructor. We don't want to have extra, redundant copies proliferate in the computer.

You can just as easily write an assignment-operator function that takes a **char*** argument. Although adding this function to the class isn't strictly necessary (because one of the constructors provides a conversion from the **char*** type), it makes evaluation of some expressions more efficient.

```
    String& String::operator=(char *s) {
        cpy(s);
        return *this;
    }
```

Both of these functions are short enough to be inlined.

Note ▶ If you compare the definitions of the copy constructor and the assignment-operator function (which calls the cpy member function), you'll see that they do similar things. There is an important difference, however: The cpy member function assumes that the current object has already been created and initialized. It therefore uses the delete operator to free the memory currently pointed to by ptr. The copy constructor makes no such assumption, since the object is new.

Writing a Concatenation Function

This String class is already getting to be a lot more useful. But we can make the String class even better still. What you'd really like to do is write statements like this:

```
String a("the ");
String b("end.");
String c = "This is " + b + c;
```

What you have to do, of course, is write an `operator+` function for the String class. Just to make things easier, let's start by writing a cat (short for "concatenation") member function. Writing the `operator+` function will then be a breeze.

The basic problem to solve here—as with most String member functions—is just how much string space to allocate. That's not too difficult, fortunately, because all you have to do is use the **strlen** library function to determine string lengths and then add them.

The algorithm for the "cat" function is therefore as follows:

1 Set N to the length of the current string plus the length of the string data to be added.

2 Allocate a new **char** memory block of size N, and set a pointer P1 to point to this block.

3 Copy current string data to this memory block (pointed to by P1) and concatenate the new string data onto the old.

4 Delete the old memory block pointed to by the data member, ptr.

5 Set ptr to the same address as P1.

This algorithm is designed so that the old memory block (pointed to ptr) is not deleted until its data is copied to the memory block. That means you can't use the **delete** operator right away, and you have to temporarily store the new address in another pointer—P1.

Here is the C++ code that implements this algorithm:

```
void String::cat(char *s) {

    // Allocate sufficient room for new string data.

    int n = strlen(ptr) + strlen(s);
    char *p1 = new char[n + 1];

    // Copy data to this new memory block.

    strcpy(p1, ptr);
    strcat(p1, s);
```

```
                  // Release old memory block and update ptr.

                  delete [] ptr;
                  ptr = p1;
            }
```

Now, writing the **operator+** function is a piece of cake. The only twist is that the function must return a new String object.

```
            String String::operator+(char *s) {
                  String new_str(ptr);
                  new_str.cat(s);
                  return new_str;
            }
```

This is a pretty simple function, thanks to the existence of the cat member function. But note this function cannot return a reference. That's because the + operator creates a new object, not equal to either of the operands, and that object must be returned to the caller of the function.

A good rule of thumb is as follows:

✳ **When a member function needs to return an existing object (as in an assignment-operator function), a reference return type is sufficient. But this doesn't work when a function needs to return a new object.**

Example 14.3. *The Complete String Class*

It's easy now to present a fairly complete String class, although there is lots of room for you to add functionality of your own. To complete the String class, we need only add the member functions described in the last several sections.

As usual, the lines that are in bold contain statements that have been added to the previous example, Example 14.2.

---

string2.cpp

```
   #include <iostream>
   #include <string.h>
   using namespace std;

   class String {
   private:
        char *ptr;
```

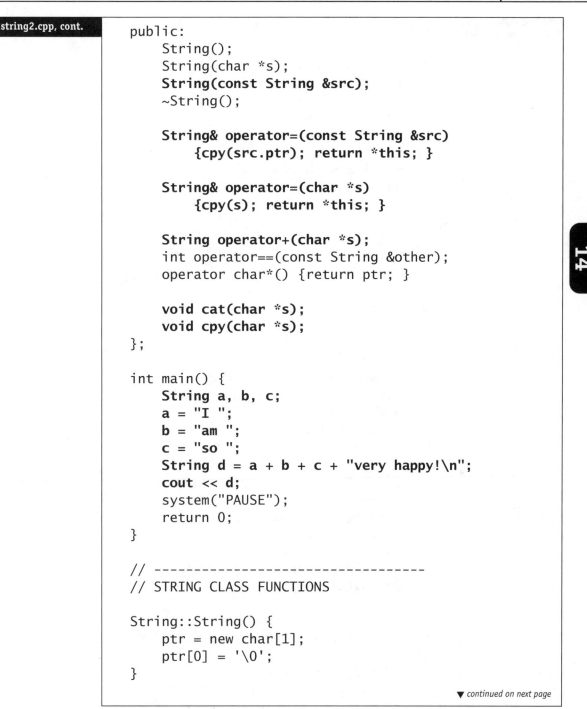

```cpp
public:
    String();
    String(char *s);
    String(const String &src);
    ~String();

    String& operator=(const String &src)
        {cpy(src.ptr); return *this; }

    String& operator=(char *s)
        {cpy(s); return *this; }

    String operator+(char *s);
    int operator==(const String &other);
    operator char*() {return ptr; }

    void cat(char *s);
    void cpy(char *s);
};

int main() {
    String a, b, c;
    a = "I ";
    b = "am ";
    c = "so ";
    String d = a + b + c + "very happy!\n";
    cout << d;
    system("PAUSE");
    return 0;
}

// ----------------------------------
// STRING CLASS FUNCTIONS

String::String() {
    ptr = new char[1];
    ptr[0] = '\0';
}
```

▼ *continued on next page*

```cpp
String::String(char *s) {
    int n = strlen(s);
    ptr = new char[n + 1];
    strcpy(ptr, s);
}

String::String(const String &src) {
    int n = strlen(src.ptr);
    ptr = new char[n + 1];
    strcpy(ptr, src.ptr);
}

String::~String() {
    delete [] ptr;
}

int String:: operator==(const String &other) {
    return (strcmp(ptr, other.ptr) == 0);
}

String String::operator+(char *s) {
    String new_str(ptr);
    new_str.cat(s);
    return new_str;
}

// cpy -- Copy string function
//
void String::cpy(char *s) {
    delete [] ptr;
    int n = strlen(s);
    ptr = new char[n + 1];
    strcpy(ptr, s);
}

// cat -- Concatenate string function
//
void String::cat(char *s) {

    // Allocate sufficient room for new string data.
```

```
        int n = strlen(ptr) + strlen(s);
        char *pl = new char[n + 1];

        // Copy data to this new memory block.

        strcpy(pl, ptr);
        strcat(pl, s);

        // Release old memory block and update ptr.

        delete [] ptr;
        ptr = pl;
    }
```

How It Works

All the functions in this example have been described in previous sections, so I won't devote space to explaining them here. There is one aspect of this example, however, that merits a little more discussion. You may notice that there is only one version of the `operator+` function.

```
String String::operator+(char *s) {
    String new_str(ptr);
    new_str.cat(s);
    return new_str;
}
```

This function assumes that the right operand has type **char***. It therefore supports operations like this one:

```
String a("King ");
String b = a + "Kong";
```

But how does the class support operations like the following, in which both operands are String objects?

```
String a("King "), b("Kong");
String b = a + b;
```

The answer is that although the class does not directly support the + operation between two String objects, the handy conversion function comes to the rescue here.

```
operator char*() {return ptr; }
```

The class knows how to convert a String object into a **char*** type, whenever such a conversion would supply the only way to legally evaluate an expression. In the "Kong" expression shown earlier, the object b is converted into a **char*** string, and the statement is executed as if it were written this way:

```
String b = a + "Kong";
```

We therefore can get away with having just one **operator+** function.

There's still a limitation with the way this function is written. Because the **operator+** function is a member function and not a global function, a String object must appear as the right operand. This means you can't execute statements such as the following:

```
String b = "My name is " + a + "Kong.";
```

The only way to support such statements—in which a **char*** string appears as the left operand in the leftmost addition (+), is to rewrite the **operator+** function as a global friend function. This is left as an exercise.

EXERCISES

Exercise 14.3.1.   Rewrite the **operator+** function as a global friend function, as just suggested. Review Chapter 13 if you need to do so. (Hint: No real change has to be made to the code other than the way the function is declared. You can still get away with having just one **operator+** function.)

Exercise 14.3.2.   In all the member functions that have a **char*** argument, change them to use an argument of **const char*** type. Does the code in the main function still work?

Exercise 14.3.3.   Add a convert-to-integer function that calls the **atoi** library function to convert the face value of the digits in the string (if any) to an integer. Also write a convert-to-double function that calls the **atof** library function. (Note: Remember to include the file stdlib.h. Also, these functions should return **int** and **double**, respectively.)

Exercise 14.3.4.   Write a **String(int n)** constructor that initializes the string data by creating a string made up of n spaces, where n is the integer specified. Write an **operator=(int n)** function that does a similar kind of assignment.

Chapter 14 *Summary*

Here are the main points of Chapter 14:

▶ Use the **new** keyword to create one more data item dynamically (that is, on the fly). Such an expression returns a pointer to the requested type. Use **delete** to release memory allocated earlier by **new**.

```
type *pointer = new type[size];
```

▶ A class destructor is called just before an object is destroyed. Writing a destructor is useful when an object owns memory or some other resource that needs to be released. A destructor has this declaration:

```
~class_name()
```

▶ A destructor is called when an object is explicitly destroyed by use of the **delete** operator or when the object goes out of scope.

▶ A *shallow copy* is a simple member-to-member copy between one object and another. For simple classes, this is often enough.

▶ A *deep copy* reconstructs the contents of one object and replicates them in another. This kind of copying—which requires the author of a class to write a copy constructor and an assignment-operator function—is often necessary for classes that manipulate system resources, such as memory or file access.

▶ The **this** keyword is translated into a pointer to the current object (that is, the object through which a member function is called).

▶ Within a member function, unqualified references to a member are equivalent to references though the **this** pointer. For example, within the String class, a call to the normalize function is equivalent to the following:

```
this->normalize();
```

▶ All versions of the assignment-operator function should end by returning a reference to the current object.

```
return *this;
```

▶ Member functions that return an existing object should have a reference return type (such as String&). This includes all assignment operator functions.

```
String& String::operator=(const String &src) {
    cpy(src.ptr);
    return *this;
}
```

◗ Member functions, such as `operator+`, that return an object with new settings should *not* have a reference return type. For example:

```
String String::operator+(char *s) {
    String new_str(ptr);
    new_str.cat(s);
    return new_str;
}
```

Two Complete OOP Examples

If you've stayed with me through the last three chapters—I call them "object-oriented boot camp"—then congratulations! I've taken you through a number of the subtleties of writing C++ classes, complete with constructors and operator functions.

But now it's time to have some fun with classes! In this chapter, we'll use classes to implement a customized linked list and to animate the Tower of Hanoi puzzle solution from Chapter 4.

Introducing Linked Lists

We've been able to use arrays to do quite a lot. With dynamic memory allocation, arrays can even be given a size determined at runtime. But there are still limitations: Once fixed, the length of an array can't be changed without destroying the array and starting over.

A linked list is far more dynamic, because its length can continually change. Every time you add another link in the chain, so to speak, capacity automatically grows…subject only to the limitations of the computer. Support for such data structures is one of the reasons C++ has pointers.

Note ▶ Although the design of a node class is simple, the ins and outs of operating on lists get a little tricky, at least with the ordered list in this chapter. If you want to avoid this logic and if your C++ compiler has STL support, you might want to turn to the linked-list example in the next chapter…or go right to the animated Tower of Hanoi later in this chapter.

Node Design

Each individual item inside a linked list is called a *node*. You design a general class for the nodes, create nodes as needed by using the **new** keyword, and finally link them together using pointers.

At minimum, a nodal class needs a data field—which we'll use to hold a **string** object—and a pointer to the next node. The class also needs a constructor, for ease of use.

```
class node {
   public:
      string name;
      node *next;
      node(string aName) {name = aName; next = NULL;}
};
```

All three members are public (remember that class members are private by default). We could protect the data. We could, for example, make "name" private and provide access through a "get" function, but it's easier for now to make everything public.

The second member, "next," may seem odd:

```
node *next;
```

What's this? We're in the middle of the definition for the node class, and here is a member that has the same type as the class itself (node)—even though we haven't finished defining the class yet!

C++ allows this declaration because it's a pointer. The compiler doesn't have to have the complete definition of node yet. There is no Alice-in-Wonderland infinite regress (as is the case of a set containing itself, which philosopher Bertrand Russell would argue is logically invalid). The compiler need only allocate enough space for a pointer.

The only constructor defined here enables the class user to initialize a node by setting the value of "name." The "next" member is initialized to NULL.

C++0x ▶ Note that if your compiler supports the C++0x specification, you should use **nullptr** instead of NULL.

```
node(string aName) {name = aName; next = nullptr;}
```

In any case, each node has a simple structure, as shown in the following image. Note that access to any node is always through a pointer. That is, you'll never see a node declared directly in the program code.

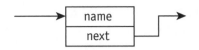

Because we're working with pointers to objects, we'll often use indirection-member operator (->). Remember that

    ptr->member

means the same as this:

    (*ptr).member

For example:

    pNode = pNode->next;   // Advance one place in list.

Implementing a Simple Linked List

You create a node by using the **new** keyword, which gives you back a pointer to the node. You can create any number of such nodes and then link them together.

You'll always need to keep a pointer to the beginning of the list (called *root* in the figure that follows); otherwise, you have no way to access the list as a whole. When a "next" member points to NULL (or **nullptr**), this indicates you've reached the end of the list. These principles enable you to traverse the entire length of the list or any part of it.

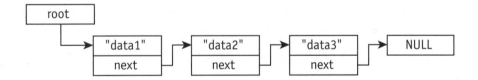

This is an example of a classic, singly linked list. You can also create doubly linked lists, but they are more work to maintain. In this chapter, we'll stick with singly linked lists.

There are different strategies for maintaining a list. The simplest approach is to add each new item, or *node*, to the end. You can either maintain a pointer to the end of the list or trace through the list to find the end.

If you're maintaining a pointer to the end of the list, the algorithm for adding a node to the end is as follows:

1 Use the "Last ptr" variable to access the node that is currently last. Assign its "next" member to point to the new node. (Skip this step if the list is empty.)

2 Assign the "next" member of the new node to point to NULL, or **nullptr**, to indicate that there is no node that comes after this one. (This is actually done automatically by the constructor.)

3 Set the "Last ptr" variable to point to the new node.

This operation is easy to picture.

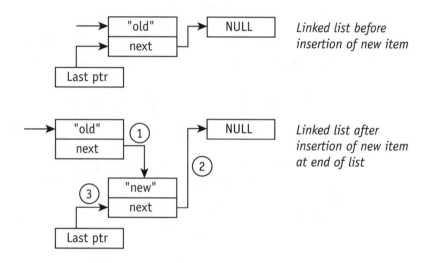

Linked list before insertion of new item

Linked list after insertion of new item at end of list

Because the second step is automatically handled by the node constructor, the procedure takes only two statements:

```
last->next = new_node;   // (1) Set existing last node
                         //       to point to new node.
last = new_node;         // (3) Adjust end-of-list
                         //       indicator.
```

If you don't maintain a "last" pointer, you can always find the last node this way:

1 Set a temporary pointer, pNode, to point to the beginning of the list.

2 Access the "next" member of the node pointed to. As long as this member does not point to NULL, advance one position in the list.

Here's the code to implement this algorithm. The effect is to end up with pNode pointing to the last node in the list, because only the last node should point to NULL in its "next" field.

```
pNode = root;   // Start at beginning of list.
while (pNode != NULL && pNode->next != NULL)
      pNode = pNode->next;
```

An Alphabetical List

Maintaining a list by adding new nodes to the end is easy. But in this chapter we're going to do something more interesting: continually maintain the list in alphabetical order.

The general strategy for adding a node is to go through the list until you find the desired insertion point and then insert the new node. But it's not quite easy. Sometimes a node is added after an existing node; other times it must be inserted before the first node. The first case—inserting a new node into the middle of the list—is a two-step procedure:

1 Set the "next" member of the new node to point to the same node as the "next" member of the existing node. For example:

```
new_node->next = p_node->next;
```

2 Adjust the "next" member of the existing node to point directly to the new node.

```
p_node->next = new_node;
```

Imagine that a list looks like this before an item is inserted after "aaa."

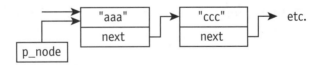

The following image shows the effect of the two statements.

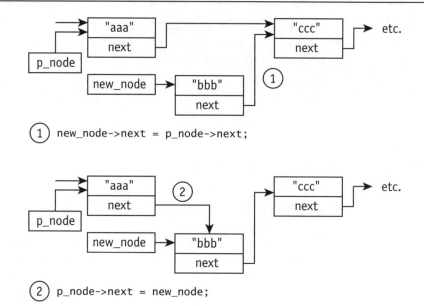

① new_node->next = p_node->next;

② p_node->next = new_node;

This insertion takes only two lines of code—wow, the program must be easy to write! But if the new node needs to be inserted at the beginning of the list, that operation must be handled separately, as a special case.

The procedure to insert a new node at the beginning of the list is:

1 Set the "next" member of the new node to point to the same node that root does. Remember that root is just a pointer to the first node.

```
new_node->next = root;
```

2 Adjust root so that it now points directly to the new node.

```
root = new_node;
```

Again, this takes just two lines of code. Assume that the current list starts with an entry that contains the string "bbb."

Now, we want to insert an item containing "aab." Clearly, this item must be inserted at the beginning of the list. The operation to insert "aab" can be pictured as shown here.

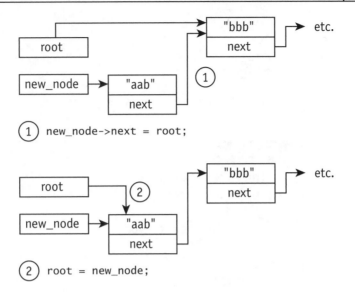

① `new_node->next = root;`

② `root = new_node;`

Armed with these programming techniques, we can now write a program that maintains nodes in alphabetical order.

Example 15.1. *Names in Alpha Order*

The virtue of this program example is that it supports any number of strings, and each of theses strings can be any size (thanks to the virtue of the STL string class, which, as we saw in the previous chapter, you can write yourself if you don't have STL support). The only restrictions are those imposed by the physical limitations of the computer, so you could—if you had time—sit down and enter millions of names.

(However, at that point you might begin to notice some degradation in performance, because the program has to traverse half the list, on average, before inserting each new name. If you have millions of entries, you ought to consider a more sophisticated data container.)

You might enter the following names:

```
Ringo
John
Paul
George
```

As soon as you are done entering names (indicating you are done by entering an empty string), the program prints out the names in alphabetical order:

George
John
Paul
Ringo

Without further ado, here is the program:

```
alphalist.cpp

  #include <iostream>
  #include <string>

  using namespace std;

  class node {
      public:
          string name;
          node *next;
          node(string input) {name = input; next = NULL;};
  };

  int main(int argc, char *argv[])
  {
      node *root = NULL;
      node *p_node, *new_node;
      string a_name;

      while (true) {
          cout << "Enter a name (or ENTER to exit): ";
          getline(cin, a_name);
          if (a_name.empty())
              break;
          new_node = new node(a_name);

          // If list is new or node goes at beginning,
          // then insert as root node. Otherwise,
          // search for a node to insert node AFTER.

          if (root == NULL || a_name < root->name) {
              new_node->next = root;
              root = new_node;
```

alphalist.cpp, cont.

```
        } else {
            p_node = root;
            while (p_node->next &&
                    a_name > p_node->next->name) {
                p_node = p_node->next;
            }
            new_node->next = p_node->next;
            p_node->next = new_node;
        }
    }
    p_node = root;      // Print out all nodes.
    while (p_node) {
        cout << p_node->name << endl;
        p_node = p_node->next;
    }
    system("PAUSE");
    return 0;
}
```

15

How It Works

The program may be longer than you expected, given that many operations take only a couple of statements, but remember that the program has to do a number of things.

First, the node class itself has to be declared. This is a simple class; its only member function is a constructor, which is convenient and saves work later.

```
class node {
    public:
        string name;
        node *next;
        node(string input)
            {name = input; next = NULL;};

};
```

The program enters a main loop that continues until broken. The first action is to prompt for a string and then break out of the loop if the string is empty (meaning the user just pressed ENTER). Otherwise, it creates a node and initializes it with the specified string.

```
              cout << "Enter a name (or ENTER to exit):
";
              getline(cin, a_name);
              if (a_name.empty())
                    break;
              new_node = new node(a_name);
```

So far, so good. The constructor made it easy to create and initialize a node. (And note that the "next" member is always initialized to NULL.) The problem remains: Where exactly in the list do we insert the new node?

One possibility is that the node needs to be inserted at the very beginning of the list. Another possibility is that the list is empty and this is the first node to be added. The following statements smoothly handle both of these cases:

```
      if (root == NULL || a_name < root->name) {
              new_node->next = root;
              root = new_node;
      }
```

If root is equal to NULL (or **nullptr**, if you are writing with a C++0x-compliant compiler), the list is empty. Alternatively, if the new name, a_name, is alphabetically less than the root node's "name" member, a_name comes before the root node in alphabetical order. In either case, the new node should become the root node.

Otherwise, the program has to search for an insertion point. That is, it searches for an existing node *after which* the new node should be inserted.

```
      p_node = root;
      while (p_node->next &&
              a_name > p_node->next->name) {
                  p_node = p_node->next;
      }
```

The first statement is obvious enough: Start traversing through the list beginning with the root (first node). Then the code asks, should I keep advancing through the list?

We already know the list is not empty and the new name is to be alphabetically placed after the first node—so it's not inserted at the beginning. The condition here asks the following: Is there another node left to compare to, and is the new string (a_name) alphabetically later than the string in the *next* node? The condition employs a look-ahead to the next node:

```
                  a_name > p_node->next->name
```

If the condition is true, a_name is not only alphabetically later than the current node (which we assume) but the next node in the list as well. In that case, the program advances one position through the list:

```
p_node = p_node->next;
```

Eventually, the correct insertion point (the point *after which* to insert the new node) is found. Inserting the new node is then easy enough, as described in an earlier section.

```
new_node->next = p_node->next;
p_node->next = new_node;
```

The list is maintained in a continually sorted order, because each new node is added in its proper place.

When the user is done entering names, the program just prints out all the values of the strings in the order found in the list. (This requires going back to the beginning and starting with the root node.)

```
p_node = root;        // Print out all nodes.
while (p_node) {
        cout << p_node->name << endl;
        p_node = p_node->next;
}
```

Dealing with Memory Leaks

The linked-list program has one defect. It causes memory leaks: It requests memory blocks and then fails to release them.

```
delete p_node;
```

Because computers come equipped with so much memory these days, you may not feel the effect of leaks for a long time. But if you run badly written programs—programs that do not properly release memory—eventually you'll get an "insufficient memory" message and wonder why you have to reboot.

So, before we go any further, it's a good idea to release memory allocated with **new**.

But once you release the memory attached to a node, you no longer can use the node, so how do you get to the rest of the list? Fortunately, there's an easy solution: Use a temporary variable.

```
void delete_list(node *p_node) {
        node *temp;
```

```
      while (p_node) {
          temp = p_node;
          p_node = p_node->next;
          delete temp;
      }
  }
```

Given this function, you delete the entire list by passing the address of the first node:

```
  delete_list(root);
```

This is an iterative solution because it uses a straightforward **while** loop that traverses the list and deletes nodes as it goes along. It works because it uses a look-ahead approach, saving the address of the next node just before deleting the current node.

A more elegant but less efficient approach is to use recursion. In this version, a call to the function deletes the portion of the list *to the right* of the node selected (through a recursive call). Then and only then does it delete the node itself.

```
  void delete_list(node *p_node) {
      if (p_node->next)                    // If not at end,
          delete_list(p_node->next);   //    delete list.
      delete p_node;                       // Delete me.
  }
```

This certainly looks more efficient, doesn't it? But this is misleading. Conceptually it is elegant because it uses the simplifying device of recursion so beautifully: We assume the problem is already solved for the N−1 case and have to solve only the Nth case. Here we assume that the program already knows how to delete the rest of the list (that is, the portion to the right of the current node).

C++ Only: Using Smart Pointers to Clean Up

C++0x ▶ This section applies to C++0x-compliant compilers only.

If you are working with a C++0x-compliant compiler, an even easier solution is open to you: Use smart pointers. C++ keeps track of all references to objects using smart pointers. When the last of those references goes out of scope, the object itself is deleted.

To use smart pointers with this example, declare all node pointers with the shared_ptr keyword:

```
  shared_ptr<type>  pointer;
```

The node class declaration now looks like this:

```
class node {
    public:
        string name;
        shared_ptr<node> next;
        node(string input) {name = input; next = NULL;};
};
```

The current node has a reference to the next node. So if the current node is to be deleted and if the next node has no other references to it that don't also need to be deleted, C++ deletes the next node. Through a recursive process, the entire list gets deleted as the variable root goes out of scope.

Note that you use a shared pointer with the same indirection operators (* and ->) you use with a standard pointer. For example:

```
p_node = p_node->next;
```

Interlude | **Recursion vs. Iteration Compared**

The recursive solution for deleting a list is tempting—the code for that approach is shorter. But is it more efficient? The truth is, as much as I pushed recursion in Chapter 4, if you have a choice between an iterative and a recursive solution, the iterative solution is usually more efficient. In these days of super-fast processors, that difference may not matter. You may prefer the recursive solution because you get to write fewer lines of code. But it's useful to consider what happens with recursion.

A recursive solution causes a function call at each level. In the linked-list example, there'd be one additional function call for each node. And if the list were a million nodes long, the system would have to execute a million function calls!

When we get into numbers like that, function-call overhead gets expensive. The program traverses the list and puts the addresses of each node on the special C++ stack segment—that's the area in memory reserved for holding arguments and local variables. The functions then return, popping addresses off the stack and deleting nodes, in reverse order. For example:

```
0x1000ff40
0x1000ff30
0x1000ff20
0x1000ff10
Etc.
```

▼ *continued on next page*

Interlude

▼ *continued*

In contrast, the iterative solution goes through the list and deletes the nodes in the order it finds them. The recursive solution, in contrast, is a "breadcrumb" solution that leaves a trail of breadcrumbs as it traverses the list (metaphorically speaking) and then goes back and picks up the crumbs, deleting nodes in the process. But that's inefficient.

Yet recursion is not only more elegant, but for a certain class of problem, it is the only practical solution. The Tower of Hanoi puzzle, which we'll return to shortly, would be vastly more difficult to solve without recursion. And there's an even bigger class of recursive problem: The C++ code that built the compiler you're using now involves a lot of recursive function calls, without which it would've been far more difficult to write.

EXERCISES

Exercise 15.1.1.   Revise the example so that it destroys nodes upon exit. If you have a C++0x-complaint compiler, use **shared_ptr** declarations; also replace NULL in the code with **nullptr**.

Exercise 15.1.2.   Revise the program so it prints nodes in reverse alphabetical order. This requires revising the insertion logic. (But, there is a shortcut that uses nearly all the existing program code yet uses simple recursion to print out nodes in reverse order.)

Exercise 15.1.3.   Write a program (or revise the existing example) to use nodes containing numeric data, such as age and salary. Keep nodes sorted first by age and then by name. (Hint: It might help to write comparison functions for the > and < operators.)

Tower of Hanoi, Animated

Chapter 4 showed how to solve the Tower of Hanoi puzzle by printing instructions on how to move the rings. But wouldn't it be more fun to *watch* the rings move around?

Of course, this requires more programming. We need to track the state of each of the three stacks. Let's say that each of the rings has a number that indicates its relative size, 1 being the smallest and 0 indicating an empty space. So, for example, if there are four rings total, then the following is true:

▶ An empty stack has array values {0, 0, 0, 0}; tos = 3.

▶ A stack with just one ring, the third largest, has {0, 0, 0, 3}; tos = 2.

▶ If the smallest ring is pushed onto that stack, it has {0, 0, 1, 3}; tos = 1.

▶ A full stack has array values {1, 2, 3, 4}; tos = -1.

The top-of-stack value, tos, is an array index one position "higher" than the top ring. Before a ring is popped, tos for the stack increases, pointing to a "lower" position. After a ring is pushed onto a stack, its tos value decreases, indicating a "higher" position.

This may seem counterintuitive, but when the stacks need to be displayed, this approach is easiest. The first array position in each stack corresponds to the physically highest position. Gravity pulls the rings down, so the top position is usually empty space (0).

1. State of stacks just prior to n = stacks[0].pop();

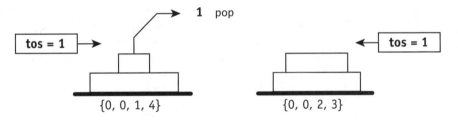

```
{0, 0, 1, 4}        {0, 0, 2, 3}
```

2. State of stacks just after stacks[1].push(n);

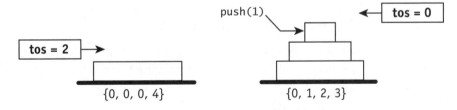

```
{0, 0, 0, 4}        {0, 1, 2, 3}
```

Mystack Class Design

To store the ring positions for the three stacks (pole positions), we need to create a data structure called a stack. Earlier, I discussed a special area of memory called "*the* stack," which stores arguments and local variables. But that's not the stack I'm talking about here.

This example calls for a special, customized stack class. Unlike most stacks, this class has to allow for empty space at the top, letting the rings fall to the bottom. The first few places may contain 0. When the program displays a picture of the three stacks, you'll see why this approach is necessary.

We need to design our own customized "stack" class—let's call it "mystack"—from which three objects will be created. The class has the design shown here.

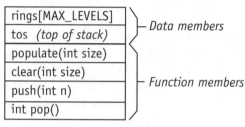

Mystack class

The rings array contains most of the data: It stores rings of different sizes by using a series of integers, 1 indicating the smallest ring and 0 indicating empty space. (So, {1, 2, 3} indicates the three smallest rings, and {0, 0, 2} indicates the second smallest ring, with two empty spaces above it.) The tos member signifies the top-of-the-stack position.

The previous section illustrated the use of the push and pop functions. These are common operations on any kind of stack.

The populate and clear functions perform initialization that's useful if you want the program to be able to reset and start over.

Using the Mystack Class

Once the Mystack class is declared, we use it by creating three of these customized stack objects and initializing them. The three objects are placed in an array.

```
mystack  stacks[3];
```

At the beginning of each animation cycle, the following happens:

▶ `stacks[0].populate( )` is called to fill the first stack.

▶ `stacks[1].clear( )` and `stacks[2].clear( )` are called to set the other stacks to the empty state.

This approach provides a lot of flexibility. As long as the size doesn't exceed MAX_LEVELS (a constant declared at the beginning of the program), the animation can be restarted with any size requested by the user. For example, if the stack size is 5, the populate and clear functions are called to fill the first stack with values 1 to 5 and to leave the other two stacks empty (0 value) in the first five positions.

stacks[0] = {1, 2, 3, 4, 5}   stacks[1] = {0, 0, 0, 0, 0}   stacks[2] = {0, 0, 0, 0, 0}

With this array of three objects in place (each of which contains its own array), we can now move rings between the three positions by calling pop and push as appropriate and then, after each move, printing a picture that represents the new state.

Example 15.2.   *Animated Tower*

With the Mystack class design in place, we can now write the animated version of Tower of Hanoi. This program builds on the Tower of Hanoi example in Chapter 4, using the recursive logic there to solve the problem of moving all the rings from pole 1 to pole 3.

Remember the two constraints: You can move only one ring at a time, and a larger ring can never be placed on a smaller ring.

This version solves the problem and displays the state of the three poles (that is, the three stacks of rings) after each and every move.

```
tower_visi.cpp

    #include <iostream>

    using namespace std;

    #define MAX_LEVELS   10
```

▼ *continued on next page*

```
// Declare three pole positions, or rather, stacks.
// Each stack is an object containing ring values.
// stacks[3] is an array three of these objects.

class mystack {
   public:
       int rings[MAX_LEVELS];  // Array of ring values.
       int tos;                // Top-of-stack index.
       void populate(int size);  // Initialize stack.
       void clear(int size);     // Clear the stack.
       void push(int n);
       int pop(void);
} stacks[3];

void mystack::populate(int size) {
    for (int i = 0; i < size; i++)
        rings[i] = i + 1;
    tos = -1;
}

void mystack::clear(int size) {
    for (int i = 0; i < size; i++)
        rings[i] = 0;
    tos = size - 1;
}

void mystack::push(int n) {
    rings[tos--] = n;
}

int mystack::pop(void) {
    int n = rings[++tos];
    rings[tos] = 0;
    return n;
}

void move_stacks(int src, int dest, int other, int n);
void move_a_ring(int source, int dest);
void print_stacks(void);
void pr_chars(int ch, int n);
```

```cpp
int stack_size = 7;

int main() {
    stacks[0].populate(stack_size);
    stacks[1].clear(stack_size);
    stacks[2].clear(stack_size);
    print_stacks();
    move_stacks(stack_size, 0, 2, 1);
    return 0;
}

// Move stacks: solve problem recursively...
// move N stacks by assuming problem solved for N-1.
// src = source stack, dest = destination stack.
//
void move_stacks(int n, int src, int dest, int other){
    if (n == 1)
        move_a_ring(src, dest);
    else {
        move_stacks(n-1, src, other, dest);
        move_a_ring(src, dest);
        move_stacks(n-1, other, dest, src);
    }
}

// Move a Ring: Pop off a ring from source (src) stack,
// place it on destination stack, and print new state.
//
void move_a_ring(int source, int dest) {
    int n = stacks[source].pop();  // Pop off source.
    stacks[dest].push(n);          // Push onto dest.
    print_stacks();                // Show new state.
}

// Print Stacks: For each physical level, print the
// ring for each of the three stacks.
//
void print_stacks(void) {
    int n = 0;
```

▼ continued on next page

```
        for (int i = 0; i < stack_size; i++) {
            for (int j = 0; j < 3; j++) {
                n = stacks[j].rings[i];
                pr_chars(' ', 12 - n);
                pr_chars('*', 2 * n);
                pr_chars(' ', 12 - n);
            }
            cout << endl;
        }
        system("PAUSE");
    }

    void pr_chars(int ch, int n) {
        for (int i = 0; i < n; i++)
            cout << (char) ch;
    }
```

How It Works

The core of this program is a recursive function that works just like the Tower of Hanoi solution in Chapter 4; see that chapter for an explanation of the logic. Much of the time this function, move_stacks, calls itself. Only sometimes does it actually get around to moving a ring.

But the difference comes when it's time to actually move a ring: Instead of just printing a message, this version calls a new function, move_a_ring, that takes care of the details of moving a single ring from one stack to another and displaying the result.

```
// Move stacks: solve problem recursively...
// move N stacks by assuming problem solved for N-1.
// src = source stack, dest = destination stack.
//
void move_stacks(int n, int src, int dest, int other){
    if (n == 1)
        move_a_ring(src, dest);
    else {
        move_stacks(n-1, src, other, dest);
        move_a_ring(source, dest);
        move_stacks(n-1, other, dest, src);
    }
}
```

Now, how exactly do we move a single ring from one position to another?

There was no way to do this in the version in Chapter 4, which just printed a general message. But now, since we have three stack objects that reflect the current state, we manipulate that state by doing the following:

1 Pop the top ring off the source stack and store its size as N.

2 Push a ring of size N onto the destination stack.

3 Print the new state.

That's exactly what the move_a_ring function does in three simple statements:

```
// Move a Ring: Pop off a ring from source stack,
// place it on destination stack, and print new state.
//
void move_a_ring(int source, int dest) {
    int n = stacks[source].pop(); // Pop off source.
    stacks[dest].push(n);         // Push onto dest.
    print_stacks();               // Show new state.
}
```

The pop and push functions are member functions defined for the class. These are short functions that use the top-of-stack indicator, tos, to get the top ring from the stack (pop) or to put a new ring onto the top of the stack (push).

Remember that member functions are defined at the class level (mystack) and used at the object level (stacks[ ]).

```
void mystack::push(int n) {
    rings[tos--] = n;
}
```

```
int mystack::pop(void) {
    int n = rings[++tos];
    rings[tos] = 0;
    return n;
}
```

The pop function has to get the size number of the ring at the top of the stack and also replace that ring with empty space, 0, thus removing the ring from the stack.

Finally, the program uses print_stacks and a convenient support function, pr_chars, to print the current state.

15

You should now be able to see why the program uses 0 to indicate empty space and why 0s must be placed "above" the positive ring values. That is, if a stack is less than full, then there will be one or more 0s in the topmost (early) positions. Where there is a 0 at a particular level (meaning no ring is there), the program prints blanks spaces. This arrangement reflects the physics of the simulation: Rings fall to the bottom!

In programmatic terms: The function accesses the rings[] array of each object, getting the value for an entire physical level before moving on to the next level. If the ring value is 0 for a particular position, nothing is printed but blank spaces. (This reflects the empty space atop a less-than-full stack.) If the ring value is greater than 0, the program prints two asterisks (*) times the size of the ring and prints spaces around it. For example, if the ring size is 3, the program prints six asterisks.

```
// Print Stacks: For each physical level, print the
// ring for each of the three stacks.
//
void print_stacks(void) {
    int n = 0;
    for (int i = 0; i < stack_size; i++) {
        for (int j = 0; j < 3; j++) {
            n = stacks[j].rings[i];
            pr_chars(' ', 12 - n);
            pr_chars('*', 2 * n);
            pr_chars(' ', 12 - n);
        }
        cout << endl;
    }
    system("PAUSE");
}
```

The pr_chars function is just a handy way of printing repeated characters.

```
void pr_chars(int ch, int n) {
    for (int i = 0; i < n; i++)
        cout << (char) ch;
}
```

EXERCISES

Exercise 15.2.1.   Prompt the user for how many rings to use in the starting position. This number should be no more than MAX_LEVELS (which we set to 10, largely because of screen-space considerations). Then repeat: If the user enters 0, then end the program; otherwise, continue with a new session. With this version, the use of the populate and clear member functions becomes evident. You need to be able to reset the initial state.

Exercise 15.2.2.   Instead of implementing rings as an array inside each object, implement it as a pointer of type **int***. Then use **new**, within the populate and clear member functions, to allocate a series of integers. Can you use the **delete** keyword to efficiently prevent memory leaks in this situation?

Chapter 15   *Summary*

Here are the main points of Chapter 15:

▶ Some C++ code deals heavily with pointers to objects. With such pointers, it's convenient to use the indirection operator -> to access a member of the object pointed to. For example:

```
// Get the num member of object pointed to.
int n = pFraction->num;

// Call the set function for object pointed to.
pFraction->set(0, 1);
```

▶ The use of dynamic memory allocation, along with pointers, to objects makes it possible to create complex structures in memory such as lists and trees. These can be as simple or complex as you choose. (Note, however, that the STL **list** class introduced in the next chapter provides a simpler way to support a standard list container.)

▶ Use the **new** keyword to dynamically allocate an object at runtime. (This keyword was first introduced in Chapter 14.)

```
Node *pNode = new Node;
```

▶ When you create your own lists and trees in memory, it becomes important to prevent memory leaks by deleting each individual object as soon as you know you no longer need it. Programs that fail to deal with memory leaks can cause your computer to prematurely run low on memory and need to be rebooted.

▶ Use the **delete** keyword to release objects and free up memory.

```
delete p;      // p points to an object
delete[] p;    // p points to an array of objects.
```

▶ Recursion is sometimes the only practical way to solve a problem, as in the Tower of Hanoi. But otherwise, if there is both an iterative (loop-based) and recursive solution, the iterative version is almost always more efficient.

Easy Programming with STL

I couldn't really introduce the Standard Template Library (STL) without first introducing the core C++ language and the basics of dealing with classes and pointers. But now that you've mastered those ideas, not only will you find the STL useful, but you may end up loving it. It makes some complex programming tasks much easier.

These days, the great majority of C++ compilers in wide use now provide full support for STL. (If you have one of the rare compilers that doesn't, of course, you may want to skip this chapter.) If your compiler is C++0x compliant, it should definitely support STL.

Introducing the List Template

STL—again, that's the Standard Template Library—provides broad support for new classes, mostly in the form of templates.

A *template* is a generalized class that can be used to create unlimited container types. The basic idea is that you specify an underlying type (**int**, **string**, and Fraction in the following examples), and STL builds a sophisticated container around this type. Here is how you use the **list** template:

```
list<int>        iList;        // List of integers
list<string>     strList;      // List of strings
list<Fraction>   bunchOFract;  // List of Fractions
```

All these create a linked list similar to the kind we developed in Chapter 15, except that (as you'll see), the STL version is more powerful and versatile.

There's no limit to how many kinds of linked lists you can create this way. You can write your own class—although, as described later, your class may need to support certain operator functions to fully work—and plug it into the **list** template. STL does the rest of the work!

413

Note ▶ All the STL names are part of the **std** namespace, which means you must either use the characters **std::** before each and every STL name such as "stack" or "list" or just keep **using namespace std;** in your programs, as I have been suggesting in every example.

Interlude

Writing Templates in C++

The earliest versions of C++ contained no support for writing templates at all. But within a few years of C++'s first appearance, programmers (especially professional programmers) were clamoring for template support.

The template technology is still one of the most advanced realizations of the philosophy of reusable code, which says once a problem has been solved, it shouldn't have to be solved again.

Templates take this idea to the level of general algorithms. Once a mechanism has been created to contain integers, for example, it should be possible to reuse the same code with other data types: **double**, for example, or strings, or objects of any class. It's as though someone took a set of container classes and related functions and did a global search-and-replace operation, replacing all instances of **int** with some other type.

C++ provides strong support for writing your own template classes and template functions. For example, you can use the template keyword to declare a generalized container class called "pair":

```
template class<T>
class pair {
public:
    T first, last;
};
```

Given this declaration, you can then declare any number of "pair" container classes:

```
pair<int>     intPair;
pair<double>  floatPair;
pair<string>  full_name;

intPair.first = 12;
```

However, for the most part, the subject of writing your own templates is outside the scope of this book. This book is intended as a general introduction to how to write programs in C++ and how to think like a C++ pro-

▼ *continued*

Interlude

grammer. Writing your own templates is a subject that—if covered in full detail—could easily add a few hundred pages.

Template writing is an advanced but fascinating topic. A number of excellent advanced texts are devoted exclusively to that subject.

But, although the subject of writing your own templates is outside the scope of this book, I encourage even relatively new C++ programmers to take advantage of the Standard Template Library as soon as they understand classes and pointers. STL classes are amazing time-savers and are easy to use. Someone else has done the work; you take advantage of that work.

Creating and Using a List Class

Before using the list template, you need to turn on support for it by using an **#include** directive.

```
#include <list>
```

Then you can create your own linked-list classes. The syntax for declaring an STL list class is as follows:

```
list<type>   list_name;
```

Here are some more examples. This is really easy to use once you understand the pattern.

```
#include <list>
...
list<int>      list_of_ints;
list<int>      another_list;
list<double>   list_of_floatingpt;
list<Point>    list_of_pts;
list<string>   LS;
```

Once you have created a list, it starts out empty, and you need to add elements to it. You can do this with the **push_back** member function. This adds elements to the end (that is, the back) of the list. For example:

```
list<string>   LS;

LS.push_back("Able");
LS.push_back("Baker");
LS.push_back("Charlie");
```

16

You can also use the **push_front** member function, which adds elements to the front of the list. If you think about it, the effect is the same except that it ends up adding the strings in reverse order:

```
LS.push_front("Able");
LS.push_front("Baker");
LS.push_front("Charlie");
```

For a numeric list, of course, you could add numeric elements:

```
list<int>  list_of_ints;
```

```
list_of_ints.push_back(100);
```

OK, we can create a linked list of any base type and add data to it. To do much more than this, you usually need *iterators*.

Creating and Using Iterators

A number of templates in STL use iterators, which are devices for stepping through a list one element at a time—that is, *iterating* through it.

Iterators look and feel a great deal like pointers—especially in their use of ++, --, and * operators—even though there are differences. You declare an iterator this way:

```
list<type>::iterator  iterator_name;
```

For example, to declare a list and an iterator for it, you could use these statements:

```
list<string>            LS;
list<string>::iterator  iter;
```

Now iter can be used to iterate through the list LS, since their underlying types (**string**) are compatible.

STL lists have **begin** and **end** functions that return an iterator to the beginning and the end of the list, respectively. The following statement uses **begin** to initialize an iterator:

```
list<string>::iterator iter = LS.begin();
```

For a string list LS with four elements, you can visualize the operation this way.

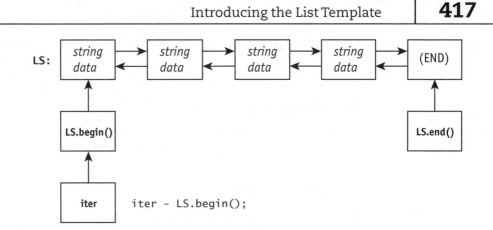

Properly initialized, iter can now be used almost like a pointer. You can make iter point to the next item by using the increment operator:

```
iter++;    // Advance one element in the list.
```

The effect of incrementing the iterator can be visualized this way.

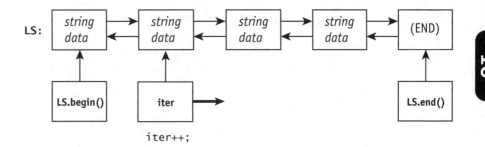

To access the data pointed to by the iterator, apply the indirection operator (*) just as you would with a pointer.

```
cout << *iter << endl;    // Print string pointed to.
```

Putting all this together, we can write a loop that prints all the elements of the list, one to a line. This works because the **end** member function produces an iterator that points to *the position just after the last element*, not the last element itself. Therefore, if we are at the end position, we've processed all the elements. We're done!

Conversely, if we haven't reached **LS.end()**, we are *not* done. That makes the loop condition easy to write.

```
iter = LS.begin();            // Start at beginning.
while (iter != LS.end()) {    // While not done,
```

```
        cout << *iter << endl;      //   Print string
        iter++;                     //   Advance to next.
    }
```

This can be written more succinctly as follows:

```
for (iter = LS.begin();  iter != LS.end();  iter++)
    cout << *iter << endl;
```

C++0x Only: For Each

`C++0x` ▶ The following paragraph applies to C++0x-compliant compilers only.

With the ranged-based **for** syntax introduced in Chapter 10, it's even easier to print out all the items in a list. You don't even need to use an iterator.

```
for (auto x : LS)
    cout << x << endl;
```

Interlude

Pointers vs. Iterators

By now you can see why I stated that iterators look a lot like pointers. The designers of STL classes deliberately made iterators look and feel like pointers in order to work smoothly with the rest of the C++ language. Reusing prefix and postfix increment (++) is convenient—they do what you'd expect them to do—as is using the indirection operator (*). And all this is supported by C++'s operator-overloading syntax.

But don't confuse iterators with true pointers, or what we might call "raw" pointers. The latter offer no protection against invalid memory access, and so (as I stressed in Chapter 6) you must be much more careful with pointers.

Iterators are safe and designed to be that way. The program can attempt to increment an iterator off the end of a cliff, so to speak (by iterating past the end of a container or list), but if it does so, nothing drastic happens. The iterator no longer accesses data inside the container. An out-of-control pointer can overwrite and corrupt memory all over the system, but an iterator on the loose can't touch anything it shouldn't.

Example 16.1. *STL Ordered List*

We now have nearly all the knowledge of iterator and list syntax to write an ordered list program, that is, a shorter version of the customized alphabetically ordered list in Chapter 15. When you see how much shorter this version is, you'll see why programmers love STL.

We need to add just one piece to the puzzle, however. STL list classes come with a built-in sort function, among other things.

```
LS.sort();        // Sort the list alphabetically.
```

Note ▶ To support this function and all the other member functions, the underlying data type of the list must define reasonable behaviors for the less-than operator (<) as well as the assignment and test-for equality operators (= and ==). The string class, of course, already defines these behaviors.

Now, here is the complete program:

```
alphalist2.cpp

   #include <iostream>
   #include <list>
   #include <string>

   using namespace std;

   int main(int argc, char *argv[])
   {
       string s;
       list<string> LS;
       list<string>::iterator iter;

       while (true) {
             cout << "Enter string (ENTER to exit): ";
             getline(cin, s);
             if (s.size() == 0)
                   break;
             LS.push_back(s);
       }
       LS.sort();        // Sort, and then print elements.
```
▼ *continued on next page*

16

```
        for (iter = LS.begin(); iter != LS.end(); iter++)
            cout << *iter << endl;

        system("PAUSE");
        return 0;
    }
```

How It Works

This is a remarkably short program considering all it does. Like the longer version in Chapter 15, this version lets the user enter any number of strings of any size (subject only to the physical limits of the system itself). After the user is done, the program prints them all in alphabetical order. For example, if I enter the following strings

```
John
Paul
George
Ringo
Brian Epstein
```

the program prints the names in this order:

```
Brian Epstein
George
John
Paul
Ringo
```

Most of this program logic you've seen before. Half the statements in **main** do nothing more than prompt the user for input and then add a string to the end of the list by using LS.push_back(). As usual, if the user just presses ENTER, resulting in a string of zero length, that is taken as a convenient "I'm done" signal.

```
        while (true) {
            cout << "Enter string (ENTER to exit): ";
            getline(cin, s);
            if (s.size() == 0)
                break;
            LS.push_back(s);
        }
```

The real power of the class is revealed by one call to **sort**, a power member function.

```
LS.sort();
```

Then finally, the iterator (iter) is used to print all the members. This is easy, because the sorting has all been done.

As explained earlier, STL iteration makes a function like this easy to write. In particular, when the iteration reaches `LS.end()`, that means the iteration has moved *one past the last element in the list*...and so the work is done.

Conversely, a condition of `iter != LS.end()` means the list has not been entirely processed, and so work should continue.

```
for (iter = LS.begin(); iter != LS.end(); iter++)
    cout << *iter << endl;
```

A Continually Sorted List

One of the virtues of the alphabetical list in Chapter 15 is that it is always in alphabetical order, because as each new string is added to the list, it is inserted into its alphabetically correct position. Consequently, the list is always sorted, and the program doesn't have to periodically sort the elements.

Theoretically, that should make program performance smoother, because there is no waiting for the entire list to get sorted. Of course, in these days of super-fast processors, you are unlikely to notice such delays anyway.

Still, it is useful to see whether you can support a continually sorted list with STL list functions. It turns out to be incredibly easy! Instead of using this statement to add a string

```
LS.push_back(s);
```

you use these statements. The **insert** function inserts a new element (in this case, a string) just before the element pointed to by the iterator.

```
for(iter = LS.begin(); iter != LS.end() && s > *iter;)
    iter++;
SL.insert(iter, s);
```

How can it be this easy? One reason is that, once again, `iter != LS.end()` is such a convenient test condition. Because `LS.end()` corresponds to *one position past the last element*, it enables the loop to test every element, from beginning to end, inclusive.

The other thing that makes this loop easy to write is that the STL **insert** function is robust, meaning it behaves well in potentially bad situations, removing the need to deal with special cases. Consider what happens if the list is empty. In that case, the **insert** function indulges you by adding s as the first element.

Or what if the iterator, iter, gets to the very end without finding an insertion point? In that case, the **insert** function does exactly what you'd want: It adds s to the very end of the list, inserting it just before the "end"—meaning just *after* the element that's currently last.

EXERCISES

Exercise 16.1.1. Revise Example 16.1 so that it uses the approach just shown in the "Variation" section, keeping a continually sorted list.

Exercise 16.1.2. Create an employee record class (emp_rec) that tracks the last name, first name, age (an integer), and job level (another integer) for each employee. Then write comparison (operator< and operator==) functions that sort them according to the order: last name, first name, job level, age. Finally, base an ordered list program around this class.

Exercise 16.1.3. Write a version of this program that works with Fraction objects. Note that you'll need to add an operator function in the Fraction calls for the less-than operator (<), or the **sort** function won't work on lists of fractions.

Designing an RPN Calculator

No, this isn't a calculator for Registered Practicing Nurses; it's the amazing Reverse Polish Notation (RPN) calculator, which can take an input line of any complexity, analyze it, and perform all the calculations specified.

This may sound daunting, and to be honest, it's a project usually reserved for very serious computer science majors at leading colleges and universities. (If that description fits you, at least you know you're getting down to serious projects.) But the STL, along with the **strtok** function from the standard C++ library, does most of the work for you.

The beauty of RPN is that it specifies mathematical and logical expressions unambiguously, removing the need for parentheses. As a grammar, it has just two rules:

```
expression → numeric-literal
expression → expression  expression  operator
```

What this says is that every expression to be evaluated is either a simple number (that's easy enough) or two expressions followed by an operator. Do you see how recursive this is? The important point is that smaller expressions can be recombined inside larger ones.

If you don't get this yet, stay with me just a bit. Most obviously, RPN notation can evaluate something like this:

```
2  3  +
```

This means "Add 2 and 3." The result is 5. This works because *expression expression operator* is valid; 2 and 3, each being numeric literals, are valid expressions and they are followed by an operator (+). So far, so good. Now consider this more complex expression:

```
2  3  +  17  10  -  *
```

When you understand RPN, this is clear. An expression can be made up of any two operands (subexpressions) followed by an operator. (In effect, the operator that is closest to the operands has precedence.) 2 3 + is a valid expression, but so is 17 10 -. These two expressions are then followed by multiplication (*), forming one larger expression.

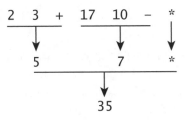

The answer is 35, and the RPN expression shown earlier is equivalent to the following input line using standard notation (also called *infix* notation):

```
(2 + 3)  *  (17 - 10)
```

And now you see the disadvantage of standard arithmetic notation. It is heavily dependent on parentheses. But RPN does away with the need for parentheses.

By the way, to complete the syntax, we ought to list the operators supported:

```
operator  →  +
operator  →  *
operator  →  -
operator  →  /
```

Or we can express this syntax in one line with "OR." Note that the uses of OR are not in bold, which means they are not intended literally.

```
operator → + OR * OR - OR /
```

Here are some more examples of Reverse Polish Notation:

```
2 10 5 4 - / +          // ==>  2 + (10 / (5 - 4))
1 2 3 * * 10 9 - +      // ==>  (1 * 2 * 3) + (10 - 9)
5 3 - 15 *              // ==>  (5 - 3) * 15
```

Interlude

A Brief History of Polish Notation

Polish Notation was invented by a distinguished philosopher, professor, and logician named Jan Łukasiewicz. Although little known to the general public in most countries, he made significant contributions to early-twentieth-century systems of axiomatic logic.

In 1920, Professor Łukasiewicz created a scheme to remove the need for parentheses from logical expressions, thus making those expressions more succinct, but the scheme is equally applicable to math. He named it Polish Notation in honor of his nationality. In his version—which we might call *forward* Polish notation—operators are prefixes, as in:

```
+ 2 3
```

In the early 1960s, computer scientists F. L. Bauer and E. W. Dijkstra invented a similar scheme but used operator suffixes rather than prefixes. They named it Reverse Polish Notation, honoring Łukasiewicz for inventing it first, albeit with prefixes.

Reverse Polish Notation (or RPN) became widely used by the public in the 1970s and 1980s when it was used in many hand-held scientific calculators. RPN (as you'll see in this chapter) is particularly easy to implement on a stack-based computing system. RPN is still the basis of some existing programming languages such as PostFix.

Is it possible for computers to implement *forward* Polish notation? Yes, but it is much more difficult because when you read an operator, you don't know what to apply it to yet. Your best bet in writing a forward Polish interpreter is to read all the items (tokens) into a list and then reverse the list!

Using a Stack for RPN

If you've read the chapters of this book in sequence, you've come across the term *stack* before. First, there's "*the* stack," which is used to store local variables, argument values, and return addresses.

Then there's the customized stack we built in Chapter 15 for the Tower of Hanoi puzzle. This is a very special stack because it does something unusual: keeping track of empty spaces. For example, if a pole for a five-ring puzzle had the two smallest rings, this state of affairs is notated as {0, 0, 0, 1, 2}.

STL provides support for a generalized stack class that does a lot of the same things as these other stacks, although it doesn't have all the features of Tower of Hanoi. An STL stack is a simple last-in-first-out (LIFO) mechanism that accountants are so familiar with.

Here's how it is used to implement an RPN calculator. Again, consider the input line:

```
2 3 + 17 10 - *
```

OK, how can we attack this? Common sense tells us a couple of things: First, when the program reads a number, it must save it for later use; second, when the program reads an operator, it should perform an operation and save the result.

The strategy is therefore as follows:

1 When the program reads a number, it pushes it on top of a stack.

2 When the program reads an operator (+, *, -, or /), it pops two values off the stack, computes the result, and pushes this result back onto the stack. Because a last-in-first-out mechanism is used, an operator will bind to the nearest two expressions that precede it, which is exactly what we want.

Let's see how this works for the line of input 2 3 + 17 10 - *.

First, the algorithm reads the numbers 2 and 3 and pushes these numbers onto the stack. (In the figure that follows, sp is the stack pointer, indicating where the next element will be pushed to. STL provides no access to this pointer, but it's useful to visualize.)

High memory addresses

Low memory addresses

Next, the program reads an addition sign (+). It therefore pops two numbers, adds them, and pushes the result back on the stack, to be used later.

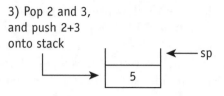

3) Pop 2 and 3,
and push 2+3
onto stack

Then the algorithm reads the next two numbers in the string, 17 and 10, and pushes these on top of the stack.

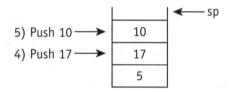

5) Push 10

4) Push 17

Next (we're almost done) the algorithm reads another operator: subtraction (-). Again, it pops the top two numbers, performs a calculation, and pushes the result onto the stack.

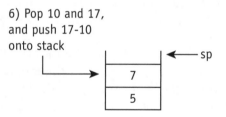

6) Pop 10 and 17,
and push 17-10
onto stack

Finally, the algorithm reads a multiplication operator (*). One final time, it pops two numbers. Then it multiplies them together and pushes the result onto the stack.

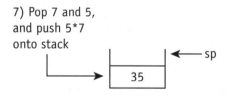

7) Pop 7 and 5,
and push 5*7
onto stack

The final result is 35, which is correct!

Introducing the Generalized STL Stack Class

In the previous section, we saw how a simple stack mechanism, storing numbers, could be used to implement a Reverse Polish Notation calculator. So, let's use an STL stack for the program.

Before using the list template, you need to turn on support for it by using an **#include** directive.

```
#include <stack>
```

You can then create a generalized stack mechanism with syntax similar to that used for STL lists:

stack<*type*> *stack_name*;

For example, you can create stacks with statements like this:

```
#include <stack>
...
stack<int>        stack_of_ints;
stack<Fraction>   stack_of_Fr;
stack<double>     xStack;
```

Each of these statements creates an empty stack. To insert elements, use the **push** member function. The most useful of the stack member functions are shown in this table:

STACK CLASS FUNCTION	DESCRIPTION
stack.**push**(*data*)	Pushes data (of stack's underlying type) onto top of stack.
stack.**top**()	Returns data (of stack's underlying type) from top of stack—but it does not remove data; for that, use **pop**.
stack.**pop**()	Removes top item of stack; does not return data.
stack.**size**()	Returns the number of items currently stored in the stack.
stack.**empty**()	Return true if stack is empty, false otherwise.

Using a stack class to push data onto the top of the stack is easy enough.

```
stack<int>        stack_of_ints;
...
stack_of_ints.push(-5);
```

However, the STL stack design splits the pop operation into two steps (and I don't know why it does this), so popping off an item requires a "top and pop" operation.

```
int n = stack_of_ints.top();   // Copy top of stack.
stack_of_ints.pop();           // Remove top of stack.
```

Example 16.2.   *Reverse Polish Calculator*

Although the following program involves about a page of code, that is still a small size for a program that does anything as useful as a calculator. The **strtok** function does most of the work of interpreting input; the STL stack class, num_stack, does most of the work of pushing and popping numbers off a stack.

```cpp
rpn.cpp

#include <iostream>
#include <cstring>
#include <stack>

using namespace std;
#define MAX_CHARS 100

int main(int argc, char *argv[])
{
    char input_str[MAX_CHARS+1], *p;
    stack<double>  num_stack;
    int c;
    double a, b, n;

    cout << "Enter RPN string: ";
    cin.getline(input_str, MAX_CHARS);
    p = strtok(input_str, " ");
    while (p) {
        c = p[0];
        if(c == '+' || c == '*' || c == '/' || c == '-'){
            if (num_stack.size() < 2) {
                cout << "Error: too many ops."<< endl;
                system("PAUSE");
                return -1;
            }
            b = num_stack.top(); num_stack.pop();
            a = num_stack.top(); num_stack.pop();
            switch (c) {
```

rpn.cpp, cont.

```
                case '+': n = a + b; break;
                case '*': n = a * b; break;
                case '/': n = a / b; break;
                case '-': n = a - b; break;
            }
            num_stack.push(n);
        } else {
            num_stack.push(atof(p));
        }
        p = strtok(NULL, " ");
    }
    cout <<"The answer is: "<< num_stack.top()<< endl;
    system("PAUSE");
    return 0;
}
```

How It Works

The program begins, as always, with **#include** directives. Note that <stack> is used to turn on support for the STL stack template.

```
#include <stack>
```

This enables a stack to be created built on any base type. What type is needed here?

Obviously, this should be **double**, the floating-point type. Integers would suffice for many calculations, but division tends to produce an unsatisfactory result with integers: C++ carries out division but then rounds down, throwing away the fractional portion. Use of floating-point ensures that division operations are accurate and precise.

The next statement creates a stack of type **double**:

```
stack<double>  num_stack;
```

Next, the program gets a line of string input from the user and starts to break it down. The **strtok** function, as explained in Chapter 7, finds the first "token" (that is, item) from the input string that is given as its first argument. The second argument lists the character or characters (in this case, a blank space) to be recognized as token separators.

```
p = strtok(input_str, " ");
```

The function returns a pointer to a substring that contains the first item token. Note that for this to work properly, each and every item must be separated by one or more spaces—including the operators. So, the following will work as expected:

```
2 3 +  17 10 -  *
```

but not this:

```
2 3+ 17 10-*
```

It might be reasonable to allow this input, but you'd need a more sophisticated lexical analyzer that you'd have to write yourself. Given the string-manipulation techniques in Chapter 7, writing such code is not that difficult: You'd need to read one character at a time and decide whether you've read an operator, space, or part of a digit string.

After the initial call to **strtok**, you get more tokens (items) by making subsequent calls to **strtok**, specifying NULL as the first argument. The program does this near the bottom of **main**.

```
p = strtok(NULL, " ");
```

C++0x ▶ If you have a C++-compliant compiler, you should use the **nullptr** keyword in preference to NULL.

The program enters a loop in which it processes the next token as long as there is another to process. The first step in responding to a token is to determine whether it is an operator (+, *, -, or /). If it is an operator, the program does several things.

The first response to an operator is to ensure there are at least two items on the stack. This is important because if you attempt to pop an empty stack, the STL **pop** function goes off into the Twilight Zone and hangs up the system. To prevent this, the program has a short error-checking section that prints an error message and exits if needed.

```
if (num_stack.size() < 2) {
    cout << "Error: too many ops." << endl;
    system("PAUSE");
    return -1;
}
```

The second response to an operator is to pop two numbers off the stack. These are put into b and a, in reverse order. Remember that a stack is a last-in-first-out device, so reverse order has to be observed.

```
b = num_stack.top(); num_stack.pop();
a = num_stack.top(); num_stack.pop();
```

With STL stack classes, you have to use a "top and pop" technique, because the two member functions—**top** and **pop**—each do only part of a "pop" operation. It's a little inconvenient, but we can live with it.

The third response to an operator is to perform the specified calculation and put the result back on the stack. The program uses **switch-case** logic explained in Chapter 9. Depending on whether the operator is +, *, /, or -, the program jumps to a different **case** statement, performs a calculation, and then breaks out of the **switch** block.

```
switch (c) {
    case '+': n = a + b; break;
    case '*': n = a * b; break;
    case '/': n = a / b; break;
    case '-': n = a - b; break;
}
num_stack.push(n);
```

OK, then, that takes care of everything that has to be done in response to an operator. If the item read (the token) is not an operator, the action to be taken is a great deal simpler. All we do is translate the item into a floating-point number and push it onto the stack.

```
num_stack.push(atof(p));
```

What if the item doesn't contain a valid number? For example, what if it contains letters instead? That's not a problem: **atof** returns 0 in that case, and there is no harm (for the most part) in operating on 0.

EXERCISES

Exercise 16.2.1.   Extend the RPN calculator in Example 16.2 by adding a unary operator signified by a pound sign (#). Have this operator take the reciprocal of its one operand. That is, x should yield 1/x. Remember that all four of the existing operators are binary operators, taking two operands. But the syntax for a unary operator is as follows:

expression → *expression*   *unary-op*

Exercise 16.2.2.   Example 16.2 is limited in its ability to process input: It can process input no longer than MAX_CHARS, which right now is arbitrarily set to 100. Revise the program so that it can input of any length whatsoever, subject only to the computer's physical capacities. (Hint: Use the STL string class. Review the previous sections in Chapter 7 if needed.)

Exercise 16.2.3.   Revise the program so that it keeps prompting the user for another line of input to calculate until the user enters an empty line by just pressing ENTER. That is to say, continue the cycle of prompting for input, interpreting it as RPN, and printing the answer, until the user wants to quit. Don't quit after one go-round. (By the way, to make sure this program works correctly every time, you ought to clear the stack before beginning a new operation.)

Correct Interpretation of Angle Brackets

Because brackets (< and >) have multiple uses in C++, ambiguity is possible when you get into heavy use of templates. The following declaration creates a problem for C++ syntax:

```
list<stack <int>>   list_of_stacks;
```

This statement should create a list of stacks. This behavior is perfectly intelligible; C++ is being directed to create a container class that contains other containers within it—which, no matter how complex that sounds, is perfectly valid.

But in this case, traditional C++ is syntactically challenged. It is used to interpreting two right-angle brackets in a row (>>) as the right-shift operator, and that causes a baffling syntax error. (This same operator, incidentally, is overloaded as a stream data in-flow operator with objects such as **cin**.)

In traditional C++, therefore, it is necessary to insert a space between the two right angle brackets to ensure correct interpretation:

```
list<stack <int> >   list_of_stacks;
```

In C++0x, however, adding this space is not necessary, because it specifies that the language must correctly interpret two right-angle brackets according to context.

Chapter 16   *Summary*

Here are the main points of Chapter 16:

▶ To enable use of the list template, use an **include** directive:

```
#include <list>
```

▶ Each use of the name "list" must be qualified as **std::list**, unless, of course, you place a **using** statement in your program.

```
using namespace std;
```

▶ You declare a list container class by using this syntax:

list<type> *list_name*;

▶ Once a list is created, you can add items to it—of the appropriate type—by using **push_back** (push to back of list) and **push_front** (push to front of list).

```
#include <list>
using namespace std;
...
list<int> Ilist;
Ilist.push_back(11);
Ilist.push_back(42);
```

▶ You can access members of a list by creating an iterator, which is not a pointer but uses several of the same operators. For example:

```
list<int>::iterator iter;
```

▶ You can loop through a list by calling the list's **begin** and **end** functions. For example, the following code prints each item in the list, one to a line.

```
for (iter = Ilist.begin(); iter != Ilist.end(); i++)
    cout << *iter << endl;
```

▶ As with the **list** class, you turn on support for last-in-first-out (LIFO) stack classes with an **#include** statement.

```
#include <stack>
using namespace std;
...
stack<string> my_stack;
```

▶ The **push** function pushes an item onto the top of the stack.

```
my_stack.push("dog");   // Put onto top of stack
```

▶ To pop items off the top of the stack, use a "top and pop" technique.

```
string s = my_stack.top();  // Get top item
my_stack.pop();             // Remove top item
```

▶ Popping an empty stack is a fatal error, so be sure to check stack size by calling the **size** or **empty** function whenever you need to do so.

16

Inheritance: What a Legacy

Inheritance (also called *subclassing*, or deriving a class) was once the most heavily promoted idea in object orientation. It promised to save a lot of work.

These days, it is more controversial; programmers debate how often to use it. Near the end of the chapter, I'll show it in the context of a carefully thought-out inheritance tree...but those take a lot of work to build an example around.

For now, we'll look at simple uses of inheritance—including new features of C++0x that make it easier to use—and consider its more sophisticated uses later.

How to Subclass

One of the themes of this book is reusable code. If a problem is solved once, you don't want to solve it again. So if a class does a particular job, you don't want to have to rewrite that class. You just want to go on reusing it in new projects.

The problem is, what if a class *almost* satisfies the needs of a new problem but doesn't quite do the job? What if you need to extend its capabilities?

You have a couple of choices. One is inheritance, or subclassing. Another is object containment. Finally, there is the use of subclassing within a well-thought-out inheritance hierarchy. We'll consider simple cases of inheritance first.

To derive, or subclass, one class from another, use this syntax:

```
class class_name : public base_class {
    declarations
};
```

The *class_name*, in this context, specifies the new class. It inherits all the members of the *base class* (except for constructors—more about that later).

The *declarations* specify additional members, which may specify new members or override old ones.

Here's an example that creates a new class based on the Fraction class:

```
class FloatFraction : public Fraction {
public:
    double get_float();
};
```

The FloatFraction class is declared as a subclass of the existing Fraction class so that each object of the new class has all the members declared in the Fraction class. In addition, each FloatFraction object supports get_float, a new member function.

Once this class is declared, you can use to create objects, just like any other class.

```
FloatFraction f1;
f1.set(1, 4);
cout << "The decimal display is " << f1.get_float;
```

This next example declares a new class, Point3D, deriving it from the existing Point class. As you may recall, the Point class has two data members: x and y.

```
class Point3D : public Point {
private:
    int z;
public:
    int get_z() {return z;}
    void set_z(int n) {z = n;}
};
```

```
Point3D    mypoint;
```

A Point3D object has *three* data members: x, y, *and* z.

Here's another example involving inheritance from the Fraction class—but this time through an intermediate class (FloatFraction):

```
class ProperFraction : public FloatFraction {
public:
    int get_whole();
    void pr_proper(ostream &os);
};
```

The base class here is FloatFraction. ProperFraction is a kind of "grandchild" class that contains every member of FloatFraction and, by extension, every member of the Fraction class as well. These declarations create a hierarchy, in which ProperFraction is an indirect subclass of Fraction.

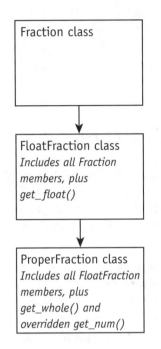

Interlude

Why "public" Base Classes?

In the syntax showed earlier for declaring subclasses, the **public** keyword was used to qualify the base class. In this context, the keyword specifies *base-class access level*.

```
class class_name : public base_class {
    declarations
};
```

Technically, you can omit the **public** keyword in favor of a straight declaration:

```
class FloatFraction : Fraction {
//...
};
```

▼ *continued on next page*

Interlude

▼ *continued*

The problem is that the default base-class access level is **private**. Private base-class access says that all inherited members become private in the new class. This is rarely what you want. Instead, stick with public base-class level, which specifies that all inherited members have the access level they had in the base class.

Example 17.1. *The FloatFraction Class*

For this example, I'm going to assume the declaration of the base class, Fraction, has been placed in the file Fract.h and that the Fraction function definitions have been compiled in a file called Fract.cpp that has been added to the project.

Here is the code that implements and tests the FloatFraction class:

```cpp
FloatFract1.cpp

#include <iostream>
#include "Fract.h"
using namespace std;

// Note: Fract.cpp must be compiled and linked into
// the project.


class FloatFraction : public Fraction {
public:
    FloatFraction() {} // Default constr:
                       // F.F. inherits no contr's!
    double get_float() {
        double x = get_num();
        return x / get_den();
    }
};

int main() {
    FloatFraction fract1;
```

FloatFract1.cpp, cont.

```
        fract1.set(1, 2);
        cout << "1/2 is " << fract1.get_float() << endl;
        fract1.set(3, 5);
        cout << "3/5 is " << fract1.get_float() << endl;
        system("PAUSE");
        return 0;
    }
```

This file is short, because it includes only the code needed for the subclass, FloatFraction. If you need to refer to the base class, Fraction, you should look at the final form of the class in Chapter 13.

How It Works

This subclass declares a default constructor and adds only one other new member: the function get_float. The function definition (which is short enough to be inlined) uses a variable of type **double** to cause floating-point division. (Remember that integer division throws the fractional portion away.)

```
    double get_float() {
        double x = get_num();
        return x / get_den();
    }
```

But why does the program use the get_num and get_den functions to get the values of num and den? Can't these values be accessed directly?

If you were writing code for the Fraction class, that would be true. But this is the FloatFraction class. And num and den, which are private members, cannot be accessed by other classes, including Fraction's own subclasses. Therefore, FloatFraction code must use get_num and get_den to get the values of these members.

The main function uses the new FloatFraction member function (get_float) as well as an inherited member function (set).

```
        fract1.set(1, 2);
        cout << "1/2 is " << fract1.get_float() << endl;
        fract1.set(3, 5);
        cout << "3/5 is " << fract1.get_float() << endl;
```

EXERCISES

Exercise 17.1.1.   Alter Example 17.1 so that it includes a set_float member function in the FloatFraction class. The function should take an argument of type **double** and use it to set the values of num and den. One way to do this is to multiply the value by 100, round to the nearest integer, and then set num to this value and den to 100 by using the set function; this will call normalize automatically. Hint: You'll need an **int** cast:

```
int n = static_cast<int>(new_value * 100.0);
```

Exercise 17.1.2.   Write a constructor for the FloatFraction class that takes a single argument of type **double**. This should be easy if you've completed Exercise 17.1.1.

Problems with the FloatFraction Class

Creating a subclass is *almost* as easy as I made it look in the previous section. But if you do some experimenting, you'll run into limitations.

The following innocent-looking code does just what you'd want it to do, given a complete Fraction class:

```
Fraction f1(1, 2);
f1 = f1 + Fraction(1, 3);
if (f1 == Fraction(5, 6))
    cout << "1/2 + 1/3 = 5/6";
```

But if you use the FloatFraction—which, according to what I've said, ought to support everything the Fraction class does—each of these statements produces errors!

```
FloatFraction f1(1, 2);          // Error!
f1 = f1 + FloatFraction(1, 3);   // Error!
if (f1 == FloatFraction(5, 6))   // Error!
    cout << "1/2 + 1/3 = 5/6";
```

The problem is that subclasses do not inherit constructors. What a letdown...although fortunately, C++0x (if your compiler supports it) offers a very easy fix. This issue with constructors is so significant it deserves to be another cardinal rule:

> ✱ **Subclasses do not inherit constructors from their base class (although C++0x provides a simple way around this).**

The missing constructors for the FloatFraction class are easy enough to supply in this case, although it is tedious extra work. These constructions need do no more than the corresponding Float constructors do.

```
FloatFraction() {set(0, 1);}
FloatFraction(int n, int d) {set(n, d);}
FloatFraction(int n) {set(n, 1);}
FloatFraction(const FloatFraction &src)
      {set(src.get_num(), src.get_den()); }
```

I also had to make one other change. You'd like to keep the definition of the copy constructor simple so that it looks like this:

```
FloatFraction(const FloatFraction &src)
      {set(src.num, src.den); }    // ERROR! Private!
```

The problem is that num and den are private members—of the Fraction class. This means they are not accessible from other classes, not even subclasses of Fraction! (That's a problem I'll revisit in this chapter.) Consequently, in Float-Fraction code, you need to use the public functions get_num and get_den, instead of referring directly to num and den.

C++ Only: Inheriting Base-Class Constructors

C++0x ▶ This section applies only to compilers that are C++0x compliant.

This is one of the most convenient and requested features of C++0x. A single statement (which should be declared in the public section of a class) causes a subclass to inherit the constructors of its base class.

```
using BaseClass::BaseClass;
```

For example, we could implement this in the FloatFraction class (with the new statements shown in bold):

```
class FloatFraction : public Fraction {
public:
    using Fraction::Fraction;   // Inherit constr's

    double get_float() {
       double x = get_num();
       return x / get_den();
    }
};
```

This is an easy solution to a lot of problems, but there are two caveats.

First, use of this syntax is all-or-nothing. If you use it, you inherit all the base-class constructors.

Second, there might be cases where a base-class constructor's behavior is inadequate. In the Point class example, none of the inherited constructors sets a value for z.

```cpp
class Point3D : public Point {
private:
    int z;
public:
    using Point::Point;        // Inherit Point constr's

    int get_z() {return z;}
    void set_z(int n) {z = n;}
};
```

This problem is easily solved by initializing z within the class declaration (which is another C++0x capability, introduced in Chapter 12), as in the following example.

```cpp
class Point3D : public Point {
private:
    int z = 0;
public:
    using Point::Point;        // Inherit Point constr's

    Point3D (int new_x, int new_y, int new_z) {
        set_x(new_x); set_y(new_y); z = new_z;
    }
    int get_z() {return z;}
    void set_z(int n) {z = n;}
};
```

This example also adds a new constructor, which initializes z as well as x and y.

Example 17.2.   *The Completed FloatFraction Class*

In this section, I use a different approach: I show both the old C++ way of doing things and the new, C++0x way.

If your compiler is not C++0x compliant, you explicitly create all the constructors for the class, because no constructors are inherited.

FloatFract2A.cpp

```cpp
#include <iostream>
#include "Fract.h"
using namespace std;

// This is the version of the program for
// compilers NOT COMPLIANT WITH C++0x.
//
// Fract.cpp must be compiled and linked into project.

class FloatFraction : public Fraction {
public:
    FloatFraction() {set(0, 1);}
    FloatFraction(int n, int d) {set(n, d);}
    FloatFraction(int n) {set(n, 1);}
    FloatFraction(const FloatFraction &src)
        {set(src.get_num(), src.get_den()); }

    double get_float() {
        double x = get_num();
        return x / get_den();
    }
};

int main() {
    FloatFraction f1(1, 2), f2(1, 3), f3(0);

    f3 = f1 + f2;
    cout << "Value of f3 is " << f3 << endl;
    cout << "Dec. format is " << f3.get_float();
    cout << endl;
    system("PAUSE");
    return 0;
}
```

17

The C++0x-compliant version is significantly shorter. Lines that are different are in bold.

FloatFract2B.cpp

```cpp
#include <iostream>
#include "Fract.h"
using namespace std;

// This version of the program is only for
// compilers THAT SUPPORT C++0x.
//
// Fract.cpp must be compiled and linked into project.

class FloatFraction : public Fraction {
public:
    using Fraction::Fraction;        // Inherit constr's.

    double get_float() {
        double x = get_num();
        return x / get_den();
    }
};

int main() {
    FloatFraction f1(1, 2), f2(1, 3), f3(0);

    f3 = f1 + f2;
    cout << "Value of f3 is " << f3 << endl;
    cout << "Dec. format is " << f3.get_float();
    cout << endl;
    system("PAUSE");
    return 0;
}
```

How It Works

This example is straightforward. The revised declaration for FloatFraction
includes all the needed constructors, so declarations such as the following are
now supported:

```cpp
FloatFraction f1(1, 2), f2(1, 3), f3(0);
```

Once the issue of constructors is cleared up, you can confidently state that the FloatFraction class inherits all of the Fraction class's capabilities, including operator functions.

Note that if Fraction was not declared as a **public** base class, then all the members declared in Fraction would become **private** when you used them in the FloatFraction class. That would make all the operations in this example (including the use of constructors) invalid.

EXERCISES

Exercise 17.2.1. Revise the main function in Example 17.2 so that it demonstrates successful use of the test-for-equality operator (==) as well as addition and multiplication.

Exercise 17.2.2. Derive a class from Fraction called FractionUnits, which (in addition to Fraction's usual behavior) contains an extra string data member called units. Let the default value be "meters." Make sure that the class has a constructor that assigns values to this string member. Also, use either the standard C++ technique or the new C++ technique for supporting all of the Fraction class's constructors.

Protected Members

The FloatFraction subclass inherits the two data members, num and den. Because these are declared **private**, they are accessible only within the base class (Fraction). In the subclass function-definition code, you have to resort to the get_num and get_den functions to get at the values of num and den.

Wouldn't it be nice to let subclasses refer to num and den directly? The ideal arrangement might be to let subclasses access the data, while restricting access from outside the class hierarchy.

There is a way to do that. C++ supports a third access level—**protected**—which is midway between private and public. If num and den had been given this access level (through the use of the **protected** keyword), then all the subclasses could refer to them directly.

```
class Fraction {
protected:
    int num, den;       // Numerator and denominator.
    //...
```

When should class members be declared protected rather than private? Although it's usually clear what should be public, the decision to make something protected or private is not as obvious. When you declare something private, you're saying you don't want anyone to alter it or pay attention to it (not even yourself) when writing a subclass. It probably makes sense, for example, to make the support functions (lcd, gcf) private, because no one should mess with these. They are called only by the normalize function, and that's the only function that should use it.

Other members might be made protected. The normalize function itself is probably a good candidate, since this function is useful generally. And authors of a subclass would find it useful to refer to the data members, num and den, as we've seen.

But problems could arise if the author of a subclass tried to set num and den directly rather than relying on the "set" function. So, it may make sense to keep num and den private, depending on how much you trust the people who might try to write a subclass.

Here's a summary of the three access levels in C++.

MEMBER ACCESS LEVEL	DESCRIPTION
public	The member can be accessed by any function, whether part of the class or not.
protected	The member can be accessed by a function only if the function is a member of the class *or a subclass.*
private	The member can be accessed by a function only if the function is a member of the same class.

Within the scope of a class, all the class's members are accessible—even if they are in another object of the same class (as opposed to "this" object). For example:

```cpp
class Node {
private:
    string my_own_business;
public:
    Node(string s) {my_own_business = s;}
    void do_some_stuff(Node other) {
        cout << my_own_business << endl; // This is
OK.
        cout << other.my_own_business;   // Also OK.
    }
};
```

Object Containment

An alternative strategy is object containment. A class can contain data of any type, including objects of other classes. There is, of course, an important restriction: You cannot create objects of a particular class before that class is declared.

Note ▶ The restriction against using a class before declaring it is necessary because it prevents you from declaring two classes, A and B, containing each other! Nor can you declare a class containing itself. Either case would lead to an Alice-in-Wonderland situation, an infinite regress like Alice looking in a mirror while holding another mirror next to her face (or taking too much potion and growing infinitely large). You can, however, declare a class that contains a pointer to a class yet to be fully declared, as shown in Chapter 15.

Suppose you wanted to customize the Fraction class by adding a string containing units ("meters," "miles," "liters," and so on) and also by adding a floating-point field. We could keep modifying the Fraction class by subclassing it and adding new fields.

Or we could instead declare a completely new class—let's call it Quantity—containing several data members: a Fraction, a string, and a **double** member. In this case, there is no inheritance. There is simply one large type containing three objects of smaller type.

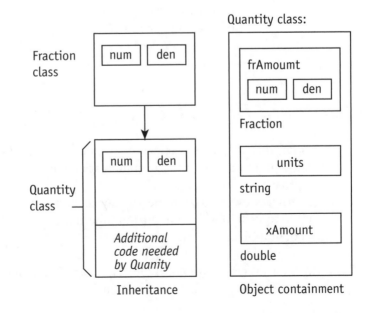

The second approach in the figure illustrates object containment. You don't have to worry about what is inherited or not inherited or how access levels change. Each object is manipulated through its public members.

But because no members are inherited, merely contained, you usually end up having to do more programming. You may have to write data-access functions just to make your larger object usable. And that's just the beginning. If you want operator functions for the new class, for example, you'll have to write them all yourself. And you have no access to private or protected data within the contained classes.

The following statements create a minimal structure for such a class, assuming the three contained objects are private. This doesn't even include constructors.

```
class Quantity {
private:
    Fraction frAmount;
    string   units;
    double   x;
public:
    set(int n, int d);
    set(int n);
    set(double x);
    set(string new_units);
    set(int n, int d, string new_units);
    int get_num();
    int get_den();
    double get_float();
    string get_units();
};
```

Safe Inheritance Through Class Hierarchies

So far, this chapter has taken an ad hoc approach to inheritance. But increasingly, programmers and computer scientists are discouraging this laid-back approach to subclassing.

Instead, most programmers today suggest inheritance should be carried out in the context of well-thought-out inheritance schemes. For example, consider a set of graphical-user interface classes.

▶ In the root class, Graphical Object, you put functionality common to all your classes: for example, a resize function.

▶ Under the root is a class named Control that has common functionality for end-user controls such as text boxes and picture boxes. Here you put functionality common to all controls, such as get_focus and lose_focus.

▶ Under Control is Text Box, Picture Box, and so on. Here you add functionality unique to each specific control type. For example, Text Box has member functions such as set_text and get_text not used by other types of controls.

The resulting class hierarchy can be pictured as shown here.

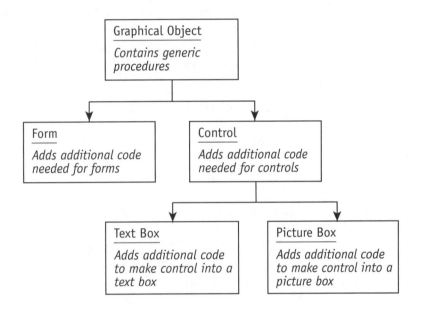

Do you see the goal here? The point of this inheritance scheme is never to have to write the same function definition more than once.

For example, the root class—Graphical Object—can declare functions common to all the classes in this hierarchy. One such function might be resize. This function is then inherited by everyone else and need not be written again.

```
void Graphical_Object::resize(int left, int right,
   int top, int bottom)
{
    x1 = left;
    x2 = right;
    y1 = top;
    y2 = bottom;
    redraw();
}
```

But there is a catch here: Each subclass will likely need to implement a different version of the redraw function, because each type of graphical object needs to display different items on the screen.

Each of the subclasses can *override* the definition of redraw in Graphical Object by supplying its own implementation, which would seem to solve the problem.

But in that case, which version of redraw gets called? What ensures that the correct version of redraw is called for any given object?

That's actually a very big issue in object orientation: The answer involves the **virtual** keyword and polymorphism, and we'll take up that matter again at the beginning of the next (and final) chapter.

For now, I'll end this chapter by showing skeletal code for this class hierarchy—which doesn't provide implementations but shows the relationships between classes.

```
class Graphical_Object {

// Root class. Put most common functions here.
};



class Form : public Graphical-Object {

// Subclass of Graphical_Object.
// Put functions here specifically used for forms,
//    such as Open, Close, Load.
};



class Control : public Graphical_Object {

// Subclass of Graphical_Object.
// Put functions here common to all controls,
//   such as get_focus, lose_focus.
};



class Text_Box : public Control {

// Subclass of Control.
// Put functions here unique to text boxes,
```

```
//  such as get_text, set_text, etc.
};


class Picture_Box : public Control {
};
```

Chapter 17 *Summary*

Here are the main points of Chapter 17:

▶ To derive a class from (subclass) an existing class, use this syntax:

```
class class_name : public base_class {
    declarations
};
```

▶ The **public** keyword in this context is not strictly required by the syntax, but it is strongly recommended (particularly when you are first learning C++). If the base-class has **private** access level (the default), all members in the base class become private when they are inherited by the subclass.

▶ All the members of a base class are inherited by the subclass—except for constructors.

▶ However, in C++0x, you can cause a subclass to inherit the constructors of a base class with this statement in the public section of the declarations:

```
using baseclass::baseclass;
```

▶ The declarations in the subclass may specify new members—which become members of the class in addition to inherited members.

▶ As always, the compiler supplies an automatic version of the default constructor, copy constructor, and the operator= function, as described in previous chapters. For subclasses, each of these compiler-supplied functions calls the base-class version. (But note: As always, the compiler supplies the default constructor only if you write no constructors at all.)

▶ Private members of a base class are inherited by a subclass but are not accessible in subclass code. To declare members that are accessible by code in any and all subclasses—but not by code outside the class hierarchy—declare members as **protected**. (These members are also accessible by code in indirect subclasses, that is to say "descendent classes," down through any number of generations.)

```
protected:
    int num, den;
```

▶ Classes (subclasses as well as ordinary classes) can contain objects as members—which means that one class can contain another. However, a class cannot instantiate an object of its own class, nor can two classes contain each other. (However, as demonstrated in Chapter 15, a class can contain a *pointer* to an object of its own class.)

▶ The general rule is that a class must be fully declared before it is used to create (instantiate) an object.

▶ Another new feature of C++0x is that in writing a constructor, you can *delegate* the work to another, existing constructor if appropriate. In the following example, the second constructor in the second line delegates its job to the constructor in the first line.

```
Point(int new_x, int new_y) {x = new_x; y = new_y;}
Point() : Point(0, 0) {}
```

Polymorphism: Object Independence

If you've made it this far, congratulations! You're about to scale the highest peak of all in the mountain range of object-oriented concepts: *polymorphism*. It is the key to making objects truly independent.

Remember that objects—which are instances of classes—are data items that have built-in behavior. More than anything else, this ability of an unknown object to bring in new kinds of behavior—essentially plugging new software into an existing framework—makes good on the promise of object orientation.

A Different Approach to the FloatFraction Class

Virtual functions are at the core of polymorphism. To understand why they are useful, let's look at an example building on the Fraction class.

The FloatFraction class in Chapter 12 calculated a floating-point (**double**) value "on the fly"—that is, whenever the user of the object asked for that value by calling get_float. But you might instead want to make the floating-point value persistent, recalculating it only when values change. To do that, you'd need to do the following:

▶ Declare a new data member, float_val.

▶ Override the normalize function so it calculates the floating-point value, in addition to performing its other tasks. Remember that normalize is called whenever a new value is set.

In the previous chapter, I barely mentioned the override ability, and for a good reason. It is dangerous to override members without using the **virtual** keyword.

Here is the overridden version of normalize. You'll notice it uses the scope operator (::) to explicitly call the base-class version of the function before doing anything else. This ensures that normalize carries out its usual activity.

```
void FloatFraction::normalize() {
    Fraction::normalize();
    int x = get_num();
    float_val = x / get_den();
}
```

But there's a catch. There are now *two* versions of normalize—Fraction::normalize and FloatFraction::normalize. Which version does the set function call? To review, here is the definition of set—inherited and used by both classes:

```
void set(int n, int d)
     {num = n; den = d; normalize ();}
```

When the C++ compiler read the definition of set in the Fraction class, it had to make a decision then and there—at compile time—about how to call the function. To do that, it had to fix the function address. The set function might as well have been written this way:

```
void set(int n, int d)
     {num = n; den = d; Fraction::normalize();}
```

Consequently, this function never calls the overridden version of normalize, and consequently, the new value of float_val is never recalculated, even for Float-Fraction objects. Fortunately, there's an easy solution.

Virtual Functions to the Rescue!

The solution is to use the **virtual** keyword, which must be applied in the base class (Fraction). This makes the function virtual both in this class and in all subclasses. Essentially, **virtual** says "Determine which version of the function to use at runtime." In other words, make sure that the correct version of the normalize function—the one defined for the object's class—gets called.

```
class Fraction {
...
protected:
   virtual void normalize();  // Put in standard form.
...
};
```

In addition to using **virtual**, I also had to use the **protected** keyword (instead of **private**) to enable overriding of the function. This reminds us of an important rule in writing object-oriented classes:

✳ **Any member function that might be overridden by a subclass should be declared virtual and protected (rather than private).**

Once a function has been declared virtual, it is virtual in all subclasses. You don't need to apply the keyword again.

There are a few restrictions:

▶ Only member functions can be made virtual.

▶ Inline functions cannot be made virtual.

▶ Constructors cannot be made virtual, although destructors can be.

It is legal for a subclass to override a function that is not virtual, but doing so creates a risk that in certain contexts, the right function might not get called (as we saw with normalize in this discussion). If you think a member function might be overridden, make it virtual.

Interlude | ## What Is the Virtual Penalty?

Although it's not necessary to know how virtual function calls are implemented by C++, it's useful to understand the trade-off: Virtual functions are more flexible, but there is a small penalty to be paid. If you're really certain that a certain function will never be overridden, there is no point in making it virtual.

The penalty, however, is small, particularly in light of the speed and capacity of today's computers. There are actually two penalties: a performance penalty and a space penalty.

When a C++ program executes a standard function call, it does what I outlined in Chapter 4: It transfers control of the program to a specific address and returns when the function is done. This is a simple action.

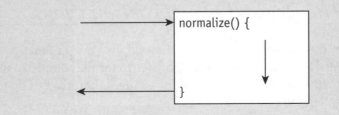

▼ *continued on next page*

18

Interlude

▼ *continued*

Execution of a virtual function is more involved. Each object contains a hidden "vtable" pointer that points to a table of all the virtual functions for its class. For example, all objects of class FloatFraction contain a vtable pointer to the table of virtual functions for FloatFraction. (If a class has no virtual functions at all, by the way, its objects don't need to have a vtable pointer, and that saves some space.)

To call a virtual function, the program uses the vtable pointer to make an indirect function call. This process, in effect, looks up the function address at runtime. (Remember, this is done under the covers and so is completely invisible to the C++ source code.) You can visualize the action this way.

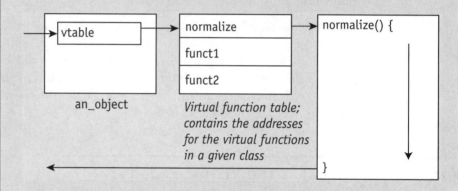

Because each object contains a vtable pointer, you can say that *the knowledge of how to carry out an action is built into the object itself*. The vtable pointer enables each object to have this "knowledge," because it points to implementations specific to its own class.

Clearly, the penalties are slight. The performance penalty arises from the greater time required to make an indirect function call (although that difference is measured in microseconds). The space penalty arises from the bytes taken up by the vtable pointer and the table itself. The moral: Make a function virtual if there's any chance it will be overridden. The cost is slight.

Example 18.1. *The Revised FloatFraction Class*

In the example here, I don't show all the code in Fraction.cpp, although it will need to be recompiled. (See Chapter 13 for the complete Fraction class.) But I do include the file Fract.h to show changes that need to be made to the Fraction declaration.

Here's the new version of FloatFraction, which contains a new data member, float_val, and overrides the normalize function. Lines that are different from the earlier version of FloatFraction (from Chapter 16) are in bold.

```cpp
FloatFract2.cpp

#include <iostream>
#include "Fract.h"
using namespace std;

class FloatFraction : public Fraction {
public:
    double float_val;

// Inherited constructors: with C++0x,
//   these can all be replaced with
//    using Fraction::Fraction;

    FloatFraction() {set(0, 1);}
    FloatFraction(int n, int d) {set(n, d);}
    FloatFraction(int n) {set(n, 1);}
    FloatFraction(const FloatFraction &src)
        {set(src.get_num(), src.get_den()); }
    FloatFraction(const Fraction &src)
        {set(src.get_num(), src.get_den()); }

    void normalize();    // OVERRIDDEN
};

void FloatFraction::normalize() {
    Fraction::normalize();
    float_val = (double) get_num) / get_den;
}

int main() {
    FloatFraction fract1(1, 4), fract2(1, 2);

    FloatFraction fract3 = fract1 + fract2;
    cout << "1/4 + 1/2 = " << fract3 << endl;
    cout << "Floating pt value is = ";
    cout << fract3.float_val << endl;
}
```

Here is the revised version of the file Fract.h, which contains the Fraction class declarations. The one line that needs to be altered is in bold.

Fract.h

```
#include <iostream>
using namespace std;

class Fraction {
private:
    int num, den;       // Numerator and denominator.
public:
    Fraction() {set(0, 1);}
    Fraction(int n, int d) {set(n, d);}
    Fraction(int n) {set(n, 1);}
    Fraction(const Fraction &src) {set(src.n, src.d);
}

    void set(int n, int d)
        {num = n; den = d; normalize();}
    int get_num() const {return num;}
    int get_den() const {return den;}
    Fraction add(const Fraction &other);
    Fraction mult(const Fraction &other);
    Fraction operator+(const Fraction &other)
        {return add(other);}
    Fraction operator*(const Fraction &other)
        {return mult(other);}
    int operator==(const Fraction &other);
friend ostream &operator<<(ostream &os, Fraction &fr);

protected:
    virtual void normalize(); // Put in standard form.
private:
    int gcf(int a, int b);   // Greatest Common Factor.
    int lcm(int a, int b);   // Lowest Common Denom.
};
```

How It Works

This program follows the strategy outlined earlier. The floating-point value is made persistent and is recalculated only as needed.

```
class FloatFraction : public Fraction {
public:
    double float_val;
//...
```

The key to this example is the overridden normalize function. The new version of normalize recalculates the value of float_val so that float_value is always updated whenever changes are made to the object.

The "set" function is inherited from the base class (Fraction), and it makes the call to normalize.

```
void set(int n, int d)
    {num = n; den = d; normalize ();};
```

This function correctly calls the new version of normalize (FloatFraction:: normalize) even though it is a Fraction member function, and *it knows nothing about the existence of any subclasses!* This works because normalize is declared with the **virtual** keyword in the Fraction class.

```
protected:
    virtual void normalize(); // Put in standard
form.
```

The main function tests the FloatFraction class by declaring FloatFraction objects and accessing the new member, float_val.

```
FloatFraction fract1(1, 4), fract2(1, 2);

FloatFraction fract3 = fract1 + fract2;
cout << "1/4 + 1/2 = " << fract3 << endl;
cout << "Floating pt value is = ";
cout << fract3.float_val << endl;
```

This code correctly prints the value 0.75.

C++0x ▶ If you are working with a C++0x-compliant compiler, you can save some work by automatically inheriting all the Fraction constructors in the subclass, FloatFraction, as described in Chapter 17. Include the statement "using Fraction::Fraction;" as mentioned in the comments for FloatFract2.cpp on page 444.

18

Remember, because the normalize function is declared virtual, the correct version is called in the derived class (FloatFraction); and that version, unlike the original, adjusts the value of the new member, float_val. To make things easier, this overridden version of normalize first calls that original version, and then it does the extra work.

```
void FloatFraction::normalize() {
    Fraction::normalize();
    int x = get_num();
    float_val = x / get_den();
}
```

Finally, remember that making this function virtual is necessary because the function is overridden in the derived class (FloatFraction).

EXERCISE

Exercise 18.1.1. In the overridden version of normalize (FloatFraction::normalize), add the following statement:

```
cout << "I am now in FloatFraction::normalize!" << endl;
```

When printed, this message tells you that the overridden version of normalize is being executed rather than the base-class version. Rebuild and rerun the program, noting how many times the message is printed. Then, alter Fract.h by removing the **virtual** keyword from the declaration. What you should find is that the message is not printed, verifying that the use of **virtual** is necessary to get the right implementation to execute. (You should also find that float_val member does not get correctly set.)

C++ Only: Requiring Explicit Overrides

C++0x ▶ This section applies to C++0x-compliant compilers only.

One of the problems with overriding functions is that if you are inheriting from a complicated base class, you can override a function without meaning to by accidentally using a name already used in the base class. Another problem is that if you mistype the name of a function you *meant* to override, you can end up creating a new function with a different name. Either case can cause serious program errors.

To prevent these problems, you can declare a derived class in such a way that it requires functions to be explicitly overridden. To do so, use the following syntax, which includes the **base_check** keyword:

```
class class_name base_check : public base_class {
    declarations
};
```

When **base_check** is in use, function declarations within the class can override a base-class function only when the **override** keyword is used. Where this keyword appears, the function name must match some base-class function name exactly (so typos are flagged). Where **override** does not appear, it is an error to reuse any member name of the base class. For example:

```
class FloatFraction base_check : public Fraction {
...
    void normalize override (); // OVERRIDE successful

    void normlize override (); // This typo would be
                               //  flagged as an error
    void set(int n, int d);    // ERROR: need override
};
```

Notice that the **override** keyword comes after the function name (normalize, in this case) but before the argument list.

"Pure Virtual" and Other Abstract Matters

So, virtual functions matter. The issue is that of always getting the right implementation to execute even when the function is overridden.

Remember, you can choose to execute the base class version of a function by specifying it in code, if that's what you want.

```
Fraction::normalize();
```

But if you don't make this specification, presumably you want an object to execute its *own* version, not that of a base class. And that's when virtual functions are necessary.

The implications of this ability go far. Inheritance hierarchies are deeply ingrained in development systems such as Microsoft Foundation Classes, Java, and Visual Basic.

With these systems, you subclass a general Form, Window, or Document class to create your own implementation. The operating system calls on your object (through your class declaration and implementation) to perform certain tasks—Repaint, Resize, Move, and so on. These actions are all virtual functions, and that is what ensures *your* functions are called using *your* implementation of *your* code.

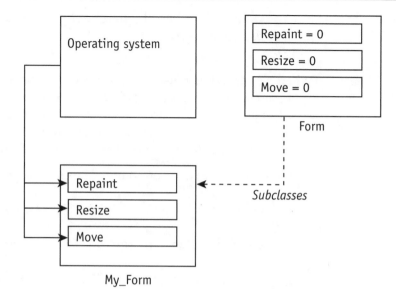

Central to this idea is the concept of *interface*, which is explicitly part of the Java language but is implemented through class inheritance in C++.

In discussing interfaces, I first need to talk about *pure virtual functions*. A pure virtual function is one that has no implementation at all—at least, not in the base class. You indicate a pure virtual function by using the notation =0. For example, a class might define normalize as follows:

```
class Number {
protected:
    virtual void normalize() = 0;
};
```

Here, the normalize function is pure virtual. The declaration has no function definition.

What is the point of such declarations? Well, it all has to do with abstract classes, which I describe next.

Abstract Classes and Interfaces

An abstract class is a class that has one or more pure virtual functions—that is, virtual functions without implementations. An important rule is that abstract classes cannot be instantiated. This means you can't use the class to declare objects.

```
Number a, b, c;    // ERROR: Number is abstract class
                   //   because it has a pure virtual
                   //   func. a, b, c cannot be created.
```

But an abstract class can be useful as a general pattern for its subclasses. Suppose you have an inheritance hierarchy for Windows development and that this hierarchy includes an abstract Form class. You can subclass this to create individual, concrete forms.

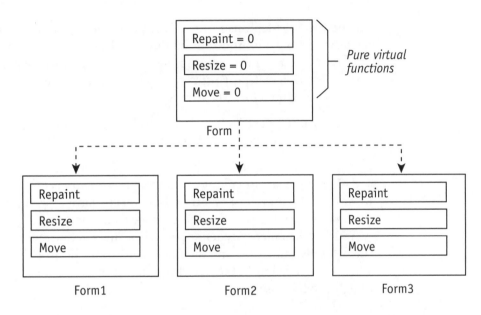

Before you can use a subclass to instantiate (that is, create) objects, it must provide function definitions for all the pure virtual functions. A class that leaves even one of these functions unimplemented is abstract and therefore cannot be used to instantiate objects.

All this is useful in turn, because it gives you a way of specifying and enforcing a general set of services, or interface. Note the following:

▶ Each subclass is free to implement all these services (i.e., pure-virtual functions) in any way it wants.

▶ Every service needs to be implemented, or the class cannot be instantiated.

▶ Every class must strictly observe type information—return type and the type of each argument. This gives the inheritance hierarchy discipline so that really stupid actions (passing the wrong kind of data, for example) are flagged by the compiler.

The author of a subclass knows that he or she must implement the services defined in the interface—such as Repaint, Move, and Load—but within that mandate, he or she is free. And because all these functions are virtual, the correct implementation is always executed, no matter how an object is accessed.

I'm about to show, I hope, an example of how all of this is useful.

Object Orientation and I/O

The best simple demonstration of the power of object orientation (OOP) may be the way it extends input/output through the use of the stream classes.

Once upon a time, there was the C language, which required the use of a library function called **printf** if you wanted print to the console. This function had cousins named **fprintf** (print to a text file) and **sprintf** (print to a string).

```
printf("Here's an int: %d", i);   // Print an integer
printf("Here's a flt pt: %f", x); // Print a double
```

The problem with these functions is that if you create your own data type—say a Fraction class or complex-number class—there is no way to extend **printf** to work with your class; **printf** and its cousins have a fixed set of data formats (%d, %f, %s, and so on), and these can never be modified.

You could, in theory, redefine **printf** by using **#define** to intercept calls, substitute your own function, and then call **printf** yourself through a function pointer when you needed to, but this is a horrendous "hack," requiring massive amounts of ugly programming.

cout Is Endlessly Extensible

C++ introduced the I/O stream classes, although it still supports the old C functions for backward compatibility. The stream classes demonstrate the extensibility of OOP beautifully.

(The new C++0x specification adds to this extensibility even further, enabling you to create user-defined literals as shown in Chapter 13.)

As we saw in Chapter 13, with C++, making a class "printable" is simply a matter of writing an **operator<<** function.

```
ostream &operator<<(ostream &os, Fraction &fr) {
    os << fr.num << "/" << fr.den;
    return os;
}
```

This operator function makes Fraction objects printable in many contexts—not only with console output (**cout**) but also any file or string using the I/O stream classes.

```
Fraction fr1(1, 2);          // fr1 = 1/2.

cout << fr1;                            // Print to console.
fout << "The value is: " << fr1; // Print to file.
```

So, in theory, one might say that for any class of object, the following statement can be made to work smoothly:

```
cout << "The value of the object is " << an_object;
```

But cout Is Not Polymorphic

However—although this is not at first obvious—there is one limitation. Stream classes can work with an object only if its type is known at compile time. The client code must know all about the object's class.

But isn't that always true? How can you even refer to an object whose type isn't fully defined?

Actually, it *is* possible to refer to an object whose type isn't defined. One way to do that is to use a **void** pointer, which is a pointer to an object of any type. If you use such a pointer and dereference it, **cout** will not know how to print the object.

```
void *p = &an_object;
cout << *p;               // ERROR! *p cannot be printed
```

Ideally, you ought to be able to do the following: You ought to be able to specify a dereferenced pointer to an object (that is, an expression such as *p) and have the object always be printed in the correct format. Another way of saying this is, *the knowledge of how to print an object ought to be built into the object itself.*

This is important in systems programming. You might get a pointer to a new type of object over the Internet. You'd like to ensure that the correct function code gets called, even if the object has a new type that the client code (the user of the object) knows nothing about.

In short, you'd like your programs to work seamlessly with new data types to be defined in the future.

To do this, we can declare an abstract class named Printable, which declares a pure virtual function named print_me. In the next example, I show that any class that subclasses Printable and implements print_me can be correctly printed by **cout** (or any instance of an **ostream** class)—even if the class is newer than the client code—so that the specific class of the object isn't even known by the main program.

The following statement will work, even though nothing at all may be known about the class of an_object beyond the fact it subclasses Printable.

```
Printable *p = &an_object;   // Object's class must
                             //  subclass Printable.


cout << *p;        // This will be printed in the
                   //  correct format,
                   //  as defined by
                   //  the class of an_object.
```

There's an important rule that makes this code possible. An object of subclass type can be passed wherever a base-class object is expected. And a pointer to an object of subclass type can be passed to a pointer of base-class type. Or, to put it more simply:

✳ **Something specific (a subclass) can always be passed to something more general (a base class).**

The converse is not generally true (passing a base-class pointer to a subclass pointer) unless there is a conversion function to support it.

Example 18.2. *True Polymorphism: The Printable Class*

This next example demonstrates a way to work with output stream classes and objects (such as **cout**) that is truly polymorphic. By observing a general interface—realized here as the abstract class named Printable—you can correctly print any kind of object, even if the exact type of that object is not known at compile time.

This approach is *polymorphic* (meaning "many forms") because a single function call can result in an unlimited number of implementations at runtime. The number of possible responses is theoretically infinite.

That may seem impossible. But I meant what I wrote. You can print an object without knowing its type or its function code, because you (that is, the client code) don't need to know how to print the object. The knowledge of how to be printed is built into the object and its class.

Printme.cpp

```cpp
#include "iostream"
using namespace std;

class Printable {
    virtual void print_me(ostream &os) = 0;

    friend ostream &operator<<(ostream &os,
                                    Printable &pr);
};



// Operator<< function:
// All this does is cause virtual function print_me
//   to be called, sending output to the stream.
//
ostream &operator<<(ostream &os, Printable &pr) {
    pr.print_me(os);
    return os;
};

// CLASSES SUBCLASSING PRINTABLE
//-----------------------------------------

class P_int : public Printable {
public:
    int n;

    P_int() {};
    P_int(int new_n) {n = new_n; };
    void print_me(ostream &os);        // override
};

class P_dbl : public Printable {
public:
    double val;

    P_dbl() {};
    P_dbl(double new_val) {val = new_val; };
```

▼ *continued on next page*

18

```
        void print_me(ostream &os);      // override
};

// IMPLMENTATIONS OF PRINT_ME
//-----------------------------------------

void P_int::print_me(ostream &os) {
    os << n;
}

void P_dbl::print_me(ostream &os) {
    os << "  " << val;
}

// MAIN FUNCTION
//-----------------------------------------
int main() {
    Printable *p;
    P_int num1(5);
    P_dbl num2(6.25);

    p = &num1;
    cout << "Here is a number: " << *p << endl;
    p = &num2;
    cout << "Here is another:  " << *p << endl;
    system("PAUSE");
    return 0;
}
```

How It Works

The code in this example consists of three major parts:

▶ The abstract class, Printable

▶ The subclasses, P_int and P_dbl, which contain an integer and floating-point value, respectively, and which tell how to print the object

▶ The main function, which puts these classes to the test

The Printable class is an abstract class, which you can also think of as an interface that defines a single service: the virtual function print_me.

```
class Printable {
    virtual void print_me(ostream &os) = 0;

    friend ostream &operator<<(ostream &os,
                                   Printable &pr);
};
```

The idea of the class is simple: Subclasses of Printable implement the function print_me to define how they send data to an output stream (**ostream**).

The Printable class also declares a global friend function. This function converts an expression such as this:

```
cout << an_object
```

into a call to the object's own print_me function.

```
an_object.print_me(cout)
```

Because print_me is virtual, the correct version of print_me is always called no matter how the object is accessed.

```
Printable *p = &an_object;
//...
cout << *p;
```

If print_me were not a virtual function, this code would not work.

The actual implementations of print_me do little in this particular example, but that's not important. Integers and floating-point values are easily printed. I put in a small difference between them—printing a couple of extra spaces for the floating-point implementation—just so you can notice a different version of print_me is being called.

```
void P_int::print_me(ostream &os) {
    os << n;
}

void P_dbl::print_me(ostream &os) {
    os << "   " << val;
}
```

Implementations of print_me for other classes can be much more interesting. Here, for example, is how you might implement print_me for the Fraction class:

```
void Fraction::print_me(ostream &os) {
    os << get_num() << "/" << get_den();
}
```

How is this useful? Well, you could have an array of pointers to objects of different types. As long as they all were instances of classes derived from Printable, you could print all of them, each in the correct format as determined by the objects' own classes.

Again, the objects know how to print themselves! The line containing "cout <<" essentially says to each object "Print yourself." The amazing thing is that each object may (in effect) execute a different piece of code, tailor-made for its own particular subclass.

```
Printable array_of_objects[ARRAY_SIZE];
//...
for (int i = 0; i < ARRAY_SIZE; i++)
    cout << array_of_objects[i]  << endl;
```

EXERCISE

Exercise 18.2.1.   Revise the Fraction class so that it subclasses Printable and implements the print_me function. Then test the results by using code such as the following to print a Fraction object:

```
Fraction fract1(3, 4);
//...
Printable *p = &fract1;
cout << "The value is " << *p;
```

If all goes well, you should find that the Fraction object is printed in the correct format.

A Final Word (or Two)

When I was first learning about object-oriented programming way back in the 1980s, I developed the idea in my mind that object-oriented programming was all about creating individual, self-contained entities that communicate by sending messages to each other. The Smalltalk language, for example, is built around this idea.

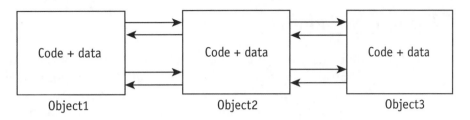

These days, I still think that's not a bad way to get a grip on some of the major concepts. Individual, self-contained entities like to shield their contents; they therefore have encapsulation—the ability to keep their data private.

I'm not sure how well inheritance is demonstrated by this model, although you can make it fit. If each of the individual objects is like a microprocessor or chip (to think of it all in hardware terms), then ideally you should be able to pop out a chip, make some modifications or improvements to it, and pop it back in.

Above all, the model of "independent entities sending messages to each other" is a good way of illustrating what polymorphism and virtual functions are all about.

Recall what I said a little earlier about the Printable interface in the introduction to Example 17.2. Here I paraphrase it in general terms:

> **You can use an object without knowing its type or what functions it calls, because the knowledge of how perform the service is built into the object itself, not the user of that object.**

This principle is consistent with the idea of independent objects that communicate by sending messages. The user of an object doesn't need to tell it how to do its job. What goes on inside another object is a mystery. You send a message, knowing that the object will respond in some appropriate way.

In essence, objects—independent units of code and data—are liberated from slavish dependence on the internal structure of other objects.

But the result is not anarchy. Object-oriented programming systems enforce discipline in the area of type checking. If you want to support an interface, you have to implement *all* the services (that is, virtual functions) of that interface, and you have to match the types in the argument lists exactly.

You can implement a function in a way that had not yet been written at the time the client code was written. Remember that the following will always work correctly—without being revised or recompiled—even if the specific type of an_object changes.

```
Printable = &an_object;
cout << *p;
```

A Final, Final Word

But what does all this mean? Why does polymorphism matter? Is it because it contributes to code reuse? Well, yes. But it's not primarily that.

Object-oriented programming is really more about *systems*—graphical systems, network communication, and other aspects of the technology we daily become more enmeshed in. Items in a graphical-user interface, or in a network, act like independent objects sending messages to each other.

Traditional programming techniques were developed for a different world, a world in which it could be a triumph just to submit a stack of punch cards and see your program have a successful beginning, middle, and end, rather than gagging and puking. In this world, you assume that you're the only game in town.

Today's software has become more complex as it has become richer. The success of Microsoft Windows, for example, stems in part from its rich set of components. And the component model is not as easy to implement with traditional programming techniques. You want to be able to plug ever newer software components into complex existing frameworks, such as Windows.

Ultimately, this way of looking at things is closer to the reality of the great wide world. One of the most exalted claims made for object orientation is that "it more closely models the real world." That's an inflated claim but one with a nugget of truth. We *do* live in a complex world. We *do* interact with things and people independent from ourselves. We *do* need to trust in specialized knowledge that others can bring. And maybe if we could liberate software objects, giving them the independence and freedom to do what each of them knows how to do best, we might feel more encouraged to liberate ourselves.

Chapter 18   # Summary

Here are the main points of Chapter 18:

▸ *Polymorphism* means that the knowledge of how to perform a service is built into the object itself, not the client (that is, the software that uses it). Consequently, the resolution of a single function call or operation can take unlimited different forms.

▸ Polymorphism is made possible by virtual functions.

▸ The address of a virtual function is not resolved until runtime. (This is also called *late binding*.) The class of an object—as known at runtime—determines which implementation of a virtual function gets executed.

▶ To make a function virtual, precede its declaration in the class with the **virtual** keyword. For example:

```
protected:
    virtual void normalize();
```

▶ Once a function is declared virtual, it is virtual in all subclasses. You don't need to use the **virtual** keyword more than once per function.

▶ You cannot make a constructor or an inline function virtual.

▶ However, a destructor can be virtual.

▶ There is a small performance penalty and a small space penalty whenever a function is made virtual. However, these losses of efficiency are minor in terms of today's powerful computers.

▶ As a general rule, any member function that might be overridden should be declared virtual.

▶ A *pure virtual function* has no implementation (that is, no function definition) in the class in which it is declared. You declare a pure virtual function by using =0 notation. For example:

```
virtual void print_me() = 0;
```

▶ A class with at least one pure virtual function is an *abstract class*. Such a class cannot be used to instantiate objects.

```
Number a, b, c;    // ERROR!
```

▶ Abstract classes are useful as a means to create a general interface—a list of services that a subclass provides by implementing all the virtual functions.

▶ In the final analysis, polymorphism is a way of liberating objects from slavish dependence on each other—because the knowledge of how to perform a service is built into each individual object. It's ultimately this feature that gives object orientation its special flavor and makes it *object* oriented, not merely class oriented.

18

Operators

Table A.1 lists C++ operators with their precedence, associativity, description, and syntax. The levels—to which I've assigned numbers—have no significance beyond the fact that all operators at the same level have equal precedence.

Associativity can be left-to-right or right-to-left. This matters when two operators are at the same level of precedence. For example, in the expression

```
*p++
```

the * and ++ operators are at the same level of precedence (level 2), so the order of evaluation is determined by associativity—in this case, right-to-left. The expression is therefore evaluated as if written this way:

```
*(p++)
```

meaning that it is the pointer p itself (not what it points to) that gets incremented.

Note that level-2 operators in this table are unary operators; that is, they operate on only one expression. Most other operators are binary, having two operands. Some operators (such as *) have both a unary and binary version—and they do very different things.

The items in the syntax column represent several kinds of expressions:

▶ *expr*: Any expression.

▶ *num*: Any numeric expression (including **char**).

▶ *int*: An integer (also includes **char**).

▶ *ptr*: A pointer (that is, an address expression).

▶ *member*: A member of a class.

▶ *lvalue*: An item that can legally be the target of an assignment. This includes a variable, an array element, a reference, or a fully dereferenced pointer. Literals and array names can never be lvalues.

475

Table A.1: C++ Operators by Precedence Level

LEVEL	ASSOCIATION	OPERATOR	DESCRIPTION	SYNTAX
1	L-to-R	()	Function call	*func*(*args*)
1	L-to-R	[]	Access array element	*array*[*int*]
1	L-to-R	->	Access class member	*ptr*->*member*
1	L-to-T	.	Access class member	*object*.*member*
1	L-to-R	::	Clarify scope	*class*::*name* ::*name*
2	*R-to-L*	!	Logical negation	!*expr*
2	*R-to-L*	~	Bitwise negation	~*int*
2	*R-to-L*	++	Increment	++*num* *num*++
2	*R-to-L*	--	Decrement	--*num* *num*--
2	*R-to-L*	-	Change sign of	-*num*
2	*R-to-L*	*	Get contents at (dereference)	**ptr*
2	*R-to-L*	&	Get address of	&*lvalue*
2	*R-to-L*	**sizeof**	Get size of data in bytes	**sizeof**(*epxr*)
2	*R-to-L*	**new**	Allocate data object(s)	**new** *type* **new** *type*[*int*] **new** *type*(*args*)
2	*R-to-L*	**delete**	Remove data object(s)	**delete** *ptr* **delete** [] *ptr*
2	*R-to-L*	cast	Change type	(*type*) *expr*
3	L-to-R	.*	Pointer-to-member (rarely used)	*obj*.**ptr_mem*
3	L-to-R	->*	Pointer-to-member (rarely used)	*ptr*->**ptr_mem*
4	L-to-R	*	Multiply	*num* * *num*
4	L-to-R	/	Divide	*num* / *num*
4	L-to-R	%	Modulus (remainder)	*int* % *int*
5	L-to-R	+	Addition	*num* + *num* *ptr* + *int* *int* + *ptr*
5	L-to-R	-	Subtraction	*num* - *num* *ptr* - *int* *ptr* - *ptr*
6	L-to-R	<<	Left shift (bitwise); also stream op	*expr* << *int*
6	L-to-R	>>	Right shift (bitwise); also stream op	*expr*>>*int*

Table A.1: C++ Operators by Precedence Level (*continued*)

LEVEL	ASSOCIATION	OPERATOR	DESCRIPTION	SYNTAX
7	L-to-R	<	Is less than?	*num* < *num* *ptr* < *ptr*
7	L-to-R	<=	Is less than or equal?	*num* <= *num* *ptr* <= *ptr*
7	L-to-R	>	Is greater than?	*num* > *num* *ptr* > *ptr*
7	L-to-R	>=	Is greater than or equal?	*num* >= *num* *ptr* >= *ptr*
8	L-to-R	==	Test for equality	*num* == *num* *ptr* == *ptr*
8	L-to-R	!=	Test for inequality	*num* != *num* *ptr* != *ptr*
9	L-to-R	&	Bitwise AND	*int* & *int*
10	L-to-R	^	Bitwise XOR (exclusive OR)	*int* ^ *int*
11	L-to-R	|	Bitwise OR	*int* | *int*
12	L-to-R	&&	Logical AND	*expr* && *expr*
13	L-to-R	||	Logical OR	*expr* || *expr*
14	*R-to-L*	?:	Conditional operator: evaluate expr1: if nonzero, evaluate and return expr2; otherwise, evaluate and return expr3	*expr1* ? *expr2* : *expr3*
15	*R-to-L*	=	Assign	*lvalue* = *expr*
15	*R-to-L*	+=	Add and assign	*lvalue* += *expr*
15	*R-to-L*	-=	Subtract and assign	*lvalue* -= *expr*
15	*R-to-L*	*=	Multiply and assign	*lvalue* *= *expr*
15	*R-to-L*	/=	Divide and assign	*lvalue* /= *expr*
15	*R-to-L*	%=	Modular divide and assign	*lvalue* %= *expr*
15	*R-to-L*	>>=	Right shift and assign	*lvalue* >>= *expr*
15	*R-to-L*	<<=	Left shift and assign	*lvalue* <<= *expr*
15	*R-to-L*	&=	Bitwise AND and assign	*lvalue* &= *expr*
15	*R-to-L*	^=	Bitwise XOR and assign	*lvalue* ^= *expr*
15	*R-to-L*	|=	Bitwise OR and assign	*lvalue* |= *expr*
16	*R-to-L*	,	Join (evaluate both expressions and return expr2)	*expr1*, *expr2*

The rest of this appendix provides more detail on some of the operators, in order of precedence:

▶ The (::) scope operator

▶ The sizeof operator

▶ Cast operators

▶ Integer vs. floating-point division

▶ Conditional (?:) operator

▶ Assignment operators

▶ Join (,) operator

The Scope (::) Operator

This operator has several related uses. First, it can be used to refer to a symbol declared in a class or namespace.

```
class::symbol_name
```

```
namespace::symbol_name
```

The scope operator can also be used to refer to a global—or rather, unqualified—name. This might be used, for example, to refer to a global symbol from within a class's member function when there is a name conflict.

```
::symbol_name
```

The sizeof Operator

The **sizeof** operator returns the size of the type of its operand in bytes:

▶ If **sizeof** is used on a pointer, it returns the width of the pointer itself (currently 4 bytes on today's 32-bit computers), not the base type.

```
Double x = 0.0;
double *p = x;
cout << sizeof(p);    // Print 4.
Cout << sizeof(x);    // Print 8.
```

▶ If **sizeof** is used on an array, it returns the total size of all the elements of the array. For example, if **sizeof(int)** is 4, then the following prints 40:

```
int arr[10];
cout << sizeof(arr);    // Print 40.
```

▶ **sizeof** can be used directly on a type name (including class names).

```
cout << sizeof(char);    // Print 1.
```

Old and New Style Type Casts

For backward compatibility, C++ supports the old-style C type cast:

(*type***)** *expression*

The C++ standards committee had long planned to deprecate this usage. A deprecated usage is one that the compiler advises the programmer against using, generating a warning message. However, because C++ is still being used to compile large amounts of C legacy code, the committee decided not to deprecate this type cast.

The four new-style casts are still preferred within the C++ community (see Table A.2). Admittedly, they are longer and take more work to put into programs, but they have the advantage of being more self-documenting. The habit of using these operators (and not the old-style C type cast) reduces the possibility of using an improper cast accidentally.

Table A.2: C++ Cast Operators (New Style)

CAST SYNTAX	DESCRIPTION
static_cast<*type*>(*expression*)	Recasts *expression* into the data format of *type*, such as casting **double** to **int** (and removing warning messages), or to cast to or from an **enum** type. Essentially, **static_cast** says, "Yes, I really do want to do this." For the cast to work, some sort of conversion must be possible between the types involved.
reinterpret_cast<*type*>(*expression*)	Recasts one pointer type to another or casts between a pointer type and **int**, or vice versa. This cast is potentially dangerous (so make sure you need it before using it), because it changes how data at a particular address is to be interpreted.
dynamic_cast<*type*>(*expression*)	Casts a base-class pointer to a subclass pointer after verifying that the object pointed to has the specified subclass *type*. Produces NULL if cast is not valid. Requires that the classes involved have one or more virtual functions. This is casting *downward* through an inheritance hierarchy; going the other way (assigning subclass pointer to a base-class pointer) is freely permitted and requires no cast.
const_cast<*type*>(*expression*)	Casts a non-**const** expression to a **const** type. It is your responsibility to make sure the expression is not one that will be changed.

Integer vs. Floating-Point Division

Most of the operators in Table A.1 are self-explanatory, but special considerations apply to some types. When one integer is divided by another, the remainder is thrown away.

```
int quotient = 19 / 10;    // quotient  = 1
```

In this case, the fractional portion (0.9) is discarded. To get a remainder resulting from integer division, use the modulus (%) operator:

```
int remainder = 19 % 10;    // remainder = 9
```

In the following example, integer division is performed, throwing away much of the result, even though quotient has floating point format and could have stored the result, 1.9.

```
double quotient = 19 / 10;    // quotient  = 1.0
```

However, if one of the operands has type **double** (which is the case when a decimal point is used in a numeric literal), the other operand is promoted to **double** and floating-point division is carried out.

```
double quotient = 19 / 10.0;    // quotient = 1.9
```

Bitwise Operators (&, |, ^, ~, <<, and >>)

Bitwise AND, OR, and exclusive OR (&, |, ^) operate on two integer expressions of the same width. If one operand has a different width (size) than the other, then the smaller of the two is promoted to the larger width. The action of these operators is to compare bit-n in one operand to bit-n in the other and set bit-n in the resulting integer. For example:

```
cout << hex;

cout << (0xe & 0x3);   // 1110 & 0011 -> 0010 (AND)
cout << endl;
cout << (0xe | 0x3);   // 1110 | 0011 -> 1111 (OR)
cout << endl;
cout << (0xe ^ 0x3);   // 1110 ^ 0011 -> 1101 (XOR)
```

Note that exclusive OR (also called XOR) means "either or but not both."

Bitwise negation (~) is a unary operator that produces a result containing the reverse setting of each bit in its operand. For example:

```
cout << hex;

cout << (~(char)0xff); // 1111 1111 -> 0000 0000 (0)
cout << endl;
cout << (~(char)0x89); // 1000 1001 -> 0111 0110 (76)
```

When used on integers, double-angle brackets (<< and >>) are not stream operators but bit-shift operators:

```
integer << number_of_positions_to_shift
integer >> number_of_positions_to_shift
```

These operators originated in the C language solely to perform bit shifts, not I/O. In C++, they are *overloaded* to work with streams—in effect becoming stream input/output operators but only through redefinition. But they retain the same precedence and associativity no matter how they are used.

Conditional Operator

The conditional operator (?) provides a way to perform if-then-else logic within an expression; it is another option for writing extremely compact code. A simple example is that of comparing x to 1 and then printing 1 or 0 depending on the result.

```
if (x == 1)
    cout << 1 << endl;
else
    cout << 0 << endl;
```

With the conditional operator, this could be expressed as follows:

```
cout << (x == 1 ? 1 : 0) << endl;
```

The general form of the operator is *condition ? expr1 : expr2*. The *condition* is evaluated. If true (nonzero), then *expr1* is evaluated and returned as the value of the overall expression; otherwise, *expr2* is evaluated and returned as the value of the overall expression.

Precedence of the conditional operator is very low, so a conditional expression (like that just shown) typically needs to be enclosed in parentheses.

Assignment Operators

All the assignment operators return the value that was assigned, thus permitting multiple assignments such as the following:

```
x = y = z = 0;
```

Many assignment operators are provided as convenient shorthand for some operate-and-assign action. For example, the expression

```
i += 1;
```

is functionally equivalent to the following:

```
i = i + 1;
```

Similarly, for all the operators such as \=, *=, -=, and so on, note that the expression

```
(i += 1)
```

is equivalent to

```
(++i)
```

because they both say, "Add 1 to the value of i, and then pass this value along to the larger expression."

Join (,) Operator

The join, or comma, operator is a way of combining multiple expressions in the space of a single expression. This is useful in **for** statements in which there's a need to initialize or increment more than one variable:

```
for (i = 0, j = 0; i <= 100; i++, j++)
    . . .
```

In general, the operation of the comma operator is to evaluate both conditions on either side of the comma (,) and then return the value of the second expression. In addition to **for**, another useful situation is the following, where the comma is used to execute several actions at the top of a loop before finally testing the condition i < 10:

```
while (i = j + 1, cout << "i", i < 10)
    i++;
```

This operator (,) has the lowest precedence of all C++ operators.

Data Types

Although the C++ specification is somewhat general when it comes to ranges of types, certain ranges are (for all practical purposes) universal on computers with a 32-bit architecture. This includes all personal computers in use today, both PCs and Macs. However, some of these ranges are subject to change. When 64-bit architecture becomes standard, for example, you should expect **int** to be identified with 64-bit integers.

The **int** and **double** types are the "natural" sizes for integer and floating-point numbers, respectively, for the computer's own architecture. This means that when any integer type is used in an expression (such as **char**), it is automatically promoted to **int** provided it can be done so without loss of information. There is never any reason to use **short** or **float** except where compact storage formats on disk or other data stream requires it.

Table B.1 lists data types and their ranges on 32-bit computers and is followed by sections describing other issues in data-type storage. I use "billion" here in the American sense: a thousand million (1,000,000,000).

Here are some notes on version support:

▶ Some types are marked "ANSI." Almost all but the oldest compilers now support ANSI-required types, so unless your compiler is very much out of date, it should support these.

▶ Some types are marked "C++0x." Compilers that are C++0x compliant support these, but some C++ vendors have been supporting these even before the C++0x specification was proposed.

Table B.1: C++ Intrinsic Data Types

TYPE	DESCRIPTION (FOR 32-BIT SYSTEMS)	RANGE (ON 32-BIT SYSTEMS)
char	1-byte integer (used to hold ASCII character value)	0 to 255
unsigned char	1-byte unsigned integer	0 to 255
signed char	1-byte signed integer	-128 to 127
short	2-byte integer	-32,768 to 32,767
unsigned short	2-byte unsigned integer	0 to 65,535
int	4-byte integer (but same as short on 16-bit systems)	Approx. ± 2 billion
unsigned int	4-byte unsigned integer (but same as unsigned short on 16-bit systems)	Approx. 4 billion
long	4-byte integer	Approx. ± 2 billion
unsigned long	4-byte unsigned integer	Approx. 4 billion
bool	Integer in which all nonzero values are converted to **true** (1); also holds **false** (0) (ANSI)	**true** or **false**
wchar_t	Wide character, for holding Unicode characters (ANSI)	Same as **unsigned int**
long long	64-bit signed integer (C++0x)	Approx. $\pm 9 \times 10^{18}$
unsigned long long	64-bit unsigned integer (C++0x)	Approx. 1.8×10^{19}
float	Single-precision floating point	3.4×10^{38}
double	Double-precision floating point	1.8×10^{308}
long double	Extra-wide double-precision (ANSI)	At least as great as **double**

Precision of Data Types

All integer types have absolute precision at all times. That is one of their chief advantages. For example, you can be close to the top of the **long long** range, and adding 1 to the amount is accurately reflected in the new value, whereas adding 1 to a very high **float** number might have no effect, with the added value of 1 lost because of rounding.

▶ The **float** type has 7 (decimal) digits of precision.

▶ The **double** type has 15 (decimal) digits of precision.

▶ Values in **float** format can store the value 0.0 precisely. They can also store tiny values as close to zero as 1.175×10^{-38}.

▶ Values in **double** format can store the value 0.0 precisely. They can also store tiny values as close to zero as $2.225074 \times 10^{-308}$.

Data Types of Numeric Literals

In C++ (and programming generally), a *literal* is a series of characters that the compiler immediately recognizes as a fixed value upon reading. In the core language, these are always numbers and text strings. A literal is different from a symbol (usually a variable, class, or function name), which has to have a value assigned to it.

```
int i = 23;                      // 23 is a literal
int j = number_of_students;      // Not a literal
int k = MAX_PATH;                // Not a literal
```

In these statements, 23 is the only literal that appears. MAX_PATH may be changed into a literal during preprocessing (where a **#define** statement may replace it with a literal value such as 256), but it is not yet a literal.

All literals are constants, but not all constants are literals. For example, array names are constants in C and C++, but they are symbols, not literals.

The default numeric format is decimal (base 10). The default storage for whole numbers is **int** type. But several other numeric formats may be used with literals:

▶ The **0x** prefix specifies hexadecimal (base 16).

▶ A leading 0 specifies octal (base 8).

▶ Scientific notation indicates floating-point format: The literal is stored in **double** format.

▶ Use of a decimal point, even if followed by 0, indicates floating-point format; again, the literal is stored in **double** format.

Here's an example:

```
int a = 0xff;     // Assign 1111 1111 (256) to a.
int b = 0100;     // Assign octal 100 (64) to b.
double x = 3.1415;  // Assign flt. pt. number
double y = 3.0;     // This also assigns flt pt.
double z = 1.6e5;   // Use of scientific notation:
                    //  1.6 times 10 to the fifth
```

In addition, several suffixes may affect how the value of a literal is stored. Storage of a literal can sometimes matter because it can affect the precision it has, what range is permitted, or what conversion has to be applied later on to copy the data to another location. Furthermore, some integer values cannot be represented without applying the proper suffix.

▶ The **L** suffix indicates storage of an integer in **long int** format. **long** is equivalent to **int** on most computers in use today.

▶ The **U** suffix indicates storage of an as **unsigned int**. (This doubles the range supported for positive numbers; see "Two's Complement Format for Signed Integers" later in this appendix.)

▶ The **F** suffix indicates storage in **float** format (usually 4-byte floating point) rather than **double** (8-byte floating byte). Usually this is unnecessary or even undesirable but might be necessary in a situation in which you were reading 4-byte floating-point numbers from a binary file, for example.

▶ If **long long** is supported, then the **LL** and **ULL** suffixes are supported for **long long** and **unsigned long long** formats, respectively. Some integer values are so large they cannot be written out as literals except with one of these suffixes (because otherwise the compiler attempts to fit integer literals into **int** format).

String Literals and Escape Sequences

Ordinary string literals have **char*** format. They are translated into a **char*** array with one byte allocated for each character plus an extra byte for the null terminator.

```
char str[] = "This is a string. ";
```

Wide character strings are similar, but to indicate a wide-character literal, use an "L" prefix: this causes the compiler to allocate a **wchar_t** array, which includes two bytes for each character, including the null terminator.

```
wchar_t unicode_str[] = L"This is a Unicode string. ";
```

The appearance of a backslash in a string literal indicates that the backslash itself—along with the very next character—is not interpreted as a backslash but instead has special meaning as an *escape character*. Table B.2 summarizes the meaning of escape characters.

Table B.2: Escape Characters in C++

ESCAPE CHARACTER	MEANING
\'	Literal single quotation mark.
\"	Literal double quotation mark. (This is necessary, because otherwise a quotation mark is recognized as terminating the string literal.)
\\	Literal backslash.
\a	Bell.
\b	Backspace.
\f	Form feed.
\n	Newline.
\r	Carriage return.
\t	Horizontal tab.
\v	Vertical tab.
nnn	ASCII character corresponding to number nnn, where nnn is an octal number (base 8).
\x*hh*	ASCII character corresponding to number hh, where hh is a hexadecimal number (base 16).

Two's Complement Format for Signed Integers

Virtually all personal computers in use today (including Macs) use two's complement format for storing signed integers. Two's complement is a technique for representing negative numbers along with positive numbers. Although the leftmost bit always indicates the sign of the quantity, it is not precisely the same as a sign bit.

With signed formats (for example, **int** as opposed to **unsigned int**), only the bottom half of the range is used to represent positive values, along with zero. The top half of the range represents negative values. Consequently, a pattern with leftmost bit set to 1 always indicates a negative value.

Here's how the format works. To take the negative of any number, follow these steps:

1 Reverse the setting of each bit (this is logical bitwise negation, also called the one's complement).

2 Add 1.

For example, to produce -1 for a single-byte number, first start with the bit pattern for 1. Remember, we're going to get the negative by reversing each bit and adding 1.

```
0000 0001
```

First, we reverse each bit:

```
1111 1110
```

Adding 1 then produces the *two's complement*. This is therefore the two's complement representation of -1:

```
1111 1111
```

And in fact, for every signed integer format, the setting of all 1s in every bit position always signifies -1. If we were using unsigned format, this bit pattern would instead be interpreted as 255.

Using all 1s to represent -1 is mathematically sound. If you take the negative again, you get positive 1, exactly as expected. Remember, to get the negative of any signed number, reverse each digit and then add 1. You can see how this gets us back to positive 1:

```
  1111 1111      (This is -1)

  0000 0000      Reverse each bit.
+ 0000 0001      Add 1.
  ===========
  0000 0001
```

The -1 value, of course, is not the lowest possible negative value. The lowest signed value is always a bit pattern of 1 followed by all 0s:

```
1000 0000
```

With a signed, two's complement format, this is interpreted as -128. (In unsigned format, it would be interpreted as positive 128.) Adding 1 in signed format produces -127, a slightly higher number:

```
1000 0001
```

The general rule is that any signed quantity with 1 in its leftmost bit is interpreted as a negative number.

Incidentally, taking the two's complement of 0 produces 0 itself. This is mathematically correct, because multiplying 0 by -1 should produce 0.

```
  0000 0000    // Start with 0
  1111 1111    // Reverse each bit (one's complement)
+          1   //  Now add 1 to get two's complement
============
  0000 0000    // "Flips over," producing 0 again!
```

The advantage of using two's complement format for representing signed numbers is that so many mathematical operations work smoothly with it without needing to check a sign bit. With a few exceptions, the same machine instructions that work on unsigned integers work correctly, and without change, on signed integers. For example, if you add any number to its negative, you end up with zero, exactly as expected.

```
0000 0001        1
1111 1111    Add -1
=========
0000 0000    Result "flips over," producing 0.
```

Syntax Summary

This appendix gives a general overview of the core C++ language.

Basic Expression Syntax

Except in the case of **void** expressions, an expression is something that produces a value. Expressions are the fundamental building blocks of statements, because an expression can be turned into a statement by adding a semicolon (;).

Smaller expressions can form part of larger expressions. For example, an expression is formed by addition:

```
expression + expression
```

Each of these can be any two smaller expressions that produce a numeric value. (Also, pointers may be added to integers; see Appendix A.) The result is an expression that can be used, in turn, in still larger expressions.

In C and C++, expressions can produce side effects. For example, the following decrements j by 1, multiplies the result by 3, and then assigns that result to both x and y:

```
x = (y = 3 * --j);
```

This statement contains one long expression terminated by a semicolon (;). Note that assignment is not a kind of statement but merely another kind of expression. Several of these expressions have side effects. First, --j decrements the value of j before using j in the assignment expression:

```
y = 3 * --j
```

Assignment is an expression with a side effect, in this case, setting the value of y. As with all assignment operators (see Appendix A), the value assigned is passed along to the larger expression, which in turn assigns this same value to x.

The following are all expressions:

```
literal
symbol
expression op expression        // (binary op)
op expression                   // (unary op)
expression op                   // (unary op)
function(args)
```

In addition, C++ supports one trinary operator: the conditional operator.

Basic Statement Syntax

Statements are the building blocks of C++ programs because a program consists of one or more functions, and each function consists of zero or more statements.

The most common form of a statement in C++ is an expression terminated by a semicolon (;). Notably, semicolons are statement terminators, not statement separators as they are in Pascal.

```
expression;
```

It is also valid to have a statement with no expression. This is an empty statement.

```
;
```

Any number of statements can be grouped together to form a compound statement (also called a *block*). Remember that a compound statement is valid anywhere a single statement is valid.

```
{ statements }
```

Each of the control structures (covered in the next four sections) also defines a statement. Control structures can therefore be nested to any level.

In addition to these statements and the control structures (**if, while, do-while,** and **switch**), there are several "branching," or direct-transfer-of-control statements: **break, continue, return,** and **goto.**

A statement can be labeled with a symbolic name (following the same rules as variable names), as follows:

```
label: statement
```

This syntax (like that for control structures) is recursive so that a statement can have multiple labels—a fact that **switch-case** statements sometimes take advantage of.

Control Structures and Branch Statements

This section contains a section on each of the statements that controls execution in a C++ program.

The if-else Statement

The **if** statement has two forms. The first form is as follows, in which *condition* is an expression that evaluates to true (any nonzero value) or false (a zero value):

```
if (condition)
    statement
```

Standard practice is to use relational expressions (such as n > 0), which always produce **true** or **false**, or an expression of type **bool**. It can also be effective to use a pointer as a condition in C++. If the pointer is null (for example, because a file-open attempt failed), the condition equates to false; otherwise, it equates to true.

Pointers can be compared to NULL by using logical negation (!), meaning "not." For example, in this case, several statements are executed if the file was not successfully opened:

```
ofstream fout(silly_file_name);
if (!fout) {
    cout << "Could not print ";
    cout << silly_file_name;
    return -1;
}
```

An **if** statement can have an optional **else** clause:

```
if (condition)
    statement1
else
    statement2
```

The while Statement

The **while** statement has the following syntax:

```
while (condition)
    statement
```

The *condition* is a true/false expression; see the **if** statement for rules applying to conditions.

The action of the **while** statement is to first to evaluate the *condition*. If it is true, then the *statement* is executed, and then the condition is tested again. The cycle continues until *condition* is false or unless some other action terminates the loop, such as **break**.

For example, the following code fragment prints a message five times:

```
int n = 5;

while (n-- > 0) {
    cout << "Hello.";
    cout << endl;
}
```

The do-while Statement

The **do-while** statement has the following syntax:

```
do
    statement
while (condition);
```

The operation of the **do-while** statement is the same as the **while** statement, except that with the **do-while** statement, the enclosed statement is executed at least once; the condition is evaluated afterword.

The for Statement

The **for** statement provides a compact way of using three expressions (abbreviated *expr*) to control execution of a loop.

```
for (init_expr; condition_expr; increment_expr)
    statement
```

This expression is essentially the same as the following in its behavior (except, as noted later, with regard to the continue statement):

```
init_expr;
while (condition_expr) {
    statement
    increment _expr;
}
```

The *init_expression* can declare one or more variables; if it does, the variables declared are local to the **for** statement. For example, the following code fragment prints the whole numbers from 1 to 10:

```
for (int i = 1; i <= 10; i++) {
    cout << i << endl;    // i local to this block.
}
```

For more information, see Chapter 3, which I have devoted entirely to the **for** statement.

The switch-case Statement

The **switch-case** statement is an alternative to the use of repeated if-else. It has this syntax:

```
switch (target_expression) {
    statements
}
```

Within the statements, you can place any number of statements labeled with the case keyword. A case statement has this syntax:

```
case constant: statement
```

It follows from the recursive nature of the syntax that a single statement may (optionally) have multiple labels. For example:

```
case 'a':
case 'e':
case 'i':
case 'o':
case 'u':
    cout << "is a vowel";
```

You can also include an optional default label.

```
default: statement
```

Statement labels need to be unique within the scope of the **switch** statement but not necessarily the larger program.

The action of switch is to evaluate the *target_expression*. Control is then transferred to the case statement, if any, whose constant value matches the value of *target_expression*. If none of these values matches but there is a statement labeled default, then control is transferred there. If none of the values matches and there is no default statement, control passes to the first statement after the end of the switch statement.

For example, the following code fragment prints "is a vowel," "may be a vowel," or "is not a vowel," depending on the value of c.

```
switch(c) {
    case 'a':
    case 'e':
    case 'i':
    case 'o':
    case 'u':
        cout << "is a vowel";
        break;
    case 'y':
        cout << "may be a vowel";
        break;
    default:
        cout << "is not a vowel";
}
```

Once control is transferred to any statement within the block, execution is continues normally, falling through unless a **break** statement is encountered. For this reason, each "case block" should usually be terminated with a **break** statement.

The break Statement

The **break** statement transfers execution out of the nearest enclosing while, do-while, for, or switch-case statement. Execution is transferred to the first statement past the end of the block.

```
break;
```

The continue Statement

The **continue** statement causes execution to be transferred to the end of the current **while, do-while,** or **for** statement, effectively advancing to the next iteration (cycle) of the loop.

```
continue;
```

If **continue** is used inside a **for** loop, the *increment* portion of the **for** statement is executed as part of the action of advancing to the next iteration.

The goto Statement

Traditionally, using **goto** is strongly discouraged because its overuse tends to create something called *spaghetti code*, in which the flow of control in the program resembles a tangled heap of spaghetti; these days it might also be compared to the mess of interconnected wires in the back of a home-entertainment system.

But **goto** is still useful as a way of breaking out of a deeply nested loop, since a single **break** statement would not do the job.

```
goto label;
```

The label is a symbol (that is, a name) used to label a statement within the same function. Remember that labeled statements have this syntax:

```
label: statement
```

The return Statement

The **return** statement has two forms. The first, used with **void** functions, causes immediate exit from the current function. Control returns to the caller of the function.

```
return;
```

When within functions that are not **void**, the **return** statement must return a value of the appropriate type.

```
return value;
```

Note that when used within **main**, the **return** statement returns control to the operating system. In such a case, the return value may be a success or failure code (0 usually associated with no errors, or success).

```
return EXIT_SUCCESS;
```

The throw Statement

The **throw** statement raises an exception, which must then be handled by the nearest enclosing catch block; otherwise, the program terminates abruptly. See Chapter 9 for more information on throw and catch.

```
throw exception_object;
```

The *exception_object* may have any type; **catch** statements handle an object by looking for that type. The matching catch block will have either the same type or a base-class type (that is, it must be an ancestor class of the type of object thrown).

Variable Declarations

A data declaration is a statement that creates one or more variables of a particular type. If the type is a class, the variables are objects. In the following syntax, *var_decl* is one or more variable declarations, separated by commas if there is more than one:

```
modifiers  type  var_decls;
```

Each *var_decl* is a variable declaration with an optional initialization. For the meaning of the optional *modifiers*, see the end of this section.

Either of these is valid:

```
var_name
```

```
var_name = init_expression
```

The *init_expression* is any valid expression of the corresponding type or an expression that can be converted to the type. If the variable is an array, *init_expression* may also be an aggregate:

```
{ init_expression, init_expression... }
```

For example, the following statements declare three variables of type **int**; two of them are initialized:

```
int i = 0, j = 1, k;
```

And this example declares a two-dimensional array and initializes it:

```
double[2][2] = {{1.5, 3.9}, {23.0, -8.1}};
```

If the variable being declared is an object (it has class type), it can be initialized through "function-style" syntax, which passes arguments along to the appropriate constructor.

```
Fraction fract1(1, 2);
```

The C++0x specification also allows you to use aggregate-style initialization with objects:

```
Fraction fract1{1, 2};
Fraction fract2 = {10, 3};
```

In a variable declaration, the variable name can be qualified with operators, including [], *, (), and &; these create arrays, pointers, pointers to functions, and references, respectively. To determine what kind of item has been declared, ask yourself what the item would necessarily represent in executable code. For example, the variable declaration

```
int **ptr;
```

means that **ptr, when it appears in executable code, is an item of type **int**; ptr itself is therefore a pointer to a pointer to an integer, because it would have to be dereferenced twice to produce an integer. Likewise, the following declaration creates a pointer to a function—and that function must take a single double argument and return a double return value.

```
double (*fPointer)(double);
```

Pointers to functions are used as callback functions (for example, passed to the qsort library function) and in tables of functions. A pointer to a function needs to be assigned the address of a function before being called.

```
double (*fPointer)(double);
fPointer = &sqrt;
...
int x = (*fPointer)(5.0);    // Call sqrt(5)
```

The exception to this general procedure is that the ampersand (&) creates a reference during declaration. Note that reference variables need to be initialized, or else need to be reference arguments; otherwise, they have nothing to refer to. References, unlike pointers, cannot be reassigned to refer to new data.

```
int n = 0;
int &silly = n;  // silly is a reference for n.
```

The optional *modifiers* to a variable declaration can include any of the following:

▶ **auto**: This is largely outmoded and unnecessary. It indicates automatic storage class, which local variables have by default. (Do not confuse with **auto** variable definitions permitted by C++0x, in which the **auto** keyword is used in place of a type.)

▶ **const**: A variable declared **const** is prevented from being changed by being on the left part of an assignment, incremented, or decremented. Also, a pointer or reference to a **const** variable may not be passed to a function unless that function is also declared **const** or unless the function declares the argument as **const**. Pointers and references to a **const** type may not change the data to which they refer.

▶ **extern**: An **extern** declaration gives a variable visibility among all modules of the project. (In addition to an **extern** declaration, the variable also needs to be defined in exactly one module; you can do this by initializing it and declaring it without **extern**.)

▶ **register**: A suggestion to the compiler that it should dedicate a register (onboard processor memory) to the variable. Modern optimizing compilers do this anyway when it would improve program performance and therefore may ignore this modifier.

▶ **static**: When used with a local variable or data member, it indicates there is only one copy of the variable. In the case of local variables, this means that the function "remembers" the value between function calls. It's incompatible with recursive functions.

▶ **volatile**: A rarely used but occasionally important keyword; **volatile** is an indicator to the compiler that it must not place a variable in a register or make any assumptions about when it can change. This is most often used when a variable corresponds to a location that is being manipulated by some outside hardware device (such as a port).

Function Declarations

Before a function can be called by another function, it must first be declared or defined. It can be given a type declaration first (a prototype). The definition can then be placed anywhere in the source code or another module linked into the project.

A function prototype has this syntax:

```
modifiers  type  function_name(argument_list);
```

For the meaning of the optional *modifiers*, see the end of this section. The *type* specifies the return value of the function. A function can optionally have **void** type, specifying that it does not return a value.

The *argument list* contains one or more argument declarations separated by commas if there are more than one. The argument list may be left blank, indicating that the function has no arguments. (Unlike C, C++ does not permit the use of a blank argument list to mean an indeterminate list.)

Each entry in the argument list has the following form. Declaration syntax follows other rules specified for variable declarations (see previous section), and it permits an optional initializing expression indicating a default argument. But note that each *type* and *var_decl* must be one-to-one.

```
type  var_decl
```

A more complete syntax for a function prototype is therefore as follows, in which there are zero or more occurrences of *type var_decl*. If there are more than one, they are separated by commas:

```
modifiers   type   function_name( type var_decl, ...);
```

Syntax for a complete declaration, including function definition, is the same, except that it includes a block with zero or more statements. (Note that any *modifiers* previously declared in a prototype do not, as a general rule, need to be repeated in the definition.)

```
modifiers   type   function_name(argument_list) {
    statements
}
```

A function definition does not end with a semicolon (;) after the final brace—unlike a class declaration. Also, note that names of arguments (but not types) can be omitted from a prototype but not from a function definition.

The optional *modifiers* can include any of the following:

▶ **const:** A **const** function is restricted from changing the value of its arguments and from calling other functions not declared **const**. But this permits it to be called by other **const** functions.

▶ **inline:** A suggestion to the compiler that the function be made an inline function. Modern optimizing compilers do this on their own whenever it would improve speed and compactness, making this keyword less necessary. In addition, a member function defined within its class declaration is automatically inlined.

▶ **static:** In multiple-module projects, a function automatically has external linkage unless declared with static. (Each function still needs to be prototyped in any source file that uses it, however, thus making header files necessary.)

▶ **virtual:** Used with member functions only. Declaring a function virtual means that calls to the function are handled through indirect calls that involve a vtable, which, in practical terms, means that the destination of the function call is not resolved until runtime. In C++, the details of carrying this out are invisible to the programmer, so you call a virtual function exactly the way you'd call any other function. The **virtual** keyword needs to be applied only once, when the function is first declared in the base class.

Class Declarations

A class declaration extends the language by creating a new type. Once a class is declared, the class name can be used directly as a type name, just like an intrinsic data type such as **int, double, float**, and so on. The basic syntax for a class declaration is as follows:

```
class class_name {
    declarations
};
```

Unlike a function definition, a class declaration is always terminated by a semicolon (;) after the closing brace.

The declarations can include any number of data and/or function definitions. Within the declarations, the **public, protected**, and **private** keywords can occur, along with a colon (:) to indicate the access level of the declarations that follow it. For example, in the following class declaration, data members a and b are private; data member c, as well as function f1, are public.

```
class my_class {
private:
    int a, b;
public:
    int c;
    void f1(int a);
};
```

Note when you use the **class** keyword to declare a class, members are private by default.

Within a class declaration, constructors and destructors have the following special declarations. You can have any number of constructors differentiated by argument lists. You can have at most one destructor.

```
class_name (argument_list)        // Constructor
~class_name()                      // Destructor
```

The syntax for a subclass declaration includes the name of a base class. Although the use of **public** in this context is not required, it is strongly recommended. Without it, default base-class access level is private, which makes all inherited members private.

```
class class_name : public base_class {
    declarations
};
```

Most versions of C++ support multiple inheritance, in which you list more than one base class separated by commas. For example, in this example, the class Dog is derived from both Animal and Pets and therefore inherits all members of both classes:

```
class Dog : public Animal, public Pets {
...
}
```

Note ▶ The syntax here applies to the **struct** and **union** keywords as well as **class**. A **struct** class is the same as a class defined with the **class** keyword, except that with **struct**, members are public by default, and with **class**, members are private by default. Members of a **union** class are also public by default. Members of a union share the same address in memory. (Basically, a union can be used to create a "variable data type" class in which different data formats are in use at different times.)

Enum Declarations

The **enum** keyword can be used to create a series of symbolic names (symbols) each with a constant integer value. It has this general syntax, in which *name* is optional:

```
enum name {
    symbol_decls
};
```

In this syntax, *symbol_decl* consists of one or more names, separated by commas if there are more than one. In addition, each may optionally have an assigned value:

```
symbol = assigned_value
```

If a symbol is not assigned a value (which must be a literal or other constant), its value is that of the previous symbol plus one. If it is the first symbol and not assigned a value, it is given the value zero.

For example, the following declaration creates enumerated constants rock, paper, scissors and gives them the values 0, 1, and 2.

```
enum {rock, paper, scissors};
```

Optionally, these can be given a type name, which creates a weakly typed enumeration. (For information on how to create strongly typed enumerations with C++0x, see Chapter 10.)

```
enum Choice {rock, paper, scissors};
```

Now the word Choice can be used to declare variables just like any other type name. The underlying type of an enumeration is actually integer, and you can assign enumerated constants to integer variables. However, you can't go in the opposite direction without a cast.

```
Choice my_play = rock;
int n = paper;                 // Ok without cast

// But this requires a cast...

Choice your_play = static_cast<Choice>(1);
```

Preprocessor Directives

The C++ preprocessor can perform a number of useful actions before the regular compilation phase. For example, the **#define** directive can be used to replace all occurrences of a certain word with another—creating easy-to-interpret symbolic constants rather than arbitrary-looking numbers. The directives have other uses, the most important of which are probably including header files and making sure that such header files are compiled only once.

In addition to the directives listed here, C++ also supports a **#pragma** directive, but its use is entirely implementation defined. See your compiler documentation for more information.

This appendix covers the directives in alphabetical order, followed by a list of predefined compiler constants.

The #define Directive

The **#define** directive has three forms, each of which has a different use.

```
#define symbol_name

#define symbol_name  replacement_text

#define symbol_name(args)  replacement_text
```

The first version of **#define** is used to control compilation, by affecting the behavior of the **#ifdef** and related directives later. For example, you might use the following directive to indicate that the C++0x specification is supported. See **#if**, **#ifdef**, and **#ifndef** for more information.

```
#define CPLUSPLUS_0X
```

The second version is useful in creating predefined constants to help remove "magic numbers" (that is, arbitrary numbers) from your program. For example, you might define column width just once in your program:

```
#define COL_WIDTH  80
...
char input_string[COL_WIDTH+1];
```

One of the advantages of using this approach is that if you decide to change the column width, you only need to change it in one place (namely, the **#define** directive); the change is then automatically reflected throughout the source file wherever COL_WIDTH appears.

The third version is used to define macro functions, which take one or more arguments and expand them into larger expressions. The effect is something like inline functions, which are expanded into the body of the caller. Macro functions, however, have some limitations. They are usually limited to single expressions, and they have no type checking.

The following example macro function produces the maximum of two numbers. It takes advantage of the condition (?:) operator; see Appendix A for more information on this operator.

```
#define  MAX(A, B)  ((A)>(B) ? (A) : (B))
```

The extra parentheses, though not always necessary, help ensure that the expressions A and B are evaluated in their entirety before the other operators are applied (just in case A and B are complex expressions). Here is an example that uses this macro:

```
int x, y;
cout << "Enter a number: "
cin >> x;
cout << "Enter another: "
cin >> y;

cout << "The maximum is: " << MAX(x, y);
```

During preprocessing, the compiler expands the last line shown in the previous code into the following (in which I've removed the extra parentheses for clarity). The action of the conditional (?:) operator is to evaluate the first expression (in this case, x>y) and return x if true or y if false.

```
cout << "The maximum is: " << (x>y ? x : y);
```

The ## Operator (Concatenation)

The concatenation operator is used within macros to join text together, as in this macro, designed to generate file names:

```
#define  FILE(A, B)  myfile__##A.##B
```

The expression FILE(1, doc) should generate the following:

```
myfile__1.doc
```

The defined Function

This function is almost always used in conjunction with **#if** and **#elif**. It has this syntax:

```
defined(symbol_name)
```

If *symbol_name* is defined (it doesn't matter what value, if any, the symbol was given), the **defined** function returns true; otherwise, it returns false. For example, this function can be used to turn an **#if** directive into an **#ifdef** directive:

```
#if defined(CPLUSPLUS_0x)
```

For a more complete example, see the next section.

The #elif Directive

The **#elif** directive can be used as part of a conditional compilation block. **#elif** forms the beginning of an "else if" block. In the following example, different source code is compiled depending on whether the symbol CPLUSPLUS_0x has been defined, the symbol ANSI has been defined, or neither has been defined. It does not matter what value (if any) was assigned to these symbols.

```
#if defined(CPLUSPLUS_0x)

// Here you might place code supported by
// C++0x-compliant compilers only.

#elif defined(ANSI)

// Here you might place code for compilers that are
// ANSI compliant but not C++0x compliant.
```

```
#else

// Place code here for compilers not ANSI compliant.

#endif
```

Given this conditional-compilation block, you can control what gets compiled by inserting or deleting one line that precedes this block, such as the following:

```
#define ANSI    // Use ANSI features (but not C++0x)
```

The #endif Directive

The **#endif** directive forms the end of a conditional-compilation block. It is used in conjunction with **#if**, **#ifdef**, **#ifndef**, and **#elif**. Note that the syntax used here is not like C++ language syntax; the preprocessor has a language all its own that resembles Basic more than it does C++.

For examples of use, see any of the related sections: **#if**, **#ifdef**, **#ifndef**, and **#elif**.

The #error Directive

The **#error** directive generates an error message during compilation. For example:

```
#ifndef __cplusplus < 199711
#error C++ compiler out of date.
#endif
```

The #if Directive

The **#if** directive is used to begin a conditional compilation block. It is mostly used in conjunction with the **defined** function. For example, although this is implementation specific, compilers may choose to refer to predefined constants such as __win32__ or __linix__ to indicate what operating system they are running on.

```
#if defined(__win32__)
char op_sys[] = "Microsoft Windows";
#endif
```

If the value following **#if** is true, the compiler reads and processes lines of code up until the nearest matching **#elif**, **#else**, or **#endif** directive; otherwise, it ignores those lines.

Another use for **#if** and **#endif** is to temporarily "comment out" large blocks of code. Notice that C-style comment symbols (/* and */) do not nest properly and—if you attempt to nest them—cause errors:

```
/*  (Begin a "commented-out" block...
/*
char op_sys[] = "Overco Operating System";

*/          // OOPS! This ends the first comment.
*/          // Syntax error!
```

However, **#if**/**#endif** pairs can be as deeply nested as you like. Each **#if**/**#endif** pair can be used to "comment out" lines of code that you do not want to compile at this particular time. One commented-out block can be placed inside another.

```
#if 1

// Do some stuff.
#if 1

// Do some more stuff.
#endif
...
#endif
```

The #ifdef Directive

The **#ifdef** directive begins a conditional compilation block. Although closely related to the **#if** directive, it is a more succinct way of expressing what the **#if** directive usually does. The following syntax

```
#ifdef symbol_name
```

is exactly equivalent to the following:

```
#if defined(symbol_name)
```

The first example in the previous section could be rewritten as follows:

```
#ifdef __win32__
char op_sys[] = "Microsoft Windows";
#endif
```

The #ifndef Directive

This directive is similar to the **#ifdef** directive but reverses its logical meaning; it enables conditional compilation only if the specified symbol has *not* been defined.

```
#ifndef symbol_name
```

This directive is widely used to avoid conflicts that can occur when multiple header files are in use.

For example, the following statements can be used to prevent compilation of a header file that has already been compiled. For example:

```
#ifndef FRACT_H
#define FRACT_H

// Here is the body of Fraction.h

#endif
```

The first time that the file Fraction.h is read in, it defines the symbol FRACT_H; that, in turn, prevents Fraction.h from being compiled a second time, no matter how many different files include it.

The #include Directive

The **#include** directive has two different versions. Both are almost always used to include *header files*, which contain function prototypes and symbolic constants needed to work with a project or a portion of the standard library.

```
#include <filename>
```

```
#include "filename"
```

In either case, the effect of **#include** is to suspend compilation of the current file and instead run the compiler on the named file until the end of that file is reached. Then the compiler returns to compiling the current file.

The first version (using angle brackets) searches for the named file in the directory or folder set aside for header files. In the case of MS-DOS and Windows, for example, this directory is indicated by the setting of an INC environment variable.

The second version (using quotation marks) searches for the named file in the same way but also searches the current directory or folder.

By convention, the first version is almost always used to include library header files or header files supplied by vendors (even though both versions would work), while the second version is used for header files for the project. For example:

```
#include <iostream>
#include <cmath>
#include "Fraction.h"
```

Note ▶ Each standard library file beginning with *c*, as in cmath, corresponds to a traditional .h file inherited from the C language. Another example is cctype, which corresponds to the ctype.h file used in C. With C++, the newer form is preferred, even if the older (C-style) headers still work for now.

The #line Directive

The #line directive has two forms.

```
#line   filename   number
#line   number
```

The effect is to reset the values of the __FILE__ and __LINE__ constants, as well as affecting how error messages are printed by the computer. For example:

```
#line myfile.cpp 100
```

The #undef Directive

The **#undef** directive undoes the definition of the named symbol, so it is no longer considered defined.

```
#undef   symbol_name
```

Predefined Constants

Table D.1 lists constants that all C++ preprocessors are required to support. Specific implementations of C++ may define others as well.

Table D.1: C++ Predefined Constants

CONSTANT	MEANING IF DEFINED
__cplusplus	Indicates support of a particular version of C++. Current, up-to-date compilers should define it as 199711 or greater.
__DATE__	Expands to a date string in the format mm dd yyyy.
__FILE__	Name of file being compiled.
__LINE__	Current line being compiled.
__STDC__	Defined by C compilers as 1. Usually defined by C++ compilers to indicate support for C, but this is implementation-defined.
__TIME__	Expands to a time string in the format hh:mm:ss.

ASCII Codes

This appendix presents ASCII codes according to decimal value, hexadecimal value, and corresponding character. Hexadecimal codes can be used to embed values into a string. You can also print characters by using a (char) cast. For example:

```
cout << "Hex code 7e is " << "\x7e" << endl;

// Print ASCII codes from 32 to 42.
for (int i = 32; i <= 42; i++)
    cout << i << ": " << (char) i << endl;
```

Some nonprintable characters have special meanings:

- **NUL:** null value

- **ACK:** acknowledgment signal (used in network communications)

- **BEL:** bell

- **BS:** backspace

- **LF:** linefeed

- **FF:** form feed (new page)

- **CR:** carriage return

- **NAK:** no acknowledgment

- **DEL:** delete

Table E.1 gives the standard ASCII codes.

Table E.1: Standard ASCII Codes

DEC	HEX	CHAR	DEC	HEX	CHAR	DEC	HEX	CHAR	DEC	HEX	CHAR	DEC	HEX	CHAR
00	00	NUL	26	1a		52	34	4	78	4e	N	104	68	h
01	01		27	1b		53	35	5	79	4f	O	105	69	i
02	02		28	1c	FS	54	36	6	80	50	P	106	6a	j
03	03		29	1d	GS	55	37	7	81	51	Q	107	6b	k
04	04		30	1e	RS	56	38	8	82	52	R	108	6c	l
05	05		31	1f	US	57	39	9	83	53	S	109	6d	m
06	06	ACK	32	20	space	58	3a	:	84	54	T	110	6e	n
07	07	BEL	33	21	!	59	3b	;	85	55	U	111	6f	o
08	08	BS	34	22	"	60	3c	<	86	56	V	112	70	p
09	09		35	23	#	61	3d	=	87	57	W	113	71	q
10	0a	LF	36	24	$	62	3e	>	88	58	X	114	72	r
11	0b	CR	37	25	%	63	3f	?	89	59	Y	115	73	s
12	0c		38	26	&	64	40	@	90	5a	Z	116	74	t
13	0d		39	27	'	65	41	A	91	5b	[	117	75	u
14	0e		40	28	(	66	42	B	92	5c	\	118	76	v
15	0f		41	29	)	67	43	C	93	5d	]	119	77	w
16	10		42	2a	*	68	44	D	94	5e	^	120	78	x
17	11		43	2b	+	69	45	E	95	5f	-	121	79	y
18	12		44	2c	,	70	46	F	96	60	`	122	7a	z
19	13		45	2d	-	71	47	G	97	61	a	123	7b	{
20	14		46	2e	.	72	48	H	98	62	b	124	7c	|
21	15	NAK	47	2f	/	73	49	I	99	63	c	125	7d	}
22	16	SYN	48	30	0	74	4a	J	100	64	d	126	7e	~
23	17		49	31	1	75	4b	K	101	65	e	127	7f	DEL
24	18		50	32	2	76	4c	L	102	66	f			
25	19		51	33	3	77	4d	M	103	67	g			

Table E.2 lists extended ASCII codes; note that these are somewhat implementation dependent. They are most likely to be correct for computers of American manufacturers running Windows.

Table E.2: Extended ASCII Codes for American Equipment Manufacturers

DEC	HEX	CHAR	DEC	HEX	CHAR	DEC	HEX	CHAR	DEC	HEX	CHAR	DEC	HEX	CHAR
128	80	Ç	154	9a	Ü	180	b4	┤	206	ce	╬	232	e8	Φ
129	81	ü	155	9b	¢	181	b5	╡	207	cf	╧	233	e9	Θ
130	82	é	156	9c	£	182	b6	╢	208	d0	╨	234	ea	Ω
131	83	â	157	9d	¥	183	b7	╖	209	d1	╤	235	eb	δ
132	84	ä	158	9e	₧	184	b8	╕	210	d2	╥	236	ec	∞
133	85	à	159	9f	ƒ	185	b9	╣	211	d3	╙	237	ed	φ
134	86	å	160	a0	á	186	ba	║	212	d4	╘	238	ee	ε
135	87	ç	161	a1	í	187	bb	╗	213	d5	╒	239	ef	∩
136	88	ê	162	a2	ó	188	bc	╝	214	d6	╓	240	f0	≡
137	89	ë	163	a3	ú	189	bd	╜	215	d7	╫	241	f1	±
138	8a	è	164	a4	ñ	190	be	╛	216	d8	╪	242	f2	≥
139	8b	ï	165	a5	Ñ	191	bf	┐	217	d9	┘	243	f3	≤
140	8c	î	166	a6	ª	192	c0	└	218	da	┌	244	f4	⌠
141	8d	ì	167	a7	º	193	c1	┴	219	db	█	245	f5	⌡
142	8e	Ä	168	a8	¿	194	c2	┬	220	dc	▄	246	f6	÷
143	8f	Å	169	a9	⌐	195	c3	├	221	dd	▌	247	f7	≈
144	90	É	170	aa	¬	196	c4	─	222	de	▐	248	f8	°
145	91	æ	171	ab	½	197	c5	┼	223	df	▀	249	f9	·
146	92	Æ	172	ac	¼	198	c6	╞	224	e0	α	250	fa	·
147	93	ô	173	ad	¡	199	c7	╟	225	e1	ß	251	fb	√
148	94	ö	174	ae	«	200	c8	╚	226	e2	Γ	252	fc	ⁿ
149	95	ò	175	af	»	201	c9	╔	227	e3	π	253	fd	²
150	96	û	176	b0	░	202	ca	╩	228	e4	Σ	254	fe	■
151	97	ù	177	b1	▒	203	cb	╦	229	e5	σ	255	ff	
152	98	ÿ	178	b2	▓	204	cc	╠	230	e6	µ			
153	99	Ö	179	b3	│	205	cd	═	231	e7	τ			

Standard Library Functions

The most commonly used library functions fall into a few categories: string functions, data-conversion functions, single character functions, math functions, time functions, and randomization functions. This appendix provides an overview. Note that I do not cover I/O functions such as printf or fprintf, because I assume you are using C++ stream classes.

For more information on the stream objects **cin**, **cout**, and the stream classes, see Appendix G.

String (C-String) Functions

To use these functions, include the file <cstring>. The functions apply to traditional C **char*** strings, not to the STL **string** class.

In Table F.1, s, s1, and s2 are null-terminated **char*** strings; or rather, each of these equates to the address of one of these strings. Also, n is an integer, and ch is a single character. Except where otherwise noted, each of these functions returns the address of its first argument.

Table F.1: Common String Functions

FUNCTION	ACTION
strcat(s1, s2)	Concatenates the contents of s2 onto the end of s1.
strchr(s, ch)	Returns a pointer to the first occurrence of ch in string s; returns NULL if ch cannot be found.
strcmp(s1, s2)	Performs a comparison between contents of s1 and s2, returning a negative integer, 0, or a positive integer, depending on whether s1 appears before s2 in alpha order, has same contents as s2, or appears later than s2.
strcpy(s1, s2)	Copies contents of s2 into s1, replacing existing contents.

continues

Table F.1: Common String Functions (*Continued*)

FUNCTION	ACTION
strcspn(s1, s2)	Searches s1 for occurrence of any character in s2; returns index of first matching s1 character; returns the length of s1 if none found.
strlen(s)	Returns current length of s (not including null byte).
strncat(s1, s2, n)	Same action as **strcat** but copies at most n characters.
strncmp(s1, s2, n)	Same action as **strcmp** but compares at most n characters.
strncpy(s1, s2, n)	Same action as **strcpy** but copies at most n characters.
strpbrk(s1, s2)	Searches s1 for occurrence of any character in s2; returns a pointer to first matching s1 character; returns NULL if none found.
strrchr(s, ch)	Same action as **strpbrk** but searches s1 in reverse order.
strspn(s1, s2)	Searches s1 for first character that does not match any character in s2; returns index of this character; returns length of s1 if none found.
strstr(s1, s2)	Searches s1 for the first occurrence of substring s2; returns a pointer to substring found within s1; returns NULL if not found.
strtok(s1, s2)	Returns a pointer to the first token (substring) in s1, using delimiters specified in s2. Subsequent calls to this function with NULL for the first argument find the next token within the current string—the previously set value of s1. Specifying a non-null value for s1 resets the tokenization process with a new string.

Data-Conversion Functions

To use the functions in Table F.2, include <cstdlib>.

Table F.2: Data-Conversion Functions

FUNCTION	ACTION
atof(s)	Reads a **char*** text string as a floating-point digit string and returns the equivalent **double**. The function skips past leading spaces and stops reading after the first character that doesn't form part of a valid floating-point representation (such as "1.5" or "2e1.2").
atoi(s)	Reads a **char*** text string as a digit string and returns the equivalent **int**. The function skips past leading spaces and stops reading after the first character that doesn't form part of a valid integer representation (such as "-27").
atol(s)	Reads a **char*** string and produces a **long** value; on 32-bit systems, this is equivalent to **atoi**.
atoll(s)	Similar to **atoi**, but it produces a **long long** integer value. Required in the C++0x specification

Single-Character Functions

To use any of the functions in Table F.3 or Table F.4, include <cctype>. Each of the functions in this first subgroup tests a single character and returns true or false.

Table F.3: Character-Testing Functions

FUNCTION	ACTION
isalnum(*ch*)	Is the character alphanumeric (a letter or digit)?
isalpha(*ch*)	Is the character a letter?
iscntrl(*ch*)	Is the character a control character? (These include backspace, line-feed, form feed, and tab, among others; these are nonprintable characters that perform actions.)
isdigit(*ch*)	Is the character a digit in the range 0 to 9?
isgraph(*ch*)	Is the character visible? (This includes printable characters other than a space.)
islower(*ch*)	Is the character a lowercase letter?
isprint(*ch*)	Is the character printable? (This includes space characters.)
ispunct(*ch*)	Is the character a punctuation character?
isspace(*ch*)	Is the character a white space? (This includes tab, newline, and form feed, in addition to the simple space character.)
isupper(*ch*)	Is the character an uppercase letter?
isxdigit(*ch*)	Is the character a hexadecimal digit? This includes digits in the range 0 through 9, as well as A through E and a through e.

Including <cctype> also adds declarations for the following two conversion functions.

Table F.4: Character Conversion Functions

FUNCTION	ACTION
tolower(*ch*)	Returns a lowercase letter if ch is an uppercase letter; otherwise, returns ch as is
toupper(*ch*)	Returns an uppercase letter if ch is a lowercase letter; otherwise, returns ch as is

Math Functions

To use any of the functions in Table F.5, include <cmath>. Each of the functions in this first takes an argument of type **double** and returns a **double** result, except where noted. Each of these functions returns the result of the operation, and none of them alter their argument or arguments.

In using these functions, keep in mind that an integer can be given where a **double** argument is required; the integer is promoted without C++ printing a warning message. However, to assign a double result to an integer variable causes a warning message to be issued if a cast is not used. (The new style cast useful in this case would be **static_cast**.)

Table F.5: Math Functions

FUNCTION	ACTION
abs(*n*)	Returns the absolute value of **int** argument *n*. Result has type **int**. For floating-point version, see **fabs**.
acos(*x*)	Arc cosine of *x*.
asin(*x*)	Arc sine of *x*.
atan(*x*)	Arc tangent of *x*.
ceil(*x*)	Rounds upward to nearest integer (but still returns result as a **double**).
cos(*x*)	Cosine of *x*.
cosh(*x*)	Hyperbolic cosine of *x*.
exp(*x*)	Raises the mathematical constant e to the power of *x*.
fabs(*x*)	Returns the absolute value of *x*.
floor(*x*)	Rounds *x* downward to the nearest integer (but still returns result as a **double**).
log(*x*)	Natural logarithm (base e) of *x*.
log10(*x*)	Base 10 logarithm of *x*.
pow(*x*, *y*)	Raises x to the power of y. (For example, pow(2,5) returns 32.)
sin(*x*)	Sine of *x*.
sinh(*x*)	Hyperbolic sine of *x*.
sqrt(*x*)	Square root of *x*.
tan(*x*)	Tangent of *x*.
tanh(*x*)	Hyperbolic tangent of *x*.

Randomization Functions

To use the functions in Table F.6, include both <cstdlib> and <ctime>. See Chapter 4 for more information on using these three functions.

Table F.6: Randomization Functions

FUNCTION	ACTION
rand()	Returns the next number (an integer) in the current random-number sequence. This sequence should first be set by calling **srand**. The number returned ranges in value between 0 and RAND_MAX (defined in <cstdlib>).
srand(*seed*)	Takes the seed number—an **unsigned int**—to start the random-number sequence used for calls to **rand**.
time(NULL)	Returns the system time. Calling this function is a good choice for getting the seed number to pass to **srand**.

Time Functions

To support the library functions in Table F.7, include <ctime>. The general procedure with these functions is to call the **time** function to get a **time_t** value representing the current time as a number. Then use that value as input to **gmtime** or **localtime**, which fills a **tm** structure listing specific information including month, day of the week, and so on. The declaration of the **tm** structure is shown at the end of this section.

Alternatively, you can call the **asctime** function to get a **char*** string describing the time in human-readable form—or **ctime**, which produces the same result more directly:

```
#include <ctime>
#include <iostream>

time_t t = time(NULL);    // Put time into t.
cout << ctime(&t);        // Display current time.
```

You can also use **strftime**, which returns a formatted time string.

Table F.7: Time Functions

FUNCTION	DESCRIPTION
asctime(*tm_ptr*)	Takes a pointer to a tm structure and returns a **char*** string in the format "Ddd Mmm DD HH:MM:SS YYYY\n" in which Ddd is a three-letter abbreviation for day of the week and Mmm is a three-letter abbreviation for the month. See also **ctime**.
clock()	Returns number of clock ticks on internal clock. To convert to seconds, divide by CLOCKS_PER_TICK predefined symbol.
ctime(*time_ptr*)	Takes a pointer to a time_t value (returned by the **time** function) and returns a **char*** string in the same format that **asctime** returns. This function is equivalent to calling **localtime** and then passing the resulting structure to **asctime**.
difftime(*t1*, *t2*)	Returns t1–t2 in seconds, in which *t1* and *t2* are time_t values.
gmtime(*time_ptr*)	Takes a pointer to a time_t value (returned by the **time** function) and returns a pointer to a tm structure using Greenwich Mean Time.
localtime(*time_ptr*)	Takes a pointer to a time_t value (returned by the **time** function) and returns a pointer to a tm structure using local time.
mktime(*tm_ptr*)	Converts tm structure pointed to by *tm_ptr* into a time_t value and returns that value. The tm_wday and tm_yday members of the tm structure are ignored.
strftime(*s*, *n*, *fmt*, *tm_ptr*)	Takes a pointer to a tm structure (*tm_ptr*), formats time data from that structure according to a format string *fmt*, and places the result in string *s*. See the next section for details. *n* is the maximum number of characters to write, including null.
time(*time_ptr*)	Returns the current time as a time_t value (usually **unsigned long**, although this is implementation dependent). If the argument is null, it is ignored. If it is not null, the return value is copied to the address specified.

Here is an example that uses some of these functions to print the day of the week as a number from 0 to 6:

```
#include <ctime>
...
time_t t = time(NULL);
tm *tm_pointer = localtime(&t);
cout << "The day is " << tm_pointer->tm_mday;
cout << endl;
```

The declaration of the tm structure is as follows:

```
tm struct tm {
    int tm_sec;      // Seconds, 0-59
```

```
          int tm_min;      // Minutes, 0-59
          int tm_hour;     // Hours, 0-23
          int tm_mday;     // Day of month, 1-31
          int tm_mon;      // Month,0-11
          int tm_year;     // Years since 1900
          int tm_wday;     // Days since Sunday, 0-6
          int tm_yday;     // Days since Jan. 1, 0-365
          int tm_isdst;    // Daylight Savings Time...
    }                      //    positive: DST in effect,
                           //    zero: not in effect,
                           //    negative: unknown
```

Formats for the strftime Function

The **strftime** function has the following declaration:

```
size_t strftime(
  char    *str,     // String to write to.
  size_t  n,        // Max. chars to write,
                    //    including null terminator.
  char    *fmt,     // Format string
  tm      *tm_ptr   // Ptr to tm structure.
);
```

The **strftime** function uses time data from the structure pointed to by *tm_ptr* and writes that data to string *str*. The *fmt* argument contains formatting characters determining what data to write and how to write it, using the format specifiers listed in Table F.8. For example, the following code fragment displays what day of the week it is:

```
#include <iostream>
#include <ctime>

char s[100];
time_t t = time(NULL);
tm *tm_ptr = localtime(&t);
strftime(s, 100, "Today is %A.", tm_ptr);
cout << s << endl;
```

Table F.8: Format Characters for strftime

FORMAT SPECIFIER	DESCRIPTION
%a	Day of the week, abbreviated.
%A	Day of the week, spelled out.
%b	Month name, abbreviated.
%B	Month name, spelled out.
%c	Complete month and day.
%D	Day of the month, 01 to 31.
%H	Hour, 00 to 23 (based on 24-hour clock).
%I	Hour, 00 to 11 (based on 12-hour clock).
%J	Day of the year, 000 to 366.
%m	Month, 01 to 12.
%M	Minute, 00 to 59
%p	a.m./p.m. designation.
%S	Seconds, 00 to 61 (up to two leap seconds)
%U	Week number, 01 to 53. Week 1 starts with first Sunday.
%w	Weekday, 0 to 6, in which Sunday is 0.
%W	Week number, 01 to 53. Week 1 starts with first Monday.
%x	Date.
%X	Time.
%y	Year, 00 to 09, within the century.
%Y	Year.
%Z	Time zone; blank if time zone is not known.
%%	Literal %.

I/O Stream Objects and Classes

The objects and classes in this appendix support reading and writing to the console, as well as to files and strings. To read and write to the console, include <iostream>:

```
#include <iostream>
cout << "Hello, world." << endl;
```

To write data to a string, include <sstream>. String streams support a member function (in addition to the ones listed here), **str**, which returns the data in string format.

```
#include <sstream>

stringstream s_out;
s_out << "The value of i answer is " << i << endl;
string s = s_out.str()
```

Console Stream Objects

The objects listed in Table G.1 provide predeclared streams to which to read or write text to the console. Each of them supports the appropriate stream operator (<< or >>). For example:

```
cout << "n is equal to " << n << endl;
```

Table G.1: Stream Objects

FUNCTION	DESCRIPTION
cerr	Console error-message stream. By default it writes characters to the console just as **cout** does; however, this stream may be redirected without affecting **cout**. Use of this object is fairly rare.
cin	Console input stream. Reads input from the console as a stream of ASCII (8-bit) characters.
clog	Console log stream. Similar to **cerr** and **cout**, but intended to display runtime messages that are not necessarily errors. Use of this object is rare; many programmers never use it.
cout	Console output stream. Displays output to the console as a stream of ASCII (8-bit) characters.
wcerr	Wide-character error-message stream. Similar to **cerr** but writes text as a series of wide characters.
wcin	Wide Console Output. Similar to **cin** but reads input from the console as a stream of wide characters.
wclog	Wide-character log stream. Similar to **clog** but writes text as a series of wide characters.
wcout	Wide-character Console Output. Similar to **cout** but writes text as a series of wide characters.

I/O Stream Manipulators

The I/O manipulators in Table G.2 can be used with stream objects to modify how they read or write text. For example, the following statement writes "0x1f" to the console.

```
cout << hex << showbase << 31;  // Output 0x1f.
```

Some I/O manipulators affect both input and output streams, although many affect output only. For example, if **hex** is used, input is interpreted in hex format. In this code fragment, input of 10 would actually put the value 16 into n.

```
cin >> hex >> n;
```

Table G.2: Stream Manipulators

MANIPULATOR	DESCRIPTION
boolalpha	Writes out Boolean values **true** and **false** as "true" and "false" rather than 1 and 0 (the default).
dec	Switches to decimal format (the default) for integers.
fixed	Displays floating-point numbers in fixed-point format.
hex	Switches to hexadecimal format for integers.
left	Left-justifies output. (Matters only when a minimum print-field width has been specified: see the **width** function in Table G.4.)
noboolalpha	Turns off **boolalpha**, so that **true** and **false** are not printed.
noshowbase	Turns off **showbase**.
noshowpoint	Turns off **showpoint**. Floating-point 5 is written as "5."
nouppercase	Displays numeric data in lowercase letters, so that hexadecimal FF (for example) with **showbase** on is displayed as 0xff (the default).
nounitbuf	Turns off **unitbuf**.
oct	Switches to octal format for integers.
right	Right-justifies output. (Matters only when a minimum print-field width has been specified: see the **width** function in Table G.4.)
scientific	Displays all floating-point numbers in scientific notation.
showbase	When writing octal or hex format, displays the "0x" or "0" prefix.
showpoint	Always displays decimal point when writing out a floating-point number. For example, floating-point 5 is written as "5.0."
showpos	Shows the positive sign (+) for positive numbers.
uppercase	Displays numeric data in uppercase letters, so that hexadecimal FF (for example) with **showbase** on is displayed as 0XFF.
unitbuf	For output streams, causes output buffer to be flushed after each output operation.
endl	When sent to an output stream, this prints a character.
ends	When sent to an output stream, this outputs a null terminator. This manipulator is generally used only with strstream objects.
flush	Flushes the buffer, so that any text in the buffer is immediately written out to destination.

Input Stream Functions

The functions in Table G.3 can be called by input streams such as **cin** as well as input-file streams. For example:

```
char input_str[COL_WIDTH];
cin.getline(str, COL_WIDTH);
```

Table G.3: Input Stream Functions

FUNCTION	DESCRIPTION
get()	Gets the next character from the input stream
getline(s, n)	Copies line of input to string address s, getting no more than n-1 characters
peek()	Returns the next character without removing it from the stream
putback(c)	Puts character c back onto the input stream
read(s, n)	Binary read operation: reads n bytes and places data at address s, which needs to be cast to **char*** type if the data is not in **char** format.

Output Stream Functions

The functions in Table G.4 can be called by output streams such as **cout** as well as output-file streams and string streams. For example, the following code fragment prints a number n in a print field 20 characters wide and right-justifies it:

```
cout.width(20);
cout << right << n << endl;
```

Table G.4: Output Stream Functions

FUNCTION	DESCRIPTION
base(n)	Set the radix for output operations to n, which must be 8, 10, or 16.
fill(c)	Set the fill character used to fill print fields when the output is smaller that the width. (By default, this is a space.)
flush()	Flush the output buffer, causing output to be immediately printed.
precision(n)	Set the number of digits of precision for writing floating-point numbers.
put(c)	Output character c.
width(n)	Set minimum print-field width for the next output operation.
write(s, n)	Binary write operation: writes n bytes directly from data at address s, which needs to be cast to **char*** type if the data is not in **char** format.

File I/O Functions

To enable the member functions in this section, include <fstream>.

```
#include <fstream>
```

You can create a file of type **fstream**, **ifstream**, or **ofstream** and optionally attempt opening a file when declaring the file object—or you can declare the object first and then attempt opening with the open function. The default mode is text.

```
ofstream fout(filename);
```

Note that a file object contains NULL after a file-open attempt fails. See Chapter 8 for more information on the use of file-stream objects. File-stream objects support the member functions in Table G.5, as well as the ones shown in the earlier tables.

Table G.5: File I/O Functions

FUNCTION	DESCRIPTION
open(*file, mode*)	Instead of opening a file when a file-object is declared, you can call this function separately to open the indicated *file*, a **char*** string containing a file specification. The *mode* argument takes one or more of the flags listed in Table G.6.
close()	Closes the file.
eof()	Returns true if end-of-file marker has been reached.
is_open()	Returns true if file has been successfully opened.
seekg(*pos*)	Moves input-file pointer to indicated position (an offset from beginning of the file in bytes).
seekg(*off, dir*)	Moves input-file pointer by the indicated offset *off* (which may be positive or negative) in the direction indicated by *dir*. See Table G.7 for values.
seekp(*pos*)	Same as **seekg** but intended for use with output files.
seekp(*off,dir*)	Same as **seekg** but intended for use with output files.
tellg()	Returns file position—an offset from beginning of file in bytes.
tellp()	Same as **tellg** but intended for use with output files.

The flag values in Table G.6 are used with the mode argument of the open function. They can be combined through the bitwise OR operator (|). For example:

```
// Open named file (filename) for binary input.

fstream fout;
fout.open(filename, ios::binary | ios::in);
```

Table G.6: File Mode Flags

FUNCTION	DESCRIPTION
ios::binary	Open file in binary mode.
ios::in	Open file for input operations.
ios::out	Open file for output operations.
ios::ate	Position file pointer at end of file.
ios::app	(Append.) Position file pointer at end of file after each i/o operation.
ios::trunc	(Truncate.) Remove all existing contents before doing any other operations.

The constants in Table G.7 are used in conjunction with the **seekg** and **seekp** functions.

Table G.7: Seek Direction Flags

DIRECTION VALUE	DESCRIPTION
ios::beg	Seek operation is relative to beginning of the file.
ios::cur	Seek operation is relative to the current position; the offset moves the file pointer forward if positive or backward if negative.
ios::end	Seek operation moves file pointer forward beyond current end of file if offset positive; if negative, file pointer is moved backward from end of file.

STL Classes and Objects

Although the Standard Template Library (STL) supports many useful templates, this appendix summarizes the use of just three (the ones used in this book):

▶ The string class

▶ The list template

▶ The stack template

The STL String Class

The features in this section require including <string>.

STL string objects are declared simply as **string**—or **std::string** if the **std** namespace is not being used. The simple **string** class actually instantiates the template class **basic_string** for type **char**, so the functions listed here are also supported by **basic_string** classes:

```
#include <string>

basic_string<char>     s1;    // Equivalent to string
basic_string<wchar_t>  s2 = L"Hello";  // Wide string
wcout << s2;
```

Once declared, **string** objects support copying of contents (=), concatenation (+), and comparison of contents (<, >, and =). Unlike standard C-strings (**char*** strings), STL strings can be assigned data without worrying about size considerations.

```
#include <string>
using namespace std;
```

```
...
string your_dog = "Fido";
your_dog = "Montgomery";    // String automatically
                            // grows.

string my_dog = "Mr. " + your_dog;
```

The **string** objects can be indexed as if they were **char*** strings.

```
cout << "The third character is" << my_dog[2];
```

With most of the functions listed in Table H.1, *str* may be either a STL string or a **char*** string. The return value, except where otherwise noted, is a reference to the current string object (the object through which the function is called).

In all these functions, position numbers use zero-based indexing.

Table H.1: String Member Functions

FUNCTION	DESCRIPTION
append(*str*)	Appends string *str* onto current string.
append(*str*, *n*)	Appends first *n* characters of *str* onto current string.
append(*n*, *c*)	Appends *n* copies of character *c* onto current string.
begin()	Returns an iterator pointing to the beginning of the string. This corresponds to a single character.
clear()	Clears the contents of the string. Has no return value.
c_str()	Returns the C-string (**char***) equivalent of current string.
empty()	Returns true if the string is currently empty; false otherwise.
erase(*pos*, *n*)	Erases *n* characters starting at position *pos*.
end()	Returns an iterator pointing to the end of the string (the position one past the last character).
insert(*pos*, *str*)	Inserts string *str* at position *pos*.
insert(*iter*, *c*)	Inserts character *c* at position pointed to by iterator *iter*.
find(*str*, *pos*)	Finds first occurrence of substring *str*, starting search at position *pos*. Returns position of string found; returns **string::npos** if not found.
find(*str*)	Finds first occurrence of substring *str*. Returns position of string found; returns **string::npos** if not found.
find(*c*, *pos*)	Finds first occurrence of character *c*, starting search at position *pos*. Returns position of character found; returns **string::npos** if not found.
find(*c*)	Finds first occurrence of character *c*. Returns position of character found; returns **string::npos** if not found.

Table H.1: String Member Functions (*continued*)

FUNCTION	DESCRIPTION
find_first_of(*s, pos*)	Finds first occurrence of a character that is also in string *s*, starting search at *pos*; if *pos* is omitted, search from beginning of string. Returns position of character found. Return **string::npos** if no such character found.
find_first_not_of(*s, pos*)	Finds first occurrence of a character that is *not* in string *s*, beginning at *pos*; if *pos* is omitted, search from beginning of string. Returns position of character found. Return **string::npos** if every character in string is also in *s*.
replace(*pos, n, str*)	Replaces *n* characters, starting at position, *pos* with *str*.
replace(*iter1, iter2, str*)	Replaces characters in range from iterators *iter1* to *iter2*, with *str*.
size()	Returns the current length of the string.
substr(*pos, n*)	Returns substring at position *pos* of length *n*.
swap(*str*)	Swaps existing contents with those of specified string, an STL string. Has no return value.

The <list> Template

To enable use of the list template, include <list>.

```
#include <list>
```

List classes can then be instantiated, creating a list container for the indicated base type. You can then add elements by calling any member functions such as **push_back**.

```
// Create several kinds of lists.

list<int>       list_of_int;
list<double>    list_of_double;
list<string>    list_of_string;
list<Point>     my_list;

list<int>        IList;  // Create list, add elements.
IList.push_back(5);
IList.push_back(225);
IList.push_back(100);
IList.sort();            // Sort list by value.
```

After declaring a list, you can declare an iterator and use it to step through the list.

```
list<int>::iterator  ii;   // Declare ii as
                           // int-list iterator.

for(ii = IList.begin(); ii != IList.end(); ii++){
    cout << *ii << endl;
}
```

Table H.2 lists the good majority of member functions supported for list templates. A few functions—merge, splice, and predicates—are complex and difficult to describe in a short summary. See your compiler documentation for more information on those.

Table H.2: List Template Member Functions

MEMBER FUNCTION	DESCRIPTION
assign(*n*, *val*)	Replaces entire list contents with *n* copies of *val*, a data object of the base type.
begin()	Returns an iterator that points to the beginning of the list.
clear()	Erases contents of the list.
empty()	Returns true if the list is empty; false otherwise.
end()	Returns an iterator to the end of the list (one position past the last element).
erase(*iter*)	Erases the element pointed to by iterator *iter*.
erase(*iter1*, *iter2*)	Erases the elements in the range from *iter1* to *iter2*.
front()	Returns the first element.
insert(*iter*, *val*)	Inserts indicated value just before the position pointed to by *iter*; if *iter* is equal to end(), then element is inserted at end of list.
insert(*iter*, *n*, *val*)	Inserts *n* elements just before the position pointed to by *iter*; each has the indicated value, *val*.
pop_back()	Erases the last element in the list. Behavior if "undefined" if list is empty (but don't count on your program still running).
pop_font()	Erases the first element in the list. Behavior is "undefined" if list is empty.
push_back(*val*)	Adds specified value, *val*, to back of the list.
push_front(*val*)	Adds specified value, *val*, to the front of the list.
rbegin()	Returns a (reverse) iterator that points to last element.
rend()	Returns a (reverse) iterator that points to one position before the beginning of the list.
reverse()	Reverses the current order of all elements in the list.
sort()	Sorts elements in the list, using comparison operator ($<$) defined for the base type.
unique()	Erases duplicate adjacent elements from the list.

The *<stack> Template*

To enable use of the list template, include <stack>.

```
#include <stack>
```

Stack classes can then be instantiated, with each declaration creating a stack that uses the indicated type.

```
stack<int>       stack_of_int;
stack<double>    stack_of_double;
stack<string>    stack_of_string;
stack<Point>     my_stack;
```

The stack template creates a simple last-in-last-out (LIFO) mechanism supporting just a few member functions. Because the template doesn't provide **begin** and **end** functions for iteration, a stack class is not a full container class; it cannot be used with ranged-based **for** supported by the C++0x specification.

Once you declare a stack class, you can push and pop members. Note that popping an STL stack actually requires two operations: **top** to get the top member of the stack and **pop** to remove it. So, remember to "top and pop."

```
stack<string>  beats;
beats.push("John");
beats.push("Paul");
beats.push("George");
beats.push("Ringo");
cout << beats.top() << endl;  // Print "Ringo".
a_stack.pop();
cout << beats.top() << endl;  // Print "George".
a_stack.pop();
```

Note that attempting to pop or remove an item from an empty stack produces "undefined" results, which usually means your program will happily dance off to the Twilight Zone and stay there. So, be careful not to pop empty stacks.

Table H.3: Stack Template Member Functions

FUNCTION	DESCRIPTION
push(*val*)	Pushes value (of stack's underlying type) onto top of stack.
top()	Returns data (of stack's underlying type) from top of stack—but it does not remove data; for that, use **pop**.
pop()	Removes top item of stack; does not return data.
size()	Returns the number of items currently stored in the stack.
empty()	Return true if stack is empty, false otherwise.

Glossary of Terms

This section provides an overview of terminology used in this book. For more detailed information on these topics, see the index.

abstract class: A class that cannot be used to create objects but that may still be useful as a general pattern (in other words, interface) for other classes. An abstract class has at least one pure virtual function.

access level: The level—private, protected, or public—that determines who or what can access members of a given class. Public members are freely accessible outside the class (although references to such members have to be properly qualified). Private members are accessible within the class but never from outside, and protected members are accessible within the class and any derived classes.

address: The numeric location of a piece of data or program code in memory. This location is often called a "physical location" in memory (although opening the computer to try to find this location is not likely to be helpful). Addresses, when displayed, are usually shown in hexadecimal notation (base 16) and aren't very meaningful except in the context of a program. The CPU understands only numbers, not words or letters: Numbers used by the CPU to access locations within main memory are addresses.

ANSI: American National Standards Institute. ANSI C++ is a recent specification of C++ that includes many features (such as the **bool** type and new-style cast operators) required for compilers to be up-to-date. However, it is superseded by the C++0x specification, which is even newer.

application: A complete, functioning program, as seen from the user's point of view. A word processor is an application; so is a spreadsheet. Basically, any compiled, tested program that does something useful in an application. The C++ compiler is a kind of application, although useful only to a specialized audience (programmers).

argument: A value passed to a function; also known as a parameter.

array: A data structure made up of multiple elements, in which each element has the same base type. Individual elements are accessed through an index number as well as the array name. For example, an array declared as int arr[5] is an array of five int values, accessed as arr[0] through arr[4]. In C and C++, index numbers run from 0 to n−1, where n is the size of the array.

ASCII: A coding system, adopted by convention, which assigns each printable character (and some nonprintable characters) a unique number in the 1-byte range (0 to 255). Consequently, in C++ a character is stored as **char** (a 1-byte integer), and a string is stored in an array of **char**. Use of ASCII code is built into the computer and low-level software so that when you type an H, for example, the ASCII code for H is put into the data stream and an H is displayed on the screen. (These details are far below the level of most programs, which means you don't have to worry about how all this happens.)

Some such coding system is necessary for programs to handle text, because at the level of machine code (the computer's native language), only numbers are understood. There are some other character coding systems (EBCDIC), but ASCII is universally adopted among personal computers and most mini-computer systems.

associativity: The rule (either left-to-right or right-to-left) that determines how to evaluate an expression that combines two or more operators at the same level of precedence. For example, in the expression *p++, the operators associate right-to-left, so the expression is equivalent to *(p++). (This means the pointer gets incremented to point to the next element, rather than incrementing the element itself.)

backward compatibility: The policy that states new versions of the C++ compiler should continue to support old programs even while introducing new features. C++ was intended to be largely backward compatible with the C language, although it is not quite 100 percent so. Lack of backward compatibility can cause huge problems for programmers, who may find that programs that compiled and ran perfectly well before are suddenly "broken" just because they updated their compiler, as in, "The ANSI C++ committee broke my programs!"

base class: A class from which you derive another class. All members of the base class are inherited by the derived class, except for constructors.

bit: A single digit equal to 0 or 1, stored in the CPU or in memory. Eight bits make up a byte. You cannot get access to individual bits except through bit-field and bitwise operations.

block: See compound statement.

Boolean: A true/false value or true/false operation. In ANSI C++, the **bool** type is supported; if it's not available, you can use the **int** type to hold Boolean values. C++ defines **true** and **false** (also defined in ANSI C++) as 1 and 0, respectively. Where a Boolean is expected, any nonzero value is converted to 1 and interpreted as true.

byte: A group of eight bits stored together. Memory in a computer is organized in bytes, so each byte has a unique address.

C++0x: The up-to-date specification of the C++ language that includes many new features. Some of these features—such as user-defined literals, ranged-based **for**, and ability to inherit base-class constructors—are features that C++ programmers have requested for years. C++0x is the version of the language that compiler vendors need to start implementing in order to be state-of-the-art...if they haven't already done so.

C-string: The old text-string type supported by the C language and still fully supported in C++: The format consists of an array of **char** and includes a null-terminating byte. Use of the STL **string** class offers many advantages over using C-strings, but string literals are still stored as C-strings, and some of the old-style string functions (such as **strtok**) in the standard library are still useful. See Chapter 7 for more information.

callback: A function whose address you give to another process or function so that it can *call back* your function at the specified address. An example may help clarify: To call the C++ standard library function **qsort**, you need to pass a **qsort** address of a comparison function you supply. **qsort** then calls this function in order to help determine the proper ordering of any two elements of an array.

With C++ and other object-oriented languages, callback functions are made largely obsolete through the use of virtual functions, which provide a much safer and more structured way of doing the same thing.

cast: Also known as type cast (and occasionally as data cast). An operation that changes the type of an expression. When a type with a smaller range is assigned to variable of greater range, C++ automatically promotes the smaller type, and no cast is usually necessary. However, when going in the reverse direction, such as assigning a floating-point number to an integer variable, a cast is necessary to avoid a warning message.

Casts are also useful in other situations. In writing to a binary file, a pointer of base type char is expected, so you need to recast other address types to **char***. If you are using the new style type cast, this requires **reinterpret_cast**, because it involves pointers. For examples using the new style casts, as well as the old "C-style" cast, see Appendix A.

class: A user-defined data type (or a data type defined in a library). In C++, a class can be declared by using the **class**, **struct**, or **union** keyword. In traditional programming, such a type can contain any number of data fields (called *data members* in C++); object-oriented programming in C++ adds the ability to declare functions members as well. Thus, you define a data type both by what it *stores* and how it *behaves*. Once a class is declared, you can use it to create any number of class instances, called *objects*.

code: Another word for "the program." The word code implies the programmer's point of view, rather than the user, who sees the end result at runtime. When C++ programmers speak of "the code," they are usually referring to the C++ source code, which is the group of C++ statements and functions that make up the program. This use of the word *code* originated in the early days of computer programming, when all programming had to be done in machine code. In those days, every instruction was encoded in a unique pattern of 1s and 0s.

compiler: The language translator that reads your C++ program and produces machine code and (ultimately) an executable file that can actually be run on the computer. This executable file is also called an *application*.

compound statement: A group of zero or more statements (typically more than one) enclosed in curly braces ({}). Also called a *block* or *statement block*. One of the fundamental rules of C and C++ syntax is that any place a single statement is valid, so is a compound statement. So, for example, you can use it to put any number of statements inside the body of a **while** loop so that each time through the loop, multiple statements are executed.

constant: A value that is not allowed to change. All literals are constants, but not all constants are literals. For example, an array name is a symbol (that is, a name) but is a constant.

constructor: A special member function that is automatically called when an object (an instance of a class) is created. Implicitly, a constructor returns an instance of the class, although constructors never have an explicit return type. (Syntactically speaking, every function in C++ must have a return type—even if it is void—the two exceptions being constructors and destructors.) Usually, a constructor performs initialization of some kind; note, however, that the compiler-supplied default constructor (see default constructor) performs none.

control structure: A way to control what happens next in a program rather than just "Go onto the next statement," which is usually what happens. Control structures can make decisions (albeit very limited ones), repeat operations, or transfer execution to a new program location. The **if**, **while**, **for**, and **switch-case** statements are all control structures.

copy constructor: A constructor in which an object is initialized from another object of the same type. For each class, the compiler provides a copy constructor if you don't write one: It performs a simple member-by-member copy.

CPU: Central processing unit. Although nearly all computers in use today have coprocessors that do some of the work (notably floating-point operations and graphics), a personal computer generally has one and only one central processor, which is a silicon "chip" that evaluates each machine-code instruction in a program. (Remember that all programs are translated into machine code before being run.) The central processor's execution of these instructions, one by one for the most part, is what drives a computer program—making decisions, performing arithmetic, copying values to memory, and so on.

data member: A data field of a class; each object of the class has its own copy of the data member (unless the member is declared static).

declaration: A statement that provides type information for a variable, class, member, or function. A data declaration actually—unless it is an extern declaration—creates a variable, causing the compiler to allocate memory for it. A function declaration can be either a *prototype* (which contains type information only) or a *definition* (which tells what the function does). In C++, every variable and function except for **main** must be declared before being used...although note that #**include** directives bring in declarations implicitly for large portions of the standard library.

default constructor: A constructor that has no arguments. For each class, the compiler provides an automatic default constructor if you write no default constructor of your own. As a result, if you write any other constructor, the compiler takes away the default constructor, and then you cannot create objects without explicitly initializing them. You can avoid this behavior by writing your own default constructor. Note that the compiler-supplied default constructor performs no initialization; it is essentially a no-op.

definition, function: A series of statements that tells what a function does. When a function is called, program control is transferred to these statements.

deprecate: A deprecated feature is one that the C++ design committee (yes, there are such people) strongly discourages from being used, so much so that the compiler generates a warning message that the programming feature in question may not always be supported! (This is, to say the least, strongly against the spirit of backward compatibility.) For a long time, the committee had intended to deprecate old-style C casts but changed its mind when it became clear how much C legacy code was been maintained with C++.

dereference: The process of getting data that a pointer points to. If p is a pointer that points to n, then the expression *p "dereferences" the pointer by getting the data stored in n. In theory, you can have a pointer to a pointer to a pointer...in that case, the expression ***p fully dereferences the pointer, producing data of the base type.

derived class: See *subclass*.

destructor: Not as lethal as it sounds. A destructor is a member function that performs cleanup and termination activities when an object is destroyed. The destructor is called just before an object is about to be removed from memory. The declaration of a destructor is ~*class_name*(). Writing a destructor is not required but is a good idea when objects of a class have ownership of resources (such as memory and file handles) that need to be given back so other processes can use them.

directive: A general command to the compiler. Directives affect how the compiler interprets the program but do not correspond directly to runtime actions. For example, the **#include** directive causes the compiler to include the contents of another source file.

encapsulation: The ability to hide or protect contents, exposing the underlying functionality of what is protected by providing some general (and ideally easy-to-use) interface. For example, by declaring a file-stream object, you gain the ability to read and write to files without having to deal with the operating system's low-level file commands. Encapsulating complex operations and data into classes with consistent, easy-to-use interfaces is a general goal of object-oriented programming.

end user: The person who runs a program, as opposed to writing it. Most programs are designed for end users (typically referred to as *users*) who are not experts and have no knowledge of programming. However, ironically, the first user of a program—the first person to try it—is almost always the programmer him or herself. Still, unless you are writing a program strictly for your own use and no one else's, it is wise to make the program self-explanatory, foolproof, and easy to use.

exception: An unusual occurrence at runtime, typically (but not always) a runtime error. What all exceptions have in common is that they disrupt the normal flow of the program and require immediate action. If an exception is not handled, the program terminates abruptly (and quite rudely) without so much as an explanation to the user. An example of an exception is attempting to divide by zero. C++ provides the **try**, **catch**, and **throw** keywords to let you centralize exception handling in your programs.

floating point: A data format that can store fractional portions of numbers as well as storing numbers in a much larger range than integer types (such as **int**,

short, and **long**). On a computer, floating-point numbers are stored internally in base 2 but displayed in decimal format. Rounding errors are possible. Many ratios—such as 1/3—cannot be stored precisely in floating-point format, although they can be approximated to a certain precision. The principal floating-point type in C++ is **double**, which stands for "double precision."

Rounding errors are always possible with floating-point numbers, because each floating-point format has a limited precision; very high integers may in some cases be not stored precisely, although a **long int** or **long long int** might be able to store the same number with absolute precision. Therefore, you shouldn't use a floating-point type where an integer type would be sufficient.

GCF (greatest common factor): The highest integer that divides evenly into each of two numbers. For example, the greatest common factor of 12 and 18 is 6; the greatest common factor of 300 and 400 is 100.

global variable: A variable shared by all functions in the same source file (or at least all functions whose definitions appear after the declaration of the global variable). You declare a global variable in C++ by declaring it outside of any function. In a multiple-module program, you can even share a global variable among all the functions in the program by using extern declarations. A global variable is visible from the point where it is declared until the end of the file.

A global variable automatically has static storage class.

header file: A file that contains a series of declarations and (optionally) directives; it is intended to be included (through the use of **#include** directives) in multiple files. This technique saves programmers from having to enter all the needed declarations into each module of a project and from having to declare prototypes for library functions. Remember that classes, variables, and functions all have to be declared in C++ before being used.

IDE: Integrated development environment; a text editor from which you can run the compiler as well as test your program.

implementation: A word with many different meanings, but one of the most common is this: An implementation of a virtual function provides a function definition, thereby *implementing* that function with a particular response.

index: The number used to refer to an element of an array. Index numbers are also used with **char*** strings (which are really arrays), STL string objects, and any container class that supports the brackets operator [ ].

indirection: Accessing data indirectly, through a pointer. For example, if pointer ptr points to variable amount, then the statement *ptr = 10; changes the value of amount through indirection.

infinite loop: A loop that apparently continues forever, because (for example) the **while** condition is always true. Usually, an infinite loop represents a fatal error in a program, unless there is some kind of exit condition, such as a break or return statement.

inheritance: The ability to give one class the attributes of another, previously declared class. This is done through subclassing. The new class automatically has all the members declared in the base class (except for constructors, although the C++0x specification does provide a way to inherit base-class constructors).

inline function: A function whose statements are inserted into the body of the function that calls it. In a normal function call, program control jumps to a new location and then returns when execution is complete. This does not happen with an inline function. Instead, the inline function call is *expanded* by being replaced with the statements defined for it (much like a "macro").

When you declare a member function inside a class and include its definition inside the class as well, it is automatically made an inline function.

instance/instantiation: An instance of something is a concrete realization of a general category. For example, the Sears Tower is an instance of the category "building." But in C++, the word *instance* is usually synonymous with the word *object*. Any individual value or variable is an instance of some type. The number 5 is an instance of **int**, and the number 3.1415927 is an instance of **double**. Every object is an instance of some class. When a class is *instantiated*, that means it has been used to create an object.

integer: A whole number or, rather, a number with no fractional part. This includes the numbers 1, 2, 3, and so on, as well as 0 and negative numbers -1, -2, -3, and so on.

interface: This is another word with many different meanings, depending on the context. In this book, I've used it to refer to a general set of services that difference subclasses can implement each in their own way. In C++ you can use an abstract class to define an interface.

iteration/iterative: Computing by using repeated statements (loops). An iterative—as opposed to a recursive—solution is one that repeats a series of statements over and over, usually in a **while** loop or **for** loop. Iteration is the processing of repeating a group of statements by simply jumping back up to the top of the loop after the bottom is reached.

iterator: An object or variable used to cycle through the elements of a container, typically in a **for** loop. In the case of arrays, you can use a simple loop counter as a primitive iterator, but be careful to set its beginning and ending limits carefully. With STL container classes such as <list>, STL iterators provide a safe and convenient way to cycle through all the elements. See Chapter 16 for more information.

keyword: A word (such as **if, for, while, return,** or **do**) that has special meaning to the core C++ language. Function and variable names that you come up with yourself cannot be keywords.

LCM: Lowest common multiple, the lowest number that two numbers can be divided into evenly. For example, the lowest common multiple of 20 and 30 is 60, because 20 and 30 both divide evenly into 60 (leaving no remainder). Another way of saying this is to say that 20 and 30 are both factors of 60.

LIFO: Last-in-last-out; this is a system of data management characteristic of any kind of *stack*. The last item to be put on the stack is the first item to be popped off. This is why stack operations are usually referred to as "pushing" and "popping."

literal: A fixed number such as 5, -100, or 3.1415927, or a text string such as "Mary had a little lamb." A literal is something the compiler immediately recognizes as a specific value upon reading it in a source file. A literal specifies a value; it does not need to have it looked up in a table. In contrast to a literal is a *symbol* (or symbolic name), which has to be assigned a value before it can be used. All literals are constants, but not all constants are literal.

local variable: A variable that is private to a particular function or statement block. The benefit of local variables is that each function can have its own variable x (for example) but that changes to x within one function won't interfere with the value of x in any other function. We can also say that the local variable x is visible only within its function. This feature—a right to privacy—is a cornerstone of modern programming languages.

loop: A group of statements repeated over and over: The image of "loop" comes from the way control cycles back to the top, each time the bottom is reached.

loop counter: A variable used to control the number of times a loop is executed.

lvalue: A "left value," meaning a value that can appear on the left side of an assignment statement. In other words, an lvalue is just something you can assign a value to. Variables are lvalues; literals are not. Other examples of lvalues include array members, most class data members (if they are ordinary variables, not array names), and fully dereferenced pointers. Array names, as opposed to array members, are not lvalues because they are constants.

machine code: The computer's own internal language. Such a language (different for every make and model of processor) consists of a unique pattern of 1s and 0s to carry out different actions; this is why programs are referred to as *code*...because each machine instruction is a code for a different operation. The term *code* originated in the 1950s and stuck.

Very few programmers ever write in machine code anymore—or even assembly language, which is similar to machine code but uses intelligible names for instructions, such as COPY, JUMP, or JNZ ("jump if not zero"), instead of bit patterns. Because a language like Basic or C++ is closer to human language and frees the programmer from having to worry about the processor's architecture, a programmer writing in C++ can generally accomplish the same task that a machine-code or assembly-code programmer could...only many times faster.

main function: The main function is the starting point of a C++ program, and it does not need to be declared before being used. (In a console application, a main function is required; other types of applications may use other kinds of starting points.) In a console application, main is the only function guaranteed to be run. Other functions in a program are executed only when called.

main memory: The memory in which all computer programs run. Although programs are stored in a disk file or network location, a computer must download a program into main memory before it can run that program. This area (often called *RAM* or just *memory*) is volatile and impermanent; but it is the only memory that the CPU has direct access to. Main memory must be shared with other programs running at the same time, including the operating system (such as Windows).

member: An item declared inside a class. Data members are similar to the fields of a record or structure. Member functions define operations exclusive to the class, which (generally speaking) operate on members of the class.

member function: A function declared within a class. Member functions are sometimes called methods in other languages.

memory: Although memory can either be volatile or persistent (in other words, stored in a disk file or other semi-permanent medium), the term *memory* itself usually refers to main memory.

module: A large, semi-independent division of the program. A module corresponds to one source file. In the largest programs, multiple modules may be compiled and linked together.

nesting: Placing one control structure inside another or one declaration inside another.

newline: A signal to the monitor that says to start a new line of text.

object: A unit of closely associated data that can have behavior (in the form of member functions) as well as data. The concept stems for the old concept of "data record" but is much more flexible. By writing member functions, you can define an object's ability to respond to requests. Furthermore, because of polymorphism in C++, the knowledge of how to carry out an operation is built into the object itself, not the client code (that is, the code that uses the object). The type of an object is its class, and for a given class you can declare any number of objects.

object code: The machine code generated by the compiler and stored in an intermediate file to be linked into the final executable file (EXE on Windows systems). This term has no connection to objects and object-oriented programming whatsoever. The similarity of the names is frankly unfortunate.

object-oriented programming (OOP): An approach to program design and coding that makes data objects more central, enabling you to define data objects by what they do as much as by what they contain. The object-oriented approach starts by asking, "What kinds of data does the program need, and what kinds of operations can be defined on each such data object?"

one-based indexing: A system of indexing arrays and strings, which starts at index number 1. C and C++ use zero-based indexing instead, in almost every context.

OOPS: A user's cry when he realizes he's lost the contents of his or her hard disk without having saved anything. Also an acronym for object-oriented programming system. OOP, which is just object-oriented programming, is also common.

operand: An expression involved in a larger expression through some operator. For example, in the expression x+5, the items x and 5 are each operands.

operator: A special symbol (usually a single character such as +) that combines one or more subexpressions into a larger expression. Some operators are unary, meaning they take only one operand; others are binary, meaning they take two operands. In the expression x + *p, the plus-sign is a binary operator, and the asterisk (*) is in this case a unary operator.

overloading: The reuse of a name or symbol for different—although often related—purposes. Function overloading lets you use the same name any number of times to define different functions, as long as each function has a different argument list. Operating overloading lets you define how standard C++ operators (such as *, +, and <) work with objects of your own classes.

persistent memory: Memory that forms a semi-permanent record so that after the program finishes or the computer is turned off, the data hangs around. Computers provide persistent memory in the form of disk files and other media, such as memory sticks.

pointer: A variable that contains the address of another variable, array, or function. (A pointer can also be a null pointer, in which case it "points nowhere.") Pointers have many uses in C++, as described in Chapter 6. In general, pointers are valuable because they give you a way of passing a handle to a hunk of data without having to copy all the data itself; you have to copy only the pointer value (that is, the address). A pointer tells where to go to find a piece of data. Pointers also make dynamic-memory allocation possible, as well as making it possible to create linked-lists, trees, and other data structures in memory.

polymorphism: A daunting term, but what it really means is "many forms"—in computer programming terms, this is the ability to call a function and have it respond in infinitely many ways at runtime: The implementation to be called depends on the object, and the object (which can change in response to runtime conditions) brings with it its own function code.

A more compact way of saying this is: The knowledge of how to respond to a function call is built into the object itself, not the code that uses the object. Therefore, existing software can interact smoothly with new software, yet to be written. In C++, polymorphism is made possible through virtual functions. See Chapter 18 for more information.

precedence: The rules that determine which operations to carry out first in a complex expression. For example, in the expression 2 + 3 * 4, multiplication (*) is carried out first, because multiplication has higher precedence than addition. See Appendix A for the precedence of all operators.

processor: See CPU.

program: A group of commands (or rather statements), which, taken together, perform useful actions. A word processor is a program; so is a spreadsheet. (From the standpoint of a user, a program is usually called an *application*.) C++ is a language for writing computer programs using a distinct set of keywords and syntax: This version of the program (called *source code*) is then translated into machine-readable form (machine code) that is run directly on the computer itself.

prototype: A function declaration that gives type information only (that is, it is not a function definition).

pure virtual function: A function that has no implementation (that is, no definition) in the class in which it is declared.

recursion: A programming technique in which a function calls itself. This sounds like a logical paradox leading to an infinite regress. (It would be like a set containing itself, which philosopher Bertrand Russell declared logically invalid.) But the technique is perfectly workable as long as there is a terminating condition—some condition under which the function no longer calls itself. At that point, the function calls (all stored on the stack) begin returning, one by one. See Chapter 4 for several examples of recursion. A recursive approach is typically less efficient than an iterative approach, but some problems (notably the Tower of Hanoi problem from Chapter 4) are extremely difficult to solve without recursion.

reference: A variable or argument that serves as a handle to another variable or argument. A reference variable is an alias for another variable. If you understand pointers, references are easy to grasp: Essentially, they behave in a way almost identical to pointers but without pointer syntax. The important difference between pointers and references (beside the syntactic ones) is that once a reference is initialized, it cannot be made to refer to something else.

scope: The area over which a given symbol (variable or function) is visible in a program. Local variables have local scope, which means that changes to a variable inside a function have no effect on code outside the function; therefore, every function can have its own local variable i, for example, without affecting the value of i in other functions. Scope can also be defined by namespaces and classes, in which case the scope operator (::) can enable visibility of a symbol, as can the **using** statement.

source file: A text file containing C++ statements (and optionally, directives).

stack: The word *stack* has at least two distinct meanings in computer programming. There is a special area of memory set aside called "the stack," in which the computer places the addresses of functions to return to, as well as the values of arguments and local variables during each function call. This management of the stack is usually invisible to the C++ programmer. In addition, some programs use a stack-like mechanism for their own purposes, such a data type is provided by the STL. What all stacks have in common is that they use a last-in-first-out (LIFO) system of data management, so that the first item to be popped off a stack is the last item that was pushed on top of it. (Think of a stack of dishes.)

Standard Template Library (STL): A library of templates supported by all up-to-date versions of C++ (although not by the earliest versions of C++). STL includes the easy-to-use **string** class, which provides many advantages over the old C-string type (null-terminated arrays of **char***). It also includes a simplified stack class, as well as many useful container classes. This book covers the STL **string** class and the list and stack templates.

statement: A basic unit of syntax in a C++ program. A C++ statement is roughly analogous to a command or sentence in a natural language. As with sentences, there is no fixed length for a C++ statement. It can be terminated at any time—usually with a semicolon (;). A function definition consists of zero or more statements.

statement block: See *compound statement*.

static storage class: Storage class in which a variable is allocated at a specific location in the data area; as a result, there is one copy, shared by the whole program. Static storage differs from automatic storage class for local variables (allocating variables on the stack) and object storage (in which each object has its own copy of a member).

STL: See *Standard Template Library*.

storage class: The manner in which a variable is stored on the computer: *Static* storage class maintains just one copy of the variable in the data area used by the program; *automatic* storage class (used for most local variables) allocates space for the variable on the stack. This enables each instance of the function to maintain its own copy of the variable.

string: A series of text characters, which you can use to represent names, words, and phrases. Up-to-date C++ compilers support both C-strings, which are arrays of **char*** that include enough room for the data and a terminating null, as well as the newer STL **string** type, which supports reasonable behavior for assignment (=), test-for-equality (==), and concatenation (+). The latter is easier to use, because you can assign data to a string type without worrying about the string running out of space.

string literal: A text string enclosed in quotation marks, such as:

"Here comes the sun."

When C++ reads a text string from the source file (assuming it is not inside a comment), it stores the characters as a C string, which is an array of **char** that includes an extra byte for the null terminator. The string name is then associated with the address of this data. Note that the backslash (\\) signals an escape character in a C++ string. To represent an actual backslash, use two: \\\\. (See Appendix B for a list of escape characters.)

subclass: A class that inherits, or is derived from, another class (called the *base class*). The subclass inherits all the members of the base class except for constructors. Any declarations within the subclass create new or overridden members.

symbol: A variable, class, or function name. Unlike a literal, a symbol is just a name, and it derives its meaning and value according to context. (For example, a variable can be initialized.) Symbols (or *symbolic names*) must adhere to C++ naming rules: A symbol must begin with a letter or underscore (_), and the remaining characters must be letters, numbers, or uses of the underscore (_).

template: A generalized class, usually a container of some sort, that is built around a more specific class. For example, the STL list class can be used to create lists of any type: list<int>, list<float>, list<double>, and so on. Templates make use of a generalized algorithm or solution and apply to different kinds of data. This is the most advanced example of code reuse supported by C++. Up-to-date C++ compilers not only support template technology (although it was not present in the earliest versions of C++) but also supply a number of useful templates in the Standard Template Library (STL).

text string: See *string*.

two's complement: The most common format, especially on today's personal computers, for storing signed (as opposed to unsigned) integers. The leftmost bit in such a number is always 1 if the number is negative; it is 0 if the number is nonnegative. See Appendix B for more information.

variable: A named location for storing program data. Each variable has a unique location in program memory (its address). Other attributes of a variable include its type (for example, **int**, **double**, or **float**), its visibility (local or global), and its storage class.

virtual function: A function whose address is not determined until runtime (through a process called *late binding*). In C++, virtual functions are closely connected to the concept of polymorphism. Virtual functions have special flexibility. You can safely override a virtual function in a subclass, knowing that no matter how an object is accessed, the right version of the function will always be called. So, for example, a function call such as ptr->vfunc() will call the object's own version of vfunc rather than base-class version.

In ancient Rome, virtu meant "manliness"; in modern parlance, virtual means "to have the behavior of." This example of (otherwise regrettable) chauvinism has one redeeming feature: It suggests that to take one's place in society, a man's behavior was paramount; in ancient Rome, one had to earn one's right to be a Consul, Praetor, Senator, or Man of Respect, and that meant correct (and "manly") behavior. Thus, the connecting thread in the word "virtual" over the millenia is that it focuses on behavior and conduct. In computer technology, we say that if something is virtual, it emulates the behavior of the real. For example, a virtual function call looks just like an ordinary function call and is used just like an ordinary function call, even though it has a special implementation, but because it works just like a standard function call, it is as good as the real thing.

visibility: Closely related to scope. Global variables are visible from the place they are declared, onward to the end of the source file. Local variables are visible only within the functions they are declared.

zero-based indexing: A system of indexing arrays and strings that starts at 0 and runs to N−1, where N is the size of the container. The second element is indexed as 1, the third is indexed as 2, and so on. Although this technique may seem less reasonable at first, it makes sense when you think of indexes as being like offsets. Thus, the first element is always 0 units distant from the beginning. C and C++ use zero-based indexing for arrays and strings and almost every other context.

Index

Take the Next Step to Mastering C++

978-0-321-54372-1

978-0-201-72148-5

978-0-201-73484-3

978-0-321-70212-8

978-0-201-70073-2

978-0-13-704483-2

978-0-13-700130-9

978-0-201-37926-6

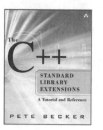
978-0-321-41299-7

978-0-321-13354-0

978-0-321-33487-9

978-0-201-63371-9

978-0-201-74962-5

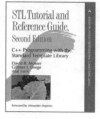
978-0-321-32192-3

978-0-321-11358-0

978-0-201-76042-2

978-0-201-61562-3

978-0-201-70434-1

978-0-201-70431-0

978-0-201-70353-5